op Cd

8⁰⁰

A H Jameson

Medina

Washington

November 1972

Reread February 1982
Laguna Hills
California

Reread December 1994.

Very interesting

Napoleon and Paris

By the same author:

NAPOLEON DEVANT DIEU: PROFIL RELIGIEUX DE
L'EMPEREUR
   (Letter of Introduction from His Imperial Highness
   Prince Napoleon) (Editions Peyronnet) 1959

NAPOLEON AND PARIS

Thirty Years of History

by
MAURICE GUERRINI

Translated, Abridged and Edited by
MARGERY WEINER

WALKER AND COMPANY
New York

First published in France as *Napoléon et Paris* in 1967.

First published in the United States of America in 1970
by the Walker Publishing Company, Inc.

ISBN: 0-8027-0196-5   Library of Congress Catalog
Card Number: 69-15726

Printed in the United States of America from type set
in the United Kingdom.

Contents

APPENDIXES

MAPS

Preface

Numerous and memorable bonds linked Napoleon with Paris. Here he came to intellectual maturity, here he married, here his son was born and here he spent more than a third of his adult life. His most grandiose schemes were conceived on the banks of the Seine where, in accordance with his last wishes, his remains are buried.

Napoleon, of all our rulers, was perhaps the one most passionately devoted to the City which was the object of his unremitting concern. Although he was always anxious about the capital's state of mind and sometimes irritated by the Parisians, he had particular regard for them and strove tirelessly to improve their lot.

Labour under the Consulate and Empire enjoyed high standing. The Parisians were deeply appreciative of the brilliant inaugural ceremonies of the laying of foundation stones of new buildings which were celebrated as national victories. Napoleon's frequent visits to the theatre were prompted by personal inclination, not to court popularity, but he also liked to meet and assess the reactions of his fellow citizens, most of whom, especially the poorest, were deeply devoted to him, admiring his genius and grateful for his tender care.

Seldom has more agonizing suspense been experienced than by the people of Paris, anxiously awaiting news of the great captain who, in burning deserts or icy wastes, gambled with the nation's destiny. Seldom also has rejoicing been more sincere than theirs when the cannon at the Invalides and the church bells gave tongue to celebrate a victory, or when the First Consul, and afterwards the Emperor, reviewed his troops on the Carrousel. This surfeit of glory led the people by natural reaction to consider victory as the norm.

To reconstruct the great moments shared by the Man and the City I have traced the stirring events which marked them in chronological order, day by day and sometimes hour by hour so that the reader may follow Napoleon from his arrival at the Ecole Militaire on 21 October 1784 to his departure from the Elysée on 25 June 1815, a period of thirty years. A few concluding pages briefly sketch the exile at St Helena and the return of the Ashes to enable the reader to accompany the Hero to the porphyry sarcophagus where he lies, not far from the place where his first night in Paris was spent.

It seemed to me that Napoleon's relations with Paris could best be understood by a parallel study of Parisian feeling for him and his achievements in the city, so the great public works are juxtaposed to the sequence of important events which had so large an influence on their development.

My main sources have been the *Moniteur*, contemporary newspapers and police reports. If my presentation shows prejudice the method does not; these eye-witness reports have the great merit of catching events on the wing and revitalizing them.

Aulard's most interesting work ends in 1808. I have followed his method to complete the documentation for the years 1809 to 1815. At the Archives Nationales I found specialized and valuable material in the reports of the administrative councils presided over by the Emperor in person. Passy's life of Frochot, written before the burning in 1871 of the archives of the City of Paris, was likewise a precious source of information. Finally, stock-exchange rates, the most sensitive barometer of public opinion, are frequently cited to allow the reader to follow closely the development of Parisian opinion from 1800 to 1815.

Most studies of Paris during the Consulate and Empire have concentrated section by section on civic undertakings, a method used in two recent and excellent works published while I was completing this book; *Paris de Napoléon* by M.-L. Biver, based on extensive research, and *Napoléon et Paris* by Georges Poisson, which summarized the outstanding events of this period in the life of Paris with a wealth of architectural and sculptural detail.

Apart from the general works of Masson and Madelin the definitive purely historical study is Lanzac de Laborie's *Paris sous Napoléon*, in eight masterly volumes, but this was published in 1907 and, as the title indicates, is mainly concerned with life in Paris; its commentary ends in 1812.

The years thereafter were the darkest of the Empire when the Parisians paid dearly for their hours of triumph but, with the exception of a handful of intriguers and careerists, they did not reproach the Emperor; as they had shared his glory so they were ready to share his misfortunes. The citizens of Paris succoured the wounded Hero and made him in truth their king. The last chapter deals with this period to bring to a close the remarkable story of Napoleon and Paris.

Acknowledgements

It is my pleasant duty to express my thanks for the help that the following have been kind enough to give me: the Curators of the Ministry of Cultural Affairs, the National Archives, the National Assembly, the Elysée, the Institute, the Louvre, the Senate, the City of Paris and the Prefecture of the Seine; and especially Madame Felkay, MM. Boussel, Roussier and de Surirey de Saint-Rémy, as well as my colleagues at the Hôtel de Ville, MM. Chiappini and Taurand and Monsieur Giudicelli, architect.

Book I

Bonaparte and Paris

I

Sojourn in Paris

L'École Militaire

To Parisians there was probably nothing exceptional about Thursday, 21 October, in the year of grace 1784. Did poetry lovers notice an ode published on the 19th in the *Journal de Paris*, celebrating the achievements of the intrepid Montgolfiers, ancestors of our cosmonauts? The poet saw the balloonists as rivals to 'the lofty eagle':

> Man soars to the ranks of the Gods
> To make the world tributary
> To the daring of his genius . . .

His readers could not guess that fifteen years later the young man who came to Paris that day would be hailed in similar fulsome terms.

It was in fact on 21 October 1784, that young Bonaparte, then 15, with four of his comrades, escorted by Father Berton, set foot for the first time in Paris. He had left Corsica on 15 December 1778, and so had spent six years on the mainland, mostly at the preparatory school at Brienne after a few months at Autun.

He landed from the old-fashioned water-coach at the picturesque port of St-Paul towards 6.0 p.m. and crossed the new bridge between the Ile[1] de Louvier and the Ile St-Louis. It is easy to fancy the young provincial's surprise at his first contact with the great capital of the kingdom. Although much in Paris was still medieval, the city had a population of over six hundred thousand inhabitants and was impressive in size when compared with Ajaccio or the small towns in France where he had been living. When the young southerner crossed the Pont Marie he may have paused to gaze at the historic green waters of the Seine, laden with history and poetry.

After a brief halt at a hostelry at the sign of the Coq Hardi in the

---

[1] Connected with the mainland in 1843 at the Boulevard Morland. Ed.

Rue des Deux-Ponts, he strolled along the quays where his studious
bent led him to buy a copy of *Gil Blas* at a second-hand bookseller's
then, continuing on his way, he and his companions came to the
'Latin country' where they rested at the Abbey of St-Germain-des-
Prés. As night fell they crossed the silent and heroic Esplanade des
Invalides to the Ecole Militaire, Gabriel's impressive masterpiece
opposite the Champ de Mars. Here Bonaparte stayed for nearly a
year almost to the day, here he was confirmed and here in March
he heard with sorrow of the death of his father, Charles Buonaparte,
at Montpellier on 24 February 1785.

Bonaparte had little opportunity for sightseeing as he threw himself wholeheartedly into his military studies and also the study of
religion; he was, in any event, subject to the strict discipline of a
boarder. His first 'authentic' home in Paris, probably giving on to an
inner courtyard, was a square cell, barely furnished with an iron bed-
stead, a wooden chair and a small cupboard. The food and arrangements at the school were excellent, as Napoleon told Las Cases in
1816: 'At the Ecole Militaire in Paris we were splendidly fed and
waited on and treated in every way like wealthy officers.'

The Duchesse d'Abrantès says that he was shocked by the 'indecent
luxury' paraded by many of his fellow-pupils who had their own
servants.

In the middle of August the young Napoleon passed an examination which admitted him to the artillery with the rank of second-
lieutenant. He had done well to come forty-second out of fifty-eight
candidates since he had only a year's preparation compared with the
others' two or three, and he was the first Corsican to graduate from
the Ecole Militaire in Paris. He left the school on 28 October and
spent the afternoon sightseeing with Lieutenant-General Rossi,
commandant of the military division of Bastia, and visited the Opéra
among other places. Next day, says Chuquet, he called on the Bishop
of Autun, Mgr de Marboeuf, brother of the Governor of Corsica,
at the Abbey of St-Germain-des-Prés.

On 30 October Bonaparte took the Lyons stage-coach for Valence
to join the La Fère regiment with which he stayed until the middle
of September 1786, when he obtained leave to return to the Ajaccio
he was longing to revisit. Here he stayed until 12 September 1787,
occupied with family matters and a history of Corsica. When his
leave expired he decided to return to Paris where he would be better

placed to watch over his family's interests. At the beginning of
October he was again an inhabitant of Paris and at once asked for an
extension of leave.

He occupied a modest room, No. 9 on the third floor of the Hôtel
de Cherbourg, 33 Rue du Four St-Honoré. For this he paid 15 frs a
month and 30 centimes each for his equally modest meals in small
eating-houses in the Passage des Petits Pères or at the Trois Bornes
in the Rue de Valois.

During his first stay in Paris the young Napoleon had lived in an
open, airy and quiet district on the Left Bank but he was now in a
densely populated part of the Right Bank, near the Louvre, the
Tuileries and the Palais Royal, in the very heart of the capital,
extremely noisy and not very salubrious. This was his first human
and social introduction to Paris as a young provincial, newly arrived
in the great city, lost in the crowd and far from home. Under low and
heavy skies, like those described by Baudelaire, far removed from
the clear light of Corsica, he spent long hours by day and even by
night alone with sheets of paper to which he feverishly confided his
nostalgia. He wandered aimlessly, given over to boredom, through
the narrow, tortuous streets of Paris, resigning himself to a life
of asceticism, always alone with his thoughts, with no outlet for
his obsession for action and longing for distraction, escape and
love.

The Palais Royal housed many attractive women of easy virtue,
game for profitable pleasure, so it was natural that, when on an
autumn evening in 1787 the young second-lieutenant left the Théâtre
des Italiens to 'stride through the walks of the Palais Royal', he
should look with desire at a pale-faced girl of whom misfortune had
made a streetwalker and that he should spend the night in her
miserable room. This casual encounter left a painful impression on the
fiercely chaste adolescent who gave vent to his distaste in a few pages,
headed 'Thursday, November 22nd, 1787, Paris, Hôtel de Cherbourg,
Rue du Four St-Honoré'.

Three other hotels

An extension of leave from 1 January 1788 gave Bonaparte the
opportunity to return to Corsica, where he stayed until 1 June when
he came back to rejoin his regiment at Auxonne. For over a year he

worked desperately, swallowing book after book to learn his profession as an artilleryman, but still remaining attentive to the serious
events in France. He was fired with enthusiasm for the revolution and
dreamed of liberating his own dear homeland, where he believed he
could become an important factor. By the end of September 1789,
he was again in Ajaccio for a stay of nearly eighteen months, ex-
ploiting a revolutionary and French policy and setting up in opposition to Paoli, the fierce advocate of an independent Corsica.

At the beginning of February 1791, Bonaparte returned to
Auxonne with his young brother, Louis, then went to Valence at the
end of September when he once again returned to Corsica to stay
until May 1792—eight months of great activity. Promoted deputy
Lieutenant-Colonel, he attempted to seize the citadel of Ajaccio, but
was struck off the strength for unauthorized leave of absence and
abandonment of his post. Only in Paris could he refute these serious
charges, justify his conduct and obtain his reinstatement and he
arrived in the city on 28 May.

From a letter written next day to Joseph we learn where he was
staying.

'I arrived in Paris yesterday and am temporarily at the same hotel as
Pozzo di Borgo, Léonetti and Péraldi, the Hôtel des Patriotes Hollandais
in the Rue Royale St-Roch.'

He ate at Justat's and the other eating-houses he had frequented
during his previous visit.

The Rue Royale St-Roch was in the Palais Royal quarter, not far
from the Place des Victoires. During the Second Empire, when the
Avenue de l'Opéra was cut, the street disappeared so that anyone
wanting to retrace Napoleon's footsteps will not find the hotel where
the young lieutenant was then living and where, no doubt, Catherine
Hübscher, the immortal *Madame Sans-Gêne*, brought him his wash-
ing.[1] However, near by, at No. 18, there is still a hairdresser's
dating from 1630, probably the oldest and smallest of its kind in
Paris, where Bonaparte often had himself shaved. This charming
shop is threatened with demolition because of its state of dilapidation.[2]

---

[1] The real *Mme Sans-Gêne* was, of course, Thérèse Figuier, who died in obscurity, but
Victorien Sardou preferred to give this name to his heroine who became the wife of
Maréchal Lefebvre.
[2] This shop has been kept for forty years by M. Prat who is very proud of it. As an
admirer of the Emperor he showed me many newspaper clippings with photographs of his
shop, particularly one from an English paper, entitled, 'Napoleon was here'.

Finding the price even of the modest rooms at the Hôtel des Patriotes beyond him Bonaparte stayed only two days. On 29 May he wrote: 'It is too dear so I shall move out either today or tomorrow'. He found a lodging at the Hôtel de Metz,[1] a six-storey building in the Rue du Mail near the home of his old school-fellow from Brienne, Bourrienne, whom he had the pleasure of seeing often.[2]

Both young men, according to Bourrienne, looked for ways to augment their slender resources,

'Every day we evolved new plans and tried to find profitable speculations.'

He adds the curious detail that, during one of their many strolls through Paris, Bonaparte 'said he would like us both to rent a certain house being built in the Rue Montauban'. This is not really surprising because later the great administrator devised financial transactions which yielded profits from property in Paris. None of these 'distractions', however, diverted Bonaparte from what was happening in the city which on his arrival he had found 'deeply disturbed'.

He witnessed the events of 20 June[3] with Bourrienne who writes:

'We had arranged to meet for our daily walk at an eating-house in the Rue St-Honoré near the Palais Royal and, as we left, we saw coming from the direction of the Halles a ragged crowd which Bonaparte estimated as of five to six thousand men . . . screaming the coarsest insults and converging rapidly on the Tuileries, a crowd which was obviously made up of the dregs of the faubourgs.
' "Let's follow this rabble," Bonaparte said to me.'

As they made for the terrace of the Louvre alongside the Seine the two young friends witnessed an outbreak of violence.

'It would be hard for me,' says Bourrienne, 'to describe his astonishment and anger. . . .'

When Louis XVI, wearing a red cap, appeared at a window overlooking the garden of the Tuileries, Bonaparte could not control his wrath. 'How could they let that rabble in,' he fulminated. 'If four or

[1] According to information given me by the Archives de la Seine this hotel, then No. 355, was on the site of two houses numbered in 1857 20 and 22. The Paris Survey for 1852 describes them thus: 'Houses consisting of a cellar, ground-floor and five square storeys with two small courtyards served by one easy staircase. To let for business.'
[2] It must have been now that he was in the habit of going to the famous Café Procope in the Rue des Fossés St-Germain (now 13, Rue de l'Ancienne Comédie) where tradition has it that he left his hat as a pledge. He may also have gone at this period to the café La Régence, 162, Rue du Faubourg St-Honoré, where I recently saw a table, carefully preserved, on which the future Consul may have played his game of chess.
[3] When the mob invaded the Tuileries. Ed.

five hundred of them had been swept away with gunshot the rest
would be running still.'

At dinner Bonaparte continued to talk about what they had seen
and presciently anticipated the result.

At St Helena Napoleon recalled the bloody riot which broke out
on 10 August.[1] 'When I heard the tocsin and that the Tuileries was
under attack I ran to the furniture shop of Bourrienne's brother at the
Carrousel. . . . It was from this house which, incidentally, I could
never find again, that I saw all that I wanted of that day's happenings.'

Just as the Fronde made a profound impression on the child Louis
XIV so these scenes of violence and disorder left a deep and painful
mark on Bonaparte and signalled the turning-point in his ideological
development. The little 'Jacobin', passionately devoted to freedom,
but with an inborn sense of order, castigated popular uprisings and
was indignant at the flouting of authority; he could not dream that
within ten years it would fall to him to restore that authority and that
as sovereign he would reign in this palace today in a state of siege.
In August 1816, he would say to Las Cases: 'When, on August 10th,
I saw the Tuileries taken by force and the person of the King seized,
I was very far from thinking that this palace would be my home.'

In the meantime he succeeded in getting reinstated in the artillery
with the rank of captain. His nomination was signed on 30 August
by Louis XVI who thus, all unknowing, appointed the man who
would take his place. This promotion did not deflect Napoleon from
his Corsican ambitions. Still intending to resume his command at
Ajaccio, he left Paris on 9 or 10 September and embarked on 10
October 1792, for Corsica, for what was to be his fourth and final
stay in his native country.

This was a highly hazardous period, including a particularly
violent confrontation with Paoli, whose arrest was ordered by the
Convention, while Bonaparte himself, threatened with death by the
Paolists, was forced to flee with his family. He landed at Toulon
on 13 June 1793, and three months later his luck changed. His
appointment as brigadier-general he owed to the siege and seizure
of Toulon. On 6 February 1794, he was named as artillery commander
of the Army of Italy and made his entry into history. . . .

Meanwhile Paris had seen the death of Louis XVI, had fallen into

---

[1] The mob attacked the Tuileries, killed the Swiss Guards, while Louis XVI and his
family became prisoners. Ed.

the clutches of the Committee of Public Safety and was living through the reign of terror. The fall of Robespierre was followed by the Thermidorean reaction (9 Thermidor Year II—27 July 1794).[1] As a friend of the dictator's brother, Augustin Robespierre, Bonaparte became suspect and was imprisoned for three weeks.

On 7 May 1795, he received the unexpected order to join the Army of the West as general of infantry. With Joseph and Sergeant Junot, his first aide-de-camp, and Captain Marmont, both of whom he had met at Toulon, he set out on the 8th for Paris, which he had not visited for almost three years, to justify his conduct and implement one of the hundred and one plans 'he made every night before falling asleep'. He arrived in Paris on 26 May and, with his companions, stayed at the Hotel de la Liberté, 11, Rue des Fossés-Montmartre.[2]

A visit to General Aubry, head of the War Department, confirmed that he had been relieved of his artillery command and put on the inactive list as a major. Lacking employment and on half-pay 'I found myself idle on the streets of Paris'. Soon he would be riding through these streets in a royal coach but now he wandered, sad and solitary, wearing a threadbare grey-green overcoat which fore-shadowed the grey greatcoat of legend. After his frugal meals at the modest eating-house of the Frères Provinciaux, where he eagerly read the newspapers as he ate, he roamed the quays, rummaging in the second-hand bookshops, to return through the winding and unlit streets to his room as darkness fell.

Bonaparte's contacts with the Parisian crowd gave him an insight into its feelings and experience of its generosity. 'In the mass,' he wrote to Joseph, 'the people of Paris are good.' He felt that Paris was the one city in the world where nothing impeded the full develop-ment of a man's personality.

'Here,' he again wrote to Joseph, 'an upright and careful man, mixing only with his friends, can live to the full in the greatest possible freedom.'

[1] The Revolutionary Calendar was adopted on 5 October 1793. Year I of the Revolution began on 22 September 1792, the date of the founding of the republic. The year consisted of twelve months, each of thirty days and six complementary days, the months divided into three decades, the tenth day being decadi, the ninth nonidi, the fifteenth quintidi and so on. The Gregorian calendar was restored on 1 January 1806. Ed.

[2] This road lay between the Place des Victoires and the Rue Montmartre. Linked with the Rues Neuve St-Eustache, des Petits Carreaux and St-Denis, on 2 October 1865, it was re-named the Rue d'Aboukir in honour of the battle gained by Bonaparte over the Turkish army on 25 July 1799.

Nevertheless, in spite of his strength of character, he felt alone in the huge city. 'As yet I had no contacts nor was I used to society.' He went occasionally to Mme Permon's house, visited by many Corsicans, where he found an atmosphere which reminded him a little of his family circle. He also strolled about the boulevards with Junot.

During one of these walks he by chance again met his friend, Bourrienne, who had just got married and was temporarily living in a small apartment in the Rue du Grenier St-Lazare.

'In the six weeks we spent in Paris we often went with him to the theatre and to the excellent concerts given by Garat in the Rue St-Marc, the first fashionable occasions since Robespierre's death.'

Bourrienne also reports that Bonaparte was always serious, no matter what the play.

'When we thought he was not in the theatre,' writes Mme de Bourrienne, 'we would catch sight of him in the second or third gallery, alone in a box, looking sulky.'

His withdrawn air was due to the difficulties he was meeting for himself and his family. At these troubled hours his favourite distraction was the theatre, which he visited several times a week, his preference being for tragedy. Visits to the theatre were also one of his ways to the heart of Paris.

One day, when Bonaparte went to a handsome new building at 19, Rue des Marais, where Bourrienne had found a first-floor apartment, he said that he would rent the house opposite for his uncle, Fesch, and Father Patrault, one of his teachers at the Ecole Militaire. 'If I had this house with my friends across the way and a gig I should be the happiest of men.'

About this time he left his little hotel room for an apartment on the first floor of 19, Rue de la Michodière (which no longer exists), perhaps because he was thinking of marrying Désirée Clary, whose sister, Julie, had married Joseph at Marseilles.

Bonaparte was nominated as brigadier-general in the Army of the West on 13 June, but he rejected this appointment as being too junior for him and applied for sick-leave.

II

General of Paris

The hour of glory at the Cadran Bleu

At the beginning of July Bonaparte left his apartment, which he found too dear, for an hotel, Au Cadran Bleu at 10, Rue de la Huchette, next door to the Hôtel de Normandie at No. 12, on the Left Bank. (This street is subject to a preservation order.) His room on the fifth floor at three francs a week enjoyed a view over the Seine. Both hotels are still in existence; the first, now known as the Hôtel de la Huchette, has a ground-floor restaurant where, up till 1962, the sign, Au Cadran Bleu, was still displayed. The Hôtel de Normandie keeps its old name but now neither hotel has a view over the river.

At the Cadran Bleu, the last of his temporary Paris homes, Bonaparte continued his modest existence; he breakfasted on a bowl of coffee and dined for 25 sous. Occasionally he allowed himself some distraction which also kept him in touch with the fashionable world of the Directory. His disconcerting manners attracted the attention of the beautiful Mme Tallien, Barras' mistress, who held sway at the Chaumière, a small house painted red near the present Place de l'Alma, where he got to know many of those—Cambacérès, Carnot, Fouché, David, to name but a few—who later played various parts in his life.

With the period of calm inaugurated on 20 May[1] Paris recovered its gaiety and revelled in pleasure at its escape from a dictatorship. Theatres, cafés and dance halls were crowded and Bonaparte was made aware that Paris was the centre of entertainment and culture. He wrote to Joseph on 18 July:

'I am amazed at the way in which luxury, amusements and the arts have revived,' and on the 30th, 'This great nation has surrendered to pleasures; balls, theatres, women, the most beautiful in the world, are

[1] Suppression of an insurrection against the government. Ed.

what count. Everything has come back to life—affluence, luxury, good taste, and the Terror is no more than a forgotten dream.'

He also observed that pursuit of pleasure did not exclude intellectual activity. 'Libraries, lectures in history, chemistry, botany and astronomy abound. . . .'

And so through the years and its various parts Bonaparte saw the many faces of Paris: in 1784 the wealth of the young aristocrats; in 1792 the fury of the famished mob; in 1795, when revolution was still in full spate, the essential goodness of the people, pleasure reigning supreme and today's enjoyments always banishing yesterday's sorrows, yet intellect still held its own and life was lived to the full in complete freedom. These lessons, learned by personal experience, he never forgot.

On 18 August fortune again smiled on Bonaparte. He had received new orders to join the Army of the Vendée but, through a recommendation to Aubry's successor, he was attached to the army's topographical bureau. Crouched over his maps in an empty room on the fifth floor of the Pavillon de Flore (the southern wing of the Louvre), Bonaparte could give rein to his strategic gifts. Hope revived; perhaps a new life was opening up, but still misfortune dogged him. His patron had left the Committee of Public Safety and, on 15 September, the Committee struck Bonaparte off the active list of generals because of his refusal to take up the command to which he had been assigned. His reaction was swift; he would go to Constantinople at the head of a mission to the Sultan to reorganize the Turkish army.

The Convention's excesses had aroused the hostility of many Parisians and brought about a revival of the royalist party. This hostility reached its peak after the constitution of the Year III (1795) had been voted. Instead of the 'new men' expected in the government the Convention, intent on hanging on to power, decreed that two-thirds of the deputies should be chosen from its own number.

A royalist-inspired wave of reaction moved Paris against the Assembly. The sections,[1] recruited solely from the nobility and the middle classes, took up arms to manifest in the Chamber. Posters on the walls of Paris adjured the French people to 'take their religion

[1] In 1792 Paris was divided into forty-eight sections in place of the sixty districts instituted for the elections of 1789. Ed.

and their King back to their hearts in order to have peace and bread'. General Menou, commanding the capital's forces, failed to hold the riot in check and was dismissed. During the night of 12/13 Ven-démiaire (4/5 October 1795) the threatened Assembly entrusted Barras with command of the Army of the Interior and the Paris garrison. At this juncture Bonaparte who, on the morning of the 4th had met the capital's new master at Chaillot, entered the scene. According to the *Mémorial de Ste-Hélène* 'he was in a box that evening at the Théâtre Feydeau where they were playing *Beverley*' when his friends told him of the unexpected turn of events. He at once rushed to the gallery 'to assess the effect of this news'. Told that Barras had suggested his appointment as second-in-command, he went home and 'for half an hour pondered on what he should do'. Morally he was reluctant to fire on some of the people, even armed and rebellious, but his sense of order, his dislike of seeing authority flouted and his fear that 'the great principles of the revolution' were melting away, dictated his decision; he accepted the appointment and rapidly left the Rue de la Huchette for the Tuileries to make his acceptance known and assume direction of operations which were then swiftly carried out.

At dawn Bonaparte, encamped on the Place du Carrousel (where soon he would inspect his legendary parades), gave his first orders. Anticipating any move by the sections' infantry, who numbered only six thousand, he ordered the impetuous Murat to transfer the forty pieces of artillery from the camp at Sablons near Neuilly to the nerve centres, the Pont de la Concorde, Pont Royal, Rue de Rohan and the Pont Tournant. Meanwhile twenty-five thousand rioters were marching in two columns on the Tuileries, seat and symbol of government. One column, including the Faubourg St-Germain section, followed the Quai Voltaire and the other, combining the Poissonière and Chaussée d'Antin sections, went down the Rue St-Honoré. The insurgents attacked at about 4.30 p.m. but were halted by fierce fire from the batteries which scattered them in disorder towards the church of St-Roch. By evening it was all over; order was restored and the Convention had triumphed. The workers of the faubourgs were not involved; they were satisfied to look on at the battle with a satirical eye.

To the Parisians Bonaparte was the saviour of the republic and the revolution and they dubbed him General Vendémiaire. His reward came next day when he was promoted general of division and confirmed in his appointment as second-in-command of the Army of the Interior; he had taken a further step on the road to glory.

Fréron, formerly commissioner in Toulon, where he had recognized the young officer's ability, paid public homage to his achievement during the session of the Convention on 10 October. The report of this session was published on 14 October and the name, 'Buonaparte' appeared for the first time in the *Moniteur* and soon was known by Paris, France and Europe. . . .

When Barras became a member of the Executive Directory the victor of Vendémiaire succeeded him on 26 October as commander-in-chief of the Army of the Interior, a post which gave him military command of Paris. His life now changed completely. Previously he had been an officer from the provinces, living in Paris like thousands of others, tramping the streets, hiding his misfortune in one hotel room after another. Today he was no longer a nobody in Paris but one of the masters of the city before becoming its supreme Master.

He was now an important personage—'essential' was the word used by the Duchesse d'Abrantès who wrote:

> 'After the 13 vendémiaire no more muddied boots; Bonaparte rode only in a handsome carriage and lived in a very good house at No. 20, Rue des Capucines,[1] belonging to the First Military Division built on the site of the former Hôtel de la Colonnade where Dupleix died.'

Desaix said that Bonaparte discharged his new duties 'with enormous success, grace and ability'. Thanks to him order was rapidly being restored. On 10 November he took his first measures to reorganize the Paris garrison in a document headed 'Paris Headquarters' which was Bonaparte's first official imprint on Paris.

During his five months in the city Bonaparte devoted himself to the reorganization of his command, which had been established by the Committee of Public Safety with no directive except that he should carry out his superior's orders in the capital. The government was in a state of sixes and sevens so that return to order was essential if Paris was to be properly administered. Thus Bonaparte was obliged for the first time to share in the administration of Paris, a valuable apprenticeship for the future.

---

[1] This street was also called the Rue Neuve-des-Capucines. It ran from the Place Vendôme (Place des Piques during the revolution), where the legendary column would be erected, and the Rue de la Paix, which was opened in 1806 as the Rue Napoléon.

It fell to him to take police action to prohibit the assembly of Jacobins following the closure of the extremist club at the Panthéon which was endangering the capital's security, but his chief anxiety was the eternal municipal problem, food supply, which later became one of the Emperor's dominant preoccupations. In 1795 this was imperative because 'frightful' scarcity and unemployment were throwing the working classes into want. Bonaparte's whole attention was given to solving the problem, seeking a reduction in the price of flour and bread and ordering distributions of bread and wood.

On foot, or more often on horseback, he toured streets, boulevards, markets and the Central Markets as far as the faubourgs, wanting to see, hear and learn everything.

This admirable diligence was noted by the people who began to take an approving interest in this young general still unknown to them, but who deserved the nickname they gave him of 'General of Paris'. One day he was accosted by a fishwife, who shouted at him. 'What do the Jacks-in-office care that we're without bread so long as they get fat?'

Like the quick-witted Ajaccian he was, Bonaparte retorted, 'Look at me, mother, and say which of us is the thinner.'

It is easy to imagine the public's response to this disarming riposte which left the fat fishwife embarrassed by her size when faced with someone so thin.

A useful adjunct to the young General's duties was his contact both with the masters of the day and with the salons of the Directory, of which Barras was king and Bonaparte now an honoured guest. He came to know a frivolous and corrupt world, previously closed to him, and at the Chaumière renewed his acquaintance with Mme Tallien. In this luxurious setting he met one of its goddesses with whom he fell passionately in love and whom he shortly afterwards married, Josephine de Beauharnais. Perhaps he was attracted by her air of being 'a real Parisienne', Napoleon's own description at St Helena of his dead wife, but as 'a lady of Paris' she roused the hostility of the whole Bonaparte family who regarded all Parisiennes as flighty and extravagant.

The marriage of Bonaparte and Josephine was celebrated by Charles Leclerc, registrar, on 9 March 1796, at the town hall of the second municipal district of the Paris canton. The eighteenth-century house at 1 and 3, Rue d'Antin, had belonged to the Marquis de Mondragon, Councillor of State, was confiscated during the revolution and was now the property of the City of Paris which, in 1795, installed the offices there of the Second Arrondissement where they remained until 1833. Today the house is owned by the Banque de Paris et des Pays Bas; the room on the first floor, formerly used for weddings, is now the office of one of the directors.

Errors are known to abound in the marriage certificate; Napoleon's address is given as 1, Rue d'Antin, which was the address of the town hall, and he in fact lived at 20, Rue des Capucines; his birthday is given as 5 February 1768, instead of 15 August 1769. He thus made himself older by eighteen months to appear only a year younger than Josephine, who is shown as being born in 1767 instead of 1763. The most titillating error is undoubtedly the one noted by G.Lenôtre, who saw an extract from the marriage certificate reproduced in the second edition of Bourrienne's Memoirs. Bonaparte is shown as having been born in Paris. Napoleon born in Paris! (It would have given me great pleasure to have unearthed this strange statement, but unfortunately I could find no trace of it, either in the extract from the birth certificate kindly given me by the Archives of the City of Paris or in the full certificates as published, for instance, in Bourrienne's Memoirs.)

Hôtel de la Victoire

Immediately after the marriage Bonaparte moved into Josephine's house at 6, Rue Chantereine,[1] between the Rue de Mont Blanc (Rue de la Chaussée d'Antin) and the Rue des Trois Frères (Rue Taitbout). This street was originally a mere country lane with nothing about it to suggest its future fame. Called Ruellette du Marais des Porcherons (Alley of the Pigkeepers' Marshes) on the plan of Jouvin de Rochefort in 1672, in 1734 it became the Ruelle des Postes, then successively Rue des Planchettes and Rue Chantereine because of the song of the frogs or *reinettes*. The district of the Chaussée d'Antin was reclaimed marshland and a fashionable building-site for big bankers, rich bourgeoisie, nobles of the old régime and actors.

In this house, sheltered from the city's noise, Josephine entertained her friends, both of the old aristocracy and of the new order,

[1] See Appendix VI for a full description of the house.

financiers, politicians or people of the theatre, making her own social contribution to her new husband's career and his imminent reign over France.

Marriage and final residence in the capital were important events in Bonaparte's life in Paris, forging a strong social and sentimental link between him and the city and one highly advantageous to his career. Now that he had a home in Paris, presided over by a woman familiar with the society of the old régime, he could from his Paris base take off for far-flung lands to which his thirst for glory and his star drew him irresistibly.

This was the prospect before him when, on the morning of 11 March 1796, after a honeymoon as brief as it was passionate, Bonaparte tore himself from his wife's arms and left Paris to take up his appointment as commander-in-chief of the Army of Italy. The heroic battles of this first glorious campaign won for the General the sunny lands of Italy and culminated in the peace treaty of Campo-Formio on 10 October 1797.

When Bonaparte, after an absence of twenty months, returned to Paris at 5 p.m. on 5 December, 1797, he found a greatly deteriorated political situation. Although Augereau's armed intervention (which Bonaparte had prompted) on 18 Fructidor Year V (4 September 1797) had preserved the republic from royalist threats, it had delivered the Directory into the hands of the army and had done little to dissipate the dark clouds on the horizon.

Bonaparte was now the glorious pacifying general whose features, reproduced from portraits painted in Milan, were becoming the object of Parisian hero-worship. His energetic intervention of 13 Vendémiaire was remembered by the citizens of Paris who today congratulated themselves that this energy was being put to the country's service. They proudly admired the works of art which filled their museum, symbols of the Italian victories whose sonorous names rang like joy-bells in their ears. Everywhere there were cries of 'Long live General Bonaparte! Long live the conqueror of Italy! Long live the peacemaker of Campo-Formio!'

This glorious picture had, however, another side. Bonaparte's position was delicate. The crowd cheered him, he was loaded with honours, given an official reception on 10 December by the Directory at the Luxembourg and on the 20th at the Louvre by the Institute of which he had just been made a member, but he was also suspect to the Jacobins, hated by the royalists and envied by the Directory. Later he told Mme de Rémusat, 'In Paris—and Paris is France— interest is taken in people rather than in things. It was greatly to the disadvantage of the Directors that nobody bothered about them and people were beginning to take too much interest in me.'

Bonaparte could not play the same part in Paris as in Milan, nor could he take any decisive action. As he was not yet 30 he could not even be a Director—'the grapes were not yet ripe'. He felt Paris weighing on him like 'a leaden coat' and knew, as he began to realize the city's weathercock temperament, that prolonged inaction would soon cause his popularity to melt away.

'Paris has no memory,' he said. 'If I remain inactive for some time I shall be lost. One notoriety replaces another in this great Babylon. When I've been seen three times at the theatre no one will look at me any more; that is why I go so seldom.'

The line of conduct he pursued was in fact to avoid flattering attentions and solicitations and live quietly at home. The *Moniteur*, reporting the General's arrival on 20 December, wrote:

'He has arrived and is staying at his wife's house in the Rue Chantereine, which is small, modest and unpretentious. He goes out rarely and, when he does, it is alone in a carriage with two horses. He can be seen fairly often walking in his little garden.'

In his honour the Central Administration of the Department of the Seine re-named the Rue Chantereine the Rue de la Victoire on 28 December 1797.

One of his rare outings was to a magnificent reception given by Talleyrand at his house in the Rue du Bac for 'the most elegant and distinguished people in Paris'. Here his rude behaviour to Mme de Staël turned her from an admirer into a passionate opponent.

On 26 March 1798, Bonaparte bought the house in which he had lived since his marriage to Josephine, and the remainder of the Bonaparte family followed him to Paris.

To keep his popularity intact and escape from the enervating air of Paris Bonaparte needed to garner fresh laurels; the expedition to Egypt offered the occasion and a glorious opportunity to give substance to his dreams of the Orient. 'All great glory rises in the east,' he had told Junot.

The Directory seized on this God-given chance of sending the too-successful General away from Paris and invested him with

command of the expedition. France and Paris welcomed the appointment and the opportunity, since invasion of England was difficult,
to take the classic way of attacking her through her commerce in
India by way of Egypt and Persia.

Bonaparte was appointed on 3 May 1798. On 1 July he landed at
Alexandria. On the 20th before the mighty Pyramids he beat the
mamelukes and, on the 24th, entered Cairo. The British destruction
on 2 August of the French fleet at Aboukir rendered him a prisoner
of the country he had conquered so, when order was restored, he
decided on 9 February 1799, to march on Syria where the Turks
awaited him. Despite some further victories his failure at Acre
forced him to beat a retreat. He again routed the Turks on 25 July
at Aboukir then left Egypt because, in dispatches and newspapers
from Paris, he had learnt of the loss of Italy and also 'the deplorable
state of France, the decline of the Directory and the successes of the
coalition'. He realized how essential swift action was for him since
Paris also moves fast.

Bonaparte embarked on the frigate *Le Muiron* on 22 August, and,
after calling at Ajaccio, reached Fréjus on 9 October. Welcoming
cries of 'Long live the Republic!' were the earliest indications of his
own immense and growing popularity in France, an impression
which deepened as on his triumphal march he met 'universal delirium'.
The announcement in the theatres of his arrival on 13 October
provoked 'general high excitement' in Paris. Bourrienne, in his
Mémoires remarks: 'No one who had not seen it could imagine such
an outburst of affection which will never be rivalled.'

Bonaparte intentionally took a route different from the one expected and thus arrived, without warning as planned, at dawn on
16 October at the Rue de la Victoire. The morning saw a veritable
siege by numerous visitors, politicians, soldiers and members of the
Institute. When, in the afternoon, Bonaparte called on the Directors
at the Luxembourg people 'crowded into the rooms and courtyards
to see him'. With many he shook hands and talked amicably to the
men who had fought with him in Italy. The *Moniteur* gives a lively
account of this visit:

> 'He was wearing civilian dress under a redingote and a Turkish scimitar
> on a silken sword belt; his hair is short and, after a year in a hot climate,
> his naturally sallow skin has acquired a deeper tone.'

The publication of this pen-portrait, simple but colourful, helped to surround the General with an exotic and romantic aura which heightened the Parisians' admiration.

On his way to Paris Bonaparte had plumbed the country's state of mind and on his arrival discovered the political temper of the capital. 'All parties wanted change and wanted that change to come with him.' The Directory was degenerating; Barras was the sole Director surviving from the previous government. Bonaparte told him that he (Barras) was 'tired and could not get used to the humidity of the capital', a polite way of getting rid of him. It was with Sieyès that the General sought a pact and 'it was agreed that some change might take place between 6 and 11 November'.

Meanwhile Bonaparte went out little, avoided public appearances (as he had done on his return from Italy) and talked only to his colleagues at the Institute, a reserve which disappointed the Parisians, who wanted to get close to the victor of Arcola and see him in action.

'The citizens were complaining about the General's incognito; he was never to be seen at the theatre or in the streets where they waited for him. . . .'

The whole city was impatient but its impatience was of short duration.

III

Master of Paris

The coup d'état

The preliminary arrangements for the change in régime were finalized on 6 November. Talleyrand, the 'great nobleman of the *ancien régime*', in charge of External Affairs, and Fouché, the powerful Jacobin, head of the General Police, both ministers of the Directory, foresaw Bonaparte's success and gave him their warm support, for which he would pay dearly in 1814 and 1815. The Council of Ancients was to order the Council of 500 to St-Cloud,[1] out of range of any possible mass rising. General Bonaparte was to take command of the army; everything had to be so arranged that Paris would accept the planned coup d'état.

During the night of 17/18 Brumaire (8/9 November) the historic meeting, lasting until dawn, at the Rue de la Victoire, determined the destiny of Napoleon, of France and of Europe. Officers and notabilities had gathered in such numbers that they overflowed from the courtyard into the lane, filled with detachments of troops. At 8.30 a.m. an official messenger brought the decree just voted by the Council of Ancients; the five clauses incorporated the agreed measures. Then Bonaparte, in the brilliant uniform of a commanding general, appeared at the top of the steps. He ordered the doors of the house, too small for such a crowd, to be opened and made a brief but stirring speech in which he appealed to their loyalty to save the nation and the republic. His words were met by unanimous cheers. When, at St Helena, he told Las Cases about this vigil, he said: 'My only part in the plot was to receive my host of visitors at the time appointed and march at their head to seize power. It was from

---

[1] [The constitution of the year III (22 August 1795) provided for two Chambers, an Upper House called the Council of Ancients and a Lower House, the Council of 500. Ed.] Article 3 of this constitution empowered the Council of Ancients to transfer both Councils outside Paris.

my own threshold, from the top of my own steps, that I led them to this victory.'

Thereafter orders were given and proclamations issued as planned. 'Legality marches hand in hand with glory.' Bonaparte mounted his horse to lead an impressive procession through the city by the Rue du Mont Blanc, the Boulevard des Capucines, the Boulevard de la Madeleine, the Pont de la Concorde and the Place de la Concorde. He was greeted as he rode past by swelling cheers from the people of Paris, eager to see and applaud the famous general and liberator on whom their dearest hopes were set.

At 10 a.m. Bonaparte entered the Tuileries, which he had saved in Vendémiaire, met in the gardens and the approaches by cheers of 'Long live the Liberator!' from the crowds who seemed in holiday mood. Before the Council of Ancients he swore a solemn oath to fulfil the mission entrusted to him then, after making a speech, he went down to the courtyard accompanied by the cheers of the Council, to be greeted by further cheers as he reviewed the assembled troops, a rapid but impressive ceremony. As he recounted at St Helena, 'The news soon got about that Napoleon was at the Tuileries and that he alone was to be obeyed.'

The Directory had collapsed, the first act was over. To ring down the curtain Fouché, already showing his acumen, had the city's barriers closed.

Bonaparte was radiant. Paris throughout the day had remained quiet but the General, concerned about the public's reactions, dictated a proclamation to Bourrienne (now his secretary), stressing the legality of the operation and calling for the 'union and confidence of the patriots'. He told Bourrienne,

'Peace is what we have now won—this must be announced this evening in every theatre, published in every newspaper, repeated in prose, in verse and even in song.'

His parting words were,

'Altogether it wasn't too bad today. We'll see what happens to-morrow. Goodnight.'

Next day, 19 Brumaire (10 November), the scene shifted to St-Cloud where fatality nearly overtook Bonaparte, greeted on his entry into the Orangery by angry demonstrations. Only the firmness of Lucien, who presided, saved his brother when he was threatened with outlawry. Bonaparte, however, pulled himself together and

succeeded in mastering the opposition of the 500. The intervention
of troops from Paris, commanded by Murat, was decisive; the hall
was quickly cleared by the grenadiers and the deputies fled in confusion, dropping their togas and toques as they ran. Bonaparte was
triumphant. At 11 p.m., still concerned about Paris, he called
Bourrienne: 'Take a note. I must issue a proclamation to the Parisians
this evening. When I get up tomorrow I shall take possession of the
whole city.'

He then dictated an account of the events of these two notable days.

At midnight by the light of candles a resolution was passed
abolishing the Directory and setting up a provisional Consular
Executive Commission of Sieyès, Roger Ducos and Bonaparte;
they were given the title of 'Consuls of the French Republic' and
invested with all the Directory's powers.

The Consuls met at 2 a.m. in the Orangery to take the traditional
oath of allegiance before representatives of both assemblies. The
presence of elegantly dressed Parisians, treating the event as if it
were a theatrical performance, made a brilliant occasion of the
nocturnal session which ended in the festive atmosphere dear to the
citizens of Paris.

Bonaparte and Bourrienne reached the Rue de la Victoire via the
Bois de Boulogne at 3 a.m. After a brief talk Bonaparte took leave
of his secretary, saying, 'By the way—we'll sleep at the Luxembourg
tomorrow.'

Paris had spent a long day of feverish anxiety and alarming
rumours when, momentarily, even the shadow of the Terror had
been glimpsed but, significantly, the faubourgs had made no move.
The populace, exhausted by a continuous and fruitless ten-year
battle, had decided to 'have no part of it'. They would wait and see,
but soon they showed Bonaparte a devotion which never wavered
even in his darkest hours.

The news from St-Cloud about 9 p.m. brought general relief and
a typical Parisian reaction, 'liveliest rejoicing succeeded acute
anxiety'. Vociferous cheers rang out in the crowded theatres. 'It was
in the theatres that public satisfaction was seen at its height.'

Next day Bonaparte's proclamation was displayed on the walls of
the capital. People snatched at the newspapers carrying reports of
the previous day's events while Paris acclaimed the brave young
general, victor of Arcola and the Pyramids, who was also the man

who had signed the Treaty of Campo-Formio, harbinger of hope for the peace to come.

A police report of 12 November stresses this state of mind in Paris:

> 'We are praying fervently that new triumphs will lead us ever nearer to the desired end; peace and Bonaparte's return to the republic are seen as a happy portent for our arms and an assurance of early and brilliant victories.'

Everyone shared the same opinion, Bonaparte, Paris and the whole of France; the foreign coalition must be beaten to end the period of disasters and usher in a lasting era of peace and prosperity.

'Long live Peace!' was the cry greeting Bonaparte who, for the mass of Parisians, was the leader whose sword was paradoxically both the instrument and the symbol of peace. This belief was the basis of a kind of tacit contract between Bonaparte and Paris but, however apparently attractive, it rested on dangerous ground. History shows that peace on earth can never be final and attempts to force its conclusion by the sword end disastrously, but for this Bonaparte is not responsible. He entered the scene when revolution was in full spate and, inheriting a situation not of his making, was inevitably led to continue fighting.

Residence in the Luxembourg

In civilian clothes and a plain carriage escorted only by six dragoons Bonaparte left the Rue de la Victoire about 10 a.m. on 11 November for the Luxembourg where Sieyès and Roger Ducos were living. He passed unobserved as the public had no notice of his departure.

At the Petit-Luxembourg at noon Bonaparte, Sieyès and Roger Ducos began a long and arduous session in the room in the palace used by the Directory. A provisional government was formed including four former ministers of the Directory. Fouché was appointed to General Police, Cambacérès to Justice, Reinhard to External Relations and Bourdon to Marine. Laplace, representing the Institute, was given the Interior, Gaudin, formerly at Posts, obtained Finance, General Berthier War, and Maret Secretary-General of the government. Talleyrand was not given office until 22 November.

By the time Bonaparte left his colleagues the people knew of the previous day's events and expressed their approval by vociferous cheers. In the evening 'public buildings and many private houses were illuminated' and long lines of people marched to cries of 'Long live the Republic! Long live Peace!' The new head of the state returned to his home for only forty-eight hours.

During the next few days Bonaparte's aim was to make direct contact with the city and so, on 12 November, he spent three-quarters of an hour at a meeting of the Institute.

> 'In the midst of his heavy preoccupations,' wrote the *Moniteur*, 'Bonaparte finds time for everything. He has not forgotten the National Institute.'

On a visit the same day he was struck by the bad condition of the Hôtel des Invalides and, anxious to honour the memory of those who had fallen in battle, asked that the church and the dome should be decorated with enemy flags taken during the revolution and antique statues ceded to France under the recent treaties. 'It will be,' he said, 'the heroes' Elysium and shed on them the most noble lustre.'

The task of restoring the building was entrusted to the man who would be official architect and enjoy Bonaparte's regard. Pierre Fontaine had attracted Josephine's notice when he was carrying out work on the house next door to her own in the Rue Chantereine.

To show his eagerness to abrogate the abominable law of hostages passed by the Directory before Novi[1] Bonaparte on 13 November went to the prisons, to see conditions for himself and question the prisoners about their food and the warders' conduct. At the Temple he sent for the keys and freed the hostages on the spot, declaring, 'An unjust law has deprived you of the freedom which it is my first duty to restore to you,' words, rapidly known in Paris, which made a deep impression.

Bonaparte was disgusted by the wretched state of these prisoners. 'What animals those Directors were,' he exclaimed when he returned to work. 'How they have left public institutions! But let's be patient. I will bring order to it all.'

He referred rather sadly to the King. 'When I was at the Temple I could not help thinking of the unhappy Louis XVI.'

His next visit was to the Botanical Gardens where he had a long and friendly conversation with the aged Daubenton, the distinguished

[1] The French were defeated by the Russian general, Suvorov, at Novi on 15 August 1799. A resolution prescribed the taking of hostages where judged necessary in the Departments on 12 July. Ed.

naturalist, who died a few days later. At the Louvre on the 15th he expressed the wish for the early admittance of the public to admire the many works of art brought from Italy. On the 13th he left his last private home in Paris, the little house in the Rue de la Victoire, for the Palace of the Luxembourg.

At the Petit-Luxembourg his rooms were on the ground floor, to the right of the Rue de Vaugirard entrance, which are now those of the President of the Senate; 'Citizeness Bonaparte' was installed in the neighbouring apartment on the first floor. The General's study was near a concealed staircase leading to his wife's rooms.

The Provisional Consulate did not last long. Bourrienne rightly called it the Preparatory Consulate since in fact it led to the Consulate for life until the advent of the Empire. Like all revolutions, the coup d'état marked the end of one era and the beginning of a new order, for which the way had to be cleared. One by one the Departments conceded this change. Paris apparently accepted it but Bonaparte knew the capital's vacillating temper and he may have asked himself this question, excellently put by Vandal: 'Is Paris capable of giving any government its consistent and unwavering support?' Bonaparte, knowing as a realist that the answer lay in his own ability to exercise power, with customary energy at once tackled the task of serving the great city.

The country was in a shocking state. Many people had been ruined by the disruption and distress caused by the revolution. Finance gave rise to special concern. The Treasury had only 167,000 frs in cash; government stocks had fallen to 2.25 frs by 20 October; the budget showed a steady deficit of 200 millions; tax collection had been systematically assigned to nominees or collectors who squeezed the last drop out of the taxpayers.

Not less distressing was Paris itself. Disorder and deficit in her finances seemed to have come to stay. There was neither a real budget nor inherited wealth; no public service was working, whether in general administration, roads, cleansing, public assistance, cemeteries, police, food supply or lighting. The city was unprotected; armed robberies took place at its gates. Public property, monuments, buildings, roads and gardens were in a state of neglect. Plinths, from which the statues had been torn down, looked desolate. Churches were ruined and desecrated and hospitals badly dilapidated. Private houses were on the verge of collapse since their owners, crushed by taxes, continually postponed even the most urgent repairs. Trade was at a standstill and unemployment rife. The difficulties of workers and small shopkeepers were increased by the rise in the price of food.

Socially the city had fallen into decadence. People thrown off balance by long years of terror and misery were receptive only to motives of profit and self-gratification. Some six hundred and forty dance-halls were crowded and dancing even took place in convents. The prosperity of the large number of places of entertainment was notorious. They numbered more than two hundred, from the great gardens of the former princely houses like Mousseaux (Parc Monceau), Bagatelle (near Longchamp), the hamlet of Chantilly (Elysée Bourbon), Frascati (at the corner of the boulevard and the Rue de Richelieu), Tivoli, the former 'folly Boutin' in the Rue de Clichy (near the present church of the Trinité), to the low eating- and public-houses of the faubourgs and the suburbs where 'dance-halls' had been set up.

Many loan-issuing houses were in operation and a whole menagerie of brokers, businessmen and speculators competed with one another in clever frauds, dragging in their wake many poor people grasping at illusory profits.

All this profoundly shocked Bonaparte's overriding passion for order. Without support of any kind he had to summon up all his innate resources to grapple with the situation. The coffers were empty and the military force of Paris reduced to five regiments and the former Guard of the Councils and the Directory, a total of some seven thousand men. Initially, therefore, Bonaparte's authority was purely moral, a historic fact worthy of recall.

Finance was the first problem tackled by Bonaparte. A law passed on 18 November abolished the graduated tax on the rich which naturally had repercussions on industry and the working class. This tax was replaced by a war contribution, raised by a surtax of 0.25 frs on the principal of other taxes. These imposts were levied on all citizens without exception, thus achieving the principle of tax equality, a step which immediately restored confidence and credit in Paris. The *Journal de Paris* of 20 November remarks:

'Before 18 Brumaire landed property near Paris could find neither purchaser nor mortgagor, but today both are available and all businessmen
are agreed that its monetary value has increased by more than the amount

of a year's rents. If, as it is to be hoped, this happens elsewhere, land-owners' capital will increase by 1,500 millions since that fortunate day. Goods of all kinds are selling better, money everywhere in good supply and cheaper. . . . Empty apartments are being re-furnished, carriages emerging from coachhouses and horses, which vanished because of the forced loan, are reappearing as if Neptune had conjured them with his trident out of the earth.'

Indeed, around the Opéra and the theatres the carriages long absent were seen again.

Bonaparte was obliged to seek from the capitalists the funds essential to run his government. On 24 November he summoned the principal businessmen and bankers of Paris to the Luxembourg (now called the Palace of the Consuls), to ask for a cash advance of 12 millions, repayable from the war contribution. According to the *Moniteur* of the 28th 'an extempore speech by Bonaparte raised enthusiasm to the skies' and the loan was granted with acclamation. In the event only three millions were subscribed which met 'our armies' most pressing needs', To pay the troops, a lottery loan with tickets at 300 frs a time was issued on the 29th.

Bonaparte, himself a witness in 1795 to the corrupt society of the Directory, was also anxious to restore morality. One cold evening at the Luxembourg he ostentatiously threw some logs on the fire, remarking pointedly for the benefit of the lightly-clad *merveilleuses*[1] present, 'Can't you see that these ladies are naked?'

Bonaparte's strictures were useful as thereafter a more suitable dress was worn by the coquettes, beginning with Josephine, who took her husband's hint. All praise is also due to her for the elegance of her receptions at the Luxembourg, which helped to strengthen his popularity in Paris. Bonaparte had a further influence on fashion; when he expressed surprise that elegant women were wearing white muslin or English organdie instead of French silks, patriotic ladies thereafter ordered their winter dresses, petticoats, wrappers, spencers and shawls in silk.

Prostitution, one of the scourges of society at the end of the eighteenth century, was among the matters dealt with by the Con-sular police; on 3 December Fouché's rounding-up of the girls at the Palais Royal caused a certain stir as it was rumoured that they were

[1] Fashionable young women who, after the end of the Reign of Terror, adopted a style of dress inspired by Greek and Roman antiquities; their dresses were of the lightest materials and highly transparent. Ed.

to be sent to Egypt to entertain the troops during their leisure hours. Credence was given to this rumour because the First Consul had lately asked Laplace to recruit a troupe of actors and suggested that it might be a good idea 'to have a few dancers'. This suggestion seemed both arbitrary and scandalous and met stern criticism which led Bonaparte to say to Roederer on 10 December, 'Where the devil have they got the idea that I wanted to send the girls arrested at the Palais Royal to Egypt?' Two days later a denial appeared in the *Moniteur*.

The Provisional Consulate was drawing to an end. In little more than a month only matters of the greatest urgency could be tackled but the speed, tact and relevance employed did much to dissipate the capital's hesitations after the coup d'état. About the consequent increase in the confidence Paris placed in the First Consul Vandal writes:

> 'Bonaparte's real conquest of Paris followed rather than preceded Brumaire. Of all the infant Consulate's achievements this is one of the most extraordinary and least known.'

I personally believe that this conquest was progressive; the groundwork was laid by Bonaparte's previous acquaintance with Paris where he had lived through times difficult but rich in experience. Its opening phase was Vendémiaire, continued thereafter with his command of the Paris garrison and the unfolding of his administrative talents. It flourished indirectly but brilliantly through the Italian campaign and reached maturity at the Peace of Campo-Formio and the Egyptian expedition, which were the basis of his popularity but, to crown his conquest, Bonaparte had to gain power and assume the government of the capital.

The hazards of provisional government were weathered when the new constitution which replaced that of the Year III (1794), now virtually moribund, was adopted on 13 December 1799 (Year VIII).

The day after the coup d'état Bonaparte had quipped to Roederer that a constitution should be 'short and obscure'. Short it may have been, but on one point at least it was clear; the concentration of all executive power in Bonaparte, appointed First Consul for ten years. The eminent lawyer, Cambacérès, representing the leftish tendency, and Lebrun that of the right, were the other two Consuls. Legislative power was shared by the First Consul, who proposed laws, the Tribunate which discussed them and the Legislature which decreed and voted them. The conservative Senate's duty was to protect the constitution and, from the lists of elected notabilities, to select the members of the assemblies.

The text of the constitution, promulgated on 15 December, was published on the 16th in the press and proclaimed all over Paris to the roll of drums and the sound of fanfares. The population, hitherto indifferent to the complex discussions preceding the voting, was now eager to hear the provisions of this notable charter and crowded round the civic officers reading it aloud in the streets.

This quotation from the *Gazette de France* of 17 December is an excellent pointer to public opinion.

'A woman said to her neighbour, "I didn't hear a thing." "Oh, *I* didn't miss a word." "Well, what's in this constitution?" "Bonaparte."'

To the people the First Consul was the blood and bones of the constitution.

The publication of the constitution overshadowed the importance of a decision taken on 16 December to restore the Ecole Polytechnique, which shortly afterwards was given a suitable home.

Bonaparte formed his government on 22 December. Lucien was given the Interior with public works, agriculture, industry and commerce in his bailiwick. His ministry was installed at the Hôtel de Brissac, 116, Rue de Grenelle. Fouché stayed at the head of the General Police at the Hôtel de Juigné, 13, Quai Malaquais, on the present site of the Ecole des Beaux-Arts. While the authority of both ministers extended over the whole of France it was particularly exercised in the capital.

Talleyrand retained the Ministry of External Relations at 73, Rue de Grenelle, a private mansion opening on the Rue du Bac, and Gaudin continued at the Ministry of Finance. The Ministry of the Treasury (set up in September 1801) with Barbé-Marbois in charge, was given offices at the Hôtel Tuboeuf, Rue Neuve des Petits-Champs, in the building now occupied by the Bibliothèque Nationale, then housed in the neighbouring Hôtel de Nevers. The Postal Department was installed in the Rue Jean-Jacques Rousseau and the Ministry of Religions at the Hôtel de Soyécourt, 51, Rue de l'Université. Maret became Secretary of State, Forfait Minister of

Marine and Abrial Minister of Justice. They were housed respectively at the Garde-Meuble, 2, Place de la Concorde, and at the Hôtel Choiseul, 13, Place Vendôme, where they remain today.

Berthier retained the portfolio of War at the Hôtel d'Orsay, 69, Rue de Varenne. In 1804 the War Ministry moved to two neighbouring buildings at 10 and 12, Rue St-Dominique and the Hôtel d'Aiguillon, Rue de l'Université. In 1818 it added the Hôtel de Brienne at 14, Rue de l'Université, formerly belonging to Lucien and given in 1806 by Napoleon to Madame Mère who, in 1817, sold it to the state. The present offices of the Ministry of the Armies are located on this site.

Today three ministries remain where they were put by Bonaparte, from whose era dates the practice of housing great Parisian administrative departments in large buildings, mainly former private residences.

On the afternoon of 22 December Sieyès selected the members of the Senate, whose president he was to be, while Bonaparte summoned the Council of State for the first time. He relieved his limited number of ministers of some of their responsibilities by assigning certain services, under their authority, to the Council of State, which played a leading part in the conduct of administration. From this arrangement sprang the ministerial directorates which were and still are one of the glories of the French administrative system.

Under his own chairmanship the First Consul likewise initiated periodical meetings of ministers, Councillors of State and high officials with a specific interest in scrutinizing decisions taken. These administrative councils were a successful innovation. At sessions devoted to internal affairs regular discussions took place about the great public works in Paris, always in the presence of the Prefect of the Seine. The first council was held on 18 January, 1800.

On 17 December when registers were opened in Paris for the public vote on the constitution, in many places so many 'ayes' were registered that there was not a single 'no'. The first Paris returns sent to the Ministry of the Interior on the 19th showed 12,440 'ayes', plus 12,000 from the garrison, to only ten 'noes'. Paris approved the constitution and the First Consul. Bonaparte, in his anxiety to implement the new constitution, anticipated the national poll and proceeded on the basis of the capital's approbation alone. By the law of 24 December the constitution came into force on the

25th. The Tuileries was allocated to the Consuls, the Palais Bourbon to the Legislature and the Palais Egalité (Palais Royal) to the Tribunate while the Luxembourg, too small for the new government, was assigned to the Senate. This personal decision made by Bonaparte was definitive as the Senate still sits at the Luxembourg where Chalgrin built a Chamber for debates and a monumental staircase.

Considerable interest attaches to the manner in which the varied and important events since 18 Brumaire were brought to the public's attention. Bonaparte, an instinctive propagandist, took personal charge of something which he thoroughly understood. He decided that the *Moniteur Universel*, which had been edited by Sieyès, should be his own newspaper and the sole official journal. From now on, he took charge of its policy, its direction and even the editing. The *Moniteur* was his favourite medium for informing and influencing public opinion both in France and abroad, but his special target was Paris where he wanted to encourage and even provoke public reaction. For fifteen years the *Moniteur* was a link between Napoleon and his capital.

The issue of 28 December, No. 97, was the first of the new paper, printed on four pages, each of three columns. Unlike the *Journal Officiel* it occasionally printed, in addition to legal and official documents, important items affecting Paris or the progress of public works in the city. The *Moniteur* was sold by subscription at 13, Rue des Poitevins at 25 frs a quarter.

The first issues contained a series of proclamations and decisions made by the First Consul, all impregnated with 'the spirit of order, justice and moderation'. Successively the government amnestied the Vendéen insurgents who 'repented', allowed the return to France of the Fructidor deportees, opened public office to those former nobles or relatives of émigrés who 'showed themselves reliable', permitted the free use of religious buildings, dispensed ministers of religion and other officials from the constitutional oath and authorized the celebration of mass on Sundays. Homage to bravery inspired other measures; the old Hôtel des Invalides, the Elysium of Courage, was elevated to a Temple of Victory, was to be improved and become the sacred repository of martial trophies; swords of honour were to be bestowed on soldiers who had performed outstanding feats of arms, anticipating the Legion of Honour. Already apparent were the great lines of the policy Bonaparte intended to pursue.

These decisions, particularly those concerned with religion, following hard on the coming into force of the constitution, created a great sensation in Paris.

'The First Consul's decree permitting freedom of worship,' notes a report of 3 January, 'has had a great effect. Attendance these last few days at church doors has been considerable. Many people shook hands and embraced.'

The Revolution was over. On 15 December there was a Consular declaration:

'The Revolution is rooted in its original principles; it is ended.'

What was excessive and injurious in the revolution did in fact disappear but what was good and noble in it survived in a purified and, it must be stressed, in a republican form. Peace replaced disturbance, order confusion, tolerance persecution, pardon hatred and so, as Jaurés said, 'the work of the revolution set itself to rights'.

Bonaparte, astonished that no organization existed to protect the capital's commercial interests, desired one to be founded as soon as possible; this was the origin of the Chamber of Commerce, set up in 1802. His most important creation, however, was the Banque de France. The chaos created by the circulation of paper money, the scarcity of capital, the excessively high rates of interest and discount urgently demanded a revival of credit. Bonaparte who, in any case, found it intolerable that the Treasury should be at the mercy of private capital, decided that the solution was to set up a bank in Paris, essential for so large a business centre. On 21 February the Banque de France discounted its first bills with immediate and substantial benefits to the Parisian economy which were subsequently extended to the whole country.

An announcement made by the Paris Tax Commission on 31 December ended with these words:

'You expect the government to give you all the benefits of peace; the government expects from you the prompt payment of your taxes,'

an indication that Bonaparte intended the people to show their solidarity with the administration. Later, a decree of 8 March promised that

'The department which, by the end of April, will have paid the largest part of its taxes will be cited as having deserved well of the country.'

The Department of the Vosges won this distinction and gave its name to the Place Royale—still the Place des Vosges—in the heart of one of the city's busiest districts.

In establishing his authority firmly and achieving internal pacification Bonaparte met resistance from revolutionaries and those royalists who regarded the Consular government as a passing phase but, as a whole, the population of Paris had become indifferent to politics and immune to any political virus. This political apathy is an important sign of the nation's fear of any kind of extremism and its trust in Bonaparte whose popularity continued to grow.

Evidence of this was given at an early session of the Assemblies when the vote was taken on the law governing the relationship between the various authorities. In spite of an eloquent and lively speech to the Tribunate by Benjamin Constant, lover of Mme de Staël, the government carried the day.

Mme de Staël had reopened her salon which had become a centre of opposition and was frequented by those whom Bonaparte called 'the ideologues', a revival of parliamentary strife which evoked unhappy memories and was resented by Paris. The Press reflected public opinion and criticized the Tribunate with such vehemence that Bonaparte, anxious to maintain public order, had to curb its freedom, but the decree of 17 January which reduced the number of newspapers from seventy to thirteen aroused little public reaction. Bonaparte contented himself with imposing on Mme de Staël a temporary withdrawal to her 'folly' at St-Ouen.

Residence at the Tuileries

The First Consul considered his power to be sufficiently established for him to take up residence in the home of the kings. For more than a century the château, completed by Louis XIV in 1672, had been abandoned when the Sun King with his Court made his home at Versailles. During Louis XVI's occupation little improvement had been made to the Tuileries which, moreover, had suffered much damage during the revolution; the walls still bore the scars of 10 August. Empty since 20 January 1793, the palace looked ruined and devastated.

Some hasty work, mainly painting, had been carried out during the winter of 1800 by Leconte, architect of the Tuileries, for its new master, who visited it several times with his secretary to supervise the alterations he had ordered. Bourrienne reports that, when the Consul saw the many Phrygian caps painted on the walls by the sansculottes, he exclaimed, 'Get rid of all this—I won't have such filth!'

The rough wooden fence separating the palace courtyard from the Place du Carrousel was replaced by an iron grille with guardrooms at either end. On the southern guardroom was inscribed:

'On August 10th, 1792, royalty was abolished in France. It will never be restored.'

Few of the trees which had once graced the courtyard remained except in the centre where two slender poplars, stripped of their skeletal branches, had been spared because of their resemblance to 'trees of liberty'.

Bonaparte took over the royal apartments in the left wing of the palace, himself occupying the first floor which communicated by a small staircase with the ground floor which was to be Josephine's. The Pavillon de Flore[1] was temporarily assigned to Lebrun who shortly after moved into the Hôtel de Noailles[2] in the Rue St-Honoré while Cambacérès took up residence in the Hôtel d'Elboeuf on the Place du Carrousel opposite the château.

The people saw the First Consul's installation in the Tuileries as a symbol of the accession to power of the citizen they had chosen as their leader. As Cambacérès said, 'Bonaparte himself wanted to be the head of a magnificently well-ordered republic. He was a republican as the workers and soldiers were republicans, that is, their conception of a republic was France without a king and a conqueror of kings.'

In 1799 Bonaparte was not yet dreaming of an empire, only that France should be well governed and that order should prevail. His residence at the Tuileries showed that he intended Paris to be the seat of government and the nation's capital in every sense.

In the fortuitous accident of Washington's death on 14 December 1799, he found an opportunity to clothe his own advent with solemn democratic significance, and, as Bourrienne says, decided to 'dazzle the Parisians with a brilliant ceremony', in which he commemorated

[1] Southern wing of the Louvre on the Seine side. Ed.
[2] Now the Hotel St-James and Albany. Ed.

simultaneously the death of the founder of the great American democracy and the laying up of flags taken from the Turks and brought from Egypt to Paris.

Fontaine's aid was enlisted to make the solemn ceremony on 9 February one of great pomp. 'On a fine clear day' Lannes handed over the seventy-two flags taken by the Army of the Orient to Berthier, who laid them at the feet of the statue of Mars in the presence of ministers, Councillors of State and the civil and military authorities. The *Moniteur* of the 24th described this 'majestic scene' in these terms:

> 'Thousands of enemy flags hung from the columns and the vaulting. On either side of the Minister Berthier stood two old soldiers, each over a hundred, whose memories of Denain and Fontenoy blurred at the sight of the trophies of Arcola and Aboukir. The sound of martial music and the presence of the heroes whose surprise return sealed the destiny of France, the sight of these aged warriors, their strength frozen by time but their hearts still beating for glory, all combined to lend a mysterious aura of charm and a certain religious awe to this setting.'

After Lannes' speech, to which Berthier replied, Fontanes delivered Washington's funeral oration, linking in the same grandiloquent homage 'this American hero' and 'the genius whose triumphant hands healed the nation's wounds'. Then black crêpe was hung on all the flags to remain there for ten days.

Bonaparte had wanted the result of the votes cast for the constitution to be published on the day preceding his residence in the Tuileries, so this proclamation was made on 18 February. To the sound of trumpet and drum civic processions made their way during the afternoon to the twelve Paris arrondissements, to the Palais Bourbon, the Luxembourg, the Palais Royal, the Tuileries and the Hôtel de Ville. The crowd at the Central Markets showed its delight by striking up the 'Ça ira'. In the Tuileries garden Murat, commandant of the Consular Guard, inspected the troops taking part in the following day's ceremony and, at the end of the evening, the First Consul, wrapped in his grey greatcoat and attended only by two officers, made a reconnaissance of the capital to sound out public opinion.

In accordance with Bonaparte's wishes the *Moniteur* published next day a five-column supplement devoted to the ecstatic speech made by Fontanes ten days earlier, intended to impress the people. A large crowd gathered round the Luxembourg to see the departure of the First Consul, making his first ceremonial appearance since his advent to power. He awoke in excellent spirits and said to Bourrienne, 'Well, it's today that at last we are going to sleep at the Tuileries. It's all right for you—you haven't got to make a show of yourself. . . . I've got to go in a procession which impresses the people. Everyone discounted the Directory because of its lack of ceremony. Simplicity is all very well in the army but, in a great city and a palace, the head of a government must do everything possible to attract the public, but it must be done warily . . .'

The Consuls, the ministers and the Councillors of State gathered at the Luxembourg in ceremonial dress. Bonaparte, in his official uniform of red velvet laced with gold, wore the sabre presented to him by the Emperor of Austria after the Treaty of Campo-Formio. At 1 p.m. precisely, to the thunder of cannon and the sound of fanfares, the orderly procession of twenty carriages moved off, preceded by a picket of hussars. The escort consisted of three thousand picked men including a superb detachment of Guides. Bonaparte, with Cambacérès on his left and Lebrun opposite, sat in a carriage, also a gift from the Emperor, drawn by six white horses.

Between lines of grenadiers of the Consular Guard the Consuls rode through the capital by way of the Rue de Thionville (Rue Dauphine) and the Quai Voltaire to the Pont Royal; as they went the people, with eyes only for the First Consul, hailed him joyously, many of them clinging like human bunches of grapes to windows, paying a high price for those overlooking the Place du Carrousel.

Josephine, surrounded by elegant ladies dressed *à la grecque,* was at the Pavillon de Flore. Joy was at its height, 'hope and happiness shone on every face' and the crowd shouted tirelessly, 'Long live the First Consul! Long live Bonaparte!'

The Consular carriage passed through the new grille to stop below the Pavillon de l'Horloge. Bonaparte descended quickly and jumped on his horse to review the assembled troops. Since he went down every rank, saying a few flattering words to the commanders, the inspection was prolonged. He then took up his position at the pavilion entrance, with Murat on his right and Lannes on his left and round him the army leaders and their glittering staffs of young warriors tanned by the suns of Egypt and Italy. Bonaparte watched the troops march past impassively but, when the torn and powder-blackened flags of the 96th, 43rd and 30th half-brigades went by, he took off his hat and bowed as a mark of respect, a gesture which evoked redoubled and frenzied cheers.

When the parade was over Bonaparte 'briskly' mounted the Tuileries staircase to meet in his study both Consuls, the ministers and Councillors of State. The Council of State was officially installed in part of the Grand Gallery, where the archives had been housed, next to his own apartments. To show how much weight the government attached to the capital, Lucien presented the administrative authorities of Paris and the evening ended with a state dinner.

After his first night in the royal palace, now given the democratic name of 'Palace of the Government', Bonaparte confided to Bourrienne his pleasure at the evidence of his increasing reputation among the people of Paris. 'I am very pleased. Yesterday went very well. The people were genuinely happy and with reason . . .'

He also congratulated himself on the rise in stock-exchange prices. 'Consult the great barometer of public opinion. Look at the price of stocks—11 frs on 8 November, 16 frs on the 20th and today 21 frs— so I can let the Jacobins cackle—but let them not do it too loud!'

When Bonaparte was dressed, he and Bourrienne went to the Galerie de Diane where he scrutinized the many busts he had placed there, among them Scipio, Brutus, Cicero, Cato, Demosthenes, Hannibal, Alexander, Caesar, Washington, Frederick the Great and Mirabeau. For a moment Bonaparte mused and then said, 'It isn't everything to be in the Tuileries; one must stay there.'

Looking out of a window in the Galerie he recalled his youth and remarked to Bourrienne, 'Look, there's your brother's house. Wasn't it from there that I saw the assault on the Tuileries and good Louis XVI carried off?'

He added, frowning and drawing himself up, 'But don't worry, let them just come . . .'

Centralization of Paris

The First Consul's occupation of the Tuileries coincided with the famous law of 28 Pluviôse Year VIII (17 February 1800), which reinforced the new constitution. Paris, the political capital, was to be also the administrative capital, inaugurating a régime of total centralization. This law, which owed much to Bonaparte's feeling for order and authority, still governs administrative life in France. It

enshrines two principles; the government is the sovereign administrator and administration is delegated to a single agent of the central
government by whom he is appointed. In the Departments this agent
is the Prefect who acts as the lynchpin of the government and is in
fact what Napoleon soon called him, 'an emperor in miniature'.

The City of Paris and the Department of the Seine owe their
status, carrying the imprint of the Napoleonic system, to this law of
Pluviôse. To appreciate its importance and understand its structure
the previous history of Parisian administration is worth resuming
briefly.

During the monarchy Paris was always subject to a special régime
under the authority of two officials, one appointed by the central
government and the other chosen by the people and assisted by a city
council.

The revolution swept away the institutions of the old régime and
the Convention set up an authoritarian and centralized government to
assume direction of the administration of the city. On 24 August
1794, the sections were abolished, to be replaced by twelve arrondissements, the origin of the present arrondissements. Under the
Directory both Paris and the Department of the Seine were under the
thumb of the Directors.

The law of Pluviôse did not set the Department of the Seine and the
City of Paris outside the common law. Both Parisian administrative
units were included in the dispositions of Articles XVI and XVII.
While the law was under discussion Senator Daunou, in his report on
12 February, put forward reasons which are still valid, 'In the very
heart of the republic there is a city whose great size, huge population
and the presence of the nation's leading authorities make it difficult
for it to conform exactly to an administrative régime suitable for
other parts of the country. . . .'

Despite the criticisms levelled at the system it is extremely
well organized; freedom may be curbed but anarchy is wholly
absent.

In place of the central administration of the Directory two prefects
were nominated by the government as heads of the Department of
the Seine; the Prefect of the Seine, invested with administrative
functions properly so called, and the Prefect of Police.

The law of 28 Pluviôse Year VIII is silent on the civic duties of
the Prefect of the Seine, but those of the Prefect of Police are the

subject of Article XVI, paragraph 2, which lays down that 'In Paris a Prefect of Police shall be in charge of all police matters'. The Prefect of Police had a decided advantage in the explicit definition of his functions by the decrees of 1 July 1800, still in force, extended by a decree of 25 October 1800.

This dichotomy is justified both for reasons of history and convenience. One person could scarcely carry out the vast prefectoral duties in the Department of the Seine; the merits of the system exceed its demerits. The two Prefects, constantly in touch with the capital, are fully cognizant of Parisian aspirations, which they sincerely try to meet. The abuse a single mayor, elected by the people of Paris, might make of his office to become a disruptive force in the nation is obviated by the appointed of the Prefects by the central government to whose authority they are subject. The Prefects differ in functions but are equal in importance; neither can impose his will on the other so that power is always balanced between them and the citizens benefit by the friendly rivalry of their administrators.

Without one mayor for the whole city Paris, like the Department of the Seine, came under the jurisdiction of both Prefects. The Prefect of the Seine centralized the powers of the twelve boroughs, while the Prefect of Police was heir to the powers parcelled out under the Directory among members of the cantonal central office.

A Departmental or General Council was to fulfil the duties of a Municipal Council. Its twenty-four members, appointed by the head of state, like those in other communes in France, acted in an advisory capacity to the Prefects. In Paris this was a purely consultative body, particularly in financial matters. It met annually at a date fixed by the government but its general session lasted several months against the fortnight taken by other civic assemblies. In this way the government of the city was totally dependent on the central power which eliminated any danger of anarchy or dictatorship of the people. A special council of the Prefecture had charge of administrative disputes.

This arrangement has often been criticized as a trick played on Paris, but this argument is invalid when it is recalled that Paris at that time included the two suburban arrondissements of St-Denis (or Franciade) and Sceaux, which were largely rural with a population of barely eighty-four thousand.

The division of Paris into twelve arrondissements was maintained, each with a mayor and two deputies, making twelve mayors and twenty-four deputies. Each arrondissemnet had four sectors, forty-eight sectors in all, which corresponded to the revolutionary sections and, in 1811, became the present Paris districts.

The original government of Paris

The First Consul wanted all the posts in Paris and the Seine to be filled as soon as possible and, three weeks after the law of Pluviôse, between 2–10 March, he signed the appointments of both Prefects, the five councillors of the Prefectures, the twelve mayors and twenty-four deputies and the twenty-four General Councillors.

Frochot was the first Prefect of the Seine. Born in 1761, a good bourgeois from Dijon, with fine features, simple in dress, he was 'a man of parts and good manners', considered to be a model patriot. His stormy political career had been devoted to combating extremism of whatever origin. In 1785 he was a notary and royal provost at Aignay-le-Duc and in 1789 became a member of the Constituent Assembly, where he got to know Talleyrand, Sieyès, Maret and Cambacérès. Frochot was singled out by Mirabeau to become his closest associate, thus gaining some acquaintance with the workings of the Paris administration, of which Mirabeau was a member, failing in 1791 to become mayor of the city.

When the Constituent Assembly was dissolved Frochot was imprisoned as suspect under the Terror, but returned to politics as a member of the Directory of the Côte d'Or. In 1799 he happened to be in Paris where he met his old friends, all now in positions of authority, who secured his nomination by the Senate as a member of the Legislature.

Frochot's qualifications had been brought to Bonaparte's attention by his associates and the First Consul had been quick to seize on his moderation, courage and devotion to the public weal, but primarily he saw Frochot as the closest collaborator of Mirabeau, for whom he cherished the highest regard. Had he not had his bust placed in the gallery at the Tuileries?

When he received some twenty prefects at 4 p.m. on 5 March 1800, he said to Frochot, the first to be presented to him. 'I know who you are and I can foresee what you will be, but my prime motive in entrusting you with the Prefecture of Paris—and one I want to mention now—is that, although the revolution treated you badly, you have nevertheless remained attached to its principles and, appointed administrator of your Department after a long period of persecution, you persecuted no one.'

Bonaparte cast a long keen look at the other prefects and added: 'Be men of the government, never men of the revolution. . . . Remember that you stand above intrigues just as the government stands above factions. The administration must be the government's right hand and France must date her happiness from the founding of the prefectures.'

Frochot set up his offices in a private house, 17, Place Vendôme (now the Ritz Hôtel), leased to him by the City Domains. He at once set to work with determination, devoting his days and even some of his nights to the government of Paris, anxious to justify the First Consul's confidence. Frochot regarded himself as the servant of the public with whose problems he sought personal acquaintance. He had the following notice inserted in the *Moniteur*:

> 'The Prefect will receive the public on primidis, quintidis and nonidis from 2 p.m. till 4 p.m.'

Frochot's assistant as Secretary-General was Méjan who had also worked with Mirabeau.

The first Prefect of Police was Dubois, then 43, energetic and ambitious. He had been an attorney at the Châtelet in 1797 and in 1799 an official at the Central Office of the Paris canton, which accounts for his being chosen in preference to the supposed 'reactionaries', Roederer and Regnault de St-Jean d'Angély. In the submission for his appointment he was noted as 'active and indefatigable; friend of liberty; knows Paris very well'. Dubois was appointed on 8 March and on the 11th took office which he held until 1810. The Duchesse d'Abrantès reports that Bonaparte said of him, 'We must not take the man whom the office suits but the man who suits the office.'

The original home of the Prefecture of Police was in the former residence of the First President of the Parlement, behind the Sainte-Chapelle in the Rue de Jérusalem (also called the Rue de l'Arcade), which ran from the Quai des Orfèvres and disappeared after the fire in 1871 when the Palais de Justice was extended.

Frochot had begun work without fuss but Dubois announced himself to the Parisians on 15 March in a portentous and highly 'official' declaration:

'Citizens, this city is enormous and the police must act swiftly. It is my
desire to justify the government's choice in entrusting police matters to
me so I call on your advice and I welcome your complaints.'

He affirmed his interest in good conditions in the prisons, said that
seditious meetings would be suppressed, that the liberty of the press
would be respected, in a word that order should prevail. Dubois'
Secretary-General was Citizen Piis, appointed on 14 March; he was
45, a compulsive rhymester and author of thousands of poems. The
Prefect of Police was also assisted by forty-eight commissioners
divided among the twelve arrondissements.

On Bonaparte's instructions the mayors were chosen among the
city's notables and appointed by a collective decree on 9 March.
Although their duties were restricted to registration and charities,
under the Empire they did exert great moral influence. As representatives of their arrondissements and familiar with the people's needs
they acted in some ways like the present Municipal Councillors and
constituted the Mayoral Corps, which played a large ceremonial and
representational role. The mayors were initially housed in public
buildings on lease but later, as Napoleon wished them to have
permanent offices, Frochot bought buildings at the city's expense.

Among the General Councillors appointed by collective decree on
10 March were Josephine's notary, Raguideau, and the lawyer,
Bellart. Bonaparte had no inkling when he signed this appointment
that he was empowering a man who became one of his most inveterate
enemies nor that, in 1814, Bellart would play a decisive part in the
events leading to his fall.

Frochot was officially installed in office on 14 March by Lucien
Bonaparte. The Prefect's speech was fervent but betrayed some of
the anxiety always felt by an official when he assumes the formidable
responsibilities of a prefect in Paris: 'And what greater proof could
be given of the confidence inspired by the strength and wisdom of this
government than my temerity in assuming alone the weight of so
immense a task?'

He ended with a glowing tribute to the First Consul and recalled
his latest speech: 'Let him know, however, that whatever is the
outcome of our endeavours France will always date her happiness
from the day when, after voyaging through seas now friendly, a frail
bark landed on our shores a hero whose whole heart was dedicated
to the peace of his country and the repose of the world.'

To the civic magistrates whom he installed on 9 March Lucien said: 'The mayors and their deputies are the men of the people, a character they must always preserve in their dealings with all citizens. More than anyone else they stand in need of individual respect and above all they must inspire confidence.'

Bonaparte and the Parisians

The Parisians, who had suffered too much and too long from disturbance and neglect, were gratified by all these appointments which promised order, stability and prosperity. Indifferent now to political strife, they were ready to entrust themselves to the officials charged with their protection, in whose installation by the First Consul they saw their most reliable guarantee.

The press reported this happy atmosphere with pleasure, the *Journal de Paris* writing on 18 March:

'The general feeling is shown by signs which never deceive an observer; all Paris welcomes the appointment of the mayors and their deputies. For the last ten years the people in look and word have shown successively surprise, fright, displeasure, resignation and even the indifference which arises from despair, but today they exhibit the confidence which is greater even than hope.'

Every day the Consular government gave proof of strength and sagacity and added to its prestige which, nevertheless, varied among the social classes. In banking, big industrial and commercial circles there was a certain reserve and hesitation, but serious opposition was found only in an extremist minority, the terrorist or 'exclusive' Jacobins and the ultra royalists.

The majority of citizens, especially the lower middle class and the populace, gave the First Consul their genuine and wholehearted support. 'At the Central and other markets,' notes a contemporary, 'morale is high; at Garchy's detestable.' (Garchy's was the most fashionable and exclusive haunt of pleasure in Paris frequented by the *muscadins*[1] who by no means represented the city.)

Police reports are unanimous about the people's enthusiasm:

'Everyone is drawn to the First Consul because of his devotion to the public well-being,' remarks a report on 30 January. 'Everyone discusses

[1] The male equivalents of the *merveilleuses*, so called because they perfumed themselves with musk. Ed.

his indefatigability, his concern to stamp out every iota of our dissensions, and the force with which he inveighs against dishonest traders. Hope springs anew in every heart.'

And next day:

'The people's apathy towards 18 Brumaire was due to their uncertainty as to its outcome, but now the lofty conduct of the government, its impartial justice and ascetic mien inspire confidence. On a decadi the citizens of the Faubourg St-Antoine, drinking together, have been heard to cry, "War to the death on the English government, war on this rule of tyrants who refuse the peace offered them by the First Consul!' while elsewhere others were heard to shout, "Long live Bonaparte! Long live the Government!" and they all spoke with approval of the First Consul whom the royalists delight to calumniate.'

The people were pleased to fancy that he had the air of 'a true republican magistrate'. The *Ami des Lois*, which had announced that Bonaparte had ordered a festivity costing 200,000 frs, drew down on its head this retort:

'This is untrue; the First Consul is aware that 200,000 frs is the cost of a half-brigade for six months.'

The press, indeed, never tired of praising his deeds, his manner and his words, daily quoting his individual remarks and lively and witty repartee, for which Bonaparte shared a talent with the Parisians.

Bonaparte's capacity for work, his integrity and strength of character were the principal source of surprise and the Parisians were impressed by his brisk and decisive manner and sober dress since, apart from the charm of his look and smile, his physical appearance was not obviously attractive. His youth also was much admired; Bonaparte was not yet 30. Respect and reverence may be felt for a leader full of years, but admiration is greater when that leader is in the flush of youth and shows great maturity of judgement and foresight.

There was yet another facet to the relationship between Bonaparte and Paris. The capital loves show, the more perhaps because its daily life is one long show. Balzac wrote that this great city's boulevards were the scene of 'a continuous drama' and spoke of the 'million actors' who make up the great dramatic company of Paris. The effect of Bonaparte's advent was to bring this drama to a climax and endow the city's 'play' with unusual vigour and attraction.

In the First Consul the Parisians now had a hero whose great

deeds inspired boundless admiration as they breathlessly followed
the course of the battles he fought to bring them peace and glory.
They were thrilled as they read his famous war bulletins and when,
in the theatres, they heard the announcements of the victories he had
won. For fifteen years the heart of Paris beat in unison with Napoleon's
spirited footsteps.

The strength and radiance of Bonaparte's genius drew Parisians
to him and his brilliant theatrical talents increased his attraction for
them. Chateaubriand said of him that he liked to play his own
personage—and that his favourite audience was the citizens of Paris.

In palace or bivouac what Paris was thinking was always in the
forefront of Napoleon's mind. Aware of the city's febrility he
constantly wanted to know its reactions, whether of the masses whose
devotion he cherished or the Faubourg St-Germain whose enmity
and sarcasms haunted him.

'What are they saying about me in Paris? What does Paris
think?' were questions continually on his lips. This interest was a
source of pride to the Parisians.

Bonaparte was rarely seen in public places and promenades. When,
preceded by a mameluke at the gallop, he occasionally drove through
the boulevards, the people, who yearned for a sight of him, only
glimpsed the First Consul's Roman profile, but they gazed long after
the carriage had passed as if it held a loved one.

Bonaparte often suggested to Bourrienne about 8 p.m., 'Let's go
for a stroll.'

He would then in his grey greatcoat set off on his secretary's arm
to bargain for trifles in the shops in the Rue St-Honoré as far as the
Rue de l'Arbre Sec near St-Germain-l'Auxerrois.

'While the things I was supposed to buy were being displayed,' relates
Bourrienne, 'he asked questions and nothing was more amusing than his
trying to adopt the light, quizzing tone then fashionable. Bonaparte liked
to ask shopkeepers their opinion of the First Consul. "Well, Madame,"
he would say, raising his cravat to hide his face. "What's new? What's
being said about Bonaparte? Your shop looks very well set out, citizen;
you must get a lot of customers here. What do they say about that ass,
Bonaparte?"

'Once, when walking with Bourrienne, he was delighted to be thrown out
of a shop for his disrespectful way of talking about the First Consul.'

Evening receptions at the Tuileries were few but dignified and
unostentatious; they were held in the yellow drawing-room on the

ground floor where Josephine, with her elegant female entourage, was learning her future duties as Empress. The guests came from all walks of life, officials, high civil servants, literary and artistic personalities, among them the singer, Garat, of whom Bonaparte was particularly fond.

Occasionally the First Consul went to parties given by his ministers. On 26 January it was to a reception in his honour at Lucien's Hôtel Brissac, where he had his one and only meeting with Mme Récamier.

Naturally he went often to the theatre and, on 3 March, was present at a concert to applaud Garat and other famous singers. His presence at the Théâtre Feydeau was noted by the *Journal de Paris*:

'An additional interest attached to such an admirable display of talent; all eyes turned towards the smallest box in the house where Bonaparte was seen to be.'

In this way with tact and discretion Bonaparte kept in touch with various strata of Paris society; he realized the contradictions prevailing in fashionable circles and that frivolity went hand in hand with a sense of tradition. He had observed, on becoming Consul, the need felt by Paris for enjoyment after long years of suffering and scarcity and the revival of old habits of amusement and amenity. Dancing especially was a universal addiction but does not every era have its 'dance mania'? One may read in the *Journal des Débats* of 13 February:

'The scraping of a wheezy fiddle calls to the tavern transformed into a dance hall the artisan, the soldier, the little milliner and the water-carrier.'

Among the upper classes only the décor was different; in the luxurious salons at Frascati or Tortoni's the passion was just as intense.

As an official mark of understanding of Parisian feeling Bonaparte, despite the austere Fouché's reluctance, gave permission for four masked balls and a dress ball to be held annually at the Opéra but, as usual seeing the question from all sides, with the proviso that a quarter of the takings should be given to the poor. On Thursday, 25 February, at the beginning of Lent Josephine, accompanied by the Murats, was present at the first masked ball to be held since 1790. Dancing began at midnight and attracted a large crowd; the ball, essentially Parisian of its time, created a great sensation. People were heard to say, 'This is the first thing we have enjoyed for ten years and we owe it to Bonaparte. If we have peace how things will go like a bomb!'

The newspapers gave the ball a great deal of space.

'This novelty,' wrote the *Moniteur*, 'should interest those who like to observe changes in manners and modes; it is one of a thousand events competing to make 18 Brumaire one of the most signal moments in our history. The doors of the Opéra open and on the instant it is filled; people come in crowds and enter in floods; between 5,000 and 6,000 people are concentrated in an area too small to hold them all. . . . Reckon what happiness and alleviation the 25,000 to 30,000 frs paid at the door will spread among a hundred families of artistes and workers connected with this theatre; calculate the yield to Paris shops of these expensively trimmed costumes and fancy dresses hired out at such a high figure (they say for as much as 48frs). . . .'

The ministers were anxious not to fall behind their master in reviving brilliant social gatherings in Paris. Talleyrand was the first to open his magnificently decorated rooms at Neuilly where, on the same evening as the Opéra masked ball, he held an exclusive reception for many distinguished personalities in Parisian society and members of the highest aristocracy of the old regime. One of the evening's attractions was Vestris, king of the dance.

The First Consul was present with a friendly word for everyone, which displeased Jacobin circles, but was his way of inducing the old aristocratic world to rally to him. When, next day, he sent for a report on the Opéra ball he congratulated himself on its success, saying to Bourrienne, 'While they're talking about the ball they won't chatter about politics, which is what I want. Let them enjoy themselves, let them dance so long as they don't stick their noses into government business. And I have other plans and I see other advantages, Bourrienne. Trade is stagnating and Fouché tells me that the shopkeepers are complaining. This at least will keep some money circulating and a fat lot I care about the Jacobins. Has a thing got to be bad because it isn't new? I much prefer Opéra balls to their saturnalia of the Goddess of Reason. I have never been so warmly cheered as at my last review.'

Bonaparte indeed set the greatest store by the reviews held at noon every decadi and sometimes also on a quintidi as they enabled him to keep vital and regular contact with the people and the army. Every French regiment came in turn to Paris to take part in the review as the Consular guard.

'The army identified itself with its chief and drew him to itself,' wrote the Duchesse d'Abrantès. 'To the army its chief was the nation incarnate. Paris learnt to know the army and the troops and they, as they passed in turn through the capital, ceased to regard it as another continent to which as it were they had become alien.'

These reviews are historic; Napoleon, wearing his black beaver hat and grey greatcoat, astride his white horse, followed by a brilliant staff, galloping down the ranks, dismounting opposite the Tuileries, ordering rapid manoeuvres in a resonant voice and watching impassively as the troops, led by a band with their bayonets glittering amidst their colourful flags, marched proudly past under the eagle eye of the hero they served. Crowds from every part of Paris pressed against the railings, fascinated as they watched the march past, heady evidence of the national glory. The Parisians deplored the fact that the Carrousel was too confined a space to allow more than a minority the eagerly prized pleasure of watching a parade at close quarters.

Bonaparte took advantage of the recall to Paris of various units from the west to hold a review on 16 March on the Champ de Mars of all the troops then in the capital. From early morning a huge crowd gathered on the slopes round the esplanade where eighteen thousand men were drawn up. Cambacérès, Lebrun and Josephine 'with a large entourage' had taken their places on the balcony of the Ecole Militaire.

'The air was still, the sun half obscured, when a sudden cannonade announced the First Consul in his red ceremonial uniform, riding among generals dear to fame and warriors of all ranks famous for their conquests and honoured by their wounds,' writes the *Journal de Paris*. 'When the troops had marched past, spectators rushed down the slopes towards Bonaparte. Only a review had been announced, and this review had turned into a celebration.'

In a few minutes the whole area of the Champ de Mars was a mass of people.

'Towards the Ecole Militaire a passage had to be opened to enable the First Consul to return to the Tuileries. Cries of 'Long live Bonaparte!'' rang out on all sides.'

The paper also reports conversations which reveal that Bonaparte was becoming the object of a cult.

'An old soldier exclaimed, "One would think something had been added to this Champ de Mars." And his daughter answered, "There is Mars." '

Bonaparte's appeal for brave men for a great reserve army revealed to what extent the city was imbued with martial spirit. All the finest young men, including the dandies, nicknamed the *incroyables*, wanted to join up.

'The extraordinary eagerness shown by the young men of Paris and old soldiers to respond to the First Consul's appeal,' wrote the *Moniteur* on 27 March, 'has been much discussed in Paris during the last few days.'

The Parisians were gratified by Bonaparte's decision to allow entertainments at Longchamp, popular with the society of the old régime but since the revolution fallen into neglect. Despite bad weather the number of spectators was 'prodigious'. In the Champs-Elysées and the Bois de Boulogne there was a great rush to watch the carriages pass and observe the rivalry in picturesque displays. As in the past the crowd admired the changes in dress ordained by fashion and once again their gratitude went out to Bonaparte, without whom 'this could not have been seen'.

This indulgence was allowed the Parisians by the First Consul who had, however, no intention of letting liberty degenerate into licence. He let it be known through Lucien on 5 April 1800 that no play might be performed without his approbation and that the official in charge of Public Instruction at the Ministry of the Interior,

'would be personally responsible for any theatrical performances which offend good taste and are contrary to the spirit of theatrical licences.'

He asked for a report to be sent to him on the decadi 'on steps to be taken to restrict the number of theatres'.

Lucien, therefore, sent Frochot this note on 18 April:

'Plays, citizen, have attracted the interest of the government. It shows respect and esteem to keep from the people whatever does not merit their attention and which might offend or corrupt morals. . . . From now on only those plays which I have authorized can be performed in the Departments.'

The morality ousted from Parisian society by the Directory's depravity was gradually being restored.

The health and security of Paris also occupied the government's attention, necessitating its intervention in public highways. Streets, bridges and quays were obstructed by stalls and barrows which impeded traffic and destroyed quiet; these obstructions, typical of Paris in 1800, caused many accidents. Most stall-keepers did not hold licences nor did their public displays of goods and stuffs pay any duty which did damage to the shopkeepers. On 22 April Dubois issued a regulation cancelling all previous licences and requiring the stall-keepers to seek new ones. If a licence was refused the stall-keeper had to withdraw within twenty-four hours. No disturbance followed the execution of this measure since those involved appreciated the motives of public order which had prompted it.

From Paris to Marengo

The great improvement in internal affairs in France was not matched abroad; the Treaty of Campo-Formio was seen as no more than a truce. When England and Austria rejected the First Consul's peace overtures a resumption of hostilities was inevitable. War broke out on two fronts, in Germany and Italy, where France was threatened with invasion by two Austrian armies.

Masséna, in command of the Army of Italy, was attacked by the main Austrian forces under Mélas and found himself blocked at Genoa on 15 April, but managed to hold the enemy for two months. Moreau, however, commanding the Army of the Rhine, gained a notable victory on 6 May at Stockach. Bonaparte's feverish impatience was relieved in the evening by a telegraphic message which gave him great satisfaction. He went to the Opéra where the communiqué announcing the victory was read amid general rejoicing.

Bonaparte then decided to assume personal command of the Army of Reserve to take the Austrians in the rear and win a decisive victory. At a ministerial meeting at the Tuileries he handed over his powers to Cambacérès, to whom he gave his final instructions, 'Say, without being precise, that I shall be away only for a short time.'

Knowing how excitable Paris was he wanted to leave at a good moment to avoid any anxiety about his departure. Next day he left at 3 a.m. with Bourrienne for Dijon.

Thus, seven months after his return from Egypt, and for the first time since he assumed power, Bonaparte left Paris in the first of a stirring series of departures for the battlefield where he would stake his own and the country's fate on a single encounter. The thoughts and good wishes of all Frenchmen went with him, but it was the

Parisians, among whom he lived, who were able to see him frequently, albeit briefly, who had earliest news of his movements, who
would be most nervous and would live with greater intensity through
the historic hours of suspense which characterized Napoleon's life.

The citizens of Paris, although aware of the adamant stance taken
by France's enemies against Bonaparte's wish for peace, themselves
longed deeply for peace but peace which would be both glorious and
final. Peace could be won only by victory on the field and for this
victory they relied implicitly on the First Consul. They prayed with
greater fervour for his success because governmental stability
seemed imperilled by his absence while his presence among them
was a guarantee of safety.

Bonaparte knew exactly how difficult a hand he had to play and
that the destiny of France depended on how he played it. Abroad
the eyes of Europe were fixed on him, while at home his enemies
were spying out any signs of weakness. As he advanced through
Switzerland his thoughts constantly reverted to Paris and each day
he avidly read the news arriving from the capital. His energy and his
faith in victory were boundless. The young army he commanded
fell completely under his influence and, full of ardour, felt itself to
be moving irrevocably to victory.

Napoleon's correspondence shows an obsessive need for news of
Paris, but his anxiety about public opinion in the capital was justified.
Chouans and Jacobins were plotting in the shadows, under the keen
eye of Fouché, who kept the balance between both factions, while
holding out a friendly hand to Bernadotte whom he knew to be
popular with the army.

Talleyrand's moves were less obvious but of deeper significance.
He sidled into the centres of opposition, preaching patience to all,
lavishing encouragement and seeking to make himself indispensable.
As everyone knew that Bonaparte was exposed to the hazards and
uncertainties of a campaign they tried to find a successor to him, a
search which continued for fifteen years whenever Napoleon was at
war. The names recurring most frequently at secret meetings were
those of Carnot, Minister of War, and Lafayette, who had returned
to France after the amnesty. Certain police reports reveal this latent
unrest—on 21 May 'the factions continue to work in the shadows and
hope to find causes to instigate a rising' and on the 2nd 'the plotters
are in despair that their attempts are fruitless'.

That this unrest was limited to opposition circles and that as a whole Paris was unmoved is confirmed by police reports.

'So far from the First Consul's absence giving rise to disturbance and popular unrest as some disaffected people hope,' observes the report for 29 May, 'all that he is doing and the progress of the army he is leading with all speed to victory has aroused the admiration of the whole capital.'

Bonaparte believed in two-way traffic; he wanted to know what was happening in Paris but he also wanted the Parisians to know how the campaign was progressing. His favourite means of imparting information was to insert a communiqué in the *Moniteur*. The colourful style employed in his dictation was designed to make a special impact and foreshadows the famous communiqués of the Grande Armée. To give the widest possible publicity to a communiqué he had it printed on loose sheets distributed gratis, especially to the poor, that is to the people whose simple and devoted hearts beat with the greatest sincerity and to whom his own heart went out.

'In the midst of a people overcome with joy' he made his entry into Milan on 2 June, triumphantly announced in two communiqués. This news say the police reports,

'has electrified all the good citizens and disconcerted all the agitators. It has just been broadcast all over the city and made an excellent impression, particularly in the faubourgs,'

but the staunchness of the public was to be put to a severe test. Almost before they were given time to rejoice at this success they heard of the fall of Genoa on 4 June, but on the 9th came news of a new victory at Montebello.

From Stradella Bonaparte announced that he was on his way to Tortona and Alexandria, news which appeared in the *Moniteur* of the 16th, with a report that the French army had fought a battle on the 14th at the village of Marengo. Official confirmation did not reach Paris for five days, during which, writes Fouché,

'Paris was in a ferment; the disaffected hoped that the man they called the French Cromwell would be halted in his course and that, as he had been elevated by war, so he would perish in war.'

Anxiety increased and the atmosphere had become oppressive when a letter, dated 14 June from Milan, reached the Tuileries on the evening of the 20th. It mentioned a great and bitterly fought battle but that the outcome was as yet in the balance. Still there was no official confirmation and anxiety gave place to restlessness; false rumours permitted every kind of intrigue and speculation. Tension was at its height throughout the night until, towards 11 a.m. on the following morning, a dusty dispatch rider arrived with the uplifting news that on 14 June the French army had won a victory at Marengo (they called it Maringo) which spread through the city; this name, now and for ever famous, was on everybody's lips.

Bonaparte's final phrase in the communiqué of 15 June made a deep impression,

> 'I have signed peace and I hope the French people will be satisfied with their army.'

Salvoes of artillery announced the glorious victory at noon. 'The general happiness, delight and surprise were indescribable and shouts of "Long live Bonaparte!" were heard everywhere.'

That an armistice and suspension of hostilities followed the victory increased the rejoicing but it was clouded by the grievous news of Desaix' death.

The news of Marengo was cheered at the Bourse, where consols rose from 29 to 37 frs. Dubois, as Bonaparte had ordered, posted up the army communiqués all over the city and had them distributed widely. In the popular quarters, especially the Faubourg St-Antoine, 'the glorious faubourg', to use the name bestowed on it by the revolutionaries, joy reached a peak of delirium. People were struck by the frank admission of the numbers of men lost or taken prisoner. 'It's not as it used to be,' they were saying in the Rue Victor. 'Now at least we know everything.'

Bonaparte had kept his word; he had not deceived them.

Palaces and the main public buildings were illuminated in the evening and private individuals spontaneously lit up their houses. Although the evening was cool a huge crowd was present at a concert given on the terrace of the Tuileries. Contemporary memoirs are a better indication of the Parisians' happiness than the police reports and the Duchesse d'Abrantès' account of 21 June is worth quoting:

> 'When we heard the news there was an outburst of rejoicing which in-toxicated the people of the faubourgs, always so free and warmhearted in showing their feelings . . . Everyone congratulated everyone else as if for some personal or family happy event. Yes, at this period I am describing and of which the recollection is still so vivid, the people of Paris, I repeat,

on this day when they learned of their deliverance and their glory, was devoted and grateful.''

Further evidence of the people's happiness was given by the hasty Te Deum sung at 6 p.m. in the church of St-Gervais and next day at Notre Dame.

'The church wanted to participate in this manifestation of the people's rejoicing.'

IV—Part I

Administrator of Paris

The ensuing period was not entirely peaceful but at least the First
Consul did not have to make personal visits to the front. The four
years from 2 July 1800, when he returned from Italy, to 18 May
1804, when the Empire was proclaimed, were the most fruitful of the
Napoleonic era, the years of the Concordat, the Legion of Honour,
the Civil Code and the reorganization of secondary education. Apart
from a few journeys to Rouen, Boulogne, the north of France and
Belgium,[1] most of Bonaparte's time was spent in Paris and a large
part of his energies devoted to improvements in the city.

The chapter of great public works in Paris opened in 1801.
Inauguration and completion were made ceremonial occasions,
regarded by the government in the same light and treated to the same
official honours as victories in war. In the citizens they aroused feelings of patriotic pride as they joyfully took part in successive ceremonies which gave Paris moments of exaltation unique in her annals.

A glance at Paris in 1800

Before turning to Consular achievements in Paris one should take a
look at the city in 1800. From the few descriptions existing—the
best is Mercier's *Tableau* (1780–1788)—we see that it bore no
resemblance to the city as it is today. According to André Halloys:

'Paris was an inchoate but picturesque jumble of houses dating from every
period; houses with pointed gables, houses with turrets, shacks of wood
or brick, mansions with pilasters and pediments.'

Its distinguishing features were the concentration in a confined

---

[1] This naturally includes the time spent by the First Consul at the château of St-Cloud
and Malmaison (which Josephine acquired on 21 April 1799) and which he visited regularly
three or four times a week until 1804, when he ceased to go as he considered it no longer
appropriate to his position.

area of buildings and people, while beyond the central zone were many open spaces, gardens and fields; the scarcity of wide thorough-fares and the prominence of palaces and monuments rising among squat houses, mainly of two storeys, or on waste lands. Upstream of the Ile St-Louis a third island, the Ile de Louvier, was not yet connected to the Arsenal bank. A few notes and figures will help to reconstruct the city as it was.

Paris was shut in by the Farmers-General's enclosure, correspond-ing roughly to the line of the outer boulevards. An enclosing wall, 8½ feet high and 17 miles long, had been built between 1782 and 1787 during the reign of Louis XVI as a defence against the smugg-ling then rife. The wall also served to facilitate the levying of inter-nal customs dues which, under the Empire, yielded the greatest revenue for the Paris budget and were always one of Napoleon's main concerns. An important fact bearing on the invasions of 1814 and 1815 is that Paris, with no defensive wall, was an open city. Merchandise entered Paris at fifty-eight fixed points or barriers, which took the place of the modern gates; there were also two water-gates at La Rapée and the Invalides. Ledoux, philosopher, architect and poet, was responsible for the excellent construction of the barriers in contemporary and tasteful imitation of the antique.

The area enclosed was divided into twelve arrondissements,[1] sub-divided into districts, nine on the Right and three on the Left Bank, corresponding roughly to the present first twelve arrondisse-ments. Today they are numbered concentrically, but in 1800 they were numbered going upstream on both banks of the river.

At the 1801 census the population of Paris was 547,756, high for its own times if small compared with the 1962 figure (2,800,000). Paris, now outstripped by many larger capitals, then ranked second

---

[1] The 1st arrondissement was made up of these districts: the Roule, the Champs-Elysées, Place Vendôme; the 2nd, the Chaussée d'Antin, the Palais-Royal, the Feydeau, the Faubourg Montmartre; the 3rd, the Faubourg Poissonière, Montmartre, St-Eustache, the Mail; the 4th, St-Honoré, the Louvre, the Central Markets (the Halles), the Bank; the 5th, the Faubourg St-Denis, the Porte St-Martin, Bonne-Nouvelle, Montorgueil; the 6th, the Porte St-Denis, St-Martin des Champs, the Lombards, the Temple; the 7th, St-Avoye, the Mont de Piété, the St-Jean and Arcis markets; the 8th, the Marais, Popincourt St-Antoine, Quinze-Vingts; the 9th, the Ile St-Louis, the Hôtel de Ville, the Cité, the Arsenal; the 10th, the Monnaie (the Mint), St-Thomas d'Acquin, the Invalides, the Faubourg St-Germain; the 11th, the Luxembourg, the Ecole de Médecine, the Sorbonne, the Palais de Justice; the 12th, St-Jacques, St-Marcel, the King's garden and the Observatory.

among world cities, after London but before Vienna and Moscow, while its population was considerably greater than that of other French cities, much smaller than they are today.

Given that, at Colbert's first census under Louis XIV, the population of Paris was 720,000, at the second census of 1762 under Louis XV 600,000 and in 1784, according to Necker's estimate, 620,000, the number of Parisians in 1800 was not excessive.

These half-million-odd inhabitants occupied an area of about 12 square miles (about a third of the present area of 36 square miles), their density of 167 to two acres being considerably lower than the modern density of 322 to two acres (excluding both Woods) for Paris as a whole and 340 to two acres for the first twelve arrondissements inhabited by approximately 1,250,000 people. Nevertheless, this comparison fails to show the real distribution of population, of which in 1800 70 per cent was concentrated on the Right Bank, in two sectors bounded by the northern boulevards (the present Grands Boulevards). The first sector, including the 4th arrondissement and both palaces, lay between the Seine and the boulevards, a core small in area but dense in population. The sector between the boulevards and the enclosing wall was more sparsely populated but was growing, mainly eastwards, and included the new districts, all being heavily built over, like the rich and fashionable quarters of the Chaussée d'Antin, the Porcherons d'Angoulême, where the bankers lived, the Rue du Mont Blanc and pretty little villas like Bonaparte's; the faubourgs occupied the remainder of the section.

To the west of the Left Bank, where fewer people lived, was the noble Faubourg St-Germain, and to the east the working-class Faubourg St-Marcel, extending to the Place d'Italie. The new or southern boulevards ran almost parallel with the Farmers-General's wall. By no means all the terrain within the enclosure was populated. More than 20 per cent was open space, mainly on the fringes (farmland, vineyards, pleasure gardens, meadows, marshes, nurseries and orchards), a high percentage when compared with 1962 which was 9 per cent of 36 square miles. A memorandum of Frochot's reveals that there were some 25,000 houses (a figure confirmed by a census taken in 1807), corresponding roughly to those in the modern first twelve arrondissements. Before the revolution these houses accommodated 700,000 people, but housing for over 100,000 was now vacant. Housing presented no quantitative problem, but difficulties did arise from the age and dilapidation of buildings which their owners were too poor to repair.

Roads also were in a bad state. There were some 1,100 streets compared with 3,940 in 1964. These streets were winding and narrow, badly lit (there were only 9,890 lamp-posts and 4,500 oil lamps or lanterns) and their average width did not exceed 24 feet. Pavements were few and milestones abutting from houses on to the roads were a permanent hazard to traffic. Including the great central sewer there were only 15 miles of primitive sewers against 130 miles in 1964. There were 18 bridges (29 in 1964) and barely six miles of quays.

Some 20,000 vehicles were in circulation, 4,600 elegant and fast cabriolets, 1,100 public carriages, 9,000 carts, and so on . . . and 1,600 horses. Although the roads were used chiefly by pedestrians and riders the Parisians nevertheless complained bitterly of 'congestion' and hoped that an east-west road would be built across Paris.

Reconstruction of the capital was a larger and more urgent problem which had been under discussion for over a century. Many plans had been drawn up, including the 'Artists' Plan' of 1793, commissioned by the Convention. This plan could have been implemented at no cost to the state by utilizing confiscated and nationalized church and émigré property, but unfortunately this was not done.

Bonaparte's Ideas

Among the problems demanding a speedy solution this renewal of Paris was one of the most inspiring. Bonaparte found Paris much as it had been under its kings although still suffering from the damage done during the revolution. The modernization and embellishment of Paris was a formidable undertaking but one well within the scope of his wide vision, the distinction he was anxious to lend his government and his obsession with action. All honour is due to Bonaparte for making Paris a modern city.

Already in 1798, as he was sailing towards Egypt, he was planning, if ever he became master of France, to make her capital 'not only the most beautiful city in being but the most beautiful which had ever been or would ever be'.

He knew full well the Parisian tendency to carp, which he sometimes mistrusted, but he did not share the fears of Louis XIV, which had led him to transfer his court to Versailles to minimize the capital's political importance. Bonaparte's ambition was to make Paris 'something fabulous, colossal and entirely new', not the wild dream of a megalomaniac but the penetrating and even prophetic vision of a man of action. He believed Paris should have a population of three to four millions, and extend as far as St-Cloud, which was merely anticipating the city's surge to the west.

Napoleon appreciated the difficulties of building anew in old Paris, chockful of men and ancient stones, nor did he want to destroy traces of the past. The empty spaces of the city's western end were the ideal site for the new city of his dreams. Part of this splendid concept was the plan for the grandiose Palace of the King of Rome which, from the heights of Chaillot, would have dominated the Champ de Mars where, on either side of the Ecole Militaire, would have risen a vast administrative city, enshrining a palace for each ministry.

It was in the nature of Napoleon's genius that his plan for transforming the capital was two-fold; to enrich it with monuments and to improve its citizens' standard of living by civic undertakings, both ideals expressed in contemporary language as 'embellishments'.

Bourrienne says that 'Bonaparte had the same affection for large constructions as for great battles, an essential element in his temperament', but this preference does not indicate a purely pagan admiration for huge buildings; for him they were a means of immortalizing and perpetuating the names and work of great men. In 1809 he would say that 'Men are great only by the monuments they leave behind'. To Bonaparte the soil of Paris was a pedestal waiting to carry monuments such as these. One February evening in 1806, after Austerlitz, he declared, 'The city of Paris is short of monuments; she must have them.'

He believed that a monument should be evocative, appeal to the intellect and strike the imagination, an ideal conception demanding greatness and beauty, even truth. On 5 February 1810, he told Fontaine, 'What is great is always beautiful,' and, in 1813, 'What is true is always beautiful.'

His liking for ancient architecture was shared by his contemporaries. As models he took the pure lines of Greek and the imposing style of Roman art which seemed to him to be the best interpreters of the majesty of his reign. From his artists he demanded respect for his ideas but, trusting their ability, left the execution to them. While

he was meticulous about detail in preparing his battle plans he
attached little importance to it in building.

Bonaparte shared the view of modern architects that a building
should be a mirror to its age, even if it was not in harmony with
buildings erected in the past. 'The monuments of bygone centuries
have the colour and the form of their time.' The tremendous ruins
he had seen in Egypt had impressed him greatly and durability was a
primary condition he demanded of builders; a building should defy
time.

Napoleon also planned to wage war on the unhealthy parts of the
city. Fain's *Mémoires* give an insight into his ideas, which anticipate
the work of Napoleon III and underline its breadth. 'To beautify
Paris,' said Napoleon, 'more must be demolished than built. Why
not disengage all those buildings which people seem to have taken
delight in hiding, and those little streets, carefully shut off from
heat and cold when behind them are large courtyards and vast
gardens in which to breathe? Isn't it imperative to purify them with
great draughts of air now that all the intervening area is full and
overfull? How can the needs of our long wide vehicles, heavy stage-
coaches and carts be met by what was adequate for loads carried by
mules and pack and led horses? Ought not some positive decision be
taken about it all? Havering about this problem only increases its difficulties the longer the remedy is postponed. Unless we are to suffocate,
we must clear this congested area; the ant-hill cannot breathe.'

A programme of this magnitude, however, required large invest-
ments which Napoleon was unwilling to make.

As well as building monuments and improving housing conditions
Napoleon was eager to ameliorate the Parisians' lot. His humanitarian and social sense led him to initiate many works of public
utility; supply of water, markets, slaughterhouses, quays, bridges,
roads and sewers.

'Be exceptionally careful in building the markets,' he said one day
to Frochot. 'See that they are sanitary and that the Corn and Wine
markets are beautiful. The people also must have their Louvre.'

When disasters revealed to him the vanity of glory he gave
preference in building to works of utility. 'It is not the moment
when one has undertaken to supply Paris with water, roads, slaughterhouses, sewers, markets and public granaries to begin vast operations
of prestige building.'

An important factor in his plans was providing employment for the working population of Paris. Keeping the workers busy was one of the Emperor's permanent preoccupations. The upheavals he had witnessed as a young man during the revolution had left their mark on him, and he knew from experience that a hungry and idle populace can lend itself to the worst excesses.

Bausset writes that:

'Napoleon's good city and ways to remedy its deficiencies to keep it worthy of him and his great people were always in the forefront of his mind. In the midst of great military operations the Emperor was constantly thinking about works and improvements in Paris.'

When Napoleon returned from a campaign it was with a host of plans. Fontaine mentions a number which circumstances prevented his beginning or completing: schools for the daughters of soldiers killed on the battlefield; prisons; hospitals; cemeteries at the four corners of Paris; mansions for the ministers; a palace for the arts and another for the University; retirement homes for emeritus professors; archives for official documents; barracks; establishments for posts, public domains and every kind of 'beautification of squares and public promenades in the city'.

Speed was Napoleon's first requisite in carrying out any enterprise; a time limit was set for everything.

'When orders were given,' writes Beugnot, 'no one breathed until they had been fulfilled.'

Napoleon also liked personally to supervise work in hand and encourage productivity.

'His incredible energy infected everyone near him,' writes Bourrienne. 'With what pleasure, when he came home from a fresh victory and a new peace, did he inspect the work done in his absence.'

Wherever in Europe he might be, he sent note after note from his bivouac, asking question after question. Lavedan says with justice, 'The Emperor himself, even more than Louis XIV, intervened continually.'

In pursuit of his plans Napoleon met an obstacle more powerful than himself—time. The wars in which he was engaged never gave him time enough.

'How often,' writes Fontaine, 'in the midst of the anxieties and fatigues of war did he not say to us, when postponing a plan found too costly,

"When we have peace then we must busy ourselves in making Paris the most beautiful city in Europe." '

Napoleon's bent towards economy was another handicap; he was extremely strict about keeping within the estimates made for any work he had ordered, nor would he incur any expense unless it was covered by a corresponding receipt nor allow any overspending.

'This over-scrupulous economy,' continues Fontaine, 'forced government architects to suspend work in hand, and in many cases splendour and magnificence had to bow to the strict rules of budgeting.'

Any recourse to loans imposing burdens on future generations was forbidden; cash payments alone were allowed. Napoleon's distrust of architects was proverbial. He said that they had 'ruined Louis XIV', which he believed would not have happened if the great King had 'known how to draw up a budget'. The future Emperor thought less of architects than of the engineers of the Highways Department who, during his reign, were given great responsibilities. Fontaine, however, was an exception to this rule.

This concern about money explains why Bonaparte, who excelled in planning, was not, like Napoleon III, the author of a master plan for transforming the capital. Plans submitted to the Convention and Directory he rightly believed impossible to implement because of their astronomical cost. He contented himself with treating them, together with various plans made under the monarchy, as bases of study for given enterprises. Under the Consulate and then the Empire decisions governing large public works specified 'plans for the embellishment of Paris'.

As a pragmatist, the First Consul embarked only on projects for which money was guaranteed. Minute study preceded the preparation in detail of any plan, either for monuments or public utility works.

'Napoleon's improvised notes,' writes Bausset, 'were not orders for work to begin. His ideas came swiftly but were never given concrete form without much thought. The plans which had been drawn up were examined carefully and discussed by the ministers, the Building Council and the Emperor himself. Approval was given and money allocated only after preliminary discussion.'

The Arc du Carrousel was one of the rare cases when the Emperor took a final decision without previous consultation.

14 July 1800

Impatience in Paris to see Bonaparte again became more lively after the victory of Marengo. He, too, was anxious to return to the city but intended, as usual, to arrive unexpectedly and astonish by the lightning speed of his journey. He wrote to Lucien from Lyons on 29 June:

'I shall arrive in Paris without warning and I want neither a triumphal arch nor ceremony of any kind. I have too high an opinion of myself to trouble about such baubles. Public approval is all the triumph I need.'

On the night of 1/2 July he was back at the Tuileries.

When the booming of guns at the Invalides informed the public of his return a tidal wave of people rushed to the Tuileries, but not this time to riot, for it was no longer the seat of oppression and despotism but of a benevolent power. Within minutes the garden was invaded and Bonaparte had to appear on the balcony several times, on each occasion raising a storm of wild cheers.

The city of Paris was anxious to do homage to the conqueror and testify to its love and happiness. At 1 p.m. Frochot, on foot and in ceremonial dress, accompanied by Méjan, the Council of Prefecture, the twelve mayors of Paris and their deputies went to the Tuileries where Lucien presented them to the First Consul, whom the Prefect addressed in these words: 'General Consul, the city of Paris, happy above all other cities, henceforth claims you for its own. Now that your eagerly awaited return is a fact its walls echo our rejoicing and speak our gratitude. Though we cannot present you with laurels meet for your glory we can at least offer you our good wishes as a sign of our affection.'

A concert was given at the Tuileries in the evening and all the streets, 'without any order having been given', were illuminated. As usual the Faubourg St-Antoine, once the centre of popular sedition, was most vociferous in expressing its delight in Bonaparte who was now its idol.

Marengo marks an important stage in Bonaparte's career; the victory consolidated his power and led the way to the Empire, but it also sealed his hold over Paris. The salons, without giving up their opposition, were deeply impressed. 'This man,' wrote Mme de Staël to Mme Récamier, 'really does possess the will to shift the world.'

Immediately after Marengo Bonaparte began to think about the solemn commemoration of 14 July. He had written to the Consuls from Milan on 22 June,

'You must consider how this celebration can be made outstanding without imitating what has previously been done. A display of fireworks would be a good idea.'

The solemnity of this commemorative ceremony, now called the Fête de la Concorde and Fête de la Paix Intérieure, was to be enhanced by a simultaneous celebration of the victory of Marengo, the pacification of the Vendée, the erection of patriotic columns, the arrival of the Consular Guard with captured Austrian flags and, finally, the inauguration of public works at the Quai de la Pelleterie (between the Notre Dame bridge and the Place de Grève, forming part of the Quai de Gesvres). The practice now instituted of co-ordinated celebrations of the government's achievements in all spheres lasted until the end of the Empire. Like the reviews at the Carrousel they were designed to maintain public fervour at a high pitch and to be a permanent and vital link between people and Bonaparte.

On the afternoon of 13 July, while the guns boomed to announce next day's celebrations, both Prefects, with the civic and Departmental authorities, proceeded to the Quai de la Pelleterie, which was to be re-named the Quai Desaix. An hour later Lucien arrived to lay the first stone. At 6 p.m. the theatres opened for free public performances.

14 July 1800 was to be the apotheosis of 14 July 1789. When the 'sweet sun of Messidor' (July) began to shine the Parisians were awakened at 5 a.m. by the sound of artillery salvoes. Squares and thoroughfares rapidly filled with people. At 9 a.m. Frochot and the Paris notables went to the Place Vendôme, hung with flags and lined with troops and the National Guard. Each borough was represented by a deputation of its citizens together with representatives of 'French actors'. In the middle of the Place the Prefect laid the foundation stone of a column to be raised 'to the memory of the brave men of the Department of the Seine who died in the defence of liberty'. At this moment the Consular Guard, in torn and dusty uniforms, entered the city after forced marches from Marengo, to the applause of the populace.

At 11 a.m. a further ceremony took place on the Place de la Concorde. Bonaparte, dressed in red and gold, with the Consuls, ministers and several Councillors of State, arrived on horseback. When the three Consuls had taken their places on a dais Lucien made a long speech, then laid the foundation stone of the nation's column. On the stone was placed a mahogany casket containing a number of commemorative medals, inscribed simply 'Bonaparte First Consul, Cambacérès and Lebrun Second and Third Consuls.' At the end of the ceremony the First Consul remounted to lead a long and brilliant procession to the Invalides. He was cheered all the way, and some of the crowd, at the risk of injury from the horses, fanatically kissed his saddle.

At 2 p.m. all the officials, joined by the Diplomatic Corps, assembled at the Invalides where

'the nave and the galleries were filled with ladies and gentlemen who had been invited; the glow of beauty and exquisite dress added to the charms of this celebration where the old servants of the nation were given seats of honour.'

Bonaparte in fact had insisted on having the oldest soldiers seated next to him.

Chalgrin (a former pupil of Servandoni and architect of the Luxembourg) had decorated 'the Temple of Mars' with sober pomp. Two large orchestras each of a hundred and fifty and a third of twenty musicians played and triumphant airs were sung in honour of the liberation of Italy. For the first time the Parisians heard in a duet by Méhul the voices of the celebrated Grassini and the tenor Bianchi, 'who had come to Paris to add their talents to the brilliance of this commemorative celebration'. The indefatigable Lucien made another speech after which the orchestras played the 'Song of 25 Messidor', set by Méhul to words by Fontanes.

When the music ended Bonaparte proceeded to the courtyard behind the Invalides to review the pensioners. Five severely wounded men, chosen by their comrades 'as most deserving of the nation's gratitude', were presented to him and awarded gold medals, inscribed with their names, ages, places of birth and battle honours.

Next the scene moved to the Champ de Mars where the entire Paris garrison and part of the National Guard were drawn up under arms. Carnot, the Minister of War, presented the Consuls with the captured enemy flags and introduced the colour bearers. After this

presentation the crowd surged forward, breaking through the
cordons of troops.

> 'At that instant,' says the *Moniteur*, 'everyone was raised to a peak of
> delirious exaltation as he pushed headlong to greet these heroes, eager to
> see the man who led them in battle and whose glory now belongs to the
> people who chose him as their first magistrate. On all sides resounded
> cries of "Long live the Republic! Long live Bonaparte!" the two names
> equally dear to Frenchmen.'

From the balcony of the Ecole Militaire the Consuls witnessed
this unprecedented eruption of enthusiasm. Towards 7 p.m., as a
symbol of rejoicing, a balloon ascended into the air where it caused a
loud explosion.

> 'In the evening Paris was on fire [sic]. Even the oldest inhabitants said
> they had never seen illuminations so brilliant; public buildings and
> private houses all offered an astonishing sight.'

At 10 p.m. fireworks were let off on the Pont de la Concorde
followed by a public concert on the terrace of the Tuileries and,
throughout the night, the people danced to the bands in the Champs-
Elysées.

At the Tuileries which 'glittered with light and joy' the First
Consul gave a great banquet to a hundred people, among them the
pensioners he had decorated that afternoon. He lifted his glass with
obvious happiness to propose a ringing toast 'To the French people—
sovereign of us all'. At this moment Bonaparte and France, liberty
and authority, melted into one sublime whole.

Six days later the General Council held its first session in the Great
Chamber of the Prefecture in the Place Vendôme. Bonaparte could
not receive the Council in May as he was leaving for the front.
The Council, therefore, sought an interview to receive his official
blessing on the beginning of their task. At 2 p.m. on 24 July Bonaparte welcomed them at the Tuileries. They were led by Frochot and
Anson, their president, who expressed their satisfaction that their
assembly coincided with the 'forerunners of peace and that they had
begun their discussions under the auspices of an armistice concluded
between France and Austria'.

In his reply Bonaparte defined the part to be played by the
Departmental assembly and expressed the hope that it would be

an example to the provincial assemblies. He stressed that: 'constitutionally a council should act as a natural counterweight to the Prefect's authority and should be the eye of the government just as the Prefect was its right arm. . . .'

Another anniversary commemorated that year in the heroic manner typical of the Consulate was that of the founding of the republic on 1 Vendémiaire, 22 September 1792. The programme arranged by Lucien was approved by Bonaparte on 5 September when he ordered monuments to be erected in the Place des Victoires to the memory of Desaix and Kléber; he himself would lay the foundation stones.

To underline the military aspect of the ceremonies, and to pay simultaneous homage to the martial prowess of both the monarchy and the new régime, Turenne's remains were to be transferred to the Temple of Mars from their temporary resting place in Lenoir's Museum of French Monuments in the Rue des Petits Augustins. This ceremony, attended by the Ministers of War and the Interior, took place on 22 September. In the evening there were free performances at the theatres. Bonaparte himself went to the Théâtre Français to see *Le Cid* and *Tartuffe* where his presence attracted nearly fifteen thousand people who overflowed from the auditorium to the foyers and the porches. 'He could not escape the heartfelt evidence of public gratitude.' The Opéra, the Théâtre des Italiens, the Feydeau and the Vaudeville played to full houses where 'joy and unity reigned supreme and the need to love and to rejoice'.

When at 5 a.m. next morning the salvoes of artillery began the streets filled rapidly. At the Place des Victoires a monument had been erected, designed like an Egyptian temple beneath which were placed statues of Desaix and Kléber. About 11 a.m. Lucien arrived, preceding Bonaparte on horseback with the other two Consuls, members of the government and Councillors of State.

'Windows, balconies, even attics in the Place were filled with spectators who demonstrated their feelings when the First Consul arrived by cries of "Long live the Republic! Long live Bonaparte!" '

When he had laid the foundation stone of the monument he proceeded to the Invalides where a huge crowd was assembled, including deputations from the Departments. Lucien, as Minister of the Interior, read out the names of the ten Departments which had raised the largest number of conscripts. A large orchestra then played a sacred hymn, dedicated to the God of the Nations, an indication of the First Consul's future religious policy. Once again Lucien made a patriotic speech, then came the reading of Bonaparte's message recalling the recent signature of peace preliminaries (by which three Bavarian fortresses were ceded to France) and announcing that British envoys had been admitted to the conference at Lunéville, to be followed by negotiations. This news, as Bonaparte had foreseen, provoked unanimous applause.

'Everyone was moved; every eye was focused on the hero; feelings of gratitude mingled with those of love, admiration and patriotism. . . .'

Bonaparte's departure at the end of the ceremony was accompanied by tumultuous cheers.

The people had their own part in the day's rejoicings. After this function at the Invalides there were sports on the Champ de Mars,

'the races greater in number and better organized than ever before, the chariots better decorated and more eye-catching'.

According to the *Moniteur*:

'More than 200,000 people had assembled in the Champ de Mars, without a single incident or accident to mar the games . . . similar quiet and order had prevailed on the previous evening at all the free performances. . . . In many other states of Europe greater efforts to maintain order meet with less happy results.'

These were all signs of the mutual confidence between Bonaparte and Paris.

The people's participation in all these ceremonies did make of the régime what Vandal calls 'the Consular republic'. Of this Bonaparte was well aware and did his utmost to put a brake on the movement forcing him towards a dictatorship. With this aim in view Lucien had published an ill-conceived pamphlet, entitled *Parallel between Caesar, Cromwell, Monk and Bonaparte*, written by Fontanes, a move which the First Consul greatly deplored. On 6 November 1800, he deprived Lucien of the portfolio of the Interior to give it to the eminent scientist, Chaptal, a Councillor of State.

The Plots

Bonaparte's growing popularity only intensified the hatred and criminal designs of his enemies. The 'exclusives' plotted, unsuccessfully, to stab him to death. While the First Consul and Josephine were attending the first performance of *Les Horaces* at the Opéra on 10 October, the Roman sculptor, Ceracchi, was arrested in a box with his accomplices, among them Adjutant-General Arena. Much excitement and alarm was aroused by this plot and at the review on the 15th there was a larger crowd than usual and spontaneous and loud cheering.

The constituted bodies came in turn to the Tuileries to express their indignation and to assure the First Consul of their loyalty. Among the most fervent was the Paris Corps of Mayors, whose spokesman on the 17th was Frochot. To his speech Bonaparte replied,

'The government deserves the Parisians' love. It is true to say that your city is responsible to the whole of France for the safety of the first magistrate of the republic. . . . It is my duty to tell you that this vast community has never shown greater loyalty to its government; never has there been less need for troops of the line to police the city. My own confidence in all classes of the population of the capital is unlimited. Were I away and felt the need of shelter it would be in the heart of Paris that I should seek it.'

An early consequence of the plot was an extension of the powers of the Prefect of Police. By a decree of 25 October 1800, Dubois was given jurisdiction over the Department of the Seine, and the communes of St-Cloud, Meudon and Sèvres in Seine-et-Oise.[1]

Bonaparte made no pause in his work in Paris. A pressing problem was the arrangement of the Louvre. The palace may, since the end of the seventeenth century, have ceased to be a royal residence but, by virtue of a decree of the Convention on 27 July 1793, it had become the 'Central Museum of the Arts'. The official opening on 10 August 1793 was, however, merely a gesture, since the classification of the pictures and other works of art was a long-term undertaking, now considerably extended because artistic conquests had gone side by side with Bonaparte's military victories in Italy. Clauses in the armistices of Piacenza and Bologna and the Treaty of Tolentino required the Duke of Parma and the Pope to hand over

---

[1] This extension of powers extended to diverse sectors; policing the prisons, public meetings, printing and bookselling, émigrés, prisoners of war, public health, supervision of public places and so on.

to France paintings and statues. So many art treasures had flowed into Paris that, in spite of his devoted labours, Raymond, the architect of the Louvre, was rapidly overwhelmed.[1]

On his many visits to the Museum Bonaparte was appalled by the prevailing chaos, particularly the storage on the ground floor of paintings, statues, bas-reliefs and marbles, products of his Italian campaign, still in their packing-cases. He ordered these masterpieces to be classified methodically and distributed in specially assigned rooms. As the Salon Carré, the Galerie d'Apollon and the available part of the Grande Galerie were full, Raymond made use of the summer apartments of Anne of Austria, especially the Salle de Mars, the Salle de Mécène and the Salle d'Auguste (Salles des Antiques), where the Apollo Belvedere was placed in a special niche. On 7 November the First Consul, accompanied by Josephine, Lebrun, Murat and Benezech, Councillor of State and chief of protocol, visited the first Salon where Guérin, Gérard, Girodet and David exhibited. These artists were warmly congratulated by Bonaparte, who was highly pleased with what he saw and ordered a bonus to be given to the workers. He himself opened the Museum officially on 18 Brumaire (9 November), the anniversary of the coup d'état, and with Josephine and a large entourage toured the rooms. This first exhibition was most successful and the large attendance of visitors went into ecstasies at the sight of this rich collection.

By virtue of the law of 28 Pluviôse Year VIII Frochot convened the Municipal Council of Paris which held its first session in the Place Vendôme. The Directory had left the city's affairs in such disorder that the Council's task would clearly be difficult but it had the advantage of Frochot's help. The Prefect was wholly devoted to his duties, which he carried out efficiently and diligently, and he enjoyed the First Consul's complete confidence. Bonaparte had laid down the broad lines of policy and Frochot was given great leeway in implementing them. At this period Bonaparte both sought and followed advice when it seemed sensible to him; it was only from 1806 that he personally took in hand and imposed his own wishes on the major administration of Paris.

Frochot announced that he was preparing measures for the reorganization of primary education, hospital administration and

[1] See Appendix V.

burial services, which developed into the great civic services of the capital. During the final session the first real budget for the city of Paris was drawn up in the form of a statement of receipts and disbursements made by the Prefect and, after discussion at the Municipal Council, was submitted to the Minister of the Interior. The gross figure was 9,156,886 frs, of which tolls to the amount of nine millions represented almost the total revenue. Charitable institutions accounted for 60 per cent of the costs while maintenance and repairs for public works amounted to barely 212,000 frs. The state assumed the major costs of the works of improvement set in hand.

On Christmas Eve, 1800, a further attempt, which almost succeeded, was made on the First Consul's life by enemies who refused to give up. While he was driving through the Rue St-Nicaise to hear Haydn's *Creation* at the Opéra a violent explosion broke his carriage windows, wounding or killing about thirty people, destroying several houses and shattering windows on that side of the Tuileries. Bonaparte, who had miraculously escaped death, ordered his coachman to drive on.

When the First Consul entered his box with Josephine he looked quite calm as he bowed graciously to the crowded auditorium and was rapturously applauded by the audience unaware as yet of the attempted assassination. The news quickly filtered into the theatre.

'Immediately,' writes the Duchesse d'Abrantès, 'some electric impulse sparked off unanimous cheers as the whole audience turned its eyes towards Napoleon, to cover him, as it were, with the protection of their love. Women were seen to burst into tears and men to tremble with rage.'

Until the curtain fell Bonaparte remained impassive but, when he returned to the Tuileries where the great salon was already filled by the many high officials who had flocked to see him, he declared, 'You should not have come to see me. You should go immediately to help those poor wretched people wounded by the infernal machine.'

He then, with the belief that this attempt was the work of revolutionaries, shouted at Fouché, 'This is Jacobins' work—not that of nobles, priests or Chouans. If they are not arrested they must be crushed.'

Next day Paris was greatly disturbed; the civic authorities were the first to express their horror. When the mayors and the general

council were introduced by Lucien into Bonaparte's presence the
Secretary General, speaking in Frochot's absence through illness,
ended his speech with words which for fifteen years were echoed by
the people of Paris: 'Citizen Consul, the people of Paris implore
you to take care of yourself. Everyone's happiness depends on your
life and the citizens of Paris will make it their business to see that
you are happy.'

In his reply the First Consul said, 'I am touched by the proofs of
affection shown me by the people at this juncture. I feel I deserve
them because my sole ambition and everything I do is designed to
add to their prosperity and glory. . . . Tell the people of Paris for
me that these hundred or so wretches who have besmirched liberty
by the crimes committed in its name will never again be in a position
to do any harm.'

Punishment of the malefactors was extremely severe; thirty
'anarchists' held responsible for the crime were deported, all members of the 'ultra' Jacobin party. In fact the real culprits were
Cadoudal's Chouans who were soon unmasked, arrested and executed.
Bonaparte was now able to throttle all opposition from royalists
or republicans, the salons or the assemblies where it tended to increase. The Christmas Eve attempt at assassination not only caused
great alarm but raised a more urgent and agonizing question.
Who was to succeed Bonaparte?

Peace, bridges, economic prosperity

The suppression of the plot served some purpose since internal
order was strengthened and Bonaparte left free to continue his peace-
making abroad. After Marengo fighting had gone on in Germany
where Moreau gained a great victory of Hohenlinden on 3 December
1800, forcing Austria to yield. A peace treaty was signed at Lunéville
on 9 February 1801, which sealed the French triumph by recognizing
the left bank of the Rhine as her natural frontier and establishing her
sovereignty over the territory conquered in Italy.

Bonaparte personally gave Chaptal his instructions on 17 February
1801 for the solemn proclamation of peace.

'You will be given, Citizen Minister, the government's resolution concerning the proclamation of peace which will be made in Paris on 21
March. You will then make this proclamation known to the Prefects of

the Seine and the Police, the Council of the Prefecture, the General Council of the Department and the mayors of the twelve arrondissements. Next you will instruct the Prefect of Police to publicize it in the commune of Paris; he will be accompanied in his progress through each borough by its mayor.'

The choice of Dubois to make the proclamation settled the division of powers between the two Prefects. At an earlier audience of the Prefect of Police and Roederer, Bonaparte seemed to minimize Frochot's responsibilities, 'I'm not very interested in the Prefect of the Department. It is the Prefect of Police who protects me and he will always get what he wants from me.'

At other times, however, he did favour the Prefect of the Seine, as administration and maintenance of order were both equally dear to him and he gave priority to whichever Prefect was involved.

At 6 a.m. on 21 March salvoes of artillery announced the ceremonies for the proclamation of peace. Joy was at its height as repeated cries of 'Long live the Republic! Long live Bonaparte!' broke out everywhere, but rejoicing and amusements were greatest in the faubourgs. The procession took six hours to pass and, at the end of the day, Dubois gave a banquet to three hundred people. His plan for illuminating the houses was frustrated by an unfortunate wind which got up. In the evening theatres gave free performances which attracted large crowds.

From a youth spent by the restless waves of the Mediterranean Napoleon loved the waters of sea or river. As an adolescent he had been deeply impressed by the Rhône, a river as turbulent, he said, as the blood which coursed through his veins. Obviously he was attracted by the charm of the Seine, the most exciting highway in Paris, nor could he be indifferent to the place it occupied in the city's life. To regulate its course and facilitate its crossing were of primary importance to him.

At the end of the eighteenth century connections between the two banks of the river were poor; crossing often had to be made by ferry or skiffs. This Bonaparte determined to alter and, by a law of 15 March 1801, implemented by a decree of 25 March, ordered the building of three bridges; one bridge (which would be called the Pont d'Austerlitz) for vehicles; the second, the Pont St-Louis, between the Ile de la Cité and the Ile de la Fraternité (the Ile

St-Louis) and the third, the Pont des Arts,[1] from the Louvre to the
Palace of the Four Nations for pedestrians only.

The government was authorized to deal with concessionaires who
would furnish the capital necessary for building these bridges. They
were to recoup their costs from tolls levied over a period of twenty-
five years, after which the bridges would become public property.
To meet the First Consul's wish for speed it was determined that the
bridges should be built and ready for use 'in eighteen months at the
latest'.

Work began on 8 August on the Pont des Arts, the first to be
built. The public's interest, according to the *Journal des Débats* of
29 March, was shown by their spontaneous association in groups of
shareholders 'to provide the capital'.

The signature of the Treaty of Lunéville stimulated the growth
and extension of the economic revival which had followed Brumaire.

'Everyone's help is needed,' wrote the Duchesse d'Abrantès, 'to dress an
elegant woman—florists, hairdressers, dressmakers and perfumiers. Most
of the money they earn is passed on to their employees, which applies
equally to the superior branches of commerce—jewellers, goldsmiths,
manufacturers of porcelain, crystal, upholstery and furniture, all this vast
part of the population of this great city.'

Parisian factories and workshops were now extremely busy. After
the revolution they were in a parlous condition; they numbered 890,
exclusive of 47 in the rural cantons. The number of workers in the
big establishments had fallen from 7,053 in 1791 to 1,722. A revival
of confidence was necessary to promote recovery. New factories
were set up, furniture workshops in the Faubourg St-Antoine, gauze
factories in the Faubourg St-Marcel and, all over Paris, a variety
of factories for making japan, leather goods, porcelain, crystal, gold
and silver plaques, cotton spinneries and foundries, all employing
newly invented techniques.

The working classes, who numbered some eighty thousand and
were an important part of the adult population of Paris, benefited
considerably from increased purchases of luxury goods. They had
suffered more than any other class so that the revolution should

---

[1] Originally this bridge was to be the Bridge of the Four Nations but it was called the
Pont des Arts because it established communication between the Louvre Museum,
designated as Palace of the Arts, and the College of the Four Nations where it was
intended to install the Ecole des Beaux Arts.

triumph, for which their recompense had been starvation, vilifica-
tion and loss of electoral rights. Demoralized by their sacrifices and
the way in which they had been duped, they had become lazy and
sluggish. Jaurès would write that:

> 'The disillusioned and exhausted proletariat sought nothing but the
> restoration of order. They were passionately Bonapartist, ardently
> nationalistic.'

It is easy to appreciate the depth of their satisfaction when work was
again to be had and honoured and the extent of their devotion to the
First Consul who had wrought this change.

Bonaparte took an active part in promoting the rise of industry
and commerce; industry, albeit after agriculture, was to him a
privileged enterprise. Himself a great captain, he regarded the
captains of industry, because of their ingenuity and pugnacity, as
supporters as valuable as generals in his struggle against England.
The industrialists were loyal and admired the First Consul, who did
not, however, care for business people whose absence of civic spirit
and greed for profits he deplored. He called them *i mercanti*.

'A businessman,' he would say, 'should not make a fortune in the
way a battle is won. He should earn a little at a time but continuously.'

He himself did much to help business and re-establish credit. One
measure, decreed on 4 March, instituted, as part of the anniversary
celebrations of the foundation of the republic, an annual five-day
exhibition in Paris of products of French industry.

A commercial stock exchange was set up in Paris by a decree of
22 June and the stockbrokers' association reorganized; in future
members were to number not more than eighty. Frochot carried out
the First Consul's wishes by setting up a council of arts and commerce which foreshadowed the Chamber of Commerce; it included
government representatives, a member of the Tribunate, a member
of the Institute, a manufacturer, a General Councillor and two actors.
At the first meeting on 11 July the Prefect paid tribute to the First
Consul's work in Paris. If his forceful phrases were lavish in praise,
the praise was deserved.

'The Consular government was not satisfied with having established the peace of the continent on the most solid foundations of
victory and moderation; it appreciated that it had another task more
difficult but even nobler; to do for the people's happiness what it had
done for their glory.'

The government not only fostered the capital's economic life but also tried to remedy the deplorable condition of the Paris hospitals where the sick were shamefully huddled together without consideration for age, sex or the nature of their illness. Action was taken to create specialized hospitals and services to relieve the congestion in the general hospitals, the Hôtel Dieu, the Charité, St-Louis, Necker and Cochin.

A General Council for civil hospices was set up in Paris on 17 January and thereafter two homes for incurables were founded, for men in the former Couvent des Récollets in the Faubourg St-Laurent and for women in the Rue de Sèvres (now the Hôpital Laënnec). A decree of 11 October 1801 consigned the aged and penniless to the Hospice des Ménages aux Petites Maisons (in the Rue de Sèvres where the Bon Marché is now) while old people of small means but able to make some personal contribution were sent to a home in Montrouge.

Similar steps were taken to give Paris proper cemeteries. An order made by Louis XVI on 10 March 1776 confirming a decree of the Parlement in 1775, had required the closure of all Paris cemeteries but the oldest, the Innocents, lasted another twenty years. While waiting for new arrangements to be made, the repugnant practice of common graves was followed. During the revolution a decision was made to open two cemeteries outside the city limits but, in practice, bodies were still thrown one on top of the other in large open holes dug haphazardly, in defiance of all laws of hygiene. When judged to be full they were covered over. To end this practice, Frochot on 12 March 1801, ordered three cemeteries to be built north, east and south of the city—Montmartre, Père Lachaise and Vaugirard.

Bonaparte continued to hold regular reviews of troops on the Carrousel. His failure to appear at the parade on 4 July, because of the recurrence of an illness contracted at the siege of Toulon, so alarmed the people that the *Moniteur* had to publish a special bulletin on the 17th, stating:

'The First Consul has for some time been suffering from a rheumatic complaint contracted during his army service. His doctor, Citizen Corvisart, thought this a suitable time to treat it with "blisters" on his chest and arms. Although much improved thereby the First Consul was unable to attend the last parade. Today he will receive the ambassadors as usual, nor has he missed a day working with his ministers. Citizen Corvisart thinks that no harm will be done if the First Consul is present at the celebrations of 14 July.'

Illness did not prevent Bonaparte from signing the decree of 6 July which gave Paris a corps of firemen, to be commanded by the Prefect of Police and administered by the Prefect of the Seine.

Applause was universal when, on 14 July, Bonaparte made his entry on to the Place du Carrousel to inspect the troops drawn up near the railings. The celebrations of the national holiday were particularly brilliant because on the following day he signed the Concordat. They were held on the 'huge site' which extended from the Place de la Concorde as far as the Etoile, where the famous Arch would soon be erected.

'It is the first time,' wrote the *Moniteur*, 'that this site has been chosen as the sole meeting place for national holidays and it must be agreed that nothing could be better from the point of view of position and lie of the land.'

For the occasion Chalgrin had built a Temple of Peace in the Champs-Elysées and on the brow of the hill, whence it could be seen all over Paris, a thirty-foot statue of Fame standing on a high rock. The evening illuminations were magnificent and the press called it a 'truly national and truly popular' holiday.

Almost immediately after the gaieties of 14 July the government began to organize the first public industrial exhibition which opened on 23 September. On the 22nd Bonaparte, with the other two Consuls, spent three hours at the exhibition, stopping at each of the one hundred and four stands and putting questions to each manufacturer. The large influx of foreigners was amazed at the speed with which everything had been done.

'Paris is a real fairyland,' was the description given by some of them to the exhibition.

On 1 October 1801, England, at Bonaparte's instigation, agreed to negotiate peace and signed the Preliminaries of London, which was known in Paris in the middle of the afternoon. The gun salutes fired on the Quai des Tuileries and at the Invalides gave the signal for public rejoicing as the Parisians filled public gardens, squares and streets. 'They stopped one another to ask questions and then rushed

in a body to the theatres' to hear the news. Official notification, read
and repeated in all the theatres in the course of the evening, was
greeted with 'lively applause'. After the performances the people
filled the districts round the theatres and the Tuileries and watched
a long parade of the police commissioners of Paris, escorted by
detachments of light infantry and dragoons, preceded by drums and
greeted by shouts of 'Long live the Republic! Long live Bonaparte!'

To the nation the First Consul was the incarnation of the republic
and France.

Administrator of Paris

The Rue de Rivoli

The advent of peace was an auspicious moment to initiate new public works. A decree of 9 October 1801 provided for the cutting of a street from the Place Vendôme to the Tuileries (Rue de Castiglione) through the grounds of the Feuillants and the Riding-School; the making of a square opposite the garden entrance of the Tuileries and a street to abut on the Rue St-Honoré (Place and Rue des Pyramides); the opening of a street along the whole length of the Passage du Manège to the Passage St-Florentin (Rue de Rivoli). This last project was far and away the most important. It had been discussed for over a hundred years and had figured on the 'Artists' Plan', although in a slightly different form.

This decree was the first attempt to solve the problem of east-west traffic at the traditional centre of Paris where the old highway Faubourg St-Honoré–Faubourg St-Antoine lost itself near the Louvre in a jumble of small and squalid streets. The new Rue de Rivoli would ease traffic on the whole of the Right Bank, the city's most populated area, and create a new district west of the old part of Paris. It foreshadowed Haussmann's alterations and, as the first great enterprise in modern Parisian town planning, should figure on Napoleon's roll of building honours.

If the making of roads was utilitarian the First Consul wished at the same time to beautify and aerate Paris; the new streets were to be wide and open. Bourrienne reports that:

> 'Bonaparte wanted all Paris streets to be 40 feet wide with pavements; nothing was too beautiful or majestic for the nation's capital.'

Aesthetically, and to make the new buildings a setting worthy of the palace and garden of the Tuileries, purchasers of land along the

new streets were obliged to erect at their own expense buildings
conforming to 'plans and façades drawn up by the official architect'.
Percier and Fontaine drew plans for arcaded houses, similar to the
old squares in the South or in Italy. Shops were not to be leased to
'anyone working with hammers' or 'making use of ovens'. Paris
owes this handsome street and elegant district, so greatly admired
by tourists, to Bonaparte's southern genius or possibly to his
memories of campaigns in Italy.

Opening the Rue de Rivoli and the side streets was part of a
complex and comprehensive overhaul of the district. A glance at a
few facts makes clear what and how much had to be done and its
importance. On Turgot's plan there is a rough square bounded on the
east by the colonnade of the Louvre, on the west by the Place de la
Concorde (Place Louis XV), on the south by the gallery running
parallel with the Seine and the southern limits of the Tuileries, and
on the north by the Rue St-Honoré. Between the Rue St-Florentin
and the northern wall enclosing the Tuileries and its garden was
property belonging to the convents of the Assumption, the Capucines
and the Feuillants, divided by a grassy lane which was to be the Rue
de Castiglione. Next came the Hôtel de Noailles, between which
and the garden wall of the Tuileries, opposite the Rue d'Alger,
was the royal riding-school where the revolutionary assemblies had
held their meetings. Thence a long path led to the royal stables.
This section ended at the Pavillon de Marsan[1] and the Rue de
l'Echelle.

The Rue de Rivoli was to extend on this site from the Rue St-
Florentin to the Rue de l'Echelle.

The Place du Vieux Louvre was in front of the façade of the Horloge
and opposite the Tuileries was the central court, the Cour Royale,
flanked by two secondary courts, the Cour des Princes on the
Pavillon de Flore side and the Cour des Suisses next to the Pavillon
de Marsan.

From east to west of the courtyards of the Louvre and the Tuileries
on one side, and the Rue St-Honoré and the Rue des Orties on the
other, was a dense area with a fantastic assortment of buildings (the
Hôpital des Quinze-Vingts,[2] the Hôtels de Longueville, de Brienne

---

[1] On the northern side of the Louvre.
[2] The expression 'quinze-vingts', that is fifteen twenties or three hundred, is an example
of the old system of counting by twenties. The Hôpital des Quinze-Vingts was for three
hundred blind people. Ed.

and d'Elboeuf, the churches of St-Nicolas and St-Louis, houses, shanties and so on.

This conglomeration was crossed north to south by three lanes (Rues Fromenteau, St-Thomas du Louvre and St-Nicaise) making in modern parlance a slum, which urgently called for redevelopment. Immediately after the bomb explosion in the Rue St-Nicaise Bonaparte ordered the approaches to the Tuileries to be cleared and, on 5 January 1801, the demolition of houses damaged in that explosion. This plan was published so that the Parisians should realize the necessity for undertaking public works in the city. The First Consul now dismissed Leconte, appointing Fontaine in his stead as architect of the Tuileries.

Orders were also given for enlarging and clearing the Place du Carrousel. In the presence of the Minister of Finance on 21 April Bonaparte dictated a note, confirming in principle the making of a road from the Tuileries to the Louvre, to be called the Rue Impériale. In line with these changes a new entrance was made in the railings round the Tuileries. Instead of erecting the Venetian horses at the Tuileries Bonaparte decided to mount them on stone piles of arms which flanked the new entrance. The transformation of the area also called for the restoration of both great palaces, especially the Louvre, and of their approaches.

Fontaine says that, at Bonaparte's advent, the Louvre offered:

'the sad and lamentable spectacle of a great colossus, dismembered and fallen into ruin without ever having been completed'.

It was hemmed in by ramshackle little buildings while, for over a century, dealers had squatted in the entrances, including those of the Cour Carrée, where in squalid booths they had set up a kind of market which seriously interfered with traffic. Many artisans and artists had either installed themselves and their families or their studios within the palace itself, which Bonaparte found shocking. On 20 August he ordered the eviction of the artists, who were partially re-housed in the studios of the Capucines, the church of the Sorbonne and the College of the Four Nations.

The First Consul, always concerned with the internal arrangements of the palace, ordered the transfer to the Louvre of the National Library from the Hôtel de Nevers, a building too small, badly organized and a fire risk. This transfer was made in preference to an earlier plan for utilizing the Madeleine (which will be dealt with in a later chapter).

Since the First Consul had taken up residence in the Tuileries various improvements had been made; in May 1801 the façade was adorned with busts in the antique style. On 2 November the last remaining trees in the great courtyard were felled and, in view of the imminence of the commemoration of 18 Brumaire, work on the demolition of the houses cluttering the Carrousel was speeded up.

This anniversary intended by the government to be dedicated to peace and joy was celebrated 'with great pomp, and was perfectly organized'. Gun salutes and the carillon of the Samaritaine opened the festivities which drew a huge crowd, including many foreigners, to gaze at the impressive symbolic constructions devised for the occasion. Among them were a triumphal arch opposite the Pont Neuf, a Doric temple dedicated to commerce, boats moored together on the Seine and, on the Place de la Concorde, a huge theatre enclosing three temples, the largest consecrated to peace and two smaller ones to the arts and industry. Many public buildings included in their decorations inscriptions and transparencies in praise of the First Consul, such as 'To Bonaparte, conqueror and peacemaker, a grateful country' and 'His repose is the repose he had given us.'

Paris did indeed feel deep gratitude and admiration for Bonaparte. On 27 October its Municipal Council adopted the proposal that a monument should be erected to his glory, 'in praise of his outstanding efforts to embellish the capital and improve its trade'. This monument was to be a 'triumphal archway' and a fountain built on the site freed by the demolition of the Grand Châtelet. Bonaparte appreciated this gesture but, in his reply on 24 December, he returned thanks only for the flattering motive which inspired it: 'I am grateful for the sentiments expressed by the magistrates of the city of Paris. I accept the offer of the monument you wish to raise to me—let its site be the one you suggest, but let its erection be left to future generations, if they confirm the good opinion you have of me.'

The year 1802, a year of peace, work and harmony, was the most glorious of the Consulate. On 8 January Bonaparte left Paris for Lyons where he inaugurated the Italian republic and assumed its presidency. On his return to Paris this increase in authority enabled him to put pressure on England to sign the Peace of Amiens on 25

March, a treaty which caused much excitement in Paris and great popular rejoicing. Yet again it was the populace in particular which was most eager to show its gratitude and affection for the First Consul; the debt they owed him for their contentment was their sole topic of conversation.

The government won another bloodless victory on 8 April when the Legislature ratified the Concordat (including the organic articles), which put a seal on long and arduous negotiations. The previous day Cardinal de Belloy had been named as Archbishop of Paris.

The Assemblies had been so obstructive that Bonaparte was obliged to 'purge' the Tribunate. Thanks to the fact that their constitutional term had been reached, a fifth of the members retired, to be replaced by men with a greater sense of reality and the common good.

The peace treaty and the Concordat were celebrated simultaneously on Easter Day, 18 April, by order of the First Consul. To enhance the effect of the Concordat Bonaparte had a notice inserted in the *Moniteur* of the publication of Chateaubriand's *Génie du Christianisme*.

Great ceremony marked the proclamation of the Concordat. From 6 a.m. an hourly salvo of sixty guns was fired, echoed by the great bell of Notre Dame, silent for ten years. At 8 a.m. the Prefect of Police, with the twelve mayors and their deputies, the commissioners of police and the constabulary, proclaimed the Concordat in every municipal district in Paris. Between ten and ten thirty the Parisian notables, members of the Tribunate, the Legislature and the Senate took their seats in the choir of Notre Dame. At 10.30 in the courtyard of the Tuileries Bonaparte, in ceremonial dress with the famous Regent[1] in his sword hilt, presented colours to the assembled troops then, to a salute of sixty guns which 'made all the windows of Paris shake', left for Notre Dame in a magnificent procession, preceded by squadrons of hussars, chasseurs, dragoons and battalions of grenadiers of the Paris garrison. Beside his carriage rode the generals commanding the city, the First Military Division and the Consular Guard. The green liveries seen that day in Paris would be worn by the Imperial household.

---

[1] The magnificent diamond so called because it belonged to the Regent, Philippe d'Orléans, who bought it for the royal crown in 1717 during Louis XIV's minority. Hidden during the revolution, it was found again and pledged by the government.

Another sixty salvoes saluted Bonaparte's entry into the metropolitan church where the Archbishop of Paris received him and offered him holy water.

'It would be hard to describe a sight more impressive than yesterday's solemnities,' wrote the *Journal des Débats* on 20 April. 'Both going and coming the First Consul heard only one continuous acclamation of "Long live Bonaparte!" He bowed affectionately to this vast crowd of citizens, whose love he has won by so many exertions and by such unstinting devotion.'

Assured of peace, territorial and spiritual, the First Consul could turn to his constant care, the large-scale promotion of public welfare. On 26 April, by a senatus consultum, émigrés were permitted to return within specified time-limits to France. This bold act of clemency was favourably welcomed by the majority and provoked a reaction only in those salons which were the haunt of the higher echelons of the emigration, where they affected to regard this concession as humiliating.

A law of 1 May laid down the bases of secondary education; the colleges of the old régime and the central schools of the revolution were replaced by lycées, the mould in which Bonaparte intended to fashion the country's youth; the first lycée was opened shortly thereafter in Paris.

The moment was now opportune for the people to show Bonaparte an exceptional mark of their appreciation; it fell to the Senate to suggest that the First Consul's powers be extended for ten years, which Paris considered inadequate and came out for a vote on his holding office for life.

'Everyone is dissatisfied with the senatus consultum which does not interpret the general feeling,'

notes a police bulletin of 9 May. Dubois made himself the city's spokesman at a meeting of the Senate on the 10th, when Cambacérès' proposal was adopted of taking the people's vote on the question, 'Should Napoleon Bonaparte be Consul for life?'

Large crowds gathered round the posters announcing this proposal.

'There was one universal desire, one universal feeling. Many people were heard to say warmly, "Whatever France can offer the First Consul will always be less than what he has done for her." '

The Corps of Paris Mayors was especially zealous and the first 'to take the citizens of the capital as a yardstick by which to measure the interest of all Frenchmen', and expressed the wish that Bonaparte should found a hereditary magistracy. He, however, did not believe that the time was yet ripe for the empire and, letting it be known that he could not entertain this proposal, forbade it to be mentioned.

Water, the quays, the theatres

A law was voted on 19 May enacting the opening of a canal from the little river Ourcq to a basin near La Villette in Paris, which would solve the critical problem of the city's water supply.

The basic supply came from the Seine through two old hydraulic machines, the pump of the Samaritaine at the Pont Neuf and the Notre Dame pump, plus the steam- or fire-pumps at Chaillot and Gros Caillou. Springs at Belleville, the Pré St-Gervais, Montmartre, Arcueil and Rungis produced a modest amount of water. In some districts wells yielded their owners an appreciable amount of water but of doubtful purity. There were also fifty-seven public fountains but these, widely dispersed, provided only a small and intermittent supply for which users had to pay. Parisians generally employed water-carriers (numbering some twenty thousand) who, for a couple of pence for five gallons, delivered water in large buckets to all floors of the houses. Each person had in practice only about a pint and three-quarters of water a day, an amount which today seems ludicrous; by the close of the Empire this quantity was tripled.

Historians are unable to decide who originated the new scheme. Chaptal, then Minister of the Interior, claims the honour. In his *Memoirs* he says that he was walking in the gardens at Malmaison one day in 1802 with Bonaparte when the First Consul said, 'I want to do something great and useful for Paris. What do you suggest?' The scientist says that his reply was, 'Give Paris water.'

Frochot also claims to have inspired Bonaparte's decision, saying that one day after the Peace of Amiens, Bonaparte had sent for him and questioned him about the capital's water supply. 'It is not enough,' the Prefect says that he answered, 'that the limpid waters of a great river should run through a great city. These waters must be taken into the homes of all its citizens. It is remarkable that no king should have thought about a matter vital to public well-being nor made any attempt to supply Paris with an element essential to health and life.'

Bonaparte is reported to have answered briskly, 'For one reason or another Paris has not and ought to have running water. It is a matter of primary importance for the civic administration.'

Nothing but plans had resulted from the monarchy's frequent consideration of this question. The plans generally referred to bringing the waters of the Ourcq, the Beuvronne, the Yvette, the Bièvre and even the Loire to the hilly parts of Paris. In point of fact no new plan had to be made, only a decision taken. Bonaparte's merit was that he took the decision.

The Legion of Honour was instituted by a law of 19 May. As a true Corsican Bonaparte had a high idea of honour and he wanted the people to have an ideal to which they could aspire, the ideal of honour. However, if the First Consul's conception of the Legion of Honour was to rally the nation, it was ill received in Paris in its early stages. The Duchesse d'Abrantès writes:

'No real idea can be given of the stir it created, an odd sort of buzzing by all classes and shades of opinion.'

The young aristocrats found it amusing to stroll down the boulevards (it was springtime) with a red carnation in their buttonholes.

'When Bonaparte heard this,' writes Bourrienne, 'he took the joke very seriously and wanted to arrest those who made fun of a new Order."

This reaction was short-lived; it was soon appreciated that the Legion of Honour was a democratic institution which took its place on the roll of signal benefits the nation had received at the hands of the First Consul whose high standing with the people continued to grow. His visit to the Opéra on 4 June to see *Hecuba* met frenzied applause. When Priam says to Achilles, 'You fulfil the hopes of the whole nation,' the cheers intensified and the audience demanded an encore.

More significant still was the poll in favour of the consulate for life; votes counted on 16 June numbered 34,135 in the affirmative on the registers opened at the Prefecture of Police, the Appeals tribunal and the Ministry of the Interior.

'There is no question,' wrote Frochot to the Minister of the Interior, 'for the citizens of the Department of the Seine, who are fortunate in being eye-witnesses of the First Consul's unremitting efforts for the glory and prosperity of the republic and the happiness and the peace of Europe.'

A week later the votes stood at 60,395 ayes and 80 noes from the largest electorate yet known in Paris.

Bonaparte had long pondered on the building of a new quay to be both useful and ornamental. On 2 July 1802, a Consular decision ordered

'the immediate construction of the Quai d'Orsay on the Left Bank of the river Seine in Paris between the Pont Royal and the Pont de la Révolution (Pont de la Concorde); the foundation stone to be laid on 13 July'.

The First Consul told Fain: 'These fine terraces which form your quays in Paris ought, generally speaking, to be given greater prominence. On the river side they should be lined with the finest houses in the city.'

He also thought of making roads like the Romans with statues of Europe's great men placed at intervals. Until 1800 only the merest sketch of a quay existed in this area, called the Quai de la Grenouillère, which shocked the Parisians who, according to Lanzac, would have liked to see the Faubourg St-Germain present a more elegant façade facing the Seine. Moreover Paris was heavily flooded during the winter of 1801–2 when the river covered part of the Champs-Elysées, the Invalides, and the Place de Grève and even lapped the Faubourg St-Honoré and the Rue du Faubourg St-Antoine.

Bourrienne recounts that one day he was standing at the window of the First Consul's study in the Tuileries when Bonaparte came in unexpectedly and asked him what he was doing.

'I bet you are looking at the pretty women walking on the terrace.'

'I do that sometimes,' was Bourrienne's answer, 'but I can assure you, General, that I was not thinking of them at this moment. I was looking at this miserable Left Bank of the Seine whose uneven quays and filth have always irritated me and I was going to talk to you about it.'

The First Consul went to the window in his turn and said, 'You are right; it *is* very ugly and it is disgusting to see dirty linen washed in front of our windows—so take this note, "The Quay must be completed next season" and send it to the Minister of the Interior.'

Chaptal made all speed as by 13 July, eve of the national holiday, the quay, called Quai Bonaparte, was ready for the official opening. Accompanied by Crétet, Councillor of State in charge of the Highways Department, Chaptal went to the Left Bank near the Pont de la Concorde, where he was received by Dubois and the mayors of the twelve arrondissements.

Chaptal spoke eloquently to the crowd of the government's plans.

'Citizens, the time has come when the authorities can turn their attention to internal prosperity and they believe that public works are the best means of ensuring it. Trade makes a nation rich and the easy communications, which alone civilize and increase people's happiness, are now the government's primary concern. Large undertakings are already under way and larger still are to come. The city of Paris, which in our own time has become the capital of the world, has tasted the fruits of the new growth. Three new bridges are rising over the Seine; canals are to be cut to bring the waters of the river Ourcq to Paris; the palace of the Tuileries stands majestically on the finest site in the universe; construction of the Quai Desaix goes on apace. . . .'

In accordance with the government's desire that morals and virtue should be specially honoured and receive public recognition, twelve young women, dowered by the commune, were chosen to be married to soldiers during the celebrations of 14 July. After the choice was made on the 13th a banquet was given by the Prefect to the couples, their families and the mayors who, on the 14th, performed the civil ceremonies followed by a religious service of great splendour in each parish church. A further banquet was given at each town hall where toasts were drunk to 'The long life and happiness of the First Consul'.

On the morning of the 14th Bonaparte in the coat of crimson satin laced with gold presented to him by the city of Lyons, inspected a grand parade on the Carrousel. When it ended Frochot and two of the Paris mayors begged him to accept as a further token of the gratitude and affection of the citizens of Paris 'a French-bred horse with trappings made by the best saddlers in the city, a gift voted by the Municipal Council'. The First Consul was deeply appreciative of the gift and told the deputation of the pleasure it would give him to mount the horse 'especially if a further opportunity presented itself of fighting for the honour of the French people'.

Reports in the press bear witness to the interest taken in Paris in public works. In the *Gazette de France* of 16 May one reads:

'Judging by the multiplicity of public and private works proceeding in the capital one would think a new city was being founded.'

The economy too was flourishing and many factories were working full out.

Progress was also being made in the hospitals. The principle of 'one patient to a bed' had been recognized. A paying clinic was opened on 21 May in the Faubourg St-Laurent for people who could not be nursed at home and who disliked the idea of going to a hospital. A hospital for sick children only, a pioneer in Europe, was founded by decree on 8 May 1802 in the Rue de Sèvres, and a midwifery school at the Lying-in Hospital at Port Royal. Thanks to donations from the First Consul, the hospice of Ste-Périne increased the number of its beds.

The city's extensive public works required funds which were largely derived from the State. To obviate stoppages the First Consul put a monthly sum of 200,000 frs at the disposal of the Minister of the Interior during 1802. New rules to implement Bonaparte's wish to reform the finances of Paris were laid down by a decree of 23 July. The budget of Paris, like that of communities of over twenty-thousand inhabitants, would be drawn up by the Prefect, but submitted for authorization to the Minister of the Interior. The Prefect of Police enjoyed the same right as the Prefect of the Seine to draw up a budget. The City's representatives were invited to seek ways and means of increasing revenue; accountancy was substantially revised and divided into two sections, one under the Prefect's authority, the other under that of a responsible municipal treasurer who acted independently except for governmental supervision. Frochot expressed his satisfaction:

'The commune of Paris,' he said, 'should congratulate itself particularly on this decree of 23 July which at last brings some order into its finances.'

A later decree of 13 August, applying the law of 19 May concerning the Ourcq canal, laid down that, until the end of 1823 a local Parisian tax of 1·25 frs per five Imperial gallons (twenty-six U.S. gallons) would be levied on wines entering the city, to be allocated exclusively to the cost of the canal, on which work should begin on 23 September for water to reach La Villette by the end of 1805. The city now had a special supplementary budget which was to be submitted annually by the Prefect to the Municipal Council and approved by the Minister of the Interior.

When the final results of the plebiscite approving the consulate for

life were published on 29 July, it was seen that 5,568,885 had voted
for and 8,374 against; on 2 August a senatus consultum proclaimed
Napoleon Bonaparte First Consul for life. The Senate simultaneously
decided that a statue of peace, with the laurels of victory in its hand,
would be a witness to future generations of the nation's gratitude.

A further senatus consultum on 4 August promulgated a new
constitution, which modified that of the Year VIII (1800) to concentrate all power in the hands of Bonaparte.

> 'This measure,' noted a police report on 5 August, 'has created a great
> sensation and seems to meet with general approval. Trade expects great
> things from it.'

Dubois solemnly proclaimed both senatus consulta in Paris on 15
August, the First Consul's birthday, which henceforth became St
Napoleon's day and the anniversary of the ratification of the Concordat. In the morning Bonaparte received the great State bodies,
the Archbishop of Paris, the Prefect of the Seine, the civic authorities
and a deputation of Paris notaries.

There was a gathering at 4 p.m. of Frochot and the Departmental
and civic officials in the handsomely decorated Place Vendôme where,
near the base of the Departmental Column erected in 1800, one
hundred and twenty-one staffs had been set up, representing the
Departments of the republic, linked by garlands and crowned by
bouquets of blue, white and red flowers. The Paris notables then
proceeded to Notre Dame to hear a Te Deum.

At 7 p.m., 40 feet above the platform of the cathedral towers, a
star, 30 feet wide, was lit up with the sign of the zodiac for 15 August
shining in its centre. A model, 42 feet high, of the statue of peace
voted by the Senate had been set up at the approaches to the Pont
Neuf. The façade of the Hôtel de Ville was illuminated as it had been
for ceremonies in days gone by.

> 'The citizens,' noted the *Moniteur*, 'seemed to regard this illumination
> as a gratifying sign that they had come into their own again.'

At 9 p.m. a brilliant firework display took place in the Place
Vendôme.

When, after his assumption of the supreme power, Bonaparte
went to the Luxembourg to swear fidelity to the constitution, he did
so in almost royal state. His procession, preceded by a mounted guard
and the mamelukes, made its way through a double line of troops

from the Paris garrison by the Quai du Louvre to the Palace of the Senate. Bonaparte took the oath and presided at a short but solemn session, then left the Luxembourg with the same ceremonial to enthusiastic cheers.

Bonaparte's position was now sufficiently assured to allow some relaxation in his governmental system. He abolished the Ministry of General Police and Fouché, its head, now became a Councillor of State together with Roederer. The First Consul was not entirely displeased to be parted from his minister who had a foot in every camp, particularly in those hostile to his régime. Méneval writes that Fouché was always suspect 'because of his ambivalent behaviour and his restless intelligence'. Réal was installed as Director-General of the Police Department, responsible to Régnier, who was appointed Minister of Justice with the title of Grand Judge.

The eve of the anniversary of the foundation of the republic on 22 September 1802 gave Bonaparte an opportunity to show the great interest he and his government took in industry, the arts and education. Accompanied by Cambacérès and Chaptal at 10 a.m. he opened the second exhibition of products of national industry in the great courtyard of the Louvre. His inspection followed the procedure of the previous year; to encourage the artists who exhibited he made a private purchase of three of the best pictures displayed.

At the end of the day Bonaparte, in ceremonial costume, made an appearance outside the pavilion of the Tuileries, where an orchestra was playing but, says the *Gazette de France*, 'he seemed to attract as much attention as the concert'. Finally he went to the Opéra where his entrance

'was greeted by universal applause in which the actors, against all the rules of the house, joined with the audience'.

This was yet a further demonstration of approval of the consulate for life and of welcome to the peace treaty.

Next day Chaptal, representing the government, solemnly inaugurated work on the Ourcq canal at La Villette while the first lycée was opened at the Prytanée (the former Collège Louis-le-Grand), which alone had preserved the tradition of classical studies.

On 28 October Bonaparte with Josephine left for Normandy, known as a royalist stronghold but where his presence soon made its impact on the disaffected. The noise of cannon announced his return to St-Cloud on the evening of 14 November.

Important decisions were taken at the end of the year. The reorganization of the Museum was the subject of a measure of 19 November; Denon was put in charge. He was one of David's protégés who had taken part in the expedition to Egypt. Visconti, the eminent Italian archaeologist, was made Keeper of Antiquities.

There was urgent need for offices suitable for the increasing importance of the Paris administration and the duties of the Prefect which were growing with the expansion of the Parisian economy. Frochot wanted his offices to be in the Hôtel de Toulouse in the Rue de la Vrillière, which would be the home of the Banque de France, but Bonaparte preferred to house the Prefect of the Seine and his staff in the Hôtel de Ville. A Consular decree of 26 November 1802 enacted that the offices of the Prefecture of the Seine, together with those of the Commission of Direct Taxes and the Council of the Prefecture, should occupy the civic mansion. This was to be extended on the north side by the buildings of the old Hôpital St-Esprit (now the northern frontage of the present Hôtel de Ville on the Rue de Rivoli, where the Prefect's private apartments were built) and on the east by the site of the disused church of St-Jean de Grève.

A further decree of that date showed the swing towards royal practice; the Prefects of the Palace, heads of the Consul's household, were entrusted with the supervision and direction of the Théâtres de la République and des Arts, a decision, says Lanzac, to which the same attention was given as to an important matter of state. The provisions of this decree were extended on 11 December to the other main theatres, the Théâtre Français, the Opéra, the Feydeau (Opéra Comique), the Opera Buffa (Italiens) and the Louvois. There were in addition about twenty minor theatres in Paris.

Bonaparte, a born actor and brilliant impresario, had a great fondness for the theatre, which was another link between him and the Parisians. As First Consul, then Emperor, he always had his box at the Théâtre Français and the Opéra for which he regularly paid rent from his privy purse. He rarely went to the small theatres since temperamentally he did not care for the plays they performed. When he did go to the Vaudeville he wore a junior officer's uniform and sat in a small screened box.

The First Consul despised comedy and thought little of melodrama; he loved Italian music and *bel canto* but his own voice, although powerful, was rarely in tune. His great passion, which he shared with

most of his contemporaries, was for tragedy. Corneille he admired
for 'his deep knowledge of the human heart and understanding of
politics'.

'A *parterre* [pit-full] of kings is needed to hear his tragedies,' he
said. 'If he had been alive now I would have made him a prince.'

For Racine he cared little, regarding him as 'bombastic' and 'the
woman's poet'. His opinion about Voltaire varied; in 1802 he said
that 'he liked him', believing him to be a writer for adults, but at St
Helena he had changed his mind and said he 'did not think much of
him', finding his work 'full of sound and fury', nor did he share the
general admiration of Molière. *Tartuffe* he considered a masterpiece
although he deplored the playwright's treatment of religion.

'It shows,' he said at St Helena, 'piety in so odious a light in my
opinion that, if the play had been written in my time, I should not
have hesitated to ban it.'

His favourite actor was Talma. The rumour ran in Paris that the
actor had been asked to give him lessons in deportment and dress, a
subject on which later Las Cases wrote:

'Napoleon, who always knew what his detractors were saying, was
teasing Talma about this rumour one day. Talma was embarrassed and at a
loss what to say.

' "You're wrong," Bonaparte told him. "It would probably have been
a good idea if I had had the time." '
'He then gave Talma some advice on acting.'

Apart from his personal fondness for the theatre Bonaparte was
aware of its influence on public opinion, especially in Paris where,
more than in the provinces, there was a real passion for drama. He
personally supervised the repertoire and frequently had a forgotten
work revived or even altered certain roles, like that of Livia in *Cinna*
for instance. Knowing himself to be a powerful centre of attraction
for the public he regarded his theatre-going as part of his duty as
sovereign, but he disliked being regularly on show and still more, as
Frédéric Masson says, 'measuring his popularity by the amount of
applause he drew'. Nevertheless, like a great star, it pleased him
when he returned from a victorious campaign to 'make his reap-
pearance' in Paris by showing himself at the Théâtre Français or the
Opéra.

The Directory had left the theatres in utter disorder; their
financial situation was parlous and their budget always in the red,

which more than justified Bonaparte's intervention in their management. He was shocked by the excessive number of free seats and
decided that, as of 26 November, all boxes were to be paid for. Two
decrees, inspired by him personally, determined the status of the
Opéra (10 January 1803) and the Théâtre Français (18 January).

Bonaparte again showed himself ahead of his times by wanting
plays for the people; he regretted that the Théâtre Français did not
on Sundays reduce the price of seats in the pit to 20 sous 'so that the
people could enjoy it'.

By the end of 1802 Paris was a city overwhelmed with good things.

'Paris,' writes the Duchesse d'Abrantès, 'had indeed realized the First
Consul's dream for his great city—that it be the capital of the civilized
world.'

The elegant carriages of the foreigners who flocked to Paris filled
boulevards and promenades; theatres played to capacity as they had
not done since the meeting of the States General; industry prospered
and public works were in full swing. Stocks reached 53 frs. According
to a contemporary newspaper 'the public gardens in ten years had
gained enormously in magnificence and amenity'. The Louvre
overflowed with masterpieces which aroused the admiration of all
who saw them; the churches were filled by the faithful. All this Paris
owed to Bonaparte and mention has already been made of the extent
of their gratitude and loyalty. Foreign visitors, for whom he was a
fascinating attraction, were not far behind the Parisians in enthusiasm
and led the rush to the Tuileries to cheer him loudly; the march past
of the Consular Guard was one of the highlights of Paris sight-seeing.

At one review an English captain was heard to say as he gazed
steadily at the First Consul, 'Good chap! May God long preserve
him!'

The Russians rivalled the British in admiration. According to a
police report,

'They praised the French government to the skies and sedulously sought
occasions for seeing the First Consul in person.'

The following year saw no relaxation in civic enterprise. While on
the Right Bank the Rue de Rivoli was taking shape and many old
buildings were being swept away from the Louvre-Tuileries district,

the Left Bank was also being transformed. The approaches to Notre Dame were being cleared and the restoration of the Palace of the Luxembourg begun so that the Senate could hold its debates as required by the constitution. Chalgrin was building a Chamber (since demolished and the site occupied by the Lobby) where the Rubens gallery had been and a monumental staircase which still exists.

A Consular decree of February 1803 confirmed a decision of October 1802 to clear the Place St-Sulpice. The demolition was put in hand of the old seminary,[1] which badly obstructed the view in front of the church, 'one of the most beautiful in Paris'.

Work on the Ourcq canal, in which the First Consul took a special interest, was advancing. On 1 March the First Consul rode out at 6 a.m. on a fine morning and for nearly five hours followed the whole proposed forty-five-mile course of the canal where work was being pushed forward on the first fifteen miles. He was pleased with the progress made and lavished praises on engineers and workmen.

Next day at crack of dawn he rode to Mareuil, where the water intake had its source and where Frochot awaited him. He did not return to Paris until 8 p.m. The *Moniteur*'s report of this inspection was encouraging:

> 'This canal will not only supply water to assuage the capital's thirst, but will also feed a considerable number of buildings in the faubourgs; the Ourcq water is very good.'

Meanwhile the First Consul was devoting much attention to the capital's business interests. The law of 24 December, instituting Chambers of Commerce in the provinces, had made no provision for Paris. A decree signed on 25 February set up in Paris a Chamber of Commerce of fifteen members elected by sixty notables, business people or bankers. The first meeting was held on 17 April at the Place Vendôme under Frochot's presidency.

Paris and the rupture of peace

Over this happy atmosphere of peace a shadow fell; the inimical attitude of Great Britain, jealous of the growing prosperity of France under the First Consul and alarmed by threats to her commercial ascendancy. The British took the island of Malta, which they refused

[1] This seminary was transferred to the Rue du Pot de Fer (Rue Bonaparte) to the house known as 'L'Instruction'.

to evacuate, as a pretext in spite of the formal clauses of the Treaty of Amiens. On 17 March the British government put an embargo on all French and Dutch ships lying in British ports. Rupture was inevitable.

Bonaparte's reaction to these alarming moves was to order the immediate arrest of all British subjects living on French soil, declaring to Junot, 'This order must be carried out between now and 7 p.m. I do not wish the most insignificant theatre or the worst restaurateur in Paris to see an Englishman in its boxes or at his tables this evening.'

Shortly afterwards in a stormy scene he shouted at the British ambassador, Lord Whitworth, 'I would rather see you occupying the heights of Montmartre!'—fatal words which found an echo in 1814 and 1815.

With the order for the occupation of Hanover and the ports of the kingdom of Naples a bitter war began.

Immediately the city of Paris ranged itself alongside the First Consul. A deputation from the electoral college of the 3rd arrondissement, including the jurist, Citizen Bellart, waited on him at the Tuileries on 10 April. One of the Councillors made a speech in which he said, ' . . . Your greatest glories are rescuing us from the abyss into which anarchy had plunged us; the suppression of our civil discords; the restoration of morality and religion; our recall to the domestic virtues; and the revival of science, the arts and commerce. These miracles you have brought about in less time than it would have taken someone else to think of them.'

Lord Whitworth's spectacular departure from Paris on 12 May, announced officially on the 22nd, signalled the definite rupture of peace and produced a strong reaction from the public which showed itself unanimously in favour of arming the navy.

The mayors of Paris, impressed by innumerable demonstrations of loyalty to the First Consul, sent Frochot this letter on 24 May:

'Citizen Prefect, Paris desires to avenge the violation of good faith. The Mayors of the city seek your permission to invite subscriptions from its citizens to build, arm and equip launches, pinnaces and transports.'

In their turn the capital's businessmen offered their support. An extraordinary meeting was convened at the Bourse by the Chamber of Commerce and the following resolution adopted:

'The commerce of the City of Paris wishes to pay its tribute to the French government in the shape of a warship of 120 guns, to be built, armed and equipped by them. The Chamber of Commerce assumes the responsibility for this offer and begs the First Consul's permission for the vessel to be called *The Commerce of Paris.*'

This resolution was approved with cheers and drowned in applause.

Bonaparte, supported by the majority of the nation, bent all his energies to preparing the bold project of invading England; with Josephine he left Paris on 23 June for the Channel coast, then made a triumphal progress in the Department of the Nord and Belgium. He returned to St-Cloud at 9.30 p.m. on 12 August; on the 15th St Napoleon's day was fêted, as in 1802, with great popular rejoicing.

The rupture of the Peace of Amiens did not slacken the rhythm of progress of public works in Paris. On Sunday, 12 June, the Pont de la Cité (Pont St-Louis), which had taken only two years to build, was opened to the public on payment of a toll. The opening of the Pont des Arts, uniting the Louvre and the Palace of the Four Nations, followed swiftly; this was the first bridge to be built in cast iron. Before the work was set in hand Napoleon asked Bourrienne to consult the architects who agreed that a bridge was needed but declared that

> 'the city would gain little in embellishment from the building of an iron bridge, of necessity extremely narrow and which would reduce the width of a good channel often utilized for ceremonial occasions, nor would its size and lightness be in harmony with the splendour of the two buildings it was to unite.'

The First Consul paid no attention to this advice as he was anxious to use the new process.

The Feuillants' building, used as a barracks for the Consular Guard (which was transferred to a new barracks in the Rue de Grenelle-St-Germain), was to be demolished. Three roads had already been opened to the right of the Rue de Rivoli—one opposite St-Roch (Rue des Pyramides), the second opposite the Rue Neuve du Luxembourg (Rue Cambon) and the third facing the Place Vendôme built over the church and gardens of the old convent of the Capucines in the direction of the boulevard.

Interest in commemorating the foundation of the republic diminished with a new monarchy in sight; 22 September 1803 was marked by no special ceremonies. This date was, however, chosen for the unveiling of a portico embellishing the Hôtel Dieu, the old seventh-century structure left in a deplorable state by the revolution.

On 1 October Bonaparte, uniting memories of the Rome of the Caesars and Charlemagne, whose successor he was to be, laid down three articles, destined to be the birth certificate of the Vendôme column:

'In the centre of the Place Vendôme in Paris a column shall be erected similar to that in honour of Trajan in Rome. This column will be 13 feet in diameter and 143 feet high. It will be encrusted with a spiral band on which will be 108 allegorical bronze figures each of three feet, representing the Departments of the republic. The column will be surmounted by a semi-circular platform decorated with olive leaves and carrying a statue of Charlemagne.'

This column was erected on the site assigned to it but its modern form differs considerably from the original plan; in any event the column underwent many changes of fortune.

Bonaparte was now engaged in planning the invasion, in which Paris and the whole of France took a passionate interest. On 6 October he visited the shipyards at the Invalides and spent some time cruising on board a gunboat on the Seine, cheered by the crowds. He paid another visit, lasting a fortnight from 3 November, to Boulogne. His extraordinary energy is recalled by Bourrienne in his *Mémoires*:

'The newspapers announced his arrival at St-Cloud and, a few days later, his return to Paris was signalized by an inspection of public works, parades, large manœuvres which he commanded and, almost immediately thereafter, a ceremonial audience preceded by a review on the Place du Carrousel. He enjoyed nothing so much as this perpetual activity.'

Bonaparte's return to Paris coincided with the installation of the Prefecture of the Seine in the Hôtel de Ville, of which the public was informed by a notice in the press:

'Instead of being open every other day the offices will now be open to the public every day.'

The foundation stone of the Hôtel de Ville had been laid on 15 July 1533, during the reign of François I, but the building was not completed until 1605 during the reign of Henri IV. The Hôtel de Ville fronted the Place of that name and had neither wings nor view over the Seine. In a spacious inner courtyard, lined with niches rich in marble and statues, were several large apartments, originally set aside for public functions. As the capital had grown so greatly the Hôtel de Ville was no longer adequate and, in addition, in common with other public buildings, had suffered much damage during the revolution. Frochot, with the aid of the civic and Departmental architect, Molinos, set to work to restore the building.

By a decree of 3 December 1803, which revived the provisions of the law of 1792 which had not been applied, Bonaparte initiated an extensive town-planning operation, which altered the appearance of part of eastern Paris and finalized the shape of one of its great squares, which was designed to be both useful and ornamental. It was to be 'lined with a double row of trees with a circular ornamental basin in the centre of the square'. A single continuous street was to be made of the Rue St-Antoine and the Rue du Faubourg St-Antoine, of which the entry was to be set back to conform with the new square.

This operation was part of the total plan for the Ourcq canal which, by cutting through the Fossé de l'Arsenal, would flow southwards into the Seine and northwards into the ornamental basin to stand at the crossroads of the inner boulevards, the canal and its towpaths on both banks. All the buildings round the square were to be symmetrical and of equal size. The cost was to be something over a million and a half francs.

Bonaparte wanted:

(1) The land freed round the Arsenal, the old Bastille and other sites by the construction of this square to be split up into lots to make them easier to sell.

(2) Cost of construction to be met by taxes on houses and buildings in the new streets and by the increase in value of land and property owned in the area by the State, particularly round the Arsenal.

This proposed tax was one of the First Consul's innovations: it established a new principle in public finance, the advantage accruing to the government of increased land values.

The year which had opened peacefully was ending in a state of tension, but the morale of the nation and its chief was in no way affected. The First Consul, deep in preparations for the invasion from which he confidently expected great results, looked the future squarely in the face and saw it lying across the Channel.

To relax and also to keep in touch with the Parisians Bonaparte paid frequent visits to the theatre, where the applause always lavished on him by the public was evidence of their confidence in him. He was also cheered when, with Josephine, he went on 17 December to the Louvre which, at Cambacérès' suggestion, had been given the name of Musée Napoléon and his bust placed in the entrance hall.

The last conspiracies

The external crisis, which had consolidated the union of Bonaparte and the nation, had also encouraged the royalist opposition and strengthened its ties with England, the headquarters of Vendéens and émigrés. Hatred of France and alarm about invasion induced the British government to give active support to a plot to kill Bonaparte and restore a Bourbon to the throne. Those principally involved were, for varying reasons, all sworn enemies of Bonaparte—Georges Cadoudal, who had landed on the cliffs at Biville on 21 August and gone on to Paris; Pichegru, Napoleon's tutor at Brienne and victor of Holland; the Comte d'Artois' aides-de-camp, the brothers Polignac and the Marquis de Rivière, who reached Paris some time between December 1803 and January 1804 and finally General Moreau.

Since Fouché's departure the police seemed to have lost heart, but Bonaparte had his own police under Duroc, Savary, Moncey and Junot. The First Consul's keen intuition led him to sense the existence of a plot and, when he heard that two Chouans had been arrested and were still in prison, he ordered them to be interrogated. One of them revealed on 28 January that Georges Cadoudal had been in hiding in Paris for several months. Bonaparte seconded Réal from the Ministry of Justice on 1 February to act as magistrate 'to examine all matters concerning the peace and internal security of the republic'.

Immediate searches made in Paris resulted in arrests, including some of Cadoudal's lieutenants, from one of whom Bonaparte was astonished to learn of Moreau's implication and his nocturnal interview on the Boulevard de la Madeleine with Pichegru. He was so overcome that he waited for forty-eight hours before taking action then, after an *ad hoc* Council, he ordered Moreau's arrest and imprisonment in the Temple.

The public reaction to the 'alleged' conspiracy was guarded; the guilt of the victor of Hohenlinden was scarcely credible, but Bonaparte was unruffled.

'I am not sufficiently known to be understood,' he told Roederer. 'My achievements are not yet great enough to be known. I respect this suspicious attitude of the Parisians, which shows that they do not act slavishly and ignorantly.'

And the citizens of Paris continued to admire him as before.

On the evening of 19 February Bonaparte paid another visit to the Théâtre Français and on the next day to the Opéra where he was greeted with unanimous and prolonged applause and shouts of 'Long live Bonaparte!' The troops, except for a republican enclave in the army, were loyal.

'Never have they shown greater devotion to the person of the First Consul,' notes a police bulletin.

Bonaparte lost not a jot of his calm despite his irritation about the plot, intensified perhaps by disillusionment with Moreau. He reiterated that his sole objective was the safety of France and his determination to pursue the lofty aims he had set himself.

'I have always told you,' he declared to Roederer, 'that I need ten years. I am only at the beginning; nothing has been accomplished.'

When, on 21 February, he returned thanks to the members of the Institute who came to express their loyal greetings after the plot which had threatened his life, 'Some storms,' he said, 'serve to strengthen a government's roots.'

These storms were being kept active by attacks made on the First Consul by all sections of the opposition. Royalists, aristocrats of the Faubourg St-Germain, 'exclusive' Jacobins, republican soldiers, discontented bourgeois, some members of the Tribunate (who included Moreau's brother) all tried to bamboozle the public into believing that the conspiracy was a 'put-up job' to discredit Moreau and eliminate him from public life. Moreau's supporters went so far as to say that 'the man who fired on the people on 13 Vendémiaire will not spare the Parisians'.

Pichegru was arrested on 29 February and his accomplices a few days later. A law inculpated those who were hiding Georges Cadoudal and the sixty-odd ruffians in English pay in Paris and its neighbourhood and rendered them liable to the same penalties. This law was printed, read and placarded at every square, bridge, crossroads, port and street. Paris was put into a state of siege; sentries were posted along its walls and an embargo placed on exits by night through the barriers and sailing on the Seine; passports were checked and houses searched; stocks fluctuated and the public began to show signs of alarm. A contemporary observed ironically that:

'to distract as much attention as possible from the great political issues there is a rumour current that the First Consul is beginning to frequent the society of very pretty women and that his passion for Mlle George is greater than ever. . . .[1]'

At last on 9 March Georges Cadoudal was arrested in the Place de l'Odéon. He confessed that he had been in Paris for several months and that in England he had been assigned the mission of assassinating the First Consul. Bonaparte's enemies were thrown into disarray; for them 'the affair was taking a bad turn'. According to a report of 10 March Cadoudal's arrest

'has electrified everyone and it is impossible to describe the people's delight when his capture was known half an hour later. All Paris knew of it and it is safe to say that rejoicing was universal.'

This satisfaction was expressed in no uncertain terms by the workers; drinking-houses and pleasure-gardens were almost as full as on Sundays.

'It is difficult today to realize,' reports Méneval, 'just how interested the people of Paris were in the unfolding of this drama. Cadoudal's arrest had stilled all doubts and raised general concern and affection for the head of state to a pinnacle. The universal desire was for the arrest and severe punishment of the instigators of the plot.'

The investigation which had led to the conspirators' arrest appeared to indicate that 'a prince', who might be hiding in Paris, was at the heart of the plot. The Duc d'Enghien was singled out by fate to be that prince. He was arrested at the Château d'Ettenheim (in the Electorate of Baden), taken to Paris, where he arrived about 3 p.m. on 20 March at the Barrière de la Villette, and conducted to the fortress of Vincennes. Here he was condemned by a military court, presided over by General Hulin, and executed during the night in the moat of the Château.

[1] One of the stars of the Comédie Française and an early mistress of Napoleon. She grew enormously fat in later life and, under the Second Empire, was glad to be an attendant in a ladies' cloakroom at the Exhibition of 1859. Ed.

This is not the place to examine the complexities of this affair, still less for a final judgement since, on his deathbed, the Emperor assumed sole responsibility. The final verdict belongs to God alone.

Earliest rumours of the execution reached Paris at dawn on 21 March and spread throughout the city until 'during the day the condemnation of the ex-Duc d'Enghien was confirmed'. More than 150,000 copies of the judgment of the Military Court were sold to a public greedy for information but 'no one hazarded an opinion'. A police bulletin reported that 'Paris has never been so utterly silent'.

The workers in the faubourgs were most vocal in their anger against the plotters and were ready to support the government's repressive action which was to them a healthy sign of strength.

'If the government needs our services,' they were saying on 24 March in the Rue du Temple, 'let it say so and it shall soon have them.'

The royalists and the émigrés were seriously disturbed; they did not dare protest but tried by circulating alarmist rumours to 'invent news'—'they are not clever enough, however, to concoct anything really to upset the public'.

Bonaparte appeared to take none of this agitation seriously.

'Although there was much talk in Paris about it,' he summed up at St Helena the consequences of d'Enghien's execution, 'what I did was to silence the royalists and the Jacobins once and for all.'

If the opposition was not crushed 'once and for all'—it never would be—it was considerably shaken. Thenceforward nothing could prevent the creation of the Empire and, on 27 March 1804 the Senate invited the First Consul to perfect his achievements by making his glory immortal.

On 5 April Pichegru (whom Bonaparte would have liked to reprieve) was found hanged in his cell, an event seized on by the opposition to spread the rumour that the General had not committed suicide but had been 'eliminated to prevent his making any public defence'. The population was only briefly affected. What people wanted was the strengthening of the régime and the suppression of all attempts to overthrow it. Bonaparte had lost not a whit of his prestige.

When, on 14 April, he went to the Opéra (soberly dressed in his Chasseur uniform), he was received with spirited applause. The public had apparently ceased to be interested in the conspiracy and even began to find it entertaining. Even the 'exclusives', according to a report of 28 April

> 'were forced to concede that public opinion, especially that of the populace, was on the First Consul's side and their loyalty to him could not be called in question.'

Bonaparte was about to climb the topmost rung of the ladder and become Imperator. This was the end sought by numerous addresses and congratulations now daily flowing in to the Tuileries, from civil, military and religious bodies as well as from the citizens of every Department and commune.

Book II

The Emperor and his Good City

I

The Emperor and the City in Time of Peace

Paris votes for the Emperor

The birth of the Empire was near and Paris would share its future
growth. It was the dream of the new Emperor, which he strove to
make a reality, that the City should be the greatest and most beautiful
in the universe. The new Caesar's supremacy would make Paris
the paramount capital of Europe, the capital of capitals, ranking
before Rome which, tomorrow, would become the second city of the
Empire. Paris was also to be his 'good city'[1] and between City and
Man would be forged bonds of affection. Napoleon would give
practical proof of his sentimental attachment in the embellishment
of the City, the conquered flags with which he would endow it and the
works of art with which he would enrich its museums.

On 23 April Curée, a former Conventionnel, laid before the
Tribunate a proposal to establish a hereditary monarchy in Napoleon's
person.

The Paris garrison, led by Murat, fervently wanted Napoleon to
be brought to the throne by its own endeavours; the proposal put
forward by the garrison was the more noteworthy because it was
signed by Masséna, Bernadotte and other generals 'always regarded
as zealous devotees of democracy'. On 4 May the soldiers at the
Invalides in their turn voted unanimously that 'Bonaparte should be
proclaimed Emperor and the Imperial honours hereditary in his
family'. Finally the City of Paris echoed this wish and recalled that,
as early as 1802, it had been the first to summon Bonaparte to the
throne:

'Two years ago, when the French people begged you to accept for life the
first magistracy of the State, the Mayoral Corps of the City of Paris,

---

[1] Revival of a medieval custom whereby certain cities were privileged and given tax
exemptions, and so on. Ed.

equating the welfare of all Frenchmen with that of the citizens of the
capital, ventured to suggest that more be asked of you and that, as some
recompense for all the benefits you have bestowed on us, you would be
able to hand on to our descendants a government strengthened by your
exertions and permanent as your own glory.'

Curée's motion was adopted on 3 May by the majority of the
Tribunate, with the exception of Carnot; a special committee drew
up the text which, on 16 May, was submitted to the Senate for the
promulgation of the organic senatus consultum which was its
constitutional duty.

Reports of the Prefecture of Police reveal the keen interest taken
by the people; the report of 17 May reads:

'Everyone is talking about the Imperial honours offered to the First
Consul, whom they all want to see as Emperor. Their impatience for the
senatus consultum cannot be put into words.'

On 18 May the resolution to proclaim Napoleon Bonaparte
Emperor of the French was adopted and the name of the new
Augustus enthusiastically cheered by all the Senators. Immediately
Cambacérès left in great state for St-Cloud, where Napoleon was in
residence; he was escorted by a regiment of cuirassiers and accompanied by a deputation from the Senate, the ministers and Councillors
of State.

Napoleon, in undress uniform, with Josephine at his side stood
waiting for the delegation and made a brief reply to the address
delivered by Cambacérès, who was the first to salute him as 'Sire'.

'Everything which can add to the country's welfare is intimately
linked with my own happiness. I accept the title which you believe
will serve the nation's glory and I submit the law of heredity to the
people's approbation.'

For the first time the cry, 'Long live the Emperor!' resounded,
that cry which millions would never tire of repeating and which was
echoed by the noise of guns thundering in the capital. Many Parisians
illuminated their houses as a sign of rejoicing and nearly everywhere
people were saying, 'At last we are delivered from the anguish of the
revolution and factions are wiped out.'

Next day the *Moniteur* published the senatus consultum, together
with the public announcement of a series of honours; Joseph and
Louis, the heirs presumptive, were created Princes of the Blood and
became respectively Grand Elector and Constable; Cambacérès was

to be Arch Chancellor of the Empire, Lebrun Arch Treasurer, Eugène de Beauharnais Arch Chancellor of the State and Duroc Governor of the Palace. Eighteen Marshals were appointed; Murat, Moncey, Masséna, Berthier, Jourdan, Augereau, Bernadotte, Soult, Brune, Lannes, Mortier, Ney, Davout, Bessières. Generals Kellermann, Lefebvre, Pérignon and Sérurier, who had been commanders-in-chief, also received the title of Marshals of the Empire.

At the same time a court was formed with Cardinal Fesch as Grand Almoner, Talleyrand Grand Chamberlain, Rémusat Chamberlain, Caulaincourt Grand Equerry and Ségur Grand Master of Ceremonies. The brilliance, pomp and etiquette of this court dazzled the Parisians who had never before seen such a display of luxury. The Salle des Maréchaux was the scene of fabulous receptions.

'On either side,' writes the Duchesse d'Abrantès, 'were three rows of ladies, decked with flowers, diamonds and waving plumes. Behind them stood a row of officers of the Imperial and Princesses' households, then the generals, glittering in gold lace, the secretaries, Councillors of State and ministers, all richly dressed, their chests covered with those plaques which the Emperor bestowed on his servitors, and those decorations which Europe offered us on bended knee.'

Josephine, dressed by the famous couturier, Leroy, succeeded marvellously in making the court luxurious beyond precedent; her perfumed path was followed by all elegant women which was a powerful stimulant for the city's trade.

To invest his accession with great lustre Napoleon ordered that the Senate should solemnly proclaim the senatus consultum in Paris, which was done on Sunday, 20 May. At 8 a.m. Fontanes, President of the Legislature, Fabre de l'Aude, President of the Tribunate, Murat, Frochot, Dubois and the mayors of the twelve arrondissements of Paris, made the first proclamation at the Luxembourg, followed by a further six announcements to the sound of trumpet and cymbals at the Place du Corps Législatif, the Place Vendôme, the Palais Royal, the Place du Carrousel, the Hôtel de Ville and the forecourt of the Palais de Justice.

'Hearty cheers and repeated shouts of "Long live the Emperor of the French! Long live Bonaparte!" greeted the good news.'

On 21 May Dubois ordered the opening of registers at the Prefecture of Police and police stations for the citizens to record their votes approving the institution of the Empire. The Parisians showed great eagerness.

'The workers particularly,' says a police report, 'make much of their right to vote for the hereditary principle in the Imperial family. They come in groups to sign, speaking warmly about the Emperor.'

Frochot, not to be outdone by his colleague, issued an important decree on the same day, authorizing the opening of a cemetery in the park of Père Lachaise, which Brongniart converted into an English garden.

From 22 May onwards imposing processions of the constituted bodies and other authorities made their way to St-Cloud to swear allegiance to the new Emperor. Frochot, the first prefect to be received in audience, took precedence of Montalivet, Prefect of Seine-et-Oise, on 27 May; a week later he was appointed a Councillor of State.

The return of spring, a season beloved of the Parisians, was a happy augury for the beginning of the Imperial régime. The *Journal des Dames et des Modes* of 20 May paints a delightful picture of life at this period in the capital:

'By 7 p.m. the promenades are crowded, fashionable riders on their way to Bagatelle, chatting to their ladies with one hand resting on the door of their sweethearts' carriages; fashionable walkers strolling along the Champs-Elysées, waiting impatiently till it is time to go to Frascati for an ice. What is known as the bourgeoisie rushes in a mass to Tivoli or the hamlet of Chantilly and other open-air places which now belong to them since they are no longer frequented by Society with a capital "S".

'All the cafés, from the Faubourg St-Antoine as far as the Madeleine, have their quota of idlers, young working girls and beer drinkers. Frascati is the only open-air place still fashionable and when Garchy gives a concert at three francs a ticket he attracts all Paris. Even those pretty women who have gone 30 or 35 miles to their country houses return for these concerts to see the latest in taste and fashion and to be seen themselves in the new Eden.'

The suppression of plots

The case against Moreau, Cadoudal and forty-eight others opened on 28 May in a special criminal court of the Department of the Seine; the hearing lasted twelve days and 139 witnesses were called. During the hearing the corridors of the Palais de Justice were crowded and the police had difficulty in tearing down all the posters stuck up in

Paris in favour of the accused. The capital, fed by rumours seeping through the walls of the Palais de Justice, showed some restlessness, apparently in Moreau's[1] favour but, in fact, it was a mere pretext for what Madelin calls 'the turbulence which our terrible capital is always ready to demonstrate'.

Napoleon, still at St-Cloud, received daily reports on the case from Bourrienne. Although he attached little importance to their effervescence he was somewhat irritated with the Parisians.

'They are taking Cadoudal's side,' he exclaimed to the Council of State. 'They're angry that I wasn't killed.'

He was annoyed with the revival of opposition among the aristocrats of the Faubourg St-Germain who were all partisans of Moreau, and he was equally displeased by fluctuations on the Stock Exchange and various demonstrations in some theatres in favour of the General.

The Tribunal pronounced sentence on 10 June at 4 a.m. Almost half the accused were condemned to death, among them Georges Cadoudal, Armand de Polignac and the Marquis de Rivière. Five others, including Moreau and Jules de Polignac, were sentenced to two years' imprisonment; twenty-two were acquitted.

To use the formula of police bulletins this verdict, as soon as it was known, 'was the subject of all public and private conversations'. The death sentences aroused dismay, but Moreau's sentence provoked varying feelings; his supporters, who had hoped for an acquittal, thought it too heavy while the government thought it too light. Although Moreau was not actively involved in the plot against Bonaparte, by his talks with the conspirators whose plans he appeared to approve he made himself their accomplice. The Emperor thought a severer sentence would both have been just and have given him an opportunity to be generous by exercising his right of clemency and even 'making peace with Moreau'.

An Imperial decision, 'eagerly read all over the city', was intended to mitigate the effects of the verdict. A series of 'acts of charity and indulgence' was announced; release of certain prisoners, amnesty for deserters, payment by the civil list of wet-nurses' fees incurred by poor citizens and the dowering of a poor and respectable girl in each arrondissement.

Napoleon had a long talk at St-Cloud on 14 June with Bourrienne,

---

[1] Moreau's counsel was Bonnet. Bellart had drawn up a brief, favourable to the General, which was perhaps at the origin of his hostility to the Emperor.

whose account of the Emperor's feelings about the trial is particularly illuminating. His first question showed his interest in the reactions of Paris. 'What's the man in the street doing and saying?'

He went on to explain his motives in punishing the dissident General.

'Could I have allowed him to conspire openly against my government? Could I foresee that, in court, Moreau would deny his previous declarations? . . . I had to agree to Moreau's arrest when I had proof of his meetings with Pichegru; a chain of consequences was set up which it was beyond human power to foresee.'

Napoleon said that his entourage had urged him to set up a military commission, which would have tried the accused within twenty-four hours.

'This I did not want; it would have been said that I fear public opinion and I do not. They can talk as much as they like so long as I don't hear them.'

He concluded, 'You can rest assured that, apart from a few hotheads whom I know how to silence, France as a whole and public opinion everywhere was on my side.'

This was neither more nor less than the truth which was confirmed by the plebiscite. The first count showed an impressive majority in favour of the Emperor, particularly in Paris, which was seen as the most Bonapartist city in France. The critical bourgeoisie, the military cliques and the sardonic Faubourg St-Germain meant little when compared with the enthusiastic masses. Napoleon's success could not but influence him to show magnanimity by pardoning or reducing the sentences of some eight of those condemned, among them Armand de Polignac. Moreau was allowed to sail for Philadelphia; he lived to betray France and die in the ranks of the enemy. Cadoudal went bravely to his death. At his execution the people showed active hostility and thousands of voices took up the cry, 'Long live the Emperor!'

So petered out the celebrated conspiracy which may have caused a slight stir round the new throne but could not shake its foundations. The young Empire, emulating the eagle which was to be its symbol, impelled by its founder's genius, was rising irresistibly upwards, for ten glory-laden years to spread its wings over Europe.

Georges Cadoudal in prison showed himself an acute psychologist when he uttered the bitter but realistic words, 'We did more than we

intended; we came to give Paris a king and we gave her an Emperor.'
Emperor of Paris Napoleon had indeed become.

Paris on the eve of the Coronation

After two and a half months at St-Cloud, giving innumerable
audiences and swearing in numbers of people, Napoleon left for Paris
where on the Carrousel on 8 July he held his first review since
becoming Emperor. His presence aroused indescribable excitement
and tumultuous cheers.

Popular rejoicing contrasted with the steady enmity of the
opponents of the régime. Their antagonism Napoleon, assured of the
nation's support, intended to scotch once and for all. He was dissatisfied with Régnier's lack of firmness and dexterity during the
Cadoudal conspiracy and decided to recall the 'inevitable' Fouché,
the minister of 'livid countenance and red-rimmed eyes'. Although in
semi-disgrace, Fouché had always maintained contact with the
Emperor and, on 30 June, he was the first to draw his attention, before
Régnier had heard of it, to the protest made in Warsaw by Louis
XVIII when the Empire was proclaimed.

When Napoleon heard of this protest he exclaimed, 'So, the Comte
de Lille[1] is up to his tricks again! The Bourbons ought to know that
I'm not afraid of them. You say that the good-for-nothings of the
Faubourg St-Germain are getting hold of and distributing copies of
his protest? Oh, for goodness's sake, let them read it freely. Fouché,
send the text to the *Moniteur* for tomorrow's issue.'

The protest was published on 1 July.

The Ministry of General Police was re-established by decree of
13 July with Fouché again as its presiding genius. To lessen the
influence of this 'fatally necessary' man, to use Méneval's phrase,
Napoleon divided the Empire into four districts, each under a
Councillor of State. The Prefect Dubois was given charge of the
fourth district, comprising the Department of the Seine and the
communes of St-Cloud, Meudon and Sèvres.

To refute the rumours cunningly spread by the opposition in Paris
that Napoleon was threatening the countries of Europe, the *Moniteur*
of 12 July published a severe warning to his enemies:

'Paris has always been the home of "they say". Every day a new rumour is

[1] Title used by Louis XVIII in exile. Ed.

born to be denied the next. "They say"—to make people believe his ambition is inordinate—that the Emperor is remaining at St-Cloud, that he is
going to the Tuileries, that he is staying at Malmaison, each remark
sillier than the next. The Emperor of the French neither wants war with
anyone nor fears it. A long period of peace is his deepest desire, but the
history of his life does not indicate that he would permit himself to be
mastered or insulted'.

The first Imperial celebration of 14 July, announced on Sunday
morning by a salute of thirty guns, was carried out with great
splendour. At 10 a.m. the troops of the Paris garrison marched past
the Emperor on the Place du Carrousel. At noon, in a procession
opened by the Chasseurs and closed by the mounted Grenadiers of the
Guard and by the Imperial Guard, Napoleon rode out of the Tuileries
for the Invalides. The troops lining the streets presented arms and
gave the general salute.

At the Invalides the Emperor was welcomed by the Governor,
Marshal Sérurier, who presented him with the keys, and by Ségur,
Grand Master of Ceremonies. Cardinal Caprara, the Papal Legate,
said mass and, after a speech by the Grand Chancellor, Lacépède,
Napoleon, covering his head like the kings of France, in a firm voice
invited those members of the Legion of Honour present, 'To swear
on their honour to dedicate themselves to the service of the Empire
and the preservation of its territory.' Their unanimous cry, 'I swear
it!' was followed by a wildly enthusiastic outburst of 'Long live the
Emperor!' from the whole assembly. The ceremony ended with a
Te Deum.

Side by side with these brilliant occasions Fouché's clever policy
was suppressing opposition activity. The city regained its calm and
the economy its upward trend. On 18 July the situation was summed
up by a police informer:

'Paris, particularly the factories and workshops, is absolutely quiet; the
workers are fully employed.'

On the same day the Emperor left St-Cloud and arrived at the
Boulogne camp on the 20th, having travelled so fast that he was
already at the port while the workers were still preparing his
welcome.

Here, where Caesar had planted his tent before invading England,
Napoleon set up his camp facing the sea at Pont de Briques, feverishly
preparing his own formidable assault on Great Britain. On his

birthday, 15 August, he made a ceremonial distribution of crosses of the Legion of Honour to eighty thousand troops assembled near the Roman Tower.

The scant confidence Napoleon had in the strategic ability of Admiral Villeneuve who, on the advice of Decrès, Minister of Marine, had been given command of naval operations, led him to postpone his invasion plans until the winter. He left the Boulogne camp for the newly annexed Rhenish territory; on 2 September he was at Mons and on the 3rd took up residence in the castle at Aix-la-Chapelle. His journey was a real triumphal progress, its high spot a pilgrimage to Charlemagne's tomb, a prelude to the coronation.

The people had endorsed his accession to power but Napoleon also wanted God's blessing from the hands of Christ's vicar on earth; he therefore planned to bring the Sovereign Pontiff to France to anoint and crown him Emperor, a ceremony which could take place only in Paris. Knowing the sardonic and frivolous temperament of the Parisians Napoleon, at a meeting of the Council of State, showed some reserve about this choice, but this was done deliberately to provoke public reaction. He knew perfectly well that no other city was in any way suitable for the grandiose plans he was making.

Some members of his entourage, mainly former revolutionaries, suggested that he should be crowned on the Champ de Mars, but this suggestion was not to Napoleon's liking. He had affection for the people but he disliked and distrusted its dregs. As he told the Council of State, 'Times have changed considerably. Once the people was sovereign and had to see everything that was done. Let's not imagine it is the same now. . . . To me twenty or thirty thousand fishwives swarming over the Champ de Mars are not the people of Paris and still less the French nation; they are only the witless and corrupt populace of a great city.'

Another reason why Napoleon rejected so ostentatious a ceremony was his desire that the coronation should be very dignified. He knew that he would be obliged to wear an elaborate costume and his acutely realistic sense made him fear lest it should produce an effect contrary to the one he wanted to make.

'When you swaddle me,' he said, 'in all those garments I shall look like a monkey. Your Imperial robes won't impress the people of Paris who go to the Opéra and see Laïs and Chéron wearing something much more spectacular and carrying it off better than I shall.'

His fears went even further that this somewhat theatrical garb, which privately he thought of as fancy dress, would make him look rather ridiculous to the Parisians, always so ready to mock. In spite of his frequent denials, he set the greatest store on public opinion which, in his view, was best represented by the Parisians whom he credited with the liveliest critical sense. In the end the Emperor, who wanted the coronation to have a religious character, decided that it should take place at Notre Dame de Paris.

Study of many police reports reveals that 'recent political disturbances have not interfered with commercial and municipal undertakings'. A report of 4 April notes that 'there is difficulty in finding workers' and that of 5 May that 'work continues to forge ahead and the workers are quiet'.

An article which appeared in the *Gazette de France* on 29 June demonstrates how great was the satisfaction with the various transformations taking place in Paris.

'People who come to Paris only occasionally and especially those who have not been here for four years could not now walk about the city without finding at every step they take something to admire. The extent to which Paris has been improved and in so short a time is barely credible, particularly as France during this period has enjoyed only one year of peace.

'The Place du Carrousel has been cleared, enlarged and embellished as if by magic; round the Louvre large numbers of hands have been employed for a year on the extensive works in preparation; spacious streets have been opened everywhere; magnificent quays are being constructed and an aqueduct, worthy of the Romans, completed under a new road which runs the whole length of the Tuileries; the palace of the Luxembourg is now one of the finest buildings in France and its gardens, extending over a wide area, have been decorated and beautified with taste and splendour. All this makes a delectable tour for the public and a magnificent panorama for the passer-by. Then there are the Botanical Gardens and finally a large regular open space is being developed on the site of the old Bastille, to which a canal, cut at great expense, will bring the pure waters of a river known until now only by name to most Parisians.'

Large improvements were needed on the Ile de la Cité because of the coronation. Balzac has written perceptively about this district between the Palais de Justice and Notre Dame. At the beginning of the nineteenth century it was a densely populated enclave, traversed by 'a congeries of sombre, narrow and tortuous streets', and a huddle of ancient buildings with jutting gables.

The work already in hand to open up approaches to the cathedral was speeded up considerably to make room for the Imperial procession to manoeuvre easily; this was done in less than two months. The tiny square in front of the cathedral, almost shut in by the dreary Foundling Hospital opposite, was enlarged by setting back the Hôtel Dieu—and southwards on the site of the garden where Charlemagne's statue stands—to make an approach 240 feet square, about a quarter of its present size. The magnificent sight presented by the cathedral was blocked by a mass of buildings, many of which, including the Chapter church, were demolished to open up the view.

If the Emperor had had more time at his disposal he would have carried out more extensive works in this area. Fain reports some of his plans: 'Why, for instance, not pull down all this part of the Cité? It's a huge ruin, good only for housing the rats of old Lutetia! The rubbishy old buildings here can't be as costly as those which clutter up the Carrousel; a few millions spread over several years would do the trick. I should like a grove of trees planted here like the one on the Champs-Elysées—it would be one of the finest promenades in Paris. The basilica of Notre Dame and the old palace of St-Louis, now devoted to Justice, would be a majestic decoration.'

In any event the alterations made were considerable and, as Lavedan says, show 'an application of the principle of the conquest of space'. They should be credited to Napoleon's civic successes. The few demolitions involved did much to purify one of the capital's most dangerous districts. Napoleon III and Haussmann continued them on a much larger scale but at the cost of destroying many buildings; their efforts resulted in the present much larger square which some people consider to be too large and an aesthetic heresy.

Among other enterprises nearing completion were the bridge, to be called the Pont d'Austerlitz; the 'beautiful Rue de Rivoli' which had been paved in its entirety; the Quai Bonaparte, called by its contemporaries, 'one of the finest undertakings of its kind', was receiving the final touches for the passing of the coronation procession. The fountain in the Place de l'Ecole de Médecine was almost finished and the Hospice des Ménages had been entirely reconstructed; a new Morgue had been built on the Place du Marché Neuf, on the north-west corner of the Pont St-Michel. A beginning had been made in house numbering; plaques of faïence in different colours were placed in the Rue Neuve des Petits Champs, an innovation of the Imperial government because the general numbering of each district, substituted by the revolution for the somewhat primitive system of the old régime, was highly confusing. Napoleon by a decree of 4 February 1805, established the system in current use, that is numbering by streets—even numbers on the right, uneven on the left. The control gained by the Napoleonic régime is shown in the names given to certain great Parisian institutions; the Lycée Louis-le-Grand in the Rue St-Jacques became the Lycée Impérial, the Opéra the Imperial Academy of Music and the National Library the Imperial Library.

The prospect of the coronation made the capital and business in particular very lively. A bulletin of 22 July notes:

'Business people's hopes are reviving; in addition to the many delegations which will come to Paris, large numbers of tourists are expected and many private individuals are furnishing their apartments to let them as a speculation. Jewellers and gem-dealers are very busy, the price of good quality diamonds has risen steeply and in general factories and workshops are very active.'

The *Gazette de France* spoke of the impetus given by the court and announced that this season would be marked

'by a general revolution in fashion. A whole flock of trades which collapsed with the fall of the monarchy are reviving with it; saddlery, lace, feathers, fur, embroidery, jewellery, buckles, watch-chains, buttons, pearls, sequins and beads, in whose manufacture so many hands are employed, and a hundred and one other articles which were considered lost to Parisian manufacture are in greater demand, dearer and better than ever. Already the daily wages of several classes of workers have increased as a result.'

Customers went to Dallemagne, the well-known artist who was to embroider the Emperor's mantle to be made of Lyons velvet supplied by Le Vacher, and to Foncier, who was making the Imperial crowns and setting the 'Regent' in the hilt of the sword fashioned by Boutet.

The numbers of provincials and foreigners arriving in Paris very soon created serious accommodation difficulties because of the limited number of hotels and furnished rooms.

In this atmosphere of great busyness an exhibition was opened on 18 September at the newly-arranged Louvre of works of living painters, sculptors, artists and engravers. Large numbers were attracted to this, the Empire's first Salon. Gros' great painting of Bonaparte visiting the Plague Hospital at Jaffa was the work most admired. The *Moniteur* reports that:

'A large group of students and artists went to the Salon to lay a wreath over this painting.'

A police report notes that:

'After gazing long and attentively at this picture people of every class seemed moved and several said with feeling, "This is the Emperor's finest deed." '

A few days later public buildings were illuminated in honour of 1 Vendémiaire (22 September); these lights cast their brilliance on a concert given in the evening at the Tuileries. This was the last official celebration of the revolutionary event, the founding of the republic.

Circles hostile to the régime disliked this atmosphere of prosperity and rejoicing.

'The temper of the salons is still very bad; everything that is done is ridiculed,' reads one of Fouché's bulletins for October.

The opposition paraded its scepticism about the English invasion plan and tried to spread rumours of a forthcoming continental war,

'but this sort of talk makes no impression on the large mass of citizens who are loyal to the government'.

The people in fact were very gay, their only disquiet caused by Napoleon's long absence; his early return was ardently desired by everyone.

The Emperor returned to St-Cloud at noon on 12 October but he had to make frequent visits to Paris. On 28 October he inspected a grand review on the Place du Carrousel; the people, deprived for several months of a sight of their hero, massed around the palace, the quays and near-by places. The Emperor was easily recognized 'by the very simplicity which distinguishes him' and immediately

'applause and shouts of "Long live the Emperor!" were heard in the distance, bringing to His Majesty positive evidence of the feelings of the capital which voiced the devotion of the whole of France.'

The Coronation

A month later, while Paris was feverishly preparing for the great day, Napoleon who, on 25 November, had gone to meet Pius VII at Fontainebleau, made his entry into the city on 28 November.

When next day the Pope appeared with Napoleon on the palace balcony he was cheered by the people. The Emperor spared a special thought that day for his 'good city'; he sent a sealed letter to the General Council, which carried out the duties of the municipal council, in this instance treating this body as the Mayoral Corps.

'Gentlemen, divine providence and the Imperial constitutions have ordained that hereditary Imperial honours should be invested in Our family and We have set aside the eleventh day of the present month of Frimaire 2 December and the metropolitan church of Paris to be the day and place of Our anointing and coronation. It would have been Our wish at this august ceremony to assemble in one building not only the entire population of the Imperial capital but also all those citizens who together make up the French nation.

'As We are desirous of showing a particular mark of Our affection to Our good city of Paris it is Our pleasure that the whole Mayoral Corps should witness these ceremonies.'

Next day the Paris municipal assembly met at the Hôtel de Ville to return thanks to the sovereign for the Imperial message and resolved that:

'The letter of His Majesty the Emperor shall be copied in full into the registers and shall remain annexed thereto as a memorial of a signal mark of favour shown to the City of Paris.'

On 1 December the Emperor received at the Tuileries a delegation from the Senate which brought the official results of the plebiscite decreed by the senatus consultum of 19 May. Ayes registered were 3,572,329 and noes only 2,579. In the Department of the Seine there were 120,947 ayes to 70 noes; the Isère had registered 82,084 ayes and 12 noes. Paris, far and away ahead of other cities of the Empire, had voted 117,504 ayes to 66 noes.

From 6 a.m. gun salutes were repeated hourly until evening and the sound of bells heralded the long-awaited ceremony. Houses were hung with flags and draperies and many shops decorated with artificial flowers. The streets filled quickly and people climbed on to

house-tops. The early morning was cold and wet but as the day wore
on the weather improved. At 8 a.m. the Councillors of State, the
members of the Legislature and the Tribunate left their respective
palaces, escorted by a hundred mounted men.

An hour later Pius VII, dressed in white and crimson, got into a
'magnificent coach drawn by eight dapple-grey horses', followed by
numbers of richly clothed clergy and escorted by detachments of the
Guard.

Any fears that the crowd might be rude were dissipated when it
showed respect and even reverence to the holy old man who joyously
scattered his blessings far and wide. The only slightly unfortunate
note struck was when the papal procession passed close to the popular
districts of the Central Markets and the Rue St-Denis where the
spectators did laugh at a prelate, wearing a broad-brimmed hat and
carrying a large gilded cross, who led the cortège on a white
mule.

At 10 a.m. through a line of troops and to the sound of bells
mingling with the noise of gun salutes the brilliant and majestic
Imperial procession set off in luxurious coaches, their occupants
gorgeously attired in velvet and satin, their gold, white and purple
competing in beauty and splendour. All along the route a crowd,
estimated at over five hundred thousand, wildly acclaimed the
Emperor whom they saw at the back of his gilded coach with eight
windows, surmounted by an imposing crown and drawn by eight
light bay horses caparisoned in white. Napoleon wore a tunic of
purple velvet, designed by Isabey and David, a short cape and a
plumed toque. He responded to the salutations of the crowd 'with a
look full of kindliness and an affectionate bow'.

The Emperor, the Empress and their suite arrived at 11.45 at the
Archiepiscopal Palace where Pius VII met them. Here the sovereigns
assumed their coronation robes and the Imperial regalia. Then,
escorted by the State dignitaries, they proceeded through a gallery
hung with tapestries to the splendidly decorated cathedral church for
the religious ceremony.

After the *Veni Creator* the Emperor, perfectly calm, kneeling with
the Empress at the altar, received the triple unction from the Pope.
Next, Napoleon removed the golden laurel wreath he was wearing
and crowned himself, then crowned Josephine—a scene which David
has handed on to posterity in his famous painting, *The Coronation*.

The Emperor, followed by his brothers, now mounted the twenty-four steps leading to the throne where he was joined by Pius VII who embraced him. The Holy Father, turning towards the congregation, pronounced the solemn formula, *Vivat Imperator in aeternum* while the choirs and orchestras resounded beneath the vaulting of the cathedral, a sound echoed by the prolonged and mighty cheers of the assemblage, to which the thundering of cannon responded. The Pope then began to intone the Te Deum and continued the mass. After the offering Napoleon swore the constitutional oath on the Bible; the ceremony was at an end.

The procession returned to the Archbishop's palace and thence to the Tuileries via the popular districts to allow the Parisians to give full rein to their excitement. As night fell thousands of torches cast an impressive glow on the crowds massing round the passing carriages.

'The illuminations on the buildings in the Tuileries gardens and the Champs-Elysées were more brilliant than ever before. The flames of Bengal lights blazed on the loftiest edifices.'

On Wednesday 5 December a ceremony devoted to 'arms, valour and fidelity' took place on the Champ de Mars. When the legislature had offered its respectful greetings in the Ecole Militaire, Napoleon and Josephine, in their robes, took their places on thrones on a stand built outside. Round them were grouped delegations from all arms of the services and the presidents of the electoral colleges.

At a given signal, while spectators and the army joined in cheers echoed by salvoes of artillery, the columns of troops advanced towards the stand. Napoleon rose and 'in a strong, vibrant and plangent voice' spoke the words of the oath, 'Soldiers, here are your flags. You swear to give your lives to safeguard them.'

Like one man, presidents, officers and the whole army, brandishing their weapons, shouted 'We swear it!' 'Their cheers mingled with the clash of arms and military fanfares' while the spectators seemed electrified into a state of enthusiasm impossible to describe, but which spread quickly to the masses on the slopes of the Champ de Mars. Then army and delegations marched past the Imperial couple, who returned at 5.0 p.m. in procession to the Tuileries, amid universal cheers.

Twenty years earlier the young Bonaparte, arriving in the capital, had made a very unobtrusive entry to the Ecole Militaire. How could he have dreamed that one day all Paris would crowd at his feet?

The City welcomes the Emperor

'Paris, ever the centre of taste, the seat of learning and the arts, the arbiter of manners and culture'

owed a duty to herself to welcome the sovereigns with suitable ceremony. As a fitting sequel to the coronation celebrations the capital on 16 December entertained the Emperor and Empress for the first time. Frochot, 'who had a gift for organizing fairy-tale festivities', took charge of the arrangements aided by the civic architect, Molinos. Two temporary wooden structures were erected on the Place de Grève, one a throne-room, the other a banqueting-hall, called the Salle des Victoires. A richly bound copy of the *Code Napoléon* was laid on the steps of the throne.

By 1 p.m. all the guests had assembled; they were drawn from the leading families in Paris and members of the administration together with the mayors of the thirty-six chief cities of the Empire. The Emperor and Empress were met on arrival in the coronation coach by the Corps of Mayors, Murat, Frochot and Dubois. They were loudly cheered on their entry into the throne-room, where Frochot greeted them on behalf of the capital.

'Sire, this people, this assembly, these walls all unite to say to you: Paris has found herself again. Yes, Sire, Paris has found herself again, not only as she was once, blindly devoted, traditionally loyal, habitually faithful, but devoted, loyal and faithful because of her gratitude. No longer is she by turns fervent and careless, arrogant and servile; she has now been made aware by your glory of the true nature of greatness, tempered by many misfortunes, matured by her own experience, influenced by the strength of your institutions, virtually reborn through the lofty effect that a great man's genius has on his times.

'As magistrates we have sworn obedience and loyalty on our own behalf and that of the great city. Today, Sire, it is Paris herself, Paris as a whole which, at this festivity, swears in its turn to be faithful to this oath.'

The Emperor replied to this speech to which he had listened with pleasure and some emotion:

'Gentlemen of the Corps of Mayors, I have come among you to assure my good city of Paris that I hold it under my special protection. Always I shall be happy to show it especial marks of my goodwill since you must know that in battle, in the midst of the greatest dangers, at sea, or even in the desert, what this great capital is thinking has ever been in the forefront of my mind—albeit taking second place to the powerful claims which the future has on my heart.'

Enthusiastic cheers, taken up by the spectators outside the building, greeted this speech.

At the reception which followed, the Emperor was particularly gracious to the mayors, to whom he expressed his satisfaction with the way in which they had for four years governed the city. He spoke in similar terms to the hospital authorities. Next came a presentation to the Imperial pair from the City of a silver-gilt table and toilet service, including two *nefs*[1], magnificently chased, one with a coronation scene and the other showing the Prefect of the Seine and the twelve mayors presenting their gift.

A banquet was then served in the Salle des Victoires, the sovereigns sitting alone at one table, the Imperial family and grand dignitaries at another and at a third the Marshals and grand officers of the Empire. During dinner an orchestra played a Haydn symphony. A firework display on the Left Bank with a set piece of the Emperor, and a ship representing the city of Paris, was followed by a concert as the Emperor walked through the rooms, with a kindly word for the ladies. A ball ended the proceedings.

Although Napoleon had agreed to the entertainments in his honour offered him by the city of Paris he did not care for displays which he thought wasteful and unproductive. At St Helena he set forth his point of view: 'I frequently objected to the entertainments the city of Paris wanted to give me—dinners, balls and firework displays costing from 400,000 to 800,000 francs; they disorganized the city for several days and cost as much to undo as to do. I proved that outlays like these could have paid for splendid monuments.'

One magnificent celebration followed another; a banquet in the Galerie de Diane at the Tuileries, a fête at the Théâtre Olympique in the Rue Chantereine, given by the generals of the Army Museum, another by the mayors and deputies of Paris, and an entertainment given in the Empress's honour at the Opéra.

The Duchesse d'Abrantès was still marvelling as she recalled this truly fairy-tale scene:

'The auditorium was decorated with silver gauze and garlands of fresh

[1] Containers in the shape of a ship for bread and salt. Ed.

flowers; myriad candles lit up magnificent jewels, groups of charming women sparkled with glittering diamonds, dresses embroidered with gems too dazzling to look at—all this in air perfumed by fresh flowers in a severe winter.'

On 27 December Napoleon went in state to open the session of the Legislature where he made a 'simple and dignified' speech, seeking from the people punishment of England's bad faith and stressing his determination to preserve the territory of the Empire intact and in peace. In the Chamber this speech aroused unanimous applause and next day it made a great sensation in Paris where 'it was the sole topic of conversation, especially in business and banking circles which were pleased with the Emperor's declarations'.

The year 1804 was ending happily and prosperously; it had been marked by events in Paris which would change the face of Europe. Its citizens, who had lived through such memorable hours and who shared to the full their sovereign's aspirations, could celebrate the New Year in a way which would help to keep the business of their city thriving.

The Louvre and the Tuileries

Napoleon had no time to give way to the intoxication he might have felt as a result of all the hero-worship lavished on him at the festivities in his honour. On 18 January 1805, he went to Malmaison, where he stayed until 25 March, pondering 'his grand designs' for Italy and England. Villeneuve's inertia at Toulon angered him and he devised a new invasion plan. Occasionally, to take his mind off his hard work, the Emperor looked back over his past and once, in an informal talk with Bourrienne, he remarked, 'When we were strolling idly through the streets of Paris what was it that told me that one day I should be master of France? My own will, but it was a will as yet vague; circumstances did the rest.'

His campaign preparations did not interfere with frequent visits to Paris where in the morning he liked to wander in civilian clothes through the streets and boulevards to inspect the works in progress. The increasing luxury surrounding his official life and court led Napoleon to improve the palaces of the Tuileries and the Louvre of which he took personal charge.

This is an appropriate moment to describe briefly the Emperor's background for fifteen years, especially the Tuileries which witnessed so much of his glory. Although his vertiginous comings and goings meant that Napoleon was not permanently in residence at the Tuileries it was there that he lived most often and he copied its décor in the various dwellings to which his campaigns took him.

The château of the Tuileries was an imposing block of buildings composed of a central section surmounted by a splendid dome featuring a clock, and with wings on either side. On the west it faced the gardens of the Tuileries, on the east the Cour du Carrousel; the wings terminated on the north in the Pavillon de Marsan and on the south in the Pavillon de Flore. In the central section were constructed the grand staircase, the grand vestibule and the Salle des Maréchaux, a huge room two storeys high with a large balcony, uniting both wings of the palace. Originally the northern wing contained the Salle des Travées (the Bow Window room) where the Council of State[1] was to hold its meetings and which was given a monumental staircase; in the rooms beyond were to be built a chapel, copied from that at Versailles, and a theatre to replace the Salle de la Convention (which had itself taken the place of the Salle des Machines).

Farther on still in the Pavillon de Marsan, facing the Rue de Rivoli, were to be housed the Grand Marshal and foreign princes. The State Apartments were in the southern wing where the Empress's apartments were on the ground floor. Facing the courtyard on the first floor was the State reception suite, consisting of the officers' salon, the Salon de la Paix (which took its name from a statue), the throne-room (formerly Louis XIV's state bedroom) with a sumptuous throne, the Emperor's State Council chamber or study which had also been used as such by Louis XIV, which was embellished by an ornate marble chimney-piece, and the Galerie de Diane used as a banqueting-room.

After a wide terrace on the garden side came the seven rooms of the ordinary apartments; the formal rooms, an antechamber or guard-room giving on to the staircase in the Pavillon de Flore, the household and the Emperor's audience salons, (the former bedroom of Louis XVI's daughter), and the private apartments, the Emperor's study, map-room, the inner study or portfolio-room, small bathroom, bedroom, dressing-room, wardrobe and ante-room. This suite was put in order to make it more comfortable; its paintings and gilding,

[1] It was here that the civil code was drawn up.

as well as those in the Galerie de Diane, were restored. Although the palace gained in splendour it was still inconvenient and sad 'as greatness' to use Napoleon's own phrase.

The Emperor's study, which he had used as First Consul since 1801, merits a pause. It was from this room, on the banks of the Seine in the very heart of Paris, that emanated those decisions which moulded Europe. Here it was that Napoleon, when not under canvas or in palaces abroad, spent most of his time.

> 'The Emperor's life was spent in his study; it was only there that he felt at home and disposed of his own time,' wrote Fain. 'When all other lights in the palace were out those in the study showed that the Emperor was still awake.'

This is how Napoleon's secretaries describe the Eagle's eyrie.

The room, of medium size, long rather than wide, was lit only by a corner window overlooking the palace garden and with a view of the river-bank. This room communicated with the salon of the ordinary apartments, of which the door was always locked. Between the study and the bedroom were the map-room and a wardrobe which had been Marie de Médicis' oratory, which had a dark alcove with a door giving on to a short lamplit staircase used by Napoleon to go down to Josephine's apartments.

In the centre of the study stood a superb desk by Biennais, deeply chased in gilded bronze and supported by gryphons. Later this was replaced by a desk of Napoleon's own design shaped like a violin with a central piece scooped out and rounded side-wings. The antique-style armchair was upholstered in green kerseymere, its folds fastened by silk cords and the arms ending in gryphons' heads. Napoleon used it only for signing documents when he then had his back to the fireplace and the window on his right. He preferred to sit on a small sofa covered in green taffeta near a little table on which were set out the letters arriving daily 'from all parts of Paris, the Empire and Europe'.

At right angles in the far corners of the room stood two large bookcases with a tall clock between them on a large mahogany table on which lay maps and reports. Along the wall facing the desk and the fireplace was a bookcase whose marble shelves were full of books. Next to it, and a little to the right, a second large door opened on to the bedroom, through which one entered the great audience chamber leading to the guard-room and thence to the Grand Staircase of the

Pavillon de Flore. In the window recess, close to the Emperor's desk, stood his secretary's small work-table, occupied by Bourrienne until 1802, Méneval until December 1812, and Fain until the fall of the Empire.

The Tuileries gardens, 'the most frequented and famous promenade in the capital' had also been extensively improved and were now 'in an admirable setting of beds planted with the finest shrubs and brightly coloured flowers'. The cutting of the Rue de Rivoli had freed land and buildings along the whole length of the Feuillants' terrace which was now bordered by high railings interspersed with stone pilasters supporting marble vases.

> 'Napoleon,' wrote Percier and Fontaine, 'was so enchanted with the Tuileries gardens that on various occasions he made us draw up tentative plans for temples, kiosks for cafés and bubbling fountains. He asked us to make extensive improvements to the approaches to the palace, new ornamental basins, and so on.'

If today's visitor to the Tuileries or Carrousel gardens is not deafened by noise he can conjure up the great days of the Empire but, in so doing, he will inevitably feel moved and regretful when he gazes at the vacuum which once was occupied by the palace of the Tuileries.

By order of the Emperor work on the Louvre Museum was speeded up. Percier and Fontaine ornamented the walls of the Cour du Sphinx with bas-reliefs and renovated the decoration of the Grande Galerie by finishing the part which abutted on to the Tuileries. This enabled the paintings of the Italian School, temporarily housed in the Salon Carré, to be moved to the Grand Galerie together with many other pictures which were arriving daily from every part of Europe.[1] Important restoration work was also carried out on the façade facing the Seine.

The two most urgent problems were the completion of the great courtyard, the Cour Carrée, of the Louvre and junction of the Louvre and the Tuileries. In attempting to solve the first problem first, Napoleon encountered serious difficulties because the Louvre had been built and enlarged over a period of centuries by the kings who succeeded Philip Augustus. Two totally different decorative schemes and designs had been used for this courtyard, now four times its original size. The first scheme, devised by Pierre Lescot, architect

[1] See Appendix V.

of François I, had been partially continued by Lemercier under Louis XIII; this concerned the west wing (the Pavillon de l'Horloge) and several frontages to the north and south. The west wing was built in two ornate orders of architecture, Corinthian on the ground floor and composite on the first floor; an attic floor with a richly ornamented pitched roof formed the second storey.

During the reign of Louis XIV the second scheme was executed by Le Vau, Claude Perrault and d'Orbay, succeeded by Gabriel and Soufflot. This scheme applied to other frontages or parts of frontages, some of which were incomplete; the three classic orders had been used, finished off by a balustrade with no visible roofing. Put in hand a century after the first scheme, this second scheme concentrated solely on the construction of a colonnade to which everything was sacrificed, and no attention was paid to earlier work or to the possibility of harmonizing both schemes.

Thus Napoleon was faced with a problem of completion and co-ordination which the kings, his predecessors, had been unable to solve. Exclusive use of either Lescot's or Perrault's plans under a plea for harmony and uniformity would necessitate horrible mutilation of the building. The architects wanted to follow Perrault's plan to complete the Louvre and, in the interests of conformity, to substitute a third order throughout the courtyard to match the eastern frontage. To this Napoleon would not agree, and here he showed an undeniable inspiration; a century ahead of his times, he insisted that the original character of both schemes should be respected, and thereby taught his architects a lesson.

His point of view is summed up in a letter sent to Champagny, now Minister of the Interior:

'The architects wanted to employ one order only and, so they said, alter it all. Economy, good sense and good taste decide otherwise; the existing parts should each preserve their contemporary character and for new work the most economical style should be employed.'

Meanwhile, nothing was to be destroyed and a committee of architects was set up to give him their suggestions.

Napoleon went on characteristically:

'It is also essential to have proper control of the order in which the work is done; first and foremost comes what has to be done to house the Library in the Louvre; ornamentation and artistry can come later.'

Special funds were allocated to meet the cost of this project, derived from the sale of the Capucines and the houses in the Rue des Orties:

'The Capucines are probably worth three millions and the Library's present site about the same; these sums, which should be available in the course of six years, ought to be sufficient to guarantee reasonable progress in this work. When the sale of the Capucines is concluded, the lands of the Filles St-Thomas can be sold and this money applied to completing the Louvre. This site was sought for the Bourse which must temporarily be housed in a theatre and the Petits Pères (Notre Dame des Victoires) re-consecrated as a church.'

In fact the Emperor was envisaging a huge programme of monumental building.

Bausset says that, on 28 February, Napoleon

'studied most attentively some of the plans presented to him and seemed inclined to transfer the Library to the Louvre without making any external changes to the frontages or to the mass of the buildings but to use the existing accommodation'.

This plan provided for:

'the placing of *objets d'art*, sculpture, antiquities and curios on the ground floor, books on the first floor and manuscripts, engravings, drawings and maps on the second floor'.

The Emperor, always in love with unity, wanted there to be a connection between the Library, 'fabulous repository of all human knowledge', and the Louvre whose galleries housed so many masterpieces, but there was something further underlying this idea. The Emperor's plans were founded on a cultural policy derived from an ideal of human progress inherited from the revolution with the ultimate aim of making Paris the supreme home of learning and the bright star of the human spirit. This conception, together with his religious ideals, is undoubtedly one of the most striking aspects of Napoleonic thought.

A decree on 26 March 1805 ordered the Institute, which had been holding its meetings in the Salle des Cariatides in the Louvre, to be transferred to the College of the Four Nations; the artists who, despite eviction orders, were still living in the Louvre, were to be turned out immediately. The architect, Vaudoyer, a former scholar of the Ecole des Beaux Arts, was given the task of adapting the College of the Four Nations to its new functions.[1]

Only a few days later a decree of 30 March ordered the transfer of the Ecole Polytechnique from the Palais Bourbon to the Collège de Navarre (Rue Descartes). These two institutions remain where Napoleon put them and should be listed with those which owe him their sites.

While Napoleon was putting to good use the period of peace France was enjoying and giving his attention to improving his capital, he learned that Villeneuve, commanding the Toulon squadron, had put to sea, reinforced by the Spanish fleet. This led him to believe that the new invasion plan he had perfected might be implemented during June; Nelson and his fleet might set off in pursuit of Villeneuve which would leave Ganteaume free to make for the English coast from Brest.

The Emperor at once made up his mind to leave for Italy, there to be proclaimed king; on 31 March, having taken leave of the Pope who was returning to Rome, he left Paris.

Napoleon entered Milan in triumph on 8 May. On the 26th he assumed the iron crown to become King of Italy, an event which made a great impression on Paris. From the month of July onwards the great city began to long for the Emperor's return, a wish gratified on 11 July when, during the night, Napoleon arrived at Fontainebleau.

No special celebrations marked 14 July; these were now reserved for 15 August. Moreover, the Imperial régime, bent on enforcing the rule of law, was in no wise eager to commemorate an event symbolical of the people's revolt against its masters.

On 2 August Napoleon left again for the Boulogne camp where he arrived at 3 a.m. on the 6th. Paris, which had immediate news of his departure, continued to put its trust in the Empire's destiny. Everyone hoped that his enterprise of striking a blow at England would be successful and lead to peace. A police bulletin of 4 August observed that:

'Never have the people of Paris shown more confidence in and loyalty to the Head of the State.'

[1] He made the former chapel into an assembly hall necessitating alterations which disappeared when the Institute was recently restored. Virtually nothing is left of Vaudoyer's work except a fountain in the second courtyard, called the Cour des Elèves, but there is a bust of Napoleon near Mazarin's mausoleum.

Still more gratifying was the report sent on 9 August by the mayor
of the 9th arrondissement to the Minister of Justice:

'Everyone in our arrondissement is worrying about what is happening at
sea. Most fathers, mothers and householders are more concerned about
the safety of the head of the government than about the enterprise. If real
and deep affection is seen in moments of danger then we are indeed happy
to recognize what devotion is shown to the Emperor and what prayers for
him are now being uttered.'

This feeling was manifest in the progressive rise in consols which
touched 61.72 frs.

During the Emperor's absence, 15 August in Paris saw much
popular rejoicing but this happy atmosphere of gaiety and exuberance
was marred by the difficulties created abroad. A third coalition,
inspired as always by England, had been formed by Russia, Prussia,
Sweden, the kingdom of Naples and Austria, with nearly five hundred
thousand men under arms. At sea Villeneuve, anxious about Nelson's
impetuosity, failed to carry out the manoeuvres ordered by the
Emperor. Instead of making for the harbour at Brest where Ganteaume awaited him to sail up Channel, he made in desperation for
Cadiz where he found himself blockaded.

The Emperor's reaction to this news which reached him on 25
August was prompt and angry; his eagle eye was withdrawn from
London to the Continent. He decided to make the Army of Boulogne
turn on its heel to throw it against Germany. He, therefore, immediately dictated his orders, a masterpiece of conciseness and
precision, to Daru, the Intendant-General of the army. The order to
march was given on 27 August, the signal for a war which would last
for ten years and end only with the drama of Waterloo.

II

Triumphs and Triumphal Arches

Austerlitz

The splendours of the coronation, the happiness inspired by the Emperor's presence and confidence in the 'invasion' had raised morale in Paris high, but the prospect of a continental war created some anxiety, heightened by a serious financial crisis.

Heavy increases in public expenditure had been incurred by the coronation, the Sovereign Pontiff's journey and the encampment at Boulogne; the 1805 budget had been balanced by temporary expedients, but the position of the Banque de France had rapidly deteriorated while business was stagnating, so that Barbé-Marbois, Minister of the Treasury, found his coffers almost empty. He was an upright man and loyal to the Emperor but his lack of decision left him at the mercy of events.

Napoleon, deep in his military preparations at Boulogne, still kept in touch with events in Paris, sending Fouché a number of memoranda about misrepresentations in the press and the harmful effect of the spleen lavished by the salons on the court.

'... It is out of the question,' he wrote on 29 August, 'that when I am a thousand miles away at the other end of Europe I should leave the field free for ill-disposed citizens to disturb my capital.'

Napoleon returned to Malmaison at 2 p.m. on 3 September. At a council of ministers held at St-Cloud on the following day he was soon made aware of the uneasiness prevailing in certain sections of Paris, particularly among the middle classes. He was also worried about the financial crisis whose magnitude his minister had not dared reveal.

After Brumaire the destiny of France was linked with Napoleon and both rested on the fate of the army so now, as at the time of Marengo, recovery could come only through a victorious campaign which would impress England and intimidate the monarchs of Europe who were jealous of the new Empire's greatness.

On 15 September Napoleon made a rousing speech, promising a speedy peace. To bring the tranquillity universally desired to the country and the capital, and restore confidence and prosperity, he would throw his legions and his eagles into a decisive battle. His own deep conviction was that the order for which he and his people yearned could be restored only by a great battle, of whose victorious outcome he had not the shadow of a doubt.

On 23 September Napoleon went to Paris to announce to the Senate the rupture with Austria and his departure for the front. On arrival at the Ecole Militaire at 12.30 p.m. he was received by Frochot, who handed him the keys of the city, the Corps of Mayors, the General Council and many other Departmental officials. Frochot's speech expressed his loyalty but betrayed some anxiety:

'Sire, here are the keys of Paris, of the capital of your Empire, of that city which you have made pre-eminent in the world. In offering you this ancient symbol of the city's submission and attachment we cannot, Sire, conceal from Your Majesty that today the happiness which always accompanies Your Majesty's arrival in His capital is mingled with feelings of deeper import which Your Majesty may regard as not less worthy of his attention.

'The rumours preceding the announcement of an Imperial session of the Senate and the announcement itself . . . have created some uneasiness which needs one word only to become a wholehearted upsurge of nationalistic feeling. This, Sire, is the word we await and the huge crowd about to surround you is eager to know what it must do to show its anger and its loyalty. . . . Wherever we must march we beg you to believe that all will soon be ready to follow, to serve and to avenge you.

'These are the feelings which inspire your good city of Paris.'

An enormous crowd cheered the Emperor wildly as he left the Ecole Militaire in state for the Luxembourg, where gun salutes greeted his arrival. A deputation of Senators welcomed him at the entrance to the palace and led him and his suite by the monumental staircase completed in the previous year to the Chamber, both built by Chalgrin.

From the throne[1] Napoleon announced the military decisions he

---

[1] In the *Livre d'Or* room (which dates back to Marie de Médicis) at the Luxembourg there is a chair which, according to tradition, was used by Napoleon when he presided at sessions of the Senate.

had taken. In an impressive session the Senate approved the decrees calling for eighty thousand conscripts and the reorganization of the National Guard.

Towards 5 a.m. next day, 24 September, the Emperor left for Strasbourg, a departure pregnant with consequences. While at Paris or St-Cloud his presence and prestige kept the people confident but, once he had gone, great apprehension was everywhere manifest. The rumour even ran that he had emptied the Bank's coffers to supply his army. On the day the Emperor went away a crowd began to gather outside the Banque de France to change their bank notes into specie. By 8 a.m. there were two hundred and an hour later four hundred people; this continued for several months.

Nevertheless, public order was in no wise disturbed nor were there any scenes when lots were drawn for conscripts for 1805. Uneasiness was, in fact, confined to business circles and manufacturers.

Meanwhile, Napoleon and his army were winning their first victory at Wertingen in Bavaria and the *Moniteur* now began to publish the legendary bulletins from the Grande Armée which made Parisian hearts beat faster and increased their admiration for the Emperor. The first bulletins appeared on 13 October and next day the guns thundered out the news of victory. They were heard with relief.

'The Emperor is in command of his armies,' people said. 'We shall hear only of victories.'

The bulletin of the 24th was exultant.

'Heavy rain has not slowed down the forced marches of the Grande Armée. The Emperor sets the example. Day and night he is on horseback among his troops or wherever he is needed. He has ridden 35 miles.'

In his triumphal progress Napoleon did not forget his good city. On 10 October he wrote from his headquarters at Augsburg to Frochot and the mayors of Paris (but not this time to the General Council) to inform them that he was dispatching eight captured enemy flags.

'Prefects and Mayors of Our good city of Paris. Our troops at the battle of Wertingen defeated twelve battalions of grenadiers, the flower of the Austrian army, took a number of prisoners and eight flags, which We have resolved to present to Our good city of Paris together with two pieces of cannon to be set up at the Hôtel de Ville.

'It is Our wish that Our good city of Paris should see in this thought and this gift a token of the love We bear it; this gift should be valued the more as it was the Governor of Paris [Murat] who commanded Our troops at the battle of Wertingen. . . .'

After several days of intensive fighting, particularly at Elchingen, Napoleon on 20 October took Ulm, where the main Austrian forces were concentrated. It was here that, for the first time, he tore the cross (of the Legion of Honour) from his own breast to bestow it on a soldier.

News of this victory first reached Paris on 23 October where it created a great sensation. Stocks rose from 59.40 frs to 59.60 frs and then to 61.00 frs. Although the financial depression continued fewer people went to the banks. The masses were jubilant.

The victory of Ulm was officially announced next day; the cannon boomed three times and a Te Deum was sung at Notre Dame. During the evening the 6th bulletin, 'joyful, terrible and restrained', in Rostand's words, was read out in all the theatres to which news of victory had drawn large crowds. Loud applause punctuated the reading. Great enthusiasm was aroused by accounts such as this:

'When the Emperor rode through a crowd of enemy prisoners an Austrian colonel expressed his astonishment that the Emperor of the French should be seen, wet through, spattered in mud and as weary as the most lowly drummer in the army.'

Confidence was restored except in the salons which were dismayed; their typical reaction was to paint a gloomy picture of war and its consequences. Royalist circles tried to propagate bad news, alleging serious losses, which caused Talleyrand to say, 'The tongues of the Faubourg St-Germain have killed more generals than the Austrian guns.'

By 6 November the Grande Armée had reached the outskirts of Vienna, which fell into French hands on the 13th. For the first time Napoleon set up his quarters in the palace of Schönbrunn (where his son was to die) and it was here that he received the dispatch announcing the disaster of Trafalgar. He succeeded in mastering his severe shock and made a show of minimizing the seriousness of this defeat. Only a great fighter such as he would not allow himself to be shaken by the simultaneous news that his Minister was powerless to cope with the worsening crisis at the Treasury.

The Emperor had now only one wish; to return to Paris to restore order.

'Not for a single moment has the Bank done what it should,' he wrote on 12 November to Barbé-Marbois. 'It has always done the opposite of what was intended when it was founded. I hope to be in Paris in the course of this month and I can assure you that the lack of order obvious in fiscal matters makes me most anxious to be there.'

Joy reached a new height in Paris when the *Moniteur* on 26 November published the 22nd, 23rd and 24th bulletins of the Grande Armée. People rushed in the evening to theatres which were giving free performances, to hear the news read. Before the curtain rose at the Opéra a silver star, wreathed in laurel, was hung over Napoleon's box. Cries of 'Long live the Emperor! Long live the Grande Armée!' rose from all parts of the house and continued for a long time as the play began.

Napoleon, before returning to Paris, wanted to strike a decisive blow on land which would wipe out the naval disaster and put him in a position to restore peace. On 2 December, the anniversary of his coronation, he fought on the plain of Austerlitz the battle where the Grande Armée decimated the Austro-Russian divisions and created a legend. A special courier brought news that evening to Paris (as yet unaware of the battle) that the Emperor of Austria had sent plenipotentiaries to Napoleon to negotiate and sign a final peace, a message received with exuberant signs of joy and shouts of 'Long live the Emperor!'

Napoleon's satisfaction with his resounding victory did not wipe out his concern about the salons' critical attitude and, on the very evening of Austerlitz, he read with great attention Fouché's reports which repeated the difficulties experienced by the Banque de France. Talleyrand, however, says that the report the Emperor singled out was one from Mme de Genlis who talked about:

'the tone in Paris, and quoted several insulting remarks made in the houses of the Faubourg St-Germain. The virulent language reported by Mme de Genlis sent Napoleon into an unprecedented rage. He swore and fulminated, "If those gentlemen of the Faubourg St-Germain think they are stronger than I am, we shall see! We shall see!" And this threat came when? . . . A few hours after a decisive victory.'

Talleyrand concludes with astonishment,

'So great an effect did the force and power of public opinion have on him, especially that of a few noblemen who had done nothing but keep their distance from him.'

A telegraphic dispatch dated 4 December from Strasbourg, was published in the *Moniteur* on the 11th:

'The Emperor has beaten the Russians near Olmütz; half their army is destroyed and the remainder is in full flight.'

On the same day Napoleon wrote from Brünn to the Cardinal Archbishop of Paris:

'We took forty-five enemy flags on the anniversary of Our coronation, of that day when the Holy Father, his cardinals and the assembled clergy of France offered up prayers in the sanctuary of Notre Dame for Our prosperous reign.
'We have resolved that these flags shall be laid up in the church of Notre Dame, metropolitan church of Our good city of Paris.'

Dubois had the Strasbourg telegram posted up on the walls of Paris next day, when he reported: 'I am daily in receipt of petitions from citizens of various parts of Paris that the honours of a triumph should be accorded to His Majesty.'

Napoleon, again at Schönbrunn, received dispatches from Paris which told of the rejoicing at the premature announcement of the opening of peace negotiations. He expressed his displeasure in two letters written on 11 December.

To Joseph he wrote:

'It was quite unnecessary to make so much fuss about the sending of plenipotentiaries and to fire salutes; it merely sends the patriotic spirit to sleep and gives people abroad a mistaken idea about our internal situation. Peace can't be got by crying "Peace". I didn't want to insert it in the bulletin, still less to have it announced in the theatres. Peace is a word without meaning; we need a glorious peace. To me nothing could have been more ill-advised and misleading than what was done in Paris at this time.'

In his second letter the Emperor reproved Fouché for

'having misdirected public opinion by so much talk of peace', and he concluded with annoyance, 'It is utterly absurd to have greeted the arrival of two poor plenipotentiaries with a salute of a hundred guns.'

On the following day honours were paid to Paris at Schönbrunn where Napoleon received a deputation of Paris mayors who had come to thank him for sending the flags and guns taken at Wertingen. Murat presented the deputation to the Emperor. Dupont, mayor of the 7th arrondissement, on behalf of the city, made a speech in the servile and fulsome language current among the officials of the Empire.

'. . . Sire, it would be vain on our part to attempt to describe to Your Majesty the exuberant happiness, the cries of joy and the unanimous enthusiasm aroused in Your good city of Paris when it learned the contents of that immortal letter with which Your Imperial and Royal Majesty honoured in this instance His Prefects and Mayors. . . .'

The Emperor heard the Parisian representatives with pleasure and then informed them of his intention to pay homage to the cathedral church of Paris by presenting it with the flags taken from the Russians on the anniversary of his coronation. He charged the deputation to take these trophies to the Cardinal Archbishop. His parting words were: 'Although I am receiving you in the palace of Maria Theresa, the day when I shall again find myself among my people of Paris will be for me a day of rejoicing.'

The 30th, 31st and 32nd bulletins, describing the battle of Austerlitz, and Napoleon's proclamation to his army, were published in the *Moniteur* on 16 and 17 December. The combination of heroic language and poetry in the 32nd bulletin, illustrated by a brief extract from the five long columns in the official journal, was calculated to fire even the coolest head:

'Dawn broke at last on 2 December with a radiant sun and that anniversary of the Emperor's coronation, which was to witness one of the century's most valiant deeds of arms, was one of the finest of autumnal days. . . .'

Paris, delirious with joy, was unable to think of an adequate way in which to glorify the Emperor. The General Council of the Seine on 18 December suggested the erection of an equestrian statue in the middle of a new square, to be called the Place d'Austerlitz. Simultaneously Poyet was entrusted by a 'number of distinguished inhabitants of the Department of the Seine' with the erection of a monument to the Emperor.

Next day the Senate debated the question of 'according the honours of a triumph to His Majesty the Emperor and King' and the *Journal de Paris* published a suggestion that a monument be erected near the Barrière du Trône to the glory of the Emperor Napoleon.

Bank notes regained their value and the moment when the Bank would resume its normal discounts was impatiently awaited.

The Grand Duchy of Berg, the principality of Neufchâtel and the vice-royalty of Italy were ceded to France by the Peace of Pressburg, signed on Christmas Day.

On 31 December, at a session convened for a manifestation of patriotism, the Tribunate voted unanimously for the ceremonial transfer to the Senate of the flags taken at Austerlitz, and the erection of a monument 'to the glory of the Emperor and King and to commemorate the triumphs of the Grande Armée.'

The Senate next day officially sanctioned the construction of a triumphal monument to Napoleon the Great and, so that the year, 1806, should begin with a substantial achievement, the Pont du Jardin des Plantes was opened to pedestrians, and shortly after to wheeled traffic. This bridge soon proved its utility since, for a toll of five centimes per head and per horse, it yielded a daily average of 400 to 500 frs, representing ten thousand crossings daily.

Four months had now elapsed since the Emperor's departure and the Press made itself the voice of

'the impatience felt by all Parisians to see again in their midst the conqueror and pacifier of Europe'.

On 17 January Napoleon left Munich (where he had attended the brilliant wedding of Eugène de Beauharnais and the Princess Augusta Amelia of Bavaria) and, with the Empress, arrived at the Tuileries during the night of Sunday, the 26th, several days ahead of Talleyrand and Murat. He had written to Cambacérès from Karlsruhe on the 21st:

'I am longing to be in Paris and you will see that I shall arrive in a few days' time.'

As usual he arrived late at night 'to avoid the homage all Paris wanted to pay him of their admiration, love and respect'. Some citizens, however, learnt of his return and, to show their joy, illuminated their houses in the evening.

Napoleon's first task was to redress the financial situation. He set to work with Gaudin and, on the following day, presided over a finance council, which sat for nine hours from 8 a.m. Present were Barbé-Marbois, Gaudin and Mollien, director-general of the Caisse d'Amortissement.

The Emperor conceded Barbé-Marbois' integrity but his anger was aroused by his minister's weakness and lack of foresight. He lashed out at him, 'I had a thousand times rather you were a thief; roguery at least has limits; stupidity has none.'

Barbé-Marbois was replaced as Minister of the Treasury by Mollien, to whom the Emperor said, 'You must take the oath this evening and be at your post at once.'

Next day, 28 January, the Emperor in great state received the homage and congratulations of the constituted bodies. Using his habitual adulatory language Frochot spoke of his happiness:

'in gazing for a moment on the victorious countenance of the august sovereign,'

but made a covert allusion to:

'certain fears felt by the people of the Department of the Seine and the good city of Paris'

about the new dangers the Emperor was to face.

Napoleon answered that he was fully conscious of the devotion of the good city of Paris and, if he avoided public demonstrations of rejoicing, it was to enable him to set to work immediately to further the interests of his subjects.

The Emperor was equally aware that, during his absence, the opposition salons had continued their 'spiteful gossip' and had exerted themselves to make capital out of the Treasury's difficulties. Fouché, who looked with a jaundiced eye on the possibility that the 'former nobles' might rally to the Emperor, had been swift to denounce the Faubourg St-Germain to the Master and suggested that a number of them should be exiled, which was done early in 1806. Although Napoleon ordered that too much stringency should not be applied, the orders did have great effect on royalist circles.

Fouché expressed himself as satisfied: 'Sire, Austerlitz has perturbed the old aristocracy; the Faubourg St-Germain has ceased its plotting.'

In fact the old nobility soon flocked to the Tuileries and sought office.

The Cour Carrée and the budget of the City of Paris

Purgative measures of this kind left Napoleon free to devote his powerful and fertile genius to Paris, where he remained for five months. As always on his return from a victorious campaign, after Austerlitz he was full of plans greater even than those after the coronation. Paris was to play the part of capital of the west, for which she must be beautified, enriched with monuments and splendid palaces prepared to receive sovereigns coming to Paris to salute the Emperor.

While the guns were still thundering to announce his return, Napoleon, on the day after his arrival, had made a quick inspection of the interior of the Tuileries, then gone on to the Louvre to see how work was progressing.

Bausset says that

'M. Fontaine was somewhat worried because he had not carried out exactly his orders to make no alterations,'

particularly in the Cour Carrée.

Napoleon, who had requested that nothing be destroyed,

'made a careful inspection of everything and, without betraying his thoughts, made a silent comparison with what had been'.

The Emperor turned to other matters, particularly the Library, which was a project very near his heart. He had given up the plan of housing it in the wing of the colonnade of the Louvre; this was now to be arranged as a large suite for a visiting monarch.

Fontaine says that, when Napoleon had received a progress report on 29 January, he decided to preserve the western façade of the Cour de l'Horloge to represent the old Louvre, which he preferred to the new. The other three frontages, south, north and east, largely built under Louis XIV, should be completed, improved and connected with the western façade with all the artistry, good taste and economy possible. Contrary to what has often been said, the Emperor did take into account the recent report submitted to him by the Committee of Artists set up in 1805. The present architecture of the Cour Carrée is evidence that Napoleon's wishes were carried out, for which credit is due to him.

The Parisians followed with great interest the changes improving their city and admired the builder as much as the warrior. Napoleon could assess his popularity by the delirious welcome he was given in the theatres.

A note sent to Champagny on 31 January reveals Napoleon's anxiety about the city's budget:

'Because of the importance of its budget the commune of Paris must receive special financial consideration. It is my wish that you make a careful study of the finances of this commune, both with regard to receipts and expenditure.'

Next day, to keep Champagny on his toes, Napoleon sent him a further letter:

'Let me know why work on the Quai Napoléon has ceased. Let me have your plans for an immediate start to be made on the Gare de l'Arsenal, in accordance with my decision taken two years ago. The cost is to be borne on the funds of the Paris commune. I also want to know what is happening about the sale of the Capucines property, the cutting of the Rue de Tournon, in fact everything connected with public works for the beautification of Paris.'

February 1806 was notable for the number of decisions taken by the Emperor about Paris. He took a keen pleasure 'as a relaxation from war weariness' in touring the city to sum up what had been done during his absence, particularly in the construction of quays and bridges. Both their technical and aesthetic aspects interested him and he questioned the engineers about their problems, gave them advice and urged them on to greater efforts.

Thursday, 13 February was an exceptionally busy day. As on every Thursday, the Emperor presided over a lengthy administrative council from 1 p.m. The Council, devoted to the City of Paris, was, in Fain's view, 'a monument to the memory of Napoleon as administrator'.

This was the first occasion on which the general account of the city's receipts and expenditure was submitted to Napoleon, an event of great importance and arising from Austerlitz. The French people were now his people, French institutions his and the country's destiny merged in his own. Paris was to be his capital, even 'his plaything'. No other French monarch had sought to arrogate Paris to himself in this way; one must go back to Rome to find such identity between ruler and city. I am in entire agreement with Passy when he writes:

'Under the Empire the body corporate called the city of Paris was lost in the body of Napoleon; the unity of the commune no longer resided in its institutions but in one man's mind.'

That man might well say of Paris what Sertorius said of Rome, 'Rome is no longer Rome, it is wholly where I am.'

The centralization introduced in 1799 was manifested by the drawing-up of the Paris budget by the Minister of the Interior instead of, as in other communes, by the Prefect. From 1806, until the fall of the Empire, Napoleon himself dictated the budget of the city of Paris. This was the procedure: the ordinary budget was drawn up by the Prefect, Frochot, sent up to the General Council (acting as Municipal Council), reviewed by the Emperor, reported on by the Minister of the Interior, revised by the Council of State, then finalized at the summit by the Emperor. The figures then arrived at were checked by the Cour des Comptes. The method now followed under the republican régime derives broadly from the system instituted by the Emperor.

Three essential facts have to be borne in mind when considering Napoleon's achievements in Paris. Firstly, his unique position as both conqueror and emperor (whom circumstances would lead to extend his domain over the whole of Europe). He would thus have at his disposal extraordinary revenues derived from levies on the conquered country. Secondly, and as a consequence of the extension of his dominion, his desire to make Paris the capital of the western world and, therefore, to beautify the city and carry out elaborate public works which required large resources. Finally, he was governed by certain psychological traits, passion for order and economy, impulsiveness, promptness in action and, in the fullest sense of the phrase, 'business acumen'.

It follows that his preoccupation with Paris, particularly on the financial plane, demanded means greatly in excess of those at the disposal of the civic authorities. Their part, as seen in the Imperial context, was neither to control nor direct but to support and execute, both tasks weighty enough to absorb their energies. Consequently the supreme administration of Paris must fall to the Emperor alone who, better than anyone else, knew the rôle he had assigned to his capital, the means at his disposal and what had to be done to ensure success. Napoleon gave himself up wholly to this, one of his most cherished projects; he watched over Paris like a jealous lover and often suffered in secret because of the indifference of certain sections of the community and the misunderstanding of others.

It is impractical to accept the common story that Napoleon turned municipal finance upside down. One of the best examples of his success in regulating the city's financial affairs concerns internal tolls. When he took over the government as Consul the city's ordinary budget for 1800 showed a sum total of 9,156,000 frs. Of this amount tolls, of nine millions, represented the major part of revenue. By 1806 these tolls were yielding 19,824,354, an increase of 100 per cent in six years.

The report of the Administrative Council held on 13 February 1806 is an excellent example of Napoleon's orderliness in administering the capital's affairs. Frochot's submission of his accounts drew from the Emperor remarks which merit quotation as they outline principles of public finance, from a structural and philosophical point of view.

'A budget is made up of receipts and expenditure, both of equal importance. Even were only simple disbursements involved, a mere statement of receipts would not suffice. In this instance a director, an administrator and accountancy are concerned and there is a moral lesson to be drawn from inspecting both receipts and expenditure. This inspection should reveal whether the tolls, the essential element in receipts, have been well or badly administered. A detailed statement of receipts from tolls since 1799 ought therefore to be made, listing in separate columns the gross receipts for each year, the cost of levying tolls and the net product year by year. In years when the scale of tolls changed two columns must be used for the gross receipts. In the first column should be listed the yield of the old scale and in the second column the additional receipts resulting from the new scale. The cash account must not be neglected and an appendix should be made of monthly cash entries.'

The great conqueror showed himself to be a shrewd accountant.

After making a detailed study of Frochot's budget proposals for 1806, Napoleon ordered one of the Councillors of State present to draw up a final statement, and requested that a reduction be made in expenditure to free an annual sum for building works and improvements of between 1,600,000 and 2,000,000 francs. The decisions he then took indicate what was being done in Paris at that time: a sum of 500,000 frs to be allocated to paving the Rue de Castiglione, the Place Vendôme, the Allée de Beauvais and the Allée des Veuves in the Champs-Elysées; 400,000 frs for the immediate extension of the boulevard, construction of the Quai du Mail, the junction of its approaches with the Pont du Jardin des Plantes and the cutting of a road leading from the bridge to the Rue St-Antoine.

That evening the Emperor sent for Fontaine to discuss the Louvre and the Tuileries. He had realized that the union of the two palaces would give a unique structure and the most splendid possible residence for his own magnificence. Bausset reports that the Emperor,

'seemed more than ever convinced of the necessity of joining up the two buildings to make one single edifice, devoted in its entirety to the sovereign's public life. . . . He seemed to be won over to the plan of clearing the area between the two palaces, but his own idea was to make it a large open space in the main axis of both entrances and to build porticos for a winter walk and garden.

' "We might," he said, "erect a triumphal arch at either end of this central area, one dedicated to Peace and the other to War. The city of Paris is lacking in monuments; it must have them." '

At the end of this conversation which lasted several hours Napoleon dictated memoranda to the Grand Marshal, implemented by the decree of 25 February 1806 which ordered a street 60 feet wide to be cut between the palaces (to be called the Rue Impériale) and the erection at the entrance to the Tuileries on the Place du Carrousel of a triumphal arch, dedicated to the glory of the army. Levies made by the Grande Armée would produce a credit for this project of 1,000,000 francs. Finally, the Hôtel de Brionne (occupied by Maret, Secretary of State) and all the houses around the area where these works were planned were to be demolished.

The Emperor's next decision concerned the Panthéon[1] which was to be completed,

'and used again, as its founder intended, as a church dedicated to Saint Geneviève, patron saint of Paris', but it was also to fulful the function assigned to it by the Constituent Assembly, that is to be the resting-place of the great Imperial dignitaries'.

Among other public works decreed on 14 February was a new town-planning project which, conjointly with the water-works in progress, helped to improve the Imperial capital and especially a 'long neglected business area'. Its centre was the Pont du Jardin des Plantes, now called the Pont d'Austerlitz, a change indicative of the impression made on the city by this great battle. Two semi-circular open spaces were constructed at either end of the bridge to enhance

---

[1] The name given to the new church of Ste-Geneviève, built to Soufflot's plans under Louis XV, and not used as such during the revolution. After Mirabeau's death the ashes of great men were deposited here. At the time this church was regarded as 'one of the finest in Paris'.

its stateliness; they were given the glorious names of two soldiers
who fell at Austerlitz, on the Left Bank the Place du Général Valhu-
bert and the Place du Colonel Mazas on the Right Bank. The Quai du
Mail was to be widened to 52 feet and take the name of Colonel
Morland (the colonel of Chasseurs also killed at Austerlitz); the
Quai de la Rapée, upstream of the bridge, was to be brought into
alignment.

Further plans included the extension of the Porte St-Antoine
(Boulevard Beaumarchais) through the Place de la Bastille to the
Seine where would be the Boulevard Bourdon (the name of the
colonel of the 11th regiment of Dragoons, likewise killed at Austerlitz). This boulevard, which linked the quays with the Place de la
Bastille and from it the Faubourgs St-Antoine and St-Marcel, was,
like the Avenue de l'Observatoire, one of the great arteries constructed by Napoleon to ease traffic, an example copied generously
by Napoleon III. The trees in the garden of the Arsenal had to be
cut down and the neighbouring houses demolished but, in fact, the
new boulevard was not extended to the bridge because the Arsenal
ditches had to be reserved for the Ourcq canal and the basin for the
mooring of boats.

Napoleon's desire to share his glory with the valiant troops whom he
led to battle had resulted in the proposal to erect a great triumphal
arch at the entrance to the Tuileries but, in emulation of the Romans,
he wanted the general's valour and that of his legions to be recognized simultaneously. Paris, the new Rome, was to give the Grande
Armée the honours of a triumph.

Napoleon dictated his instructions for this ceremony to the Minister
of the Interior on 17 February:

'Some part of the army will be stationed in Paris during May and it is
advisable to prepare now for its suitable reception.'

He laid down in remarkable detail the various forms the festivities
should take: first was the award by the City of Paris of golden crowns
for the eagles of the Grande Armée; next, an industrial exhibition
with a ceremonial prize-giving, then a splendid banquet to be given
by the City to the army and lastly the distribution of a commemorative
medal.

Always looking ahead and imbued with a spirit of economy, he

added a reminder to his note that it would be the City which would
entertain the army,

> 'The City of Paris will reimburse itself for the cost by an increase in tolls,
> which should benefit by the fact that officers and other ranks will then be
> receiving a gratuity and extra pay and will spend a lot of money.'

Another suggestion bore the imprint of his powerful imagination
and sense of theatre:

> 'The soldiers would like some bull fights, similar to those held in Spain,
> and contests of wild beasts. No better moment could be found for laying
> the foundation stone of a monument. Bull and even chariot races might
> also be a great attraction. At concerts at the Tuileries, the Luxembourg or
> elsewhere, appropriate martial airs must be sung which can be picked up
> by ear and remembered.'

His final words were:

> 'Everything must be done to make the heart beat faster and to add
> lustre to the martial spirit. Haste must be made with this year's exhibi-
> tion at the Salon and the Museum seen in all its glory.'

Triumphal arches

The plans concerted in February 1806 for monuments and institutions
in Paris were impressive. On the 17th the Emperor asked Champagny
'to let him know how the column dedicated to Charlemagne in the
Place Vendôme was progressing'. The original plan had not yet
been put in hand and an idea was current that the three projected
columns, of which the foundation stones had been laid on 14 July 1801,
should be fused into one; these were the Departmental column in
the Place Vendôme, the national column in the Place de la Concorde
and the Charlemagne column. Napoleon soon reached a decision.

He wrote to Denon, recalling the general opinion expressed on his
return from Austerlitz:

> 'I have read what you say about the column to be erected by the City of
> Paris, but it all sounds very vague to me; let me have something more
> precise. When the Senate voted for a statue of peace they were following
> a Roman custom. I believe that if the four angels at the Museum belong to
> me and are not *objets d'art* they might be used for this monument. None
> of my orders must be neglected; everything must be carried out.'

Fresh instructions sent by Napoleon on 18 February to Champagny
included various steps to be taken for the capital.

'During March, work on the Panthéon must be substantially expedited as I wish it to be completed as soon as possible. Of the sum of 5,000,000 at the Caisse d'Amortissement derived from export taxes on cereals, 20 per cent I intend to devote to the purchase of 50 tons of wheat and 20 per cent to improvements in Paris, which adds up to a million to buy wheat and a million for public works in Paris. All future receipts from the same source will be devoted in these proportions to these two projects.'

This last Imperial decision was most important since it resulted in one of the most fabulous monuments in Paris, the Arc de Triomphe de l'Etoile.

'The million allocated to public works in Paris will be used thus: half a million for the work to be done at the Panthéon this year—half a million to erect a triumphal arch where the boulevards begin, near the site of the Bastille, so that entry to the Faubourg St-Antoine is via this arch.'

It was only some months later that the Champs-Elysées was chosen as the site for this arch.

The decree of 9 October 1801 had made no provision for linking the Place Vendôme with the boulevard. This gap was filled on 19 February by a decree which prescribed the cutting of the Rue Royale, which would become the Rue Napoléon (under the Restoration the Rue de la Paix) and the Rue Daunou (between the Rue Louis-le-Grand and the boulevards). The Capucines buildings and lands were put up for sale and the purchase price devoted to meeting the costs of finishing the Louvre.

At an administrative council on the 20th Napoleon took yet another series of decisions about Paris. His concern about traffic congestion, already obvious, led him to order the construction of a new bridge. He wrote to Crétet:

'Work on a new bridge facing the Ecole Militaire is to begin in June.'

The Parisians could not but be struck by Napoleon's gigantic exertions on their behalf. Their applause showed their appreciation at the parade on 23 February, 'one of the most brilliant,' says the *Gazette de France*, 'for a long time'. Repeated cheers greeted the hero of Austerlitz on his famous white horse, 'magnificently harnessed', as he rode down the ranks of the glorious battalions just arrived from the Moravian front.

A further great demonstration of the people's affection was given on the following day at the Théâtre Français where the Emperor himself had ordered a revival of *Athalie* with Talma as Abner. At the

end of the first act Napoleon received a dispatch with news of a great
victory won in Italy on 15 February. He at once sent the message to
Talma who read it from the stage.

> 'The French army has entered Naples; all the fortresses and palaces of
> this capital, Capua and the fortified places of this kingdom are in our hands.
> The whole Neapolitan army are prisoners of war.'

The audience was delirious with joy.

Further decrees ratified previous decisions or initiated new ones.
The decree of 26 February embodied the decision of 13 February to
build an arch at the entrance to a triumphal way to the Tuileries,
and ordered the construction of a covered sewer to carry away the
waters from the Rue Froidmanteau, the first step of its kind in a vast
enterprise carried out during the Empire. The Paris sewer was still
the same fifteen miles in length as under the monarchy; by the fall
of the Empire, in under ten years, another half-mile had been added.

The *Courrier Français* described thus the ceremonial opening of the
session of the Legislature:

> 'From early morning a vast crowd had gathered at all the points where
> the procession would pass. To one who loves his country it is most
> gratifying to see the citizens' eagerness to approach the victor of
> Austerlitz.'

In the course of the Session Champagny, with great solemnity,
presented a report on the state of the Empire, including a first list of
the 'embellishments' made in Paris by the Emperor:

> 'New quays border the banks of the river Seine; two bridges have already
> been built, a third is on the point of completion. The bridge will be
> enhanced by a new district planned around it. Alterations have been made
> both to the Capucines and the Madeleine; the Louvre is being rapidly
> completed and the work begun by François I and Louis XIV is now
> reaching its conclusion.
> 'Since his return the Emperor has devoted his days and nights to meticu-
> lous supervision of every branch of the administration. The city's finances
> have been regulated by an audit over which the Emperor deigned to
> preside in person. This has produced new resources and valuable econo-
> mies which have made possible the carrying out of projects which will add
> to the city's splendour and prosperity. . . .'

A site for the Arc du Carrousel was considered at a working session devoted to Paris on 8 March, presided over by Napoleon. The decision reached was to erect it where railings had been put up at the beginning of the Consulate facing the guard-room. Work began immediately to Fontaine's plans and the decoration was entrusted to Denon. The estimated cost of a million francs was to be met from war levies on the conquered territories. Bausset reports that, at this meeting, Napoleon talked about the many improvements he wanted to make in Paris, repeating, 'Paris lacks great buildings; we must see that she has them. It is wrong to try to limit the size of this great city which could easily support a population twice as large as at present. It might happen that a dozen kings were here at the same time so there must be accommodation for them—palaces and all their appurtenances.'

Discussion followed on the plan for a monument at the entrance to Paris at the Barrière de Chaillot, also called the Barrière de l'Etoile, having regard to the lay-out of the roads to Neuilly, St-Germain, the Roule and Passy, which became the Avenues des Champs-Elysées, de la Grande Armée, Wagram and Kléber.

Apparently it was Napoleon's idea to build the planned arch at the Etoile, a suggestion enthusiastically supported by Percier and Fontaine, who added the rider 'that it was vital on so lofty a site for the monument to be colossal in size', a concept which attracted Napoleon who would opt for this site.

When, on 14 March, the Emperor saw Champagny's report, he ordered work to begin immediately on the Vendôme column, to be called the Austerlitz column, for which he set aside the requisite number of Russian and Austrian guns for the casings of the bas-reliefs. He had now given up his original idea and wanted the column to resemble Trajan's column, to be crowned by a statue by Chaudet of Napoleon dressed as a Roman emperor and crowned with laurels. Denon was to be the chief architect, aided by Gandoin and Lepère.

Navigation on the Seine within Paris was the subject discussed on the 17th and on 10 April at Malmaison the Emperor was again occupied with water supply to the city, about which he wrote a long memorandum to Crétet:

'My primary aim and object is that water should flow night and day in as many fountains as possible. When the amenity and health of so vast a city is at stake one cannot consider 100,000 francs.'

He asked to be shown on a map of Paris the sites of the existing fountains, emphasized the urgency and expressed his displeasure that,

'a natural product of such vital importance should cost the citizens money. In my opinion it is disgraceful that water should be sold at the Paris fountains.'

The conclusion of his letter struck a cheerful note:

'What a happy awakening for Paris if this can all be done as easily as I begin to believe it can and at so small a cost.'

On Sunday, 20 April, Napoleon returned to the city of Paris the entertainment offered him on his coronation. Imperial receptions at the Tuileries were normally the preserve of the élite of Parisian aristocracy but, on this occasion, the Emperor, to show that his régime did not spurn the egalitarian principle on which it was founded, gave a ball to which the capital's bourgeoisie was invited. Two thousand five hundred invitations had been sent out and this brilliant occasion scrupulously organized. The Emperor was present with Josephine, strolling among his guests, asking interested and kindly questions or addressing compliments 'full of grace and nobility' to the ladies.

Although work on the Ourcq canal was being expedited Napoleon did not wait for its waters to reach Paris to order the erection of new fountains. His reasons appear to have been several: 'a kind of romanticism', as Hautecoeur puts it—fountains always inspire meditation; his recollection of other capitals he had seen or his reading about the magnificent fountains of Rome; his wish to beautify Paris and make it healthier.

A sum of 540,000 francs, underwritten by the Treasury, was put at the disposal of the Minister of the Interior for these fountains which were sited as follows: Place du Grand Châtelet, Gros Caillou (opposite the hospital of the Imperial Guard); Pointe St-Eustache; Place des Trois Maries (Quai de l'Ecole); Rue de Sèvres (near the hospital for incurables); Rue de Vaugirard (at the corner of the Rue du Regard); Parvis Notre Dame; Rue du Lion St-Paul; the Horse Market; Rue d'Enfer (near Rue Mouffetard); Rue Popincourt; the Lycée Bonaparte; the Institute; Place St-Sulpice; and the water-tower at the Palais Royal.

When, on 9 May, Napoleon gave his approval to the erection of the Arc de Triomphe at the Barrière de l'Etoile, he took a historic decision.

'In view of all the difficulties involved in erecting the Arc de Triomphe on the Place de la Bastille,' he wrote to his Minister, 'I agree to its being erected beside the Chaillot grille at the Etoile, but on condition that a handsome fountain is built on the Place de la Bastille similar to the one intended for the Place de la Concorde.'

So Napoleon bestowed on Paris one of its finest and most distinguished monuments which, writes Lavedan,

'provided the appropriate closure to the great prospect, the monumental design sought in vain by the old régime, to rise on the summit of the Champs-Elysées'.

The arts, gardens and administration

Napoleon's object in decreeing the building of so many monuments was in part to encourage the arts and in part to play the part of Maecenas to artists. These were his underlying thoughts when on 14 May he dictated these instructions:

'The triumphal arches would be a waste of time and serve no purpose, nor would I have initiated them except with the object of fostering architecture. These triumphal arches will nourish sculpture in France for ten years. For the triumphal arch to be built at the Etoile the Minister of the Interior must get designs of all kinds. One arch is to be dedicated to Marengo and the other to Austerlitz. Somewhere in Paris I shall have another arch built to be the Arch of Peace and a fourth the Arch of Religion. These four arches should keep French sculptors busy for twenty years.'

During June the newspapers again raised the question of erecting a triumphal column to the Emperor's glory which the people were discussing. The Emperor's decision was made known by Champagny:

'The Emperor will not consent to monuments being put up to him in his lifetime. This honourable reward for such great exertions should come from posterity.'

At a plenary session of the Council of State Napoleon had expressed his concern about the state of the Paris theatres; their number should be reduced, although not too drastically. Twelve theatres would be adequate if they were so placed as not to compete with one another.

Plays by dead authors would be shared out among them and for new plays there would be free competition. The Emperor's ideas were embodied in an organic decree of 8 June:

> 'No theatre is to be set up in Paris without Our special authorization given on the report made by Our Minister of the Interior'.

The Opéra alone might produce ballets appropriate to the theatre and masked balls could be held there only. These arrangements, long desired by friends of the theatre, were welcomed by the press.

The newspapers also acclaimed the great activity in public works tirelessly stimulated by the Emperor himself. Napoleon was putting to good use the few months remaining of his stay in Paris or St-Cloud, carefully supervising the execution of his orders and taking decisions about fresh enterprises. A decree of 23 June concerned the Legislature and of 25 June St-Sulpice. As work on the Madeleine was to be resumed almost immediately this gave the Emperor the idea of changing the shabby façade of the Palais Bourbon to:

> 'give this building a frontage and entrance facing the Concorde suitable for the Temple of Laws'.

As Napoleon wished, Paris on 1 July did have a 'fine awakening'. The fifty-seven fountains began to flow continuously, while on the sites of fifteen new fountains still to be built, stand-pipes were set up to gush into temporary basins so that 'nothing should delay public enjoyment of His Majesty's beneficence'. To ensure this continuous flow, twice the normal amount of water had to be directed to the fountains and about a mile and a half of conduits or pipe-junctions installed.

The foundation stone of the Arc du Carrousel was laid on 7 July and work on the Arc de Triomphe at the Etoile de Chaillot pushed forward. Workmen in large numbers were digging deep foundations, building materials were arriving daily at the site and huge stones were piled up round it.

> 'Once,' writes a chronicler, 'this would have been said to be the work of the Romans; henceforward they will say—it is the work of Napoleon.'

A new source of beautification was found in the gardens which were being transformed. Napoleon's fondness for verdure was probably due to his Corsican youth spent out of doors; he had already shown himself to be a devotee of nature which lends itself to reflection. Did he not, towards the end of his exile at St Helena, become enthusiastic about creating a garden?

In addition to the improvements already made to the great garden of the Luxembourg a nursery garden was laid out in the grounds belonging to the Carthusians; this soon became a favoured resort for walks and relaxation. Magnificent railings had replaced the old wall on the south and east along the outer garden wall which ran parallel with the Rue d'Enfer (Boulevard St-Michel). The demolition of old obstructions revealed the grand entrance which was now a 'spacious and impressive' sight for strangers to Paris.

Various excrescences had been pulled down to make the terrace bordering the Tuileries gardens ('the most frequented in Paris') a pleasantly uninterrupted prospect. This was now extended by a wide circular parapet over the Place de la Concorde, terminating at the level of the great entrance grille at the foot of the statue of Fame. There were now, according to the *Journal l' Empire*,

> 'solitary retreats set with a magnificent view over both banks of the Seine, the two roads to Passy and the Bois de Boulogne and both groves of trees in the Champs-Elysées.'

The truncation of the Jardin des Plantes to make the Place Val-hubert around the head of the Pont d'Austerlitz had been compensated up to the river-bank along the Rue de la Seine (Rue Cuvier) by a large area of experimental gardens, laid out on the marshes, half of which was devoted to hothouses and subterranean gardens for growing tender plants. The other half, known as the Swiss Valley, had recently acquired a variety of buildings which made it the most interesting part of the Jardin des Plantes. New cages housed the animals formerly in the park of the Allée des Tilleuls.

This satisfactory advance in 'embellishments' in Paris went hand in hand with a happier economic situation and renewed financial stability; by mid-July stocks touched 65.00 frs. Napoleon continued to lavish encouragement on industry and to seek new processes for the manu-facture of silk and textiles.

On 19 July Junot was again appointed Governor of Paris, com-mander of the city and the First Military Division.[1] Napoleon addressed Junot thus when he informed him of this appointment: 'You are Governor of the city which I wish to make the greatest of

[1] Louis, who had held these appointments, had become King of Holland on 5 June 1806.

all cities. I have appointed you to this important post because I know you, and I know that the good citizens of Paris will be your children rather than your administrative charges.'

The laying of the foundation stone of the Arc de Triomphe on Napoleon's birthday, 15 August, was, curiously enough, marked by no special ceremony and went almost unnoticed, although the birthday itself was celebrated:

> 'by a variety of sports on the Champs-Elysées, ballets, two firework displays, one in the Luxembourg gardens and the other on the Pont de la Concorde, but what distinguished the day most was the happiness so obviously displayed by all classes of the people'.

III

Glory and the Temple of Glory

Jena

Napoleon had reached one of the peaks of his career and his popularity had possibly never been greater. Town and country were wholly devoted to him. In Paris opposition had ceased; the nobility continued to rally to him while the middle classes, the clergy, industry and commerce gave him their support. This atmosphere of confidence was reflected in a glittering series of entertainments and amusements, inspired and stage-managed by the Emperor.

> 'One had to see Napoleon,' writes the Duchesse d'Abrantès, 'in the midst of his fabulously luxurious Court, himself directing festivities, command performances, quadrilles and masked balls, a whole host of pleasures in such good taste that for seven years they made the Court of France the most consummately beautiful in the whole world.'

Could the Emperor, however, give his people the supreme benefit of peace, for which they all yearned and which was vital if he was to carry out his grand design and his great public works? Twice before he had found himself in this position, after the coup d'état and at the end of 1805. His answer had been first Marengo, then Austerlitz. It was clear that peace could be achieved only by a repetition of victories to which an inexorable destiny drove him.

The proud advance of the Great Empire ran counter to too many European interests to be allowed to proceed unchecked, yet Napoleon refused to submit and made heroic efforts to bring his adversaries to negotiate, but it was effort wasted. Russia denounced the Treaty signed by her Ambassador and joined with Prussia in the Third Coalition, while Pius VII demanded the evacuation of Ancona and asserted his immutable dominion over Rome. On 12 September, with no declaration of war, the Prussian armies invaded Saxony.

From September onwards the situation abroad caused concern in

Paris where it was generally believed that a new coalition had been formed against the Emperor and hopes of peace, which had given rise to substantial speculation, vanished. Stocks, which on 3 September stood at 67.75, fell next day to 66.60 frs. A review of the Imperial Guard with arms and baggage inspected on the Plaine des Sablons by the Emperor on the 11th aroused fresh anxiety.

Napoleon who, to the last minute, tried to avoid war, remained unmoved and showed his calmness in spite of the serious situation by a continued interest in arts and commerce. In advance of his mounted Guard and artillery he left St-Cloud for Mainz during the night of 24/25 September to take command of the Grande Armée, fully convinced of victory. Despite the hazards of campaigning he continued as usual to direct the affairs of country and capital, ruling the Empire as if from the Tuileries, as is evidenced by much of his correspondence. Dispatch riders or officers of the Council of State brought him daily messages from Paris, for which he was always eager.

Napoleon received the ultimatum of Frederick William III (of Prussia) on 7 October and left Bamberg next day for Saxony. On the 10th he routed the Prussian troops at Jena while Davout totally defeated Brunswick's corps at Auerstädt. The first news of these victories was brought by couriers to Paris where it was confidently awaited. On the 17th the newspapers reported as definite that a great victory had been won over the Prussian army, news repeated in Fouché's bulletin: 'Although the Grande Armée's success has not yet been officially confirmed everyone knows about it and is happy and excited.'

Stocks stayed at 66.60 frs. On 20 October the *Moniteur* published the first two bulletins of the Grande Armée together with the report of the distribution of prizes awarded at the recent industrial exhibition. This accorded with the Emperor's wish that economic progress, which he regarded in the same light as trophies of war, should be announced at the same time and given the same honours as victories.

The booming of cannon in Paris on the morning of the 21st signalled the victories at Jena; the press gave the first vivid details of the battle.

'. . . The battle began at first light,' wrote the *Courrier Français*, 'and by noon the enemy was in flight. Of his army of 120,000 men 30,000 were made prisoner and 100 pieces of artillery and the whole baggage-train fell to us. The Emperor in person tended the wounded; never has he shown himself so great.'

From Potsdam, on his march to Berlin, Napoleon's letter to Fouché on the 25th, shows that he had not forgotten the theatres in Paris:

'I am sending you my sanction of the expense incurred for the production of the ballet, *Ulysses' Return*. Get a detailed report and see the first performance of this ballet yourself to be sure it is acceptable. You know why I think this is a splendid subject? I gave Gardel the idea.'

At 3 p.m. on 27 October he made a triumphal entry into Berlin, which was illuminated and the streets full of people crying 'Long live the Emperor!' On the 28th General Hohenlohe capitulated at Prenzlow while the French army relentlessly pursued the enemy who, faced with annihilation, fled in disorder.

One after another the glorious bulletins arrived, the 23rd and 24th on 8 November, the 25th on Sunday, the 9th. In the morning the guns gave their message to the Parisians that

'thanks would be given to the God of battles for the victory he has bestowed on the just cause'.

A Te Deum was sung to a huge congregation at Notre Dame de Paris at noon 'for the total victory won near Jena over the Prussian army'.

The 26th bulletin in next day's *Moniteur* confirmed the entry of the advance guard into Poland and the rout of the Austrian army which seemed to have been 'struck by lightning'. At the Café Tortoni brokers predicted a rapid rise in stocks; on 12 November the 5 per cents which, a month earlier, had stood at 63.75 reached 74.70 frs.

The people's elation was at its height, but some circles stood aloof and even showed a certain apprehension. Their prophetic utterances arose from fear lest the Emperor fall victim to overweening ambition and advance too deeply into eastern territory. Echoes of similar fears and signs of deep fatigue reached Paris even from army headquarters, their truth vouched for by Napoleon who flung these words in Berthier's teeth, expressive if not polite, 'You'd be very happy to go and p... in the Seine.'

Unhappily, the peace each and every one desired could ensue only from battles.

As the Berlin campaign drew to a close and Napoleon prepared to enter Poland, he retorted to a British measure aimed at French nationals and vessels by issuing the famous Berlin decree on 21 November and creating the Continental System. To show how strictly he wished this system to be applied, 'especially in Paris', he wrote forthwith to Junot,

> 'Let your wives drink Swiss tea; it is as good as caravan tea and chicory coffee as wholesome as Arabian; let them set an example in their drawing-rooms instead of amusing themselves like Mme de Staël with crazy politics; let them take care also that I do not see them wearing dresses made of English stuffs. This is a very grave matter, a matter of life and death for France and England.'

The Emperor's arm also stretched out to the propriety of per-formances at the Opéra about which he wrote both to Cambacérès and Champagny on the same day. His letter to Champagny was very tart:

> 'I've read some very bad verses sung at the Opéra. Are they trying in France to discredit letters and since when does the Opéra ape the vaude-ville and stage improvisations? . . . Tell M. de Luçay how displeased I am and see that nothing is sung at the Opéra which is unworthy of that great theatre. There was a very natural opportunity to compose some good pieces for 2 December. As literature falls within your bailiwick I think you should see to it. . . .'

On this day, too, the press announced with pleasure that from his headquarters, Napoleon had decided to grant pensions to employees of the Prefecture of Police which it was 'his kindly intention' to extend to their widows and orphans.

> 'Although deep in war preparations,' wrote the *Journal de Paris*, 'the Emperor is still concerned with details which demonstrate his care for those who serve him in government employment.'

Financial matters, probably much more than those of the Opéra, were in the forefront of Napoleon's mind. Since the victory of Austerlitz the situation of the Banque de France had continued to improve. On 24 November he wrote to Mollien:

> 'I was most interested in your report . . . on the state of the Treasury and the Paris garrison. I am pleased that you have fulfilled my hopes. . . .'

The 32nd bulletin of 16 November and the 33rd of the 17th announced on the 25th the end of the Prussian campaign and the signature of an armistice. The vendors had sold their papers so heavily that they could no longer find buyers

'especially in the districts of St-Martin and St-Antoine and in the Halles where the working classes showed by their shouts of "Long live the Emperor!" what satisfaction news of an armistice and an early peace had given them'.

The *Journal du Commerce* observed on 28 November that the last bulletin 'has made a great impression in Paris and given Europe a striking proof of the victor's moderation'.

The Temple of Glory and the Pont d'Iéna

Napoleon from Posen, where he had arrived on 27 November, issued a decree on 2 December devoted to the Temple of Glory. In the first clause the great captain paid tribute to his soldiers.

'On the site of the Madeleine in Our good city of Paris and at the expense of Our Privy Purse, a monument shall be erected dedicated to the Grande Armée and on its frontage shall be inscribed, "The Emperor Napoleon to the soldiers of the Grande Armée." '

The second clause laid down that

'Within the monument shall be inscribed on marble tablets the names of all the men, by army corps and regiments, who took part in the battles of Ulm, Austerlitz and Jena, and on heavy tablets of gold the names of all those killed on the battlefield. On tablets of silver shall be inscribed the list of effectives supplied by each Department to the Grande Armée.'

In a letter to Champagny Napoleon remarked, 'I see nothing against calling the Pont de l'Ecole Militaire the Pont d'Iéna', the name it retains and which nearly proved fatal in 1815.

On the eve of his departure for Warsaw Napoleon wrote briefly to Cambacérès about the reconstruction of the Odéon, whose ownership had been transferred to the Senate on 13 August 1806. 'Let work at the Odéon be started.'

On 15 December the *Journal de Paris* announced with pride that the fine quadriga over the Brandenburg Gate in Berlin, which had been removed by Denon, had left for France with several other works of art collected in Prussia, which Napoleon was sending for his 'good city of Paris'.

The previous day a poster stuck up in Paris invited the young men of the Department of the Seine of the class of 1807 to register for conscription. There was no unfavourable reaction and people continued to be elated, a state the Imperial government was helping to encourage. On 28 December the *Moniteur* published a stirring appeal from Champagny to 'all the artists in the Empire' to submit plans for a competition for the Temple of Glory.

On 30 December stocks touched the record figure of 76.15 frs and the year ended with the brilliant prospects opened up by the glorious victories of the Grande Armée.

From 1 January 1807, when Napoleon set up his headquarters in the castle at Warsaw, may be said to date the period of great difficulties, which even the most resounding victories could not eliminate. The Russians initiated the tactics which later led the Emperor to disaster; by avoiding him they lured him reluctantly deeper into Polish territory because of his anxiety to bring the campaign to a close and return to Paris.

Concerned about morale in the capital, where his return was hoped for, the Emperor wrote to Fouché on 29 December: 'You may spread the rumour that the Emperor will soon be back in Paris.' As a relaxation for his heavy preoccupations he wrote to Champagny about the author of *Les Templiers* a note which incorporates his conception of tragedy:

> 'M. Raynouard can turn out something good if he really gets to the heart of classical tragedy: the Atrides were the victims of fate and heroes were guilty without being criminal—they merely took part in the crimes of their gods. This is not a suitable method for modern history which is concerned with the nature of things. If a tragedy is not based on this principle it will not be in the tradition of our great masters. . . . Time is needed to develop this thesis and you know full well that I have something else to do."

Paris was as feverishly anxious to have news of the Grande Armée as Napoleon was to have news of Paris. On 11 January dispatches, dated 26 and 27 December, told of the rout of the Russian troops and from Warsaw Napoleon wrote to Champagny about the Parisians' wish to give his name to the Place de la Concorde:

> 'The Place de la Concorde must keep its own name. Concord is what makes France invincible.'

Again from Warsaw Napoleon issued a decree on 15 January to

immortalize the great battle and the names of the heroes killed at Jena. The bridge built over the Seine opposite the Champ de Mars was to be called the Pont d'Iéna; the quay on the Chaillot side between the barrier and the fire-stations was to be named the Quai de Billy, after the general killed at Jena, and the quay itself was to be widened and reconstructed at a new angle; the road opposite the bridge from the quay to the enclosing wall and streets to be built near by were to bear the names of Colonels Houdart-Lamotte, Barbenègre, Marigny and Dulembourg, also killed at Jena.

On 31 January, when the 52nd bulletin of the Grande Armée was published in Paris, Napoleon sent his troops to attack the Russian army. The city was on tip-toe; stocks stayed steady at 75 frs but the absence of the court made itself felt. The Parisians hoped that the victories won would be quickly followed by a peace treaty and that Napoleon would at last return. A newspaper had already announced that

'when the Emperor has settled his army's cantonments he will leave for his capital and so we may hope to see His Majesty in Paris'.

From the battle of Eylau to the Carnival of Paris

Anxiety was quietened by the return from Mainz on 1 February of Josephine, who was welcomed by Frochot and the Mayoral Corps. She then received the great bodies of State in audience. Frochot told her how happy the Parisians were to have her among them again. The Empress replied with characteristic grace, 'Sharing as I do the Emperor's feelings, you cannot doubt my happiness in finding myself again in what it pleases him to call his good city of Paris.'

The *Journal de l'Empire* wrote on February 7th,

'With the arrival of Her Majesty the Empress the city at once took on a new look; brilliant festivities are announced in which most of the ministers will participate and, although the carnival will be short this year, it is likely that the usual entertainments will be numerous and very gay.'

While the carnival was at its height in Paris Napoleon fought the terrible battle of Eylau on 8 February, of which on the following evening he sent a brief account to the Empress:

'The enemy lost the battle but I have lost men—1,600 killed and 3,000 to 4,000 wounded.'

On the 11th he wrote to her that this 'memorable day' when he 'had beaten the enemy' had 'cost him many heroes'. On the 14th he allowed his bitterness to appear:

'The countryside is covered with dead and wounded; it is not the better part of war; one suffers and one's heart is heavy to see so many victims.'

In his whirlwind life moments of nostalgia were fleeting. From the humble bivouac where he had his quarters until 1 April he showed remarkable energy, dictating more than four hundred letters, notes and reports on the most varied subjects, making preparations for his army to strike a decisive blow against the Russians and to wipe out the upsurge of hostility aroused in Europe by the battle of Eylau, while waging a diplomatic offensive which resulted in the Shah of Persia becoming his ally. 'Nothing escaped him,' Fouché would write, 'his eyes were everywhere.'

On the 24th the *Moniteur* published the 56th, 57th and 58th bulletins of the Grande Armée; the 58th gave the first account of the battle of Eylau which the Emperor described as a victory and stressed 'the miracles achieved by his army', but he bluntly admitted the 'heavy losses' of the Grande Armée. Always sensitive to Parisian reactions, particularly among opposition circles, he concluded with a reassuring sentence:

'This expedition is over, the beaten enemy thrown back 250 miles beyond the Vistula. The army is returning to its cantonments in winter quarters.'

Two feelings were paramount in the capital where stocks still stood above 75 frs; first and foremost loyalty to Napoleon himself and the real terror felt by the people when they learned that, with his usual indifference to danger, he had rashly exposed himself to the enemy's fire. A letter of 15 February from Duroc to Jerome is revealing on this point:

'What makes one tremble is that the Emperor exposed himself like a common soldier. Many were killed and wounded at his side.'

The other feeling inspiring the public was hope of peace.

Aware that opposition circles would make capital out of his losses and desirous of maintaining the morale of a febrile population, Napoleon sent instructions to Fouché on 28 February:

'Let this news which, by the way, is true, circulate unofficially, first of all in the salons and then in the papers: the Russian army is so weakened that some regiments are reduced to 150 men—there are no more troops in Russia . . . the Russian army is suing for peace.'

Napoleon, always thinking of his good city and eager to give it new open spaces, formed a plan which foreshadowed the present Parc Monceau:

'The great City needs another good garden,' he wrote to Gaudin on 5 March. 'What has been done at Mousseaux is not what I intended so you must make another plan for a garden of a different kind but which will compete with the Tuileries, the Luxembourg and the Botanical Gardens. The Tuileries and the Luxembourg gardens are in the French style; a really beautiful garden in the Chinese style will be a new amenity for Paris.'[1]

On the 7th his note to Champagny outlined the setting up of

'a good newspaper, enlightened, impartial and well-disposed in tone, without the offensive brusquerie of existing papers which is in such contrast to the people's real nature'.

Next day he informed Cambacérès of his dispatch of flags taken at Eylau and harked back to the work he had ordered on the Madeleine: 'These flags are intended to be laid up in the new temple.'

That same day the exhibition of plans submitted for this great building opened in Paris and attracted a large and eager crowd. Champagny's competition had produced a number of entries, so many in fact that they spread over the whole length of the right-hand side of the gallery in the Louvre Museum. Eighty-two artists were represented and twenty-one of their plans were selected by the Fine Arts Committee of the Institute. Beaumont, formerly Inspector of the Madeleine and architect of the Palais Royal, won the first prize. Vignon, Peyre and Gisors would not accept their *proxime accesserunt*, but the final decision awaited Napoleon.

The resolution shown after the announcement of the battles at Eylau was somewhat shaken by the arrival in Paris of couriers bringing complaints voiced by generals tired of the rigours of war and young officers of the Council of State, like Barante, who painted a disturbing picture of the battle. In fact, although Napoleon was victorious, it was at the cost of many dead and wounded while, in spite of serious losses, the Russians had cleverly manoeuvred their retreat. Their general, Bennigsen, had even sent the Czar a report

[1] By a curious anomaly the Chinese garden was in Great Britain what was, and still is, called in France an English garden. This was what Napoleon meant.

alleging a French defeat, so Eylau did not enjoy the same prestige as previous victories won by the Grande Armée. Napoleon was no longer regarded as invincible, which had its repercussions on the whole of Europe.

The Paris salons tried to make capital out of the situation and revive the opposition. News of Bennigsen's report filtered through and created some unrest, of which Napoleon was informed by letters from Josephine, Fouché and Cambacérès. Stocks suffered a fall from 75.10 on 9 March to 72.50 frs on the 10th. Nothing serious resulted but Paris, which had been astonishingly quiet, began to be restless. Napoleon at Osterode was shocked by the ease with which defeatist news was credited and, on 11 March, wrote a lapidary note to Josephine:

> 'A lot of rubbish is being talked about Eylau. The bulletin tells the whole story and our losses are exaggerated rather than minimized.'

On 1 April, with Marie Walewska unobtrusively beside him, the Emperor took up residence in the castle of Finckenstein. He had decided to strike an all-out blow against the Russians and was actively preparing his troop concentrations, the vital objective being Danzig.

By means of the bulletins from the Grande Armée the Parisians were following the campaign with some anxiety and prayed every day for the cessation of war. Fouché tentatively made himself their spokesman to the Emperor, while carefully assuring him that he was certain 'of keeping Paris quiet'. In this Napoleon saw only signs of weakness and hesitancy:

> 'I scorn those who try to upset the country's morale; I have not the smallest doubt but that the conscription will be successful. If we do not take some timely measures a few gossips in the cafés and some ill-disposed people and idlers will shout even louder, but this is not of the slightest importance. . . . Talking all the time about peace is a sure way of not getting it; the way to get it is to be prepared for everything.'

Napoleon devoted as much attention to the progress of buildings in Paris as to the state of mind of the Parisians; the Temple of Glory now retained his attention and he dictated a long and detailed note to Fontaine about it on 19 April, characteristic of his many-sided genius and the minute care he gave to all business he transacted. He asked no less than thirteen questions of which the first was:

'Where will the Emperor leave his carriage when he goes in state with all the court to commemorate 2 December and where will he be seated?'

His next question concerned entry for the public and whether the Emperor and his court could get out of their carriages under cover in bad weather.

'Will the public also be under cover, especially the ladies who would be invited to these occasions during the winter?'

His concluding remarks were full of common sense and wisdom:

'The external ornamentation of the Temple must be subordinated to the demands of good taste and the laws of architecture; the interior must follow the same rules but what is done must, above all, be in keeping with the use to which this building is to be put.'

During April and May the Emperor turned his mind to a new subject of services in Paris; the lighting of the capital, in which he took a special interest. Gourgaud reports that at St Helena the Emperor recalled the tours he liked to make incognito in the capital: 'One day I went out alone with Duroc at 2 a.m.; the street lamps were out. In the morning I reproved the Prefect of Police, who could not guess how I knew.'

Napoleon replied on 21 April to a letter of Fouché's:

'I hear that the city of Paris is not lit and that the police are doing less about it than ever. Inform the Prefect of Police of my displeasure and take steps to see that the contractors fulfil the conditions of their contracts better. Tell them that if they continue to do their job so badly I shall deduct a considerable sum from their receipts.'

Again on the 23rd, when he had expressed his satisfaction to Fouché about the good progress of the conscription, he let fly at the Paris lighting contractors:

'They are rogues who think that they have done their job of lighting the Paris streets when they have bribed the offices of the Prefect of Police. Kindly pay great attention to the proper execution of this most important service in the capital.'

By the regular publication of bulletins of the Grande Armée, whose objective was still the capture of Danzig, Paris learned how the troops were faring. Meanwhile the city garnered the fruits of their heroism; a hundred enormous packing-cases were landed at the Port St-Nicolas containing antiquities and further valuable exhibits from Berlin and Potsdam, and another consignment for the Musée Napoléon to add to the magnificent paintings from the Hesse-Cassel gallery.

At the Invalides on 17 May the sword of Frederick the Great and the flags taken from the Prussians were ceremonially handed over, an occasion which drew a large crowd of spectators to the Rue St-Honoré, the Place and the Pont de la Concorde and the front of the Invalides. Rousing cheers greeted the appearance of a 'splendidly decorated triumphal chariot' loaded with 280 flags, followed by Marshal Moncey on horseback, accompanied by several officers, and carrying aloft the Soldier King's sword.

The exhibition of paintings for the competition, whose theme was 'The Emperor visiting the wounded after the battle of Eylau', opened next day. Twenty-five sketches were displayed in the Grand Gallery of the Louvre and a large attendance showed the great interest taken in the exhibition. The prize was won by Gros, who painted the picture of the Plague-stricken at Jaffa and the battle of Aboukir.

The important news of the capitulation of Danzig was announced to Paris on 4 June by the firing of salutes. Stocks rose sharply to 76 frs. On the 14th, while a Te Deum was being sung at Notre Dame, the Russian army under Bennigsen was crushed. Napoleon sent a note from the battlefield to Josephine.

> 'I am only writing you a few words because I am very tired; I have been bivouacking for a long time. My children celebrated the anniversary of Marengo worthily; the battle of Friedland will be as famous and as glorious for my people.'

He added a postscript. 'Salutes can be fired.'

The Peace of Tilsit

Napoleon set up his headquarters on 19 June at Tilsit on the river Niemen and granted the armistice sought by Bennigsen to the Russians. He accepted with delight the request for an interview made by the Czar, who was shaken by Friedland. The two Emperors met on the celebrated raft on the 25th.

The previous evening at 5 p.m. at St-Cloud Prince Borghese

brought the Empress the glorious battle bulletin. Next day the
Journal de Paris wrote:

> 'By a singular coincidence which deserves mention Friedland means
> "country of peace". This challenge can be accepted when we remember
> that the Emperor, during his most signal victories, has had no thought
> other than to give peace to his peoples and the universe.'

These victories were in fact welcomed as harbingers of the long-
awaited peace and created an atmosphere especially favourable for
the continuance of public works. In the forefront of the Emperor's
mind were those at the Louvre, the Tuileries and their environs.
The Louvre was temporarily set aside for the reception of 'eminent
personages coming to the capital of the French Empire'. The
Journal de l'Empire announced on 3 July that Napoleon had decided
on its completion and to a gallery being constructed on the Rue
St-Honoré side parallel to one on the river side. Thus was born a
new Napoleonic project in Paris; the 'grand design', in which the
kings had not succeeded, was being put in hand. The new gallery
was called the 'Napoleon gallery' and in 1807 a credit of 400,000 frs
(399.986 frs exactly) was assigned to the building.

The esplanade at the end of the terrace on the Seine side near the
Tuileries had recently been embellished by a garden drawn to a new
design. The terrace on the opposite (the Feuillants) side had been
extended across the level ground of the rear court of the Orangerie,
where the buildings had been renovated. In the course of construction was the entrance gateway to enclose the Tuileries garden at this
end, opposite the Rue St-Florentin; and 'houses built to a uniform
design and shortly to be inhabited' had been built in the Rues Neuve
du Luxembourg (Rue Cambon), des Pyramides and Mont-Thabor.

Work on the Carrousel arch was making rapid progress. The
Venetian horses on the Tuileries grille were removed to be harnessed
to a quadriga sculpted by Lemot (one of the best contemporary
sculptors); this quadriga was the first of its kind to be seen in
France. The Trajan column (the Vendôme column) had risen to a
sufficient height for its proportions to be appreciated; an internal
stairway was to lead to the top of the column. Under Chalgrin the
rebuilding of the Odéon theatre was advancing and the press was
pleased to stress that

> 'the Faubourg St-Germain, long without a theatre, would soon be able

to savour the noble pleasure given by the art of Corneille, Racine, Voltaire and Molière'.

Among traffic improvements the Pont d'Austerlitz had been opened to wheeled traffic since 4 March, a trial load having proved 'the strength and solidity of the bridge'. Work on the Pont de l'Ecole Militaire was in full swing; piles were being driven to support the arches and advantage was taken of the Seine being very low to push on 'by day and by night'. The Quai Napoléon (between the Pont Notre Dame and the new Pont de la Cité) was under construction; the Rue Clovis, to link the Place St-Etienne du Mont (near the present street of that name) and the Rue des Fossés St-Victor (part of the Rues Thouin and Cardinal Lemoine) was being opened up and the church of Ste-Geneviève, founded in the year 500 by Clovis, was being torn down.

On 30 June the *Moniteur* published the 79th bulletin, reporting the battle of Friedland, 'worthy to stand side by side with those of Marengo, Austerlitz and Jena', and emphasizing the decisive part played by the Emperor whose brilliant manoeuvres had resulted in victory: 'Rarely,' concluded the bulletin, 'have the French armies won such great victories with so little loss.'

Details of the interview at Tilsit were given to the Empress on 7 July by Montesquiou, one of the Emperor's aides-de-camp. On the following day Tilsit saw the signing of the peace which partitioned Europe and sealed the Franco-Russian alliance at Prussia's expense. That evening Napoleon set out on his homeward way and by the 14th the press was signalling his early arrival.

'The joyous news of the conclusion of peace' was sent by telegraph on the 23rd. Stocks soared from 76.50 on 15 June to 80.70 frs. A press announcement gave notice of an extraordinary session of the Senate called for the following day and that peace would be solemnly proclaimed in the city that evening. A further report stated that the Emperor had left Königsberg on the 13th for Paris.

'Judging by the feelings universally expressed, the citizens of Paris will find pleasure in showing their happiness, their admiration and their affection."

Napoleon arrived 'in very good health' at St-Cloud at 5 a.m. on the 27th, news given to Paris by a salute of sixty guns. Excitement was equivalent to that experienced after Marengo, and houses were spontaneously illuminated. The continuous and universal cheers were, as then, directed at the peacemaker rather than at the glorious general.

Dubois' bulletin of 30 July says:

'The city of Paris seems to be enjoying a family celebration. Concerts and every kind of entertainment went on far into the night, outbursts of gaiety side by side with evidence of the deepest devotion to His Majesty—in truth, the good and loving city of Paris.'

The Emperor received his ministers at 8 p.m., retaining Fouché and Talleyrand longest. Although he distrusted them both he meant to make full use of the exceptional gifts he knew them to possess. Fouché could parade the services he claimed to have rendered to the cause of peace and the régime by once again throttling royalist ambitions. Talleyrand had no such claims, but his inordinate ambition led him to seek this moment to ask for the office of Grand Elector. This was refused by Napoleon, but he created Talleyrand Vice Grand Elector with the loss, however, of the portfolio of External Affairs. Unfortunately Napoleon continued to make official use of Talleyrand and to seek his advice, a confidence of which the able diplomat took treacherous advantage to use against him.

For the moment the radiant Emperor was seen to savour the fruits of the peace he had won with a high hand, and he himself noted with pleasure the general improvement in the atmosphere. The assemblies, however, were less and less representative of the nation and shortly the Tribunate would be suppressed. Royalists were increasingly rallying to the Empire and achieving that social 'fusion' which, from the time of the Consulate, was a fundamental of Napoleon's rule, but it was a policy which proved a boomerang. When disaster struck, the old nobility quickly abandoned him and even infected his own creatures with the virus of their disaffection. The influence of the salons, still holding firm to their opposition views, was decreasing but, in spite of his bitter and powerful pen, Chateaubriand in fact inspired more liking than fear in the Emperor.

After his ten months' absence Napoleon intended to resume the reins of government and administration, although he spent only three and a half months in and near Paris, at St-Cloud, Fontainebleau and Rambouillet.

Talleyrand's dismissal necessitated a reshuffling of the Imperial cabinet; Champagny took over the Ministry of External Relations, his place as Minister of the Interior going to Crétet. Junot, who was loathed by the Minister of War, Clarke, was sent on a mission to Portugal while General Hulin assumed the military governorship of Paris. The Emperor was now free to devote himself to his capital.

'Scarcely has the Emperor returned,' wrote the *Journal de l'Empire*, 'than already one hears of the improvements he proposes to add to those which have already done so much for the city's beauty.'

On 28 July Napoleon received the eager congratulations of the distinguished personalities of the Empire. In the evening he sent for Fontaine, who found him walking in the garden outside his study. As was his custom Napoleon questioned Fontaine at great length.

'The many questions and the new ideas which sprang from these conversations,' reports Bausset, who was present at the interview, 'show that he was planning great enterprises.'

The Emperor seemed satisfied with Fontaine's replies because he ceased to give the impression

'at least for the moment, that he continued to cherish his often expressed prejudices against architects which led him to say that architecture was the ruin of monarchs.'

The Tuileries, the Louvre and the problem of their union were once again the chief subject of discussion. Napoleon expressed his pleasure that the theatre at the Tuileries and the Arc du Carrousel would be ready by 15 October.

The Emperor then wanted to know how far advanced were the works and whether the windows on the colonnade frontage were open. He decided to arrange this part of the building as 'a splendid apartment for a sovereign or great sovereign', thinking that he might probably receive the Czar in Paris. Reverting to a plan dear to his heart, he declared that the other three sides of the Louvre were to be retained for the Imperial Library.

Fontaine was unable to reconcile both plans and suggested that:

'a completely independent building be made available for the Library, either in the Museum picture gallery, as transport of the paintings elsewhere would be simple, or in the new wing (on the Rue de Rivoli) just started, or that an intermediate wing could be built between the Louvre and the Tuileries.'

It was the first time that the architect had mentioned such a wing, 'a plan he had conceived to unite both palaces in a perfect whole'.

Bausset says that Napoleon made no reply to this suggestion entailing the demolition of all the houses between the Louvre and the Tuileries, and changed the conversation. It was then that the plan for a huge open space dawned on him, indicative of his conception of greatness.

On 3 August the Emperor was disappointed when he found how the financing of public works in Paris stood; the previous year's receipts were insufficient for work to be carried out at the approaches to the Pont d'Austerlitz, the Quai Napoléon, the Quai Desaix and the special paving. A loan would be necessary. The Emperor asked his new Minister of the Interior, Crétet, what needed to be done to finish the Ourcq canal and other public works in Paris.

'Let me have this by next Thursday, 6 August, and also an outline of a loan to the City of Paris of two millions from the Caisse d'Amortissement.'

He then dealt with the cost of the new bridge just begun:

'I had monies advanced for the Pont d'Iéna but my idea was that this bridge should be handed over to a company. It seems to me that speculations in bridges have been sufficiently successful for us to find another company for this one. Has anyone tried to find one?'

He had to prepare the ground for the next administrative council, the first since his return, which was devoted to Parisian business, particularly the cost of public works in the City of Paris.

Napoleon, always deeply concerned about the provisioning of Paris, asked for a plan and estimate for building on the Arsenal site a storehouse or public granary to hold 500 tons of wheat and flour. He also asked Crétet for a report 'on the idea he had had for a warehouse for cereals on the credit principle'. Next he ordered that, of the funds accruing from the 25 per cent tax on the cutting of communal woods deposited at the Caisse d'Amortissement, a credit of a million should be taken for various projects in hand (the Etoile arch, work on the churches of St-Denis and Ste-Geneviève) or to be put in hand (the public granary near the Arsenal).

Napoleon now decided that a settlement of theatrical affairs was due; his decree of 8 August incorporated the measures taken by Champagny on 25 April and provided for strict official supervision.

'No new theatre may be built nor may any troupe of actors move from one theatre to another in Our good city of Paris without Our authorization.'

The maximum number of theatres was to be eight, the four great houses including the Théâtre de l'Impératrice, the Gaîté, the Ambigu-Comique (Boulevard du Temple), the Variétés (Boulevard Montmartre) and the Vaudeville. The most stringent measure called for the closure of 'all non-authorized theatres before 15 August'. The Emperor, who wanted to end the competition of boulevard plays, had with his own hand struck out the words, 'without delay' and substituted the irrevocable 'before 15 August'.

While the theatres were being dealt with the Minister of the Interior opened an architectural competition for a

'monumental building intended primarily as an Imperial orangery and winter garden for the citizens of Paris'

not too far from the Tuileries.

Many matters of interest to the City of Paris were discussed at an administrative council held by Napoleon on 13 August. The budget proposals were laid before him; among various measures to be taken, the most important showed the Emperor's preoccupation with increasing the water supply in Paris. A large sewer was to be built beneath the Rue St-Denis for 'the overflow into the Seine of water after its circulation in Paris'.

Fêtes, markets and slaughterhouses

While the Emperor was concentrating on matters affecting his capital 'preparations were being made all over Paris for the ceremonies on 15 August to be particularly outstanding'. When, after the usual rites of the day, Napoleon and Josephine appeared in the evening on the Tuileries balcony the crowd filling the garden gave vent to its delight.

'This crowd,' writes the Duchesse d'Abrantès, 'listened neither to the concert nor to the patriotic songs, nor looked at any of the illuminations in the garden, but fixed their eyes only on the two ground-floor windows of the château in the hope of seeing—if only for a moment—their beloved

Emperor—for at that moment, he was indeed the beloved Emperor and the nation's attachment to him was best seen in Paris.'

On 16 August a grand ball at the Hôtel de Ville was attended only by the Empress, as the Emperor's 'heavy tasks' prevented his coming. On the following day Napoleon toured various parts of Paris. Accompanied by Jerome and two chamberlains he was seen between four and five in the afternoon inspecting work at the Louvre, particularly at the Cour Carrée and the new gallery. He was recognized only when he got into his carriage but a large crowd gathered immediately to cheer him. His next visit was to the Boulevard Bourdon, where the Ourcq canal was soon to issue. He stopped for a moment at the Place des Innocents, returned to the Place du Marché St-Honoré, where the newly opened market had been built on the site of the Jacobins' convent. Noting that progress with the market was slow, he dictated this note to Crétet:

'Will you please see that a market can be held at the Jacobins by to-morrow at noon and that, by the afternoon, there are no dealers in greenstuffs in the Rue St-Honoré and the neighbouring streets.'

The Emperor took a great interest in market arrangements. Parisians, who lived outside the central area served by the Halles, had for their use only a jumble of improvised and insanitary stalls, often unprotected, set up near the busiest streets. To remedy this haphazard arrangement Napoleon decided to restore or enlarge some of the old markets such as the Innocents' and St-Jean's, and to build local covered markets, worthy of the capital. He supervised the rapid execution of these plans himself. Similar considerations determined the construction of clean slaughterhouses outside the populated areas to replace the old abattoirs in the heart of the city which were real hives of infection. This was part of the policy of utilitarian town planning initiated by Napoleon in Paris.

At 4 a.m. on 19 August when most people in the district were still fast asleep, not dreaming of the honour done them, the Emperor went to the Palais Royal where he thought of establishing the Banque de France and the Bourse. He was pleased to see that in the Rues Traversine (part of the Rue Berger) and St-Honoré the squalid stalls had all been removed. In the evening he reviewed all the troops of the Paris garrison in the courtyard of the Tuileries. 'After His Majesty's inspection on foot, rank by rank the units marched past him.' Immediately the Place du Carrousel was filled with a crowd of enthusiastic spectators.

At an administrative council held on the 20th Napoleon approved the budget for the City of Paris for 1807. Receipts were 19 millions, 18 million coming from internal customs dues, and expenditure 18,000,879 (of which 3,419,000 was extraordinary expenditure). In this budget the public works planned accounted only for 520,000 frs. For the Quais Napoléon and Desaix, the approaches to the Pont d'Austerlitz and special paving 1.4 millions were retained from customs dues. In effect the city of Paris was responsible only for 3 per cent of the total budget. All other important municipal projects were paid out of State funds or special funds set up by the Emperor. The 1807 budget for national buildings (approved by Napoleon at Finckenstein on 15 April) was 2,339,245 frs, wholly devoted to Parisian monuments—a million to build and finish the Louvre, 400,000 frs for the new wing of the Tuileries on the Rue de Rivoli, 400,000 frs for the Pavillon de Marsan, and 170,000 frs for the seventeen arcades of the Rue de Rivoli.

During the meeting on 20 August, entirely devoted to the business of the City of Paris, Napoleon expressed displeasure at the sluggish pace at which work was proceeding, which he had noted during his visits. He then considered at length the question of water supply; the fountains were to flow night and day and, if there were seasonal difficulties in their so doing, at least during the summer the maximum amount of water should be made available.

Crétet's report to the Legislature on 24 August on the state of the Empire accorded much space to 'the fabulous improvements in Paris'. He began by saying that the Emperor wished his capital to be the premier capital in the universe and that its appearance should correspond to so glorious an intention. Crétet then recited the formidable achievements to date.

The provisioning of the capital was the subject of a memorandum from Napoleon to Crétet on the same day.

'Although the price of bread in Paris is not too high, it is higher than it ought to be. Think about this and see if some reduction can be made, while allowing enough profit to the bakers.'

Next day it was the management of the Opéra which again claimed his attention. He wrote to Cambacérès:

'I am sending you last month's schedule of free and paid tickets to the Opéra; this seems to me excessive. Let me know the various prices of seats. Could they not be charged at less than other theatres and so abolish free seats?'

On the 27th he sent a note to the Minister of the Interior on the subject which greatly interested him, the housing of the archives and the arrangement of the Imperial Library. He ordered that 'medals and engravings should be dealt with separately as they bear no more relation to the Library than statues and paintings'. The Emperor issued a continuous flow of interventions, always to the point and always emphatic in every conceivable sphere of the city's affairs.

On 4 September Napoleon embodied the decisions taken at the administrative council in a decree, by which the old and new water supply was combined in a single municipal service, to be operated at the expense of the city of Paris. Water from the fire-pumps at Chaillot and Gros-Caillou, the hydraulic pumps and the Ourcq canal was now to be under one authority, presided over by the Prefect of the Seine, under the supervision of the Councillor of State who headed the Highways Department and the Minister of the Interior.

The basic arrangement, of special significance in the history of Paris budgets, was that the total cost of water administration in Paris should be charged to the city in a 'special budget' annexed to the commune's general budget. The Emperor, however, as an apostle of unity, upset this budgetary principle for practical reasons, which was an innovation; the present budget of the city does in fact include several budgets.

Although in residence at St-Cloud Napoleon often went to Paris where he liked to go to the theatre. On 4 September, with the Empress, he was at the Opéra to see *Les Prétendues* to the great delight of the Parisians, who had not seen him for over a year. His entry was greeted by a sonorous roll of drums and the orchestra playing the popular air, 'Where is one better off than in the bosom of one's family?' On the 19th Napoleon and Josephine went to the Théâtre Français to see Talma return to play *Cinna* and on the 20th to the Opéra-Comique. On each occasion the Emperor was rapturously applauded by the large audiences his presence attracted.

On the 21st Napoleon left St-Cloud to spend several weeks at Fontainebleau. Bainville writes that Napoleon was doing what

Louis XIV did at Versailles, adding that the Emperor 'was wary of this Paris with its bitter tongue and elusive opinions'. Even if it is true that Napoleon always feared Parisian mockery, I do not think that he was specially anxious to be away from Paris in 1807. Every year at this time when he was in France he went to the country to work in greater peace and it is known that he found the Tuileries uncomfortable. His problems at this moment were serious; abroad the exigencies of his policy of hegemony, especially those resulting from the blockade, had led him to harden his attitude to the Holy See and his relations with the Sovereign Pontiff were daily becoming more strained. And across the Pyrenees, in the expedition to Portugal which would precede war in Spain, lay the seeds of a problem even more acute.

At home Napoleon wanted to institute a new nobility which he believed would be a social bulwark for his régime. The police bulletins of 20 and 21 September reveal the anxiety felt in Paris about this innovation.

'The friends and enemies of the dynasty are much concerned with the new titles and His Majesty's intentions about them. Nothing is said, either for or against, which was not said when the Legion of Honour was instituted, although people are more inclined to accept titles than they were the Legion of Honour. The knights of the old dynasty began by laughing at this decoration, which they now solicit the honour of wearing since it has superseded all others.'

The writer of the reports continues by discussing public opinion and the people's attachment to the Emperor.

'It is a mistake to believe that people in the mass are interested in politics. Experience has cured them (and for a long time) of believing in the will-o'-the-wisps of the people's good, always awaited and never realized, conjured up by debates in the Legislative Assemblies. The Emperor is all for the bulk of the nation, which fears war because of the uneasiness it inspires; it ardently desires peace because peace is synonymous with prosperity and trade, activity in public works, reduction in taxes and the conscription. In peace the nation sees the sole augury of plenty. Anyone who makes a close study of the fluctuations of opinion can gauge to what extent the Emperor is blessed by all classes by whether his sword is more or less sheathed in its scabbard.'

Napoleon found himself once again in a situation similar to the one existing when he came to power; on his sword hung peace and the people's happiness. And once again people and nation placed all their hopes in the Emperor's wisdom and genius.

Napoleon had the secret of gestures of popular appeal. Thus, at the end of September, during a visit to the flour warehouses at Corbeil he found the flour to be of poor quality. He had it thrown out, declaring 'that he did not intend Paris to be fed with such noxious stuff'. Police reports of 27 and 28 September say that 'the Parisians were very pleased with this act'.

On 14 October an exhibition was opened at the Louvre of works of art captured during the 1806–7 campaign. Three galleries were filled with the 50 statues, 80 busts, 193 bronzes and a large number of paintings by the greatest masters, particularly of the Flemish school. In one room the colossal bust of Napoleon wearing his crown was on view. The exhibition attracted a large attendance.

Napoleon now turned his attention to the commemoration of his coronation and the victory of Austerlitz and sent instructions to Crétet that the rules laid down for the celebration should be strictly observed. The anniversary of the battle of Jena was also celebrated with the ceremonies traditional for these occasions.

In 1806 Napoleon had conceived the idea that the City of Paris should organize a festivity in honour of the heroes of Austerlitz, Jena and Friedland but, since the troops were scattered to the four corners of the Empire, he decided that the Imperial Guard should have the glorious mission of representing the Grande Armée. He himself took in hand the organization of this celebration and sent Crétet fresh instructions about it on 31 October:

'When my Guard enters Paris early in November it is my wish that it should be welcomed with great ceremony and that a triumphal arch should be erected on its route. I have instructed Marshal Bessières to give a grand dinner and ball to the officers at the Ecole Militaire. I desire that the Corps of Mayors and the General Council give a similar dinner to all other ranks on behalf of the City of Paris—I leave these bodies to decide how it shall be done. Emblems and mottoes made for this occasion should make it clear that not I, but my Guard, is concerned and they should indicate that, in honouring my Guard, the whole army is honoured. The Prefect and the Corps of Mayors will receive my Guard as it enters Paris. Finally, you will instruct the Prefect to arrange this festivity as efficiently and touchingly as possible. I need not tell you that you should have songs and poems specially written.'

*

At the beginning of November Napoleon warned Frochot to have the draft budget for 1808 for the City of Paris ready to bring to Fontainebleau on the 10th. Napoleon had hoped that some economies in the ordinary budget could be allocated to special public works in the capital and had frequently expressed the wish that municipal revenue should be increased by carefully selected new taxes, but he realized that this was difficult to achieve. On 6 August he had been forced to authorize the Caisse d'Amortissement to grant an advance to the City and he was somewhat annoyed to find that repayment could not be made as planned. Frochot had done his best to fulfil Napoleon's wishes but without success. As he said, 'To get out of trouble, somehow or other additional revenue must be found for the City of Paris.' In other words, if Napoleon wanted great things done, he himself would have to find new monies; extraordinary tasks demanded extraordinary resources. This was quite logical but the Prefect of the Seine implied thereby that the Emperor had to direct and intervene in the City's affairs.

Napoleon held an immediate administrative council and issued a decree that very day, authorizing the City of Paris to contract a loan of eight millions for special works and purchase of land. This investment budget was the origin of that now operated by the City. The loan was to be applied to the special fund to finance new works of utility selected by the Emperor.

A large proportion of the loan was assigned to work in hand for markets and slaughterhouses but also included clearing of the Pont St-Michel, building public baths, extending the Rue de Tournon, making the Place St-Sulpice and purchases of land for opening the Rue d'Ulm. This loan was repayable in sixteen years at the rate of 500,000 frs a year from 1809; loan, capital and interest were guaranteed at the Caisse d'Amortissement by the total revenue of the City of Paris.

Napoleon sent Crétet the text of the November decree and insisted that the developments planned should be accelerated.

'I take it that you plan to finish these operations speedily and increase the City's revenues. Some purely ornamental undertakings will not yield much but others, like the galleries in the markets, the slaughterhouses, and so on, should bring in much revenue, but action is needed for this. The storehouses for which I have made you an allocation of funds have not yet been begun.'

He then dealt with other subjects, the canals and their cost, and beggary, a problem to which he attached great importance, and used these memorable words,

> 'I have based the glory of my reign on changing the face of the territory of my empire. It is as vital to the wellbeing of my peoples as it is to my own sense of achievement that these plans should be carried out.'

Finally he announced his imminent departure with a parting shot at his minister, with which any head of government would agree, 'Don't fall asleep over the day-to-day work of your office.'

On 16 November at 4 a.m. he left Fontainebleau for Milan to set the kingdom of Italy in order while awaiting developments in Spain.

Because Portugal had to be incorporated in the Continental System Junot's troops occupied Lisbon on 30 November. On that day in Venice, which he had just reached after a stay in Milan, Napoleon wrote to Fouché, whose intrigues about divorce had percolated to him:

> 'I told you at Fontainebleau what I think about your indiscretions about my private affairs. As I have read your report of the 19th and know full well what you are saying in Paris I can only repeat that your duty is to follow my directives and not do as you yourself think fit. By acting contrariwise you lead public opinion astray.'

Public opinion, however, had found a choice morsel on which to feed its curiosity and royalist circles their ill-will. The police report of 4 December specifies that

> 'The moralizing ladies of the Faubourg St-Germain are raising holy hands of horror about the divorce. Mme Hamelin repeats in public what she says Her Majesty the Empress confided to her in private. This woman and several others of her kidney take it upon themselves to comment daily, to encourage and to exaggerate the Empress's complaints and distress. They say they know exactly what on such and such a day the Emperor said to the Empress, what conversations were held before and after the coronation, and what quarrels there are in the Imperial family. They claim to know that the Empress's sterility is not her fault; that the Emperor has never had any children; that His Majesty's relations with several women have never borne fruit but that, as soon as these ladies were married, they became pregnant.'

This was the tenor of gossip in the salons while the civil and military authorities in the capital were preparing to celebrate the anniversary of Austerlitz and the coronation in the traditional way. On 3 December Marshal Bessières gave a dinner for four hundred people, served 'elegantly and efficiently', at the Ecole Militaire. The City of Paris was singled out for a special compliment; the two Prefects and the mayors sat next to the ministers and the Marshals. Music to recall the victories of the Grande Armée was played during the banquet, which ended with hearty toasts drunk to the Emperor, the Grande Armée and the City of Paris.

Bessières gave another entertainment at the Ecole Militaire on 9 December

> 'to celebrate both the triumphs of the Grande Armée and, in the name of the Imperial Guard, to express its gratitude to the City of Paris for the welcome extended on its return to the capital. Among the brilliant illuminations the Invalides stood out and the lights linking up with those of the Ecole Militaire made a glorious sight of the whole Champ de Mars.'

In the centre of the arena rose a huge globe surmounted by a colossal statue of the Emperor, round which were grouped allegorical statues. The guard stood at the present when ar 8 p.m. the Empress arrived with the Imperial family and her court. She was accompanied by the princely grand dignitaries and 'a large number of the capital's most notable citizens'. A ballet, fireworks and a ball, where dancing was interrupted for a sumptuous banquet, added to the attractions of the fête watched by a large crowd in the Champ de Mars and the neighbouring avenues.

A week later, at noon on 26 December, the foundation stone was laid of the large public granary which Napoleon had ordered to be put up on the site of the old Arsenal near the Boulevard Bourdon.

Side by side with patriotic demonstrations went all the many festivities of the winter of 1807, particularly those given by Napoleon's sisters. The Emperor, who wanted people to be gay, had instructed each of his sisters to choose one day of the week on which to give a ball.

> 'Paris,' wrote the Duchesse d'Abrantès, 'was one vast scene of exotic pleasures and gaieties; every hour of the day brought new delights.'

At that close of the year, when work and happiness went hand in hand, universal good wishes were expressed for the nation's prosperity and the success of the head of state. His return, wrote a chronicler, would make 'a pleasant New Year's gift' for the capital; a telegraphic message announced Napoleon's arrival at Mont Cenis on 30 December and his early return to his palace.

IV

From the Bourse to the Escurial

Public works in Paris, and the Bourse

On 1 January 1808 at 9 p.m., Napoleon returned to the Tuileries where, apart from a week at St-Cloud, he stayed for three months, marked by two vital events abroad; the occupation of Rome on 2 February and the entry of French troops into Madrid on the 14th. At home an extensive plan to make Paris healthy and beautiful was put in hand, and Passy rightly says that 1808 was 'a memorable date in the story of great public works in Paris'. The scheme reveals that Napoleon, while still concerned with monuments, was turning more and more to works of public benefit.

Napoleon's first visit on his return was to the Tuileries theatre, which was on the point of completion. He disliked it on sight, saying, 'It's too big for a theatre,' but, as he continued his inspection, from one of the windows he saw that the scaffolding had been taken down from the Arc de Triomphe, now virtually finished except for the paving underneath and 'the erection of granite posts round it similar to those on the Carrousel'. Bausset, always with Napoleon on these tours, reports that the Emperor gazed silently at the arch then said only, 'The mass is too wide; it looks more like a pavilion than a gateway; the colonnades are of inferior marble and both in shape and size the Porte St-Denis is better.'

The Arc de Triomphe was, however, the first great work finished during his reign and privately he must have been very pleased. His companions were convinced 'by looking at him that this monument gave him great satisfaction'.

During the next few days Napoleon renewed contact with his capital. On 4 January, with Josephine, he went to see David's painting of the Coronation at the painter's studio in the Cluny church in the Place de la Sorbonne. Although they drove in a plain carriage drawn only by two horses the sovereigns were quickly recognized and received an ovation. David, who had given up the idea of painting the Emperor crowning himself, showed him placing the diadem on the head of Josephine at his feet. Napoleon concealed his surprise as he looked at the canvas, then said to David: 'You have guessed my thoughts; you have made me a French knight.'

For more than an hour he studied the painting in detail, naming all the persons thereon.

> 'Finally,' wrote the *Gazette de France*, 'as he was leaving, His Majesty paused, took off his hat and bowed to David, a gesture expressive of his kindly feeling to all great talent.'

At visits to the Opéra on the 5th, the Théâtre Français on the 7th and at the first performance in the new Tuileries theatre on the 9th, Napoleon received a tumultuous welcome. However, because of the bitter weather in that cold and foggy year of 1808, the performance on the 16th was a dismal failure. Napoleon had to cut it short for the sake of the ladies trembling with cold in their diaphanous evening dresses.

A great review was held on the 11th on the Carrousel which rapidly filled with spectators. The *Gazette de France* reported:

> 'The Parisians were agog to see that faithful Guard which played so dominant a part in the miracles performed by the Grande Armée. . . . When the Emperor appeared at last he was cheered as he went down the ranks by soldiers and people.'

Benckendorff, a member of the Russian delegation of officers from Moscow, repeated over and over again in admiration, 'Superb! Superb!'

When the Czar heard of the success of these reviews he decided that he would hold parades 'similar to those of the Emperor Napoleon'.

On the morning of 17 January, the Emperor, accompanied only by several officers of his household, went to the Louvre and the Tuileries, where he expressed satisfaction with the progress made. In the Colonnade Lemot had sculpted on the pediment a Minerva, crowning a bust of Napoleon (replaced by one of Louis XIV during the Restoration). Over the main entrance Cartelier had moulded a bas-relief which showed Victory distributing wreaths from a quadriga. In the Cour Carrée, which had been left unfinished, sculptural work was still in progress but on Lescot's wing the bas-reliefs were nearly ready. Busts of Glory and Peace, supporting a shield with Napoleon's cypher in the centre (effaced in 1815) had been set on the spandrel of the pediment parallel to the one over the Salle des Cariatides. The roof over this wing was under repair and skylights were being cut in the roof of the Museum gallery to improve the lighting of its wonderful exhibits. Between the Louvre and the Tuileries the houses were being demolished to enlarge the Place du Carrousel; the left wing of the façade of the Hôtel de Longueville had been torn down in November and the opening of the Rue Impériale was imminent. At the entrance to the Tuileries, giving on to the Cour du Manège, an entrance gate was being put up. On the quay parallel with the Louvre gallery lamp-posts had been placed from the Marigny entrance to the Pavillon de Flore.

During January and February the Emperor visited many other places to take note of the progress made in his plans for monuments. The Etoile arch was emerging majestically; the Place du Grand Châtelet was finished and the statue of Fame erected; the column in the Place Vendôme had been built and the bas-reliefs were being cased in bronze. Heavy mortars, part of the artillery captured during the Prussian campaign, were being delivered to the foundry in the Place du Palais to be melted down for the statue of General Desaix in the Place des Victoires.

The columns of the palace of the Legislature were already at half-way height and the pediments of the peristyle were being put in position. Progress was being made with the Odéon theatre; the Place St-Sulpice had been decorated with a handsome fountain, on which a statue was to be placed. Other fountains were being built facing the Ecole de Médecine in the Rue Popincourt, at St-Eustache in the middle of the Rue de Sèvres and on the Parvis Notre Dame. Huge masses of stone for the building of the Temple of Glory were blocking up the Boulevard de la Madeleine and Caumartin.

Road-works on the Left Bank included the restoration of the Place de la Sorbonne; part of the high wall surrounding the old Carthusian monastery in the Rue d'Enfer[1] was being torn down for a hay market; in the same street a sewer was being constructed to take away the water from the Arcueil fountain. From the Jardin des

---

[1] Now the Rue Henri-Barbusse, Rue Denfert-Rochereau and part of the Boulevard St-Michel. The Barrière d'Enfer is now the Place Denfert-Rochereau.

Plantes to the Barrièrre d'Enfer lamp-posts had been installed for
those southern districts without lighting. In the Luxembourg quarter
new roads were being opened up to give all-round access to the
Palace. A series of arches made a graceful arcade on the Quai de
Gesvres from the Pont Notre Dame to the Pont au Change. The
houses encumbering the Pont St-Michel were to be removed.

On the Right Bank the levelling of the Boulevard de la Madeleine
was nearly finished. Along the Quai Bonaparte the strand had been
paved for a port to replace the Port St-Nicolas. The foundations for
the Quai du Louvre had been dug and work was proceeding on its
construction. The Flower and Bird Markets were already installed
on the Quai Napoléon and the Quai de Billy was being straightened.
Work on the Pont d'Iéna was progressing; finally almost the whole
of the highway from the Champs-Elysées to the Versailles road had
been paved.

Napoleon felt that so many works and of so varied a nature must
be dealt with methodically.

At the end of an administrative council on 4 February he made the
following observations: 'All public works in Paris must be classified,
either as coming under the jurisdiction of the Highways Department,
the commune or special *ad hoc* grants. Works such as the Pont
d'Iéna, the Grande Armée column, Desaix' statue, and so on, must
be set out under separate headings. At the next Council a separate
report must be made for each work undertaken, showing in separate
columns the credits allocated to each.'

The three categories under which these works were classified were
placed under three separate authorities; the Director of the Highways
Department, the Minister of the Interior and the Prefect of the
Seine.

Responsibility in Paris and its suburbs fell to the Director of the
Highways Department for bridges, quays, and roads regarded as
extensions of national highways, plus everything appertaining to
water supply. Costs were met by advances from the Municipal Fund
and loans derived from the sale of canals. The Minister of the Interior
was responsible for works in the Place Vendôme, the church of St-
Denis, the Panthéon, the machine at Marly, the Jardin des Plantes,
the public granaries, the Arc de Triomphe, the fountains, the Bourse,
the Place de la Bastille and the obelisk on the Pont Neuf. These
costs were met by the Caisse d'Amortissement from the 25 per cent

tax on cutting of trees in communal woods and the product of export taxes on cereals. The Prefect of the Seine had under his charge the operations decreed on 10 November 1807, financed by a loan of eight millions advanced by the Caisse d'Amortissement—markets, slaughter-houses, public baths, and so on.

While regulating the payments for public works in Paris Napoleon at the same time was planning new enterprises. According to Bausset, he thought in turn of placing the Library and a palace of the arts on the land belonging to the Filles St-Thomas, of building an opera house in the Carrousel, of a covered gallery leading from the Rue de Richelieu to the Matignon entrance on the Quai du Louvre, of erect-ing 'a tall and handsome triumphal column' on the hill at Neuilly, of fountains to flow in the Place Louis XV (Place de la Concorde). of a 'first-class café' in the Tuileries gardens, of substituting four great hospitals for the Hôtel Dieu which would be closed, and of making 'a large and beautiful open space in front of Notre Dame'.

Napoleon's social theories (which inspired Napoleon III) also led him to suggest:

'that streets be cut in the poor districts to do away at small expense with those horrible dwellings which disgrace a beautiful city. A wise and generous government should try to eliminate the dens of pestilence created by these houses lacking air, huddled together and open only to narrow streets where the sun never shines.'

Neither the erection of the Arc du Carrousel nor the building of the parallel northern wing offered a solution to the difficult problem of the space between the Louvre and the Tuileries. As Napoleon seemed increasingly doubtful what to do he summoned all the archi-tects to ask their advice. His own preference for the gigantic led him to opt for maintaining an open space.

'The Emperor,' wrote Percier and Fontaine, 'found it distasteful to seek beauty other than in size; he could not imagine that they might be distinct. Whenever intermediary buildings were suggested to him, he deplored the loss of the large open space between both wings, reiterating, "Only what is large is beautiful; size and space compensate for many mistakes." '

The architects he consulted came down in favour of buildings which would mask the want of harmony between both palaces and the uneven levels on the north and south. The Louvre and Tuileries, built for dissimilar purposes, had been planned on different axes, and were architecturally incompatible.

Bausset says that, on 29 February, Napoleon seemed inclined to end his hesitations and reach a decision about various plans. When he had studied several of the proposals submitted by Fontaine he appeared to accept some of his arguments: (1) that the new wing under construction up to the Rue St-Nicaise should be made into apartments for the Grand Officers of the Crown, to be completed in five years at an annual cost of a million francs; (2) a re-entrant wing should be built to face the Tuileries, dividing it from the Louvre, thus providing a regular space for an opera house; within the two open spaces making a forecourt for the Louvre, there could be a public winter garden at ground-floor level, filled with shrubs and statues; on the south side stables for three hundred horses could be built with accommodation for the household staff; (3) on the Louvre side a triumphal arch should be built of comparable size with the Tuileries arch. The opera house between the Louvre and the Tuileries should be accessible on all sides. The cost of purchase of land, demolition and building was estimated at 42 millions. To avoid simultaneous disclosure of the divergent axes of the palaces Percier and Fontaine's plan provided for the erection on the Carrousel of a monumental fountain of a group of naiads with water gushing from their bosoms.

While Napoleon apparently approved the fountain Bausset says he scornfully rejected the statuary. 'Take these nursing mothers away,' he cried, 'the naiads were virgins.'

Crétet, Regnault de St-Jean d'Angély, Frochot, several Councillors of State and the architects were present at an administrative council held in the Emperor's State study in the Tuileries on 3 March. Plans for the Temple of Glory were studied first. Napoleon opened the discussion, trying to provoke an argument. Bausset says that wide divergences of view were revealed and that, after the whole subject had been ventilated, Napoleon chose Vignon's plan because nothing comparable had been done in Paris and because of its 'unique simplicity'.

Next, Chalgrin and Raymond put forward their proposals for the Arc de l'Etoile. In face of their disagreement Napoleon asked Fontaine to decide which of them was right, Chalgrin or Raymond. Fontaine himself was for a construction with no column, an opinion

with which Napoleon was the more ready to concur because his
architect had said that 'the height and dimensions should be this
monument's chief beauty'.

Napoleon therefore ordered that

'an arch should be built with one entrance only, with no decoration, and
30 foot wide openings at each façade'.

This is the present form of the Arc de Triomphe.

The Emperor, always careful when spending public money,
wanted the cost 'to be only two millions, excluding the expense
already incurred'.

Turning to the architectural style to be employed, the Emperor
asked whether the arch should have a single entrance only. The
answer was that the arches of antiquity had three entrances, one
for the triumphant general and two for the people but, as contemporary triumphal arches bore no resemblance to those of classical
times, one entrance would be sufficient. This information convinced
Napoleon but, to the suggestion of a pleasure-house at Mousseaux,
he replied, 'We have enough houses; we must repair before we build.'

The press reported the Emperor's studies 'for a monument to be
raised on the site of the Madeleine'. The *Publiciste* wrote:

'We must not forget that such a temple is a new idea for modern times;
this monument should stand to remotest ages as witness of its sublime
attribution and the state of fine arts at the time of its construction.'

Much was also made by the newspapers of the capital's gaiety.
Shrove Tuesday, 4 March, had been celebrated 'joyously' and with
ceremony. In the evening at Princess Caroline's masked ball 'ingenious and artistic quadrilles' were danced and, without contradic-
tion, it was 'one of the finest entertainments of its kind given in
Paris for a long time'. Both the Emperor and the Empress were
present. Napoleon found this type of entertainment amusing; he
liked to hide his face under a blue mask and mingle with the guests,
brusquely addressing men and women he met.

'As he wanted to amuse himself,' wrote the Duchesse d'Abrantès, 'he
disguised himself to the eyes on what he called these days of well-bred
saturnalia.'

To preserve his incognito someone—on this occasion Isabey—
had to imitate the Emperor's walk and appear prominently at the
ball.

The same concept of greatness which inspired Napoleon in building monuments led him to aggrandize his Empire by the creation of a new nobility. Those who had best served the régime were to be at the pinnacle of the nation's social pyramid. On 1 March he issued a decree creating dukes, counts and barons of the Empire. The reinstatement of titles was seen by the people and the army as, in Madelin's phrase, 'a mere whim of their little corporal's'. He saw it as an extension of the revolutionary concept of the social order.

'The French,' Napoleon said, 'fought for one thing only, equality before the law and for contact with governmental activities. What will be called an aristocracy is not, in fact, correct because aristocracy does not exist without privilege and heredity, and this nobility's sole privilege is a fortune awarded for civil or military services rendered.'

These decrees were long the main topic of conversation in Paris.

'Everyone is discussing titles,' note police bulletins of 12 and 13 March. 'Undoubtedly the aristocrats are the most bitter. The old families of the Faubourgs St-Germain and St-Honoré, who joked about the Legion of Honour, do not find the creation of titles funny. They are coming to realize that they themselves are not essential, that the creation of an Imperial nobility is the death knell of their own and that they would be wise to associate themselves with the new titles.'

Napoleon himself believed that, with the passing of the years, the two castes would fuse into a single aristocracy devoted to himself.

Every day of the next three weeks saw some action taken by Napoleon for the capital's benefit. On 5 March 1808 he decided definitely that the Bourse should be built on the Filles St-Thomas site; his scheme again demonstrated his spirit of economy and talent for finance. The State was to sell to the Banque de France for a sum of two millions the Hôtel de Toulouse now housing the National Printing Press. Of this amount one million was for building the Bourse, the other for restoring the Hôtel de Soubise for the Archives and the Hôtel de Rohan (the Palais Cardinal) for the Printing Press. Paris thus not only gained an imposing building but Napoleon also installed two important bodies (the Bank and the Archives) in the mansions they still occupy.

On the 10th the Emperor confirmed to Crétet various decisions taken at the administrative council, but he still had doubts about the final plan for the Tuileries:

'The Emperor is shocked by the suggestion of isolating the Tuileries. He would like from his balcony to see the junction with the Louvre, but M. Fontaine is to have a free hand to order this in his own way . . . it is quite obvious that the gallery can be extended. M. Fontaine will, as soon as possible, construct a plaster model of his plan for the palaces, to be put on exhibition at the next salon for the public's reaction. He will also make a relief model of an opera house to be sited anywhere. The theatre must be without columns but with good sight-lines and acoustics, with a large central box for the Emperor and a small box with a retiring room like the one in Milan.'

This theatre, which was a cherished project, was not built until the reign of Napoleon III.

Next day's decree concerned the building of a quay, the present Quai d'Orsay, from the Pont de la Concorde to the Pont de l'Ecole Militaire.

'Work will begin this season and will be completed within five years. The Quai Napoléon (Quai aux Fleurs) will be extended and that part of the Hôtel Dieu on the site demolished.'

After settling the national budget on the 11th Napoleon wrote Crétet a long letter about the Charité hospital, the Pont d'Iéna and the Bourse, asking to be informed why the Pont d'Iéna could not be built of iron like the Pont des Arts and whether it could be constructed by a company; he requested prompt action.

'Mid-Lent is a suitable time for starting the foundations of the Bourse with a celebration arranged by the brokers and other business people who use it. Send me a plan for this building which should be simple and beautiful.'

He showed his friendly feelings to Parisian business interests by granting an audience to the brokers' syndic, to whom he outlined with great cordiality his temperate views on public credit. 'One cannot have *ad hoc* laws; all laws must be interrelated. We are level-headed, we regulate our finances, we are rich and powerful; this is credit. We desire universal well-being and good laws; this needs time.' He drew a comparison between money which was now cheap and its high cost a few years previously. 'Too high or too low an interest-rate is not good; everyone has to live and there is more than one kind of revenue.'

The syndic was most impressed by the Emperor's 'kindly reception' which he reported in glowing terms to his association,

'It is absolutely true that, the nearer one gets to the Emperor, the greater is one's affection and admiration for him.'

The Wine Market

On 17 March the decree instituting the Imperial University was issued and Napoleon then bent his attention to the problem of the Wine Market. This market had been built on the Quai St-Bernard in 1664 and was too small for wholesalers to keep their stocks in warehouses, instead they were obliged to keep their stocks on the port before dispatch to Paris or the provinces. Paris, geographically and economically, was a suitable site for an entrepôt, but the need for a large market became acute with the imminent completion of the Ourcq canal which would bring larger quantities of wine from Champagne to the city.

As an administrative council was to be held shortly Napoleon hurled his usual torrent of questions at Frochot.

'Why is there no entrepôt at the wine market in Paris? This market can house 20,000 barrels but it does not take anything like this number and at the moment is neither warehouse nor entrepôt. How far does this figure of twenty thousand barrels correspond to the real needs of commerce in the city of Paris? How much wine is now in bond outside Paris, from La Rapée up to and including Bercy, and what is the maximum amount of wine that Parisian wine merchants have stored simultaneously at any period in warehouses or special stores outside Paris? Have the toll authorities, bearing in mind the revenues of Paris, any objection to the Minister of the Interior's suggestion that an entrepôt be built at the Arsenal?'

This question of the entrepôt was discussed at the administrative council of 19 March and made the subject of decrees on 20 and 21 March, when Napoleon informed Crétet of his decisions:

'I have signed the decree for the sale of ten canals; ten millions, of which two must be spent this year, are allocated to public works in Paris. I wish to be informed how this money will be utilized and that it will be spent so as to yield me some interest.'

His plan was to use these credits to provide supplementary receipts to be set aside for new enterprises.

'You appreciate that my principle is a progressive sale of the canals and other available assets in order to improve, to build and earn fresh revenue. . . .'

As an example he mentioned the bridge being built opposite the Invalides which,

'like the Pont des Arts, would cost between 6,000,000 and 7,000,000 million francs, which would soon be recouped. When the bridge is completed I shall sell the shares to build something else. As a general principle, whenever I create something that yields a return I intend to sell it and apply the capital to other projects.'

Meanwhile Murat and his staff had reached the outskirts of Madrid and affairs in Spain were approaching a climax. On 22 March Napoleon went into residence at St-Cloud where, on the 26th, he presided at a council devoted to the Ourcq canal and those important public works in Paris which throw light on the characteristics of his genius—his feeling for size and prestige, his preoccupation with public amenity, his regard for cost and demand for accuracy in estimating it.

Concerned always with water supply in Paris, Napoleon opened the meeting by requesting that the Highways Department give a prompt decision

'on the series of plans for the navigation canal from La Villette to the Gare de l'Arsenal, for the aqueduct carrying water to the Marché des Innocents and for the one to Mousseaux'.

The Emperor decreed that the waters of the Ourcq canal must reach Paris on 14 October, anniversary of the battles of Ulm and Jena, and this successful achievement should be the subject of a celebration in Paris.

Next Napoleon approved 'the new plan for the Arc de Triomphe de l'Etoile', with the exception of the proposed ornamentation. This plan provided for

'a single entrance, 42 feet wide, with lateral openings of the same size, at an estimated cost of 4,500,000 francs, including the 700,000 francs already disbursed'.

Various other matters were raised; the construction of the Quai de la Rapée with a causeway and paved port; a promenade at the approaches to the Pont d'Austerlitz; a palace of the arts on the site of the yards at the Quai Bonaparte and the completion of the hospitals. The final subject discussed was the Wine Market.

At St-Cloud on 30 March Napoleon signed a decree published next day in the *Moniteur*. Clause I laid down that:

'In Our good city of Paris a market and free entrepôt for wines and spirits will be built on the Quai St-Bernard on a site between the Rues de Seine (Rue Cuvier) and Fossés St-Bernard.'

Clause 8 read that:

'A company of shareholders is authorized to bid and assume the cost, against the tolls to be established by us.'

The other main decisions were:

'Wines and spirits in the entrepôt may be re-exported out of the city free of tax; wines for Paris will pay dues only when they leave the entrepôt.'[1]

Four eventful months

Napoleon left St-Cloud with a large suite on 2 April for Bordeaux and was away from Paris for four and a half months. He visited the southern departments before taking up residence in the Château de Marracq on the outskirts of Bayonne, there to devote himself to settling the Spanish question which looked threatening.

As usual the Emperor's departure caused some anxiety among the Parisians, who did not like his approaching the Spanish frontier.

This anxiety is reflected in a police report:

'People are afraid of his going to a country overrun with fanatical monks; loud complaints are heard that the Emperor does not protect himself adequately and seems careless of his life.'

The Faubourg St-Germain put in its usual oar.

'Gossip in the salons,'writes Fouché, 'had reached such a pitch that my 300 "regulators" in Paris were unable to control it.'

Nevertheless Paris, in spite of its fear, did not yet as a whole appreciate the seriousness of the Spanish situation.

Good weather helped public works to progress in Paris while from Marracq Napoleon needled his minister, writing on 1 June:

'Why do I not hear about institutions to stamp out beggary? Are you busy with the three great canals? Has all the money I allocated been spent? Work in Paris seems to have stopped; no money has yet been drawn from the Caisse d'Amortissement.'

Next day he followed up this note,

[1] Frochot and the General Council were opposed to this provision; they would have liked these dues to be paid when the wines entered the entrepôt.

'M. Crétet, let me have a short report on the work I set in hand. How is the Bourse getting on? Has the Filles St-Thomas convent been demolished? Is the building going up? What's happened to the Arc de Triomphe? How far advanced is the entrepôt? And the public granaries? And the Madeleine? Is everything in train? Shall I be able to cross the Pont d'Iéna when I return? That's all for Paris. How fares the work I ordered for eight millions?'

Since the Emperor's arrival in Bayonne much of great moment had happened in Spain—the revolt in Madrid put down with great severity by Murat; the exile to Valençay of Charles IV and the restoration of his throne to Ferdinand VII; cession by the old king of his crown to Napoleon who offered it to Joseph—but Fouché, in his report of 26 May, notes that all this had created little stir in Paris where Napoleon's possible divorce was the great topic of conversation.

'Everyone here believes there will be a divorce. They quote letters from Bayonne, one of which declares that it will be soon. They talk of a diadem recently bought in Paris for the new Empress. The need for a divorce is fully understood and no one in France or abroad is not convinced that the dynasty's life and prosperity is linked with the fruitfulness of the Emperor's marriage. The Parisians also believe that if he had children he would scorn dangers less and be more careful.'

Napoleon, angry about these rumours of divorce, on 17 June wrote to Cambacérès:

'I am told that the wildest things are being said at Fouché's. Ever since divorce was rumoured they say it's constantly a subject of discussion in his salon although I've told him a dozen times what I think about this. The upshot is loss of respect for the sovereign and confusion for the public. I have no doubts about Fouché's loyalty but I do fear this frivolity which, by spreading these ideas, engenders others and suppositions which later his duty obliges him to contradict.'

This decidedly eventful month of June saw the first conspiracy of General Malet who, with the help of two 'republican' generals of the Army of the Rhine, thought to profit by the Emperor's absence and the numerical weakness of the Paris garrison to overthrow the régime and re-establish the republic. Dubois was the first to get wind of the affair and dealt with it more energetically because his enemy, Fouché, was implicated. Fouché, however, was not the man to let himself be forestalled; he tried to shuffle off responsibility for this plot on Dubois only to draw down on his own head the Emperor's bitter reproaches.

'I have your letter of the 26th,' wrote Napoleon to Cambacérès. 'The report and interrogation of the Prefect of Police seem most important. Nobody could be more displeased than I with this Minister of Police who shows hostility towards the Prefect of Police instead of supporting, encouraging and directing him. I judge by my own judgement and my reason; these are my guides, not what others think.'

Again on 13 July he let fly at Fouché.

'Is he out of his mind? With whom is he angry? Can his jealousy of the Prefect of Police lead him to such lengths' and, to Fouché himself, he exploded, 'I shall never entrust you with anything again. Is it too hot in Paris this year?'

Napoleon left Bayonne with Josephine on the 20th for the west of France, the day on which Joseph entered Madrid. Spain, rising against the invader, was ablaze and on the 22nd the Grande Armée veteran, General Dupont, capitulated to the insurgents at Baylen. Napoleon heard the bad news on 2 August, the day after he reached Bordeaux. He could find no words to describe the catastrophe: 'Horrible disaster, unspeakable ineptitude . . .'

He was eager to return to Paris to allay anxiety, although he would rather have gone to Joseph's aid and take command of his army. From Bordeaux he wrote to Joseph, 'Events like these demand my presence in Paris. . . . I am terribly distressed when I think that I cannot now be with you and my troops.'

The ball at the Hôtel de Ville

Letters from Bayonne with earliest details about the capitulation reached Paris on 10 August where it caused some apprehension, especially as it was coupled with bad news from Portugal. Stocks had been hovering around 90 frs and now fell on the 8th to 84.50 frs. The ball to be given by the City of Paris on 15 August in honour of the Emperor's birthday was postponed till the following Sunday.

Napoleon spent a few days in Vendée and then on Sunday, 14 August, hurried back to St-Cloud with Josephine. Next day he received the Princes and Princesses of the Imperial Family and the Princes of the Empire, the ministers, the grand officers of State, the State bodies and the diplomatic corps. During the diplomatic audience Napoleon, who wanted to probe Austria's intentions, attacked Metternich. 'If your intentions are as peaceful as you say they are you must make them plain. I can give you all the assurances you may want from me.'

Soon afterwards Metternich said that they had had a 'lovers' quarrel'. This may have been so but love soon changed to hate.

Warm cheers showed 'the happiness people felt at Their Majesties' return' when, later in the day, Napoleon and Josephine arrived at the Tuileries. Napoleon went to one of the windows, specially illuminated that evening, to ask about progress on the Arc du Carrousel, which was on the point of completion; he wanted to know when he could see it without the scaffolding.

'Very soon,' was the answer of the Intendant-General of the Imperial Household, 'as the statue of His Majesty ordered by the Director of Museums is almost in position.'

'What statue are you talking about? I neither want nor did I order that my statue should have pride of place on a monument I have had erected, and at my own expense, to the glory of the army that I have the honour to command. It is appropriate that I appear on a bas-relief or a representation of a battle in which I took part but that, on a building, I should arrogate or be accorded the honour of immortality, is wholly out of place. If my statue has been mounted it must be removed, and if nothing better is found to fill the chariot, then let it stay empty'[1]—which, in fact, it did.

On 21 August, nearly four years after the coronation, Frochot and the Corps of Mayors gave a grand ball at the Hôtel de Ville to celebrate St-Napoleon's day and the birthday of the Emperor and King. Napoleon's attendance was partly due to his hope of raising morale in Paris so that the city would not be too seriously affected by the news from Spain. He knew, of course, of all the rumours flying about and the gossip in Paris shops, especially as a senatus consultum had prescribed the raising of eighty thousand conscripts from the classes of 1806, 1807, 1808 and 1809. He therefore asked the Duchesse d'Abrantès, whose husband, the Governor of Paris, was

---

[1] The Arc du Carrousel was to be surmounted by Lemot's quadriga, driven by allegorical figures representing Victory and Peace. The Venetian horses, removed from their pilasters on the Tuileries railings, were to be harnessed to this chariot. In October 1815 the Austrians removed the horses which were returned to their home over the entrance to St Mark's in Venice. The quadriga, destroyed in 1828, was replaced by a chariot sculpted by Bosio in which stood an allegorical statue representing either Restoration or Peace and holding in its hand an indeterminate object. In 1830 Lemot's two figures, torn down in 1815 but preserved, were placed beside this statue.

in difficulties in Portugal, to be present at the ball and do the honours.
At a long interview he reproached her with the 'conclaves of chit-
chat' in the salons, which he believed had a bad effect on the capital.
Primary responsibility he attributed to Fouché.

'How could you,' said the Emperor, 'allow so many harbours of
gossip and ill-will to exist in Paris?'

Nevertheless, the people continued to adore the Emperor who was
wildly cheered when, on 21 August, he rode out of the Tuileries to
inspect a great parade.

The city's welcome to the Emperor was magnificent; the square and
quays leading to the Hôtel de Ville were brilliantly lit up. Inside, the
rooms had been richly decorated, the ballroom in perfect taste and
lit to show the ladies' toilettes to the best advantage. Four thousand
people drawn from all classes of Parisian society, especially commerce and banking, received invitations, the ladies outstanding in
beauty and the richness of their dress. Napoleon had insisted that
the ladies of the bourgeoisie should be invited, saying, 'I see the
ladies who have been presented at the Tuileries often enough. At the
Hôtel de Ville I want to see only Parisian faces; it is the City of
Paris I want to know.'

A storm of cheering on the square signalled the arrival at 9 p.m.
of the Emperor and Empress, who were received by Frochot and the
Duchesse d'Abrantès on the grand staircase of the Hôtel de Ville.

'When Their Majesties were seen again in Paris through the eyes, as it
were, of the city's own distinguished representatives, the cheers which rose
were a sign of affection and gratitude.'

Next day the newspapers devoted great space to the fête; it was
the chief subject of Fouché's report, which quoted in detail what the
Emperor had said to various guests.

The *Publiciste* reports a scene that afternoon which demonstrates
the people's real cult of Napoleon.

'Yesterday His Majesty's statue was taken to the Place Vendôme. All
the brewers in the Faubourg St-Laurent offered their horses to transport
it from the studio of M. Delaunay where it was cast. The procession was
very odd. Twelve horses, remarkable for their size and weight, were
harnessed to a cart, with a brewer on each of the shafts. In this way they
reached the Place Vendôme at 5 p.m. to thousands of cheers of "Long live
the Emperor!" '

The police report of the 25th confirmed this popular idolatry. 'The mass is at work and prosperous; it is happy and loves the Emperor' but, nevertheless, the grave anxiety felt about the prospects of the Spanish war trickled through. 'Commerce is suffering and is afraid of war; there are fears that the Emperor may leave Paris. . . .'

Napoleon's message to the Senate on 4 September confirmed his intention to deal rapidly with affairs in Spain, but he wished first to strengthen his alliance with Russia in the hope that the Czar would help to prevent Prussia's revival and the rearming of Austria, thus leaving him free for an all-out effort beyond the Pyrenees. He sought and obtained an interview with Alexander but, before leaving for Erfurt, where they were to meet, he pushed on with his military preparations, calling new classes to the colours and sending to Spain some of his troops stationed in Germany.

The Peninsular War did not affect Parisian tranquillity. Stocks which at the announcement of Baylen had weakened stood steady at 81 frs. After the Spanish affair and the Emperor's departure conscription was one of the 'important concerns in Paris', but there was no recrimination. The advance units of the Grande Armée who arrived in Paris en route for Spain received a hearty welcome; the army's morale remained high. Lanzac writes to the point,

'No doubt the soldiers regretted their luxurious billets in Germany and began to weary of so many marches and battles, but this feeling was counter-balanced by their thirst for adventure and especially by the insouciance which is the predominant trait in the French character.'

To which should be added the prestige which surrounded them and their satisfaction with the nation's adulation.

The divisions taking part in the Spanish war paraded on Sunday, 11 September, on the Carrousel where Napoleon harangued them, promising as their reward 'a long peace and lasting prosperity'. The Emperor was still the idol of the army and the people.

Paris-Madrid and return

On 22 September at 5 a.m. Napoleon left Paris for Prussia where he stayed for several weeks. Until the end of September fresh columns bound for the Spanish front passed through Paris where Frochot and the Corps of Mayors extended to each unit 'the welcome due to their courage and sober discipline'. An entertainment and a banquet were given daily in the Tivoli gardens.

On the 27th Napoleon met the Czar at Erfurt. It was said in Paris that, before Talma with the élite of the Comédie Française left in advance of the Emperor for Erfurt, Napoleon said to him,

'You will see a parterre (pit-full) of kings'—kings on the ground (*rois par terre*) was the mordant Parisian gloss on this remark. This pithy phrase did indeed refer to one aspect of this interview, marked by entertainments of such brilliance that the German princes were very much also-rans. Nevertheless, the upshot was that Napoleon, betrayed by Talleyrand, found the Czar to be a real 'Byzantine of the decadent Empire' who managed to avoid any definite under-takings.

In spite of his other preoccupations at Erfurt the Emperor wrote Crétet a long memorandum about the Arc du Carrousel, ending with suggestions for the four inscriptions, one on each side of the arch. This was the first:

'In the year in which he was crowned Emperor, Napoleon planted his victorious eagles on the ramparts of Vienna and a year after his coronation won the victory of the Three Emperors. May the memory of these victories endure from generation to remotest generation and may every Frenchman who visits the fields of Moravia recollect his duty to cherish the honours won by the Grande Armée to whom this monument is dedicated. . . .'

With much to ponder on, Napoleon left Erfurt on 14 October, arriving at 9.30 p.m. on the 19th at St-Cloud. Simultaneously with the guns announcing the Emperor's arrival the *Moniteur* reported, as if it were a victory, the completion of an important undertaking in the capital.

'The aqueduct in the Rue St-Denis, begun at the end of June, was finished on the 14th of this month, the date fixed by His Majesty. This work in the busiest street in Paris was pushed forward with unusual speed in spite of the great difficulties encountered. The aqueduct is 1,100 yards long and was constructed in a hundred-odd days; it is the first of its kind . . . this once dirty and unsavoury street is now one of the finest in Paris.'

The Emperor went on the 22nd to see the salon of paintings in the Louvre where he was received by a 'parterre of artists', David,

Gros, Girodet, Vernet, Prud'hon, Gérard and Guérin. He is said to have remarked about a painting of the Czar Alexander at Tilsit, 'It isn't a good likeness; he is better-looking than that . . .'

On the 25th Napoleon went in state to open the session of the Legislature where he spoke of the necessity of continuing public works, interrupted for site clearance, and of the importance of the annual budgetary receipts.

'My people will not have to carry new burdens. I am leaving in a few days' time to take personal command of my army and with God's help to crown the King of Spain in Madrid and plant my eagles on the forts of Lisbon. . . .'

This speech was warmly received and the session ended to cries of 'Long live the Emperor!', echoed in the streets through which Napoleon returned to the Tuileries.

On the 27th Napoleon went to the Louvre to see the statues from the Villa Borghese, a first consignment of antiquities which had arrived a fortnight previously. He went on to the Elysée[1] and on 28 October visited various public works in Paris.

'At 8 a.m. in a plain carriage with no suite' he went to the site of the Filles St-Thomas where the Bourse was under construction, insisted on being told all about it and interrogated the workers. His next visit was to the Rue St-Denis where he surveyed the aqueduct from end to end and was apparently well satisfied. In the large crowd was one who would write with happy pride, 'I saw Napoleon in person.' The Emperor's last visits were to various charitable institutions, which he inspected attentively, made inquiries about their organization and expressed his satisfaction at the good order prevailing. He was, however, dissatisfied with the orphanage of La Pitié which took in 'the children of the Nation', and told Crétet that the cost per child was too high and that in general foundlings could be housed and fed cheaper outside Paris.

After these visits Napoleon presided over an administrative council devoted to the affairs of Paris; he was angry that work was proceeding slowly and that so little had been done to the major undertakings. Among his new proposals was one for a fountain for the Place de la Bastille and a winter promenade.

---

[1] After the signature of 15 July of the Treaty whereby Murat replaced Joseph, now King of Spain, on the throne of Naples, Napoleon had Murat cede to him all his French property, including the palace of the Elysée.

At noon next day the Emperor left for Rambouillet on his way to Bayonne where he arrived on 3 November with the intention of making short shrift of the Spanish war. 'Operations have begun and the enemy is everywhere beaten,' he wrote to Cambacérès on his arrival and to Joseph on 5 November, 'I hope that this will soon be over.' Paris shared his confidence to the full and stocks remained steady at 80 frs. Crowds continued to flock to the Louvre which Josephine herself visited several times, speaking to the artists with her habitual charm and making every effort to carry out the Emperor's wish of keeping the capital contented.

As he was preparing to cross the Somosierra Pass on 26 November Napoleon told Cambacérès that he wanted to build a new palace in Paris.

'I have raised a monument to the glory of the Grand Armée at the Madeleine. The Legislature must now erect on the heights of Montmartre a kind of temple of Janus, to be inscribed "The Departmental deputies of the Legislature and the electoral colleges of the French Empire have raised this temple etc. etc. . . ." Here will be made the first ceremonial proclamations of peace and the distribution of decennial prizes; it cannot cost less than 30,000,000 to 40,000,000 francs.'

The Emperor had devised an ingenious method of paying for this temple.

'The Legislature must send me a petition for a law enacting that each member of the electoral colleges (and they number between 30,000 and 40,000) is to be invited to subscribe 1,000 to 3,000 francs according to his means, to be paid annually in fifths. Thus in five years there will be 30,000,000 to 40,000,000 francs available for the building which will be one of the most beautiful in the universe; work will begin in 1809.'

The 1808 commemorations of 2 December followed the established tradition, with three inaugural ceremonies. At 9.30 Crétet, accompanied by Frochot, Dubois, the mayors, deputies and the members of the General Council and Girard, the water engineer, went to the esplanade near the basin of La Villette where the barrage was broken; as the waters of the Beuvronne filled the reservoir the enthusiastic crowd went wild. Towards noon the procession moved on to the Bastille where the architect, Cellerier, showed the plans for the projected fountain. As Napoleon wished, it was to be in the form of an elephant with a tower on its back in the antique manner, and water flowing from its trunk. Two hundred tons of bronze were to be set aside for this fountain and a large studio had been built on the site to protect the model of the elephant sculpted by Mouton. The final ceremony was held near the Barrière de Rochechouart where one of the six slaughterhouses planned by Napoleon was to be erected.

This was the very moment when 'in glorious weather' Napoleon had reached the heights above Madrid and summoned the military junta to lay down their arms. On 4 December at 10 a.m. when Madrid capitulated Paris woke to the sound of gun salutes to herald the celebrations of the anniversary of the coronation. The *Journal de l'Empire* made this an occasion for listing Napoleon's benefactions to the capital:

> 'Superb monuments are enriching Paris . . . the capital is witnessing the revival of the old Louvre whose decay seemed to spring from the decay of kings of the third dynasty. Napoleon commands and new districts, fountains, palaces and columns grow like mushrooms in the capital. . . . Seeing all these monuments rising everywhere and counting the victories won by the Imperial Eagle, would one not be justified in believing that the coronation was at least half a century away?'

Even while settling the affairs of Spain Napoleon did not lose sight of what was being done in Paris. Although he was electrified to learn that the English had appeared near Valladolid and were marching on Madrid—which at last offered him the opportunity to crush his enemy—the Emperor sent two memoranda to Crétet about improvements in Paris. The first was concerned with the two great Parisian palaces. Crétet was to have made 'a relief model of the Tuileries and Louvre plan and exhibit it publicly'. An examining committee was to send its findings to the Minister, who was also to note public reaction and report to the Emperor. The second memorandum dealt with the Fountain of the Elephant and water supply in Paris.

> 'I intend to use the Ourcq water to beautify the Tuileries gardens with jets of water and cascades and in the Champs-Elysées and its environs to make lakes as large as the gardens for all kinds of boats.'

Napoleon also sent Gaudin fresh instructions about clearing and financing the Place du Carrousel, but always mindful of protecting the tenants' interests.

Before he left Madrid for 'manoeuvres against the English' at Valladolid, Napoleon dictated a note to Cambacérès, leaving it to him to determine how 'to satisfy the public's impatience and dissipate causeless anxiety'. With the press in mind he ended:

> 'If the English do not fall back to the sea and do not take any territory from us they will find it difficult to escape and they will pay dearly for this foray on the Continent.'

As Napoleon had ordered, Cambacérès had a Te Deum sung on the 25th in thanksgiving for the victories of Espinosa, Burgos, Somosierra and the entry of the French troops into Madrid. In spite of the bitter weather the ceremony was very well attended.

At the annual closing session of the Legislature on the 31st Ségur made a reassuring speech.

'Gentlemen, you are returning to your homes in the knowledge that you have acted in concert with our sovereign's beneficent intentions. Within a few weeks the enemy armies have been destroyed and dispersed; Madrid has opened its gates and has been saved by the Emperor's magnanimity. Everything, therefore, inclines you to hope that your most heartfelt prayers will soon be granted by the early and triumphant return of our monarch to the bosom of his great family.'

The people of Paris were indeed impatient for the Emperor's return.

Those who knew to what dangers he exposed himself were anxious that he should father descendants. Within the government Fouché championed the idea of a divorce but Talleyrand, pursuing the subversive line he took at Erfurt, went further still and was already seeking the man to replace Napoleon in the event of his death. The two ministers, normally enemies, became accomplices in a real conspiracy to put Murat on the throne. The assemblies likewise were restive. Had not the Legislature recently rejected the bill for a Code of Criminal Investigation?

Abroad the scene was dominated by deteriorating relations with the Holy See and by feverish Austrian rearmament, tensions of which Napoleon was partially aware. In view of the possibility of an Austrian offensive and, as he was preparing to pursue the English, he ordered 180,000 men of the class of 1809 to be called up, in readiness for any move by Austria.

He was optimistic and, intent on sharing his optimism with Paris, he wrote on 13 January 1809 from Valladolid to Fouché:

'It would be helpful to publish some good articles comparing the evils afflicting France in 1709 with the Empire's prosperity in 1809, from the standpoint of territory, population, internal prosperity, finance, and so on. You have men able to write eight or nine articles on this most important subject which will influence opinion in the right direction. . . . Louis XIV was busy having Versailles and hunting-lodges built. We have busied ourselves with improving Paris, its water supply, its palaces, its markets, its Temple of Glory, its Bourse. All had to be done, all has been done.'

The urgent messages concerning war-like preparations in Vienna, which reached the Emperor on 16 January, aroused his anxiety about repercussions in Paris; he left Soult in command in Spain to return to the capital at breakneck speed. Before he left he wrote to the Grand Duke of Baden:

'I have beaten the Spanish and English armies and, hearing that Austria is stepping up its armaments, I considered it advisable to return to Paris.'

From the Palace of Schönbrunn to the Obelisk on the Pont Neuf

In spite of the fatigues of his headlong course Napoleon took no rest when he arrived at the Tuileries on 23 January. He immediately visited the palace from ground floor to attic and expressed his satisfaction with what had been done. He then went to the Rue de Rivoli where he 'seemed to approve' the seventeen arcades which were its planned decoration, noted with pleasure that some houses had already been built and hoped that there would be many more.

Back in his study again, he sent for Cambacérès, to whom he expressed his displeasure that, during his absence, intrigues should have been allowed to develop. Although the Emperor knew that war with Austria was imminent he caused the rumour to be spread that there would be no war, and that he had no intention of leaving Paris.

At a special audience of all the official bodies in Paris Frochot and Fontanes made laudatory speeches of welcome on the Emperor's return but, on the 27th, he sent for Fouché whom he upbraided severely for his lack of loyalty and threatened him with disgrace. To test the state of public opinion Napoleon went that evening to the Opéra where he was warmly acclaimed. Nesselrode, who was present, said that on the previous day he thought the Emperor looked troubled but he now seemed much more cheerful and his welcome was 'one of great warmth'.

It was at Talleyrand that Napoleon levelled bitter reproaches on the 28th, castigating him as a coward and a thief and depriving him of his office as Grand Chamberlain (which was given to Montesquiou). The Prince of Benevento remained impassive but never forgot the insult; his implacable hatred pursued Napoleon who was its victim in 1814. Talleyrand's disgrace was the sole topic of conversation for several days, but in a great city the focus of interest veers quickly and attention soon centred on Napoleon's measures to rally to his army the young nobles who had received officers' brevets.

During his short stay in Paris the Emperor was particularly attentive to the capital's business management. On 6 February he approved the civic budget which stood at the normal figure of about 19,000,000 francs (15,365,714 in ordinary expenditure and 3,364,386 in extraordinary outlays.) Although opposed in principle to fresh taxation, he did agree to institute customs dues in the suburbs to increase the city's resources.

To gratify Napoleon's wish that Paris should be gay fête followed fête during February, and the Duchesse d'Abrantès says 'that there never could be an equal to Napoleon's court in the winter of 1808-9', which was the ultimate in 'brilliance and beauty'.

From 28 February to 10 March the Emperor resided at the Elysée, and it is due to him that presidents of the Republic live in this palace. Napoleon said he did not like the Elysée, and that its damp situation made him liable to catch cold, but he often stayed there at the beginning of spring or in the autumn, probably because he enjoyed its comfortable rooms and the charm of the garden. He felt 'freer' than at the Tuileries and regarded the Elysée as his 'clinic'.

The Spanish business was at last being forgotten and the Parisians considered it at an end. Austria was now the chief topic of conversation. She had put an army of three hundred thousand men into commission, ready to move to the attack, encouraged by the Czar's attitude and egged on by England. The Austrians were also anxious to profit by the locking up of Napoleon's troops in Spain. Of this Napoleon was aware and, on 31 March, he began to put the finishing touches to his preparations for the forthcoming campaign of which Austria was to bear the brunt of total responsibility before the world. On 1 April the Emperor sent Champagny the following letter:

'Have articles published in the press about all that is being done in Vienna to provoke and offend the French nation. . . . There must be a daily article in the *Journal de l'Empire*, the *Publiciste* or the *Gazette de France*, to make it clear that war is being forced on us.'

Nor was Napoleon mistaken. On 9 April the Archduke Charles, in command of the Austrian armies, crossed the river Inn; a telegram was handed to the Emperor during a performance on the 12th of *Andromaque* at the Tuileries and, at the end of the third act, he quickly left the theatre.

For the first time he was surprised by the sudden attack but reacted promptly. After a brief ministerial council he decided to leave and at 4 p.m. set off for Strasbourg to take command of his army.

In Paris there was lively indignation against the aggressor and good wishes for the Emperor's success. Champagny's message to the Senate on the 14th echoed the general feeling, 'All benefits are misunderstood, all engagements violated. . . . Sire, your people will support you in this new struggle.'

After discussion of this message the Assembly voted eagerly for the levy demanded by the Emperor.

Napoleon won a victory at Eckmühl on 22 April and, the following day, took Ratisbon where he was wounded in the heel but wrote to Josephine on 6 May,

'. . . I am in very good health; the ball which touched me did no damage; it just grazed the Achilles tendon. You're wrong to worry, everything is going very well here.'

On the next day, which was a Sunday, a Te Deum was sung at Notre Dame in celebration of 'the victories won by the French army on the fields of Tann, Eckmühl and Ratisbon', which drew a large attendance of all classes, who thus demonstrated their interest in the for ever memorable events commemorated at this solemn ceremony.

Napoleon was at the outskirts of Vienna on 9 May and on the 10th he wrote to Cambacérès:

'We have entered Vienna. The order of the day will tell you how things stand; you can have it printed and read in all the theatres.'

From his strong position ensconced in the palace of Schönbrunn the Emperor issued a decree announcing the annexation of Rome and the Papal States.

Meanwhile in Paris Fouché, to ingratiate himself with the Emperor and even more to forestall his anger, was carefully supervizing public works, and writing to his colleague, Crétet, about the evils of dilatoriness. At Schönbrunn the Emperor was equally concerned about his good city, dictating on 18 May a further memorandum about the union of the Louvre and the Tuileries, which showed that he still clung to his idea of a vast open space between them; he was led to remark that there was a shortage of parks in Paris.

Official news of the entry into Vienna was received in Paris by Cambacérès on 18 May and celebrated in the same way as previous victories. The Archduke Charles had, in the meantime, withdrawn to the left bank of the Danube where, on 21 May, he was attacked by Napoleon whose army had been reinforced by the Army of Italy under Prince Eugène. The collapse of a bridge over the river halted the Emperor's attack before Essling on the 22nd and he retired to the island of Lobau, in spite of an apparently successful assault. Both sides suffered heavy losses. In covering the French withdrawal Lannes lost his life and Masséna and Oudinot were slightly wounded.

Two days after the Te Deum celebrating the entry into Vienna came the first reports of the battle of Essling, described as 'memorable and glorious' but, in fact, in spite of the miracles performed by Napoleon and his army, this battle was a setback, which was soon known all over Europe. Germany and Austria were preparing to react, resistance in Spain was hardening, rebellion seethed in Rome where, on 10 June, the Pope issued a bull of excommunication, and England reinforced its invasion threat. The Czar of Russia had not yet thrown off the mask and even paid 'compliments and tribute to French bravery' while, in fact, he was only waiting for an opportunity to join the allies' camp.

All these unpleasant repercussions affected Napoleon's health as well as his spirits. Dr Corvisart was summoned to Schönbrunn, but Napoleon mastered his depression and began energetically to prepare the next campaign.

To use Fouché's expression, events at Essling gave rise to 'every kind of rumour' in Paris and Napoleon was once again obsessed by the question, 'What does Paris think?' He wrote to Camabacérès,

'Your letters don't reveal much nor tell me anything about what Paris is thinking which, far away as I am, is what I am anxious to know.'

Only Napoleon's enemies, republicans and royalists, rejoiced at his difficulties. The Faubourg St-Germain, writes Fouché, had again become hostile but in Paris, as Madelin pertinently remarks, 'everyone was used to salon gossip'. The people did not doubt the Emperor's ultimate success nor his ability to retrieve the situation.

'In spite of unpleasant rumours of ineptitude, speculation and bad feeling, observed a police report, 'morale in Paris is very good and news of an early and resounding victory is confidently awaited.'

Of all the numerous daily reports the Emperor received he paid the most attention to those from Fouché who, at the beginning of June, spoke of difficulties at the Arc de Triomphe following an increase in working hours. Napoleon answered on 15 June,

'You must not alter working conditions when I am not in Paris; see that workers' customs and habits remain intact. These people believe that because I am not there they are discriminated against and that they have no redress, which gives them cause to think they are unjustly treated.'

The French troops left Lobau on 4 July and regrouped on the left bank of the Danube. Two days later came the thunderclap of Wagram. News of the battle reached Paris on the 14th. The 25th bulletin, published on the 18th, was rapturously welcomed with the usual celebrations and expressions of devotion to the Emperor, but stocks, due to the exchange manipulations denounced by Fouché, failed to rise. In fact from 79.40 frs they fell to 78.60 frs and then to 78 frs, which brought a swift and lively reaction from Napoleon who on 14 July wrote to Cambacérès:

'The criminal rumours which are circulating are not due to ill-will but to speculations on the rise and fall in stocks. This gambling which endangers public order must be stopped immediately.'

The unfavourable reaction was limited to a small financial circle but, at the usual Te Deum at Notre Dame, the absence of a Russian representative was noted. Wagram certainly deserved a glorious celebration but it was a costly victory nor, as yet, had peace been signed and the future was still clouded with doubts.

'Much care was yet required to preserve the good fortune which had now arrived, but was still frail.'

This was apparent on the 29th when the English disembarked at
Walcheren, causing some excitement in Paris, especially in the
government. Fouché alone saw in it an opportunity to increase his
influence. As Crétet was ill Fouché was temporarily acting as
Minister of the Interior and, to repel the invaders, in imitation of
1793 he ordered the *levée en masse* of the National Guard, whose
command he gave to Bernadotte although he had fallen foul of the
Emperor at Wagram. With greater boldness still, Fouché ordered
the mobilization of the National Guard of Paris and went so far as
to send the mayors a circular with this daring phrase,

> 'Let us prove to Europe that, while Napoleon's genius can cast its glorious
> shadow on France, his presence is not essential to repel the enemy.'

Whatever disarray these measures may have caused in Paris, the
Emperor's birthday was celebrated with the usual enthusiasm, and the
day was distinguished by a spectacular inauguration which realized
the hopes of Emperor and Parisians alike. At noon the taps were
opened for the waters of the Ourcq canal to feed the fountain of the
Innocents and a considerable crowd was enchanted to see water
flowing round the feet of Jean Goujon's nymphs. 'Never,' reports
the *Moniteur*, 'has a mass of citizenry expressed its affection for its
sovereign with greater eagerness.'

Napoleon, again for several months in residence at Schönbrunn,
chose this day to issue the decree to complement that issued from
Posen about the Temple of Glory.

> 'Desirous of expressing Our satisfaction with the conduct of Our Grande
> Armée and Our peoples during the campaigns of Jena and the Vistula
> by erecting an enduring monument, We have decreed and decree as
> follows: Article 1—At the approach to the Pont Neuf shall be raised
> an obelisk in Cherbourg granite 180 feet high with the inscription, "The
> Emperor Napoleon to the French people".
> Article 2—On the sides of this obelisk shall be inscribed all the deeds done
> in both campaigns which are to the honour of France.'

Both Fouché's decrees had raised an immediate storm of protest
from most of the members of the government; evidence of their
disapproval reached Napoleon, who was in a particularly bad mood
because he had just learnt of the English landing at Flushing on 18
August. He attacked 'the Paris plotters' who had taken advantage of
events to intrigue against him and had even marked out Bernadotte

should the throne 'accidentally become vacant'. Most of all he was angered by the levy of the Paris National Guard. On 3 September he called a halt to recruiting and placed Marshal Sérurier, governor of the Invalides, in command of the Guard. Next day he wrote to Fouché:

'The peasants near Paris are mounting guard; there are no brigands. What is the point of tiring out these poor peasants?'

Early in September the English, decimated by fever, had to evacuate Holland; the Walcheren affair had ended in total disaster and cost them fourteen thousand men. This defeat raised the Emperor's prestige in Europe, enabling him to urge on peace preliminaries which had been making slow progress. This was for what Paris and the whole of France was waiting. Total responsibility devolved upon the Emperor who from Schönbrunn wrote to Cambacérès on the 9th:

'Negotiations are continuing. Rumours were spread in Paris that I was ill, why I do not know. I never felt better.'

On the 25th he wrote in similar vein to Josephine,

'My health is good. I haven't felt so well for years. Corvisart wasn't wanted.'

While Napoleon was engaged in peace negotiations complaints reached him from owners of lands on the banks of the Ourcq canal about the severity with which the law regulating compulsory purchase was applied or the loopholes in it. This gave him an opportunity to develop his liberal ideas and on 7 and 27 September he sent instructions to Cambacérès, remarking,

'I do not see how there can be landowners in France if they are to be turned out of their holdings by a mere administrative decision.'

Napoleon's return was eagerly awaited in Paris; this and peace were the main topics of conversation.

'All Paris believes,' states a police report, 'that His Majesty's return is imminent. Business people are sure that the Spanish affair is over and that France has in front of her a long and prosperous future.'

Peace was in fact signed at Schönbrunn on 14 October. Napoleon at once left for Paris. At Strasbourg on his way he learned from police reports of the absurd rumour that his mental state was causing anxiety.

'It's the Faubourg St-Germain again,' he exclaimed, 'which thinks up such nonsense.'

V

The Palace of the King of Rome and the Grand Design

Public works during renewed peace

The Emperor's headlong journey brought him to Fontainebleau at 9 a.m. on 26 October 1809. He had scarcely reached his study before he dictated his only two letters of the day, one to Berthier, informing him of his arrival, the other revealing his interest in fulfilling the needs of the Parisians.

'Three fountains in the faubourgs St-Denis and St-Martin are dry. The people in these faubourgs say it is due to neglect on the part of the people in charge of these fountains. Send me a report about it.'

He was, however, more deeply concerned about something else, the break-up of his marriage. Josephine had heard of his arrival too late to meet him. Napoleon sent a message to her at St-Cloud and, while awaiting her coming, summoned Cambacérès. In an interview which must have seemed interminable to the Arch Chancellor, the Emperor questioned him closely about public opinion during his absence, a matter intimately linked with the part played by Fouché and the conduct of the Legislature. He also referred to the Roman and Spanish questions. Finally Napoleon informed Cambacérès of his irrevocable decision to part from Josephine and asked him to start proceedings for the earliest possible divorce. When the Empress arrived at 6 p.m. Napoleon greeted her coldly. He addressed her very sharply and the dread word 'divorce' was uttered.

Next day, while the cannon at the Invalides boomed the Emperor's return and the Imperial standard was hoisted over the Tuileries, Napoleon severely rebuked Fouché, whom he had already on 1 October from Schönbrunn relieved of his interim post as Minister of the Interior, which was given to Montalivet. Although it was generally believed that Fouché would be 'kicked out', his outstanding qualities made him indispensable and he was retained in charge of the general police.

Napoleon next received Champagny in audience and asked him to sound out the Czar about a possible marriage with the Grand Duchess Anne. In the course of the next few days Napoleon had several meetings with Fouché, who found him 'very bitter about the Faubourg St-Germain', and particularly irritated by the wild rumours it spread. The Emperor talked about 'dealing severely with people who tore him apart with one hand and begged with the other' but Fouché, ironically realistic, dissuaded him.

'It is the tradition,' said Fouché. 'The Seine flows, the Faubourg intrigues, demands, battens and calumniates; it is in the nature of things. Everyone has his own characteristics. Who was more vilified than Julius Caesar? In any case do not the most damaging rumours originate in Your Majesty's antechambers?'

Peace was publicly proclaimed throughout Paris on Sunday, 29 October, news received with great rejoicing and enthusiastic cheers of 'Long live the Emperor!'

As Napoleon had instructed, the proclamation was made with great solemnity by the mounted heralds, accompanied by twenty-four mounted police constables and a large detachment of troops who traversed the capital announcing the articles of the treaty.

Napoleon now decided to return to Paris, where he was eager to be and, on 14 November, rode into the Tuileries at 5.45 p.m. with a military suite, 'more like a conquering general than a superb monarch' to use Madelin's phrase. The Emperor went immediately to the Louvre and, with the prospect before him of a long and glorious reign, conceived the notion of residing at the Pavillon de Flore.

When he reached the State apartments of the Louvre he looked up at the ceilings and decided that they were not richly enough decorated, but he did admire the beauty of the bronze gateway to the colonnade. He recalled his plan to open a triumphal way, extending the Rue de Rivoli as far as the Bastille, which would have entailed the demolition of St-Germain-l'Auxerrois. In view of the huge expense involved he decided to postpone this, saying, 'Let's leave that till later and deal with the interior of the Louvre. Architects ruined Louis XIV.'

Finally, he was surprised to find that there was room in the palace only for a hundred or so beds, insufficient for the number of kings and their suites whom he thought would be increasingly taken with the idea of visiting Paris.

The court had returned with Napoleon to Paris, followed shortly by the King of Saxony who took up residence in the Elysée on the 13th, then by the King of Holland and by the Kings of Württemberg and Bavaria, housed respectively in the Luxembourg and at the Hôtel Marboeuf.

Napoleon showed off his good city with some pride to this princely flock which gave his return a triumphal air. For a fortnight the city was the almost nightly scene of magnificent entertainments. The shopkeepers and tradespeople congratulated themselves, 'predicting with pleasure that Paris would have a brilliant winter season'. Stocks rose rapidly and on 16 November touched 80.25 frs. On that day Napoleon, surrounded by the grand dignitaries of the Crown, received the homage of all the great State bodies. Many speeches were made, among them one by Frochot: 'At last the capital sets eyes on You again and Your magistrates, so long deprived of the presence of Your august person, are now able, at the foot of Your throne, to pay the homage of the respectful affection felt by Your Majesty's loyal subjects of your good city of Paris.'

Enthusiasm was at its height whenever Napoleon appeared in public, particularly during a great review on 26 November, but the Emperor's personal pleasure in this evidence of his popularity was embittered by the political necessity of informing Josephine of his determination to divorce, a decision he imparted to her in a painful interview on 30 November.

During the usual anniversary celebrations of the coronation and the battle of Austerlitz Napoleon spoke to the Legislature jubilantly about the victories won by his armies throughout Europe and stressed the Russian alliance by his reference to his 'ally and friend', Czar Alexander.

Paris has a new Empress

The fête at the Hôtel de Ville on 5 December to honour the Emperor's return to the capital recalled in its magnificence that of 1804 given by the City of Paris, but Napoleon had instructed the hostess, the Duchesse d'Abrantès, not to receive the Empress in the way etiquette demanded. He wanted the idea of a divorce to percolate. Thus, when the Empress, attended only by her lady-of-honour and two ladies-in-waiting, entered the throne-room, the resplendent flowers and lights only threw the ravages of her face into greater relief. It was a cruel experience for her but, although overwhelmed by the prospect of divorce, on this, her last public appearance, she behaved with courage and dignity.

Frochot made his usual speech of welcome referring to the Emperor's constant thought for his good city of Paris and the pleasure given by his presence. In his reply Napoleon spoke of his own pleasure in dining in the 'house of his good city': 'Its citizens should hold me in affection and I believe in the sincerity of their speeches since their welfare, their interests and their happiness are enshrined in my heart.' This speech was warmly cheered.

In the Emperor's State study in the château of the Tuileries at 9 p.m. on Thursday, 14 December, a family gathering 'registered' the mutual desire of separation expressed in turn and with great dignity by Napoleon and Josephine. An hour later this decision was conveyed to the Privy Council. Next day the Senate in an immediate senatus consultum pronounced the dissolution of the sovereign's marriage. A laconic communiqué appeared in the *Moniteur*:

> 'His Majesty the Emperor and King left today (15 December) for Trianon; Her Majesty the Empress Josephine is at Malmaison.'[1]

Although the Parisians loved Josephine, police reports for December reveal that they were already wondering about her successor.

> 'Everyone is greatly concerned about the wife who will give the Emperor heirs. They search through all the courts of Europe for a woman worthy of this great distinction but, most of all, they want her to love and think only of him.'

At this Christmas-tide Napoleon felt lonely in his gloomy palace. When, after ten days at Trianon he returned to the Tuileries, he wrote nostalgically to Josephine: 'I was displeased to return to the Tuileries; this great palace seemed empty and I felt very much alone.'

Never had New Year's Day been more lavishly celebrated nor Paris

[1] A decree of 15 December allocated the Elysée to Josephine. She took up residence there on 3 February 1810.

more brilliant than in 1810 but, while its citizens were merrymaking, Napoleon was hastening his divorce proceedings. On 12 January the metropolitan clergy of Paris confirmed the decree of the diocesan tribunal and pronounced the religious divorce.

Although the Emperor was now a free man he could not help feeling some grief, shown in a further note to Josephine:

'I must know for certain that you are strong, not weak. I also am rather weak which makes me terribly unhappy.'

His wish to find a new wife was, however, much too strong to permit indulgence in heartache. As the vacillations of the Russian court presaged a refusal Napoleon decided not to wait for the rebuff but turned to Austria to make a formal request for the hand of the Archduchess Marie-Louise.

With the prospect of this brilliant alliance his desire to augment the improvements in Paris was considerably enhanced, his primary consideration always the union of the Louvre and the Tuileries. Hitherto, in spite of many discussions with his architects, Napoleon had been unable to make up his mind as to how to use the intervening land because of his fear of excessive expenditure. Two plans had been drawn up, both providing for the purchase and demolition of the buildings on the Place du Carrousel, one to cost 51,804,325 frs and the other 34,118,075 frs. On 17 January Napoleon decided in favour of the less costly plan and allocated funds of 36 millions from the special account.

Napoleon's preoccupation with enriching Paris by monuments did not cause him to lose sight of improving amenities in general, particularly water supply. While settling Parisian questions once again he noted the permanent rivalry between Frochot and Dubois, each of whom tried to broaden his own sphere of influence. On 1 February he made observations which are still relevant:

'No one understands the government of Paris; there are two prefects, who are such great rivals that neither will concede an inch to the other. There is only a single city and there ought to be only a single administration. First one must consider how this system arose; it probably derives from the revolution. Lacking control of the Paris commune, the government wanted a central office and a prefecture of police. If this *was* the origin of the system then it was wrong because present circumstances bear no relation to those when the system was created. We now need a Prefect of Paris, with a council of mayors and a municipal council, who will administer income and expenditure and generally have charge of all administrative matters. A General Commissioner of Police should be entrusted with every branch of police matters but have nothing to do with administration.'

On 5 February a further meeting, 'livelier even than usual', took place at the Tuileries when the vexed question of the Louvre and the Tuileries was again under discussion. Napoleon, supported by Murat and Fesch, disagreed with Fontaine's expressed wish to overcome their irregularity:

'What is large is always beautiful and I cannot agree to cut in two a space whose principal merit is size. Between the Louvre and the Tuileries nothing could rival a fine courtyard. Only the architects agree with you, Fontaine; the division you want would destroy the size. A large building does not have to be absolutely regular. Artists see only the defects; this is nonsense which impresses the minority only.'

Nevertheless, he did not try to impose his own viewpoint. In face of Fontaine's insistence that the open space would make the disparities more obvious, he ended by adopting the architect's plan to build a lateral wing and gave orders for the purchase of the houses which had to come down, for the laying of the foundations of the new wing and the continuation of the Galerie Napoléon.

After further reflection Napoleon thought this plan too costly and again changed his mind, asking for a new plan. He ended his note to Daru with a warning about the stable site, which the architects had not considered:

'Is it not mistaken to put so much hay and straw in such close proximity to the gallery of the Louvre which houses so much of value? Is it not a danger to Paris to site the stables so near the city's houses?'

When, on 8 February, Napoleon dealt confidently with the budget of the city of Paris he thought he had achieved the balance which eluded him, but this budget would be in deficit to the tune of 1,300,000 frs because tolls had not yet been extended to the suburbs nor dues levied on the markets.

Because of the increased diplomatic activity which would result from his second marriage Napoleon decided on 8 February to build the Ministry of External Relations on the magnificent site between the newly built Quai Bonaparte and the Rues de Bellechasse and Poitiers. Three decrees were issued on the 9th. The first laid down the building of a mansion to house External Relations and the State secretariat of the kingdom of Italy[1]; the foundation stone was to be laid on 25 March. The second decree concerned the elephant fountain in the Place de la Bastille, which was to be finished and unveiled not later than 2 December 1811, and the third the construction of five slaughterhouses, three on the Right and two on the Left Bank. Foundation stones of these abattoirs were to be laid on 14 June, the day of the unveiling of Desaix' statue. These slaughterhouses were put into use on 15 September 1818 but none survived more than a hundred years.

On the 13th Napoleon informed Montalivet of the recent decree to erect on the Pont de la Concorde several statues of generals, plans for a palace at Chaillot and finally the Archives. At his visit on the 15th he was shocked by the disorder prevailing among important documents, including those of the Vatican of vital interest. He made various suggestions as to where they could be more spaciously housed with a warning about fire risks, but he still toyed with the idea of transferring the Archives from the Hôtel de Soubise, which he would then fit up for a princely guest.

Napoleon had now reached the apogee of his dazzling career; almost the whole of Europe bowed beneath his sceptre and tomorrow he would be united in marriage to the daughter of the Caesars.

On 17 February he ordered a senatus consultum to ordain the inclusion of the Roman states in the French Empire and Rome itself to be its second city.

'The Prince Imperial will bear the title and receive the honours of King of Rome. After their coronation in the church of Notre Dame in Paris the Emperors will be crowned in the church of St Peter in Rome before the tenth year of their reign.'

The little Corsican gentleman of twenty years ago was slightly

[1] The original plan provided also for housing the ministries of police and of the kingdom of Italy. Marescalchi, who was in charge of both these departments, occupied the Hôtel de Langeac, built by Chalgrin at the corner of the Champs-Elysées and the Rue d'Angoulême (Rue La Boëtie). This became the Hôtel de Massa and was re-erected stone by stone in the gardens of the Observatory. The Société des Gens de Lettres occupied this new building now in the Faubourg St-Jacques.

intoxicated at the prospect of wedding, as his ultimate conquest, an Austrian archduchess, with the added glory of having by her successors to consolidate his dynasty and bring peace to Europe. Because of his predilection for grandeur, his dramatic sense and his organizing ability he took personal charge of the festivities for the great ceremony of his marriage.

On one of his visits of inspection to the Louvre, Denon, the curator, spoke to him of the difficulty of removing the large paintings from the gallery which was to be converted into a chapel for the wedding ceremony.

'Well, the only thing is to burn them,' was the Emperor's brisk answer, and Bausset, who tells this story, adds: 'This retort, made in a moment of bad-temper, so frightened M. Denon that all the difficulties vanished'—as can be imagined.

On 24 February Napoleon chose the household of the Empress to whom he sent a portrait of himself by Isabey. He had become something of a dandy. To please Marie-Louise and give her a favourable impression on her first contact with Paris he ordered from the painter, Victor Jean Nicolle, fifty aquatints of Paris scenes,[1] enclosed in a magnificent coffer for her marriage casket.

A police report is instructive about feeling in Paris:

[1] These scenes were as follows: (1) Place de la Concorde, (2) Place Vendôme, (3) Palace of the Louvre, (4) Gallery of the Louvre, (5) Place du Palais Royal, (6) Church of St-Roch, (7) the Pont Neuf, (8) Cornmarket, (9) Place de l'Hôtel de Ville, (10) Linen Market, (11) Porte St-Denis, (12) Fountain of the Innocents' Market, (13) Porte St-Martin, (14) Water-tower of the Samaritaine, (15) Water-tower near the Porte du Temple, (16) Place du Châtelet, (17) Churches of St-Louis and St-Paul, (18) Pont de la Cité, (19) Basilica of Notre Dame, (20) Hôtel-Dieu, (21) Poultry Market, (22) Hay port, (23) Hôtel Soubise (National Archives), (24) Observatory, (25) Church of St-Etienne-du-Mont, (26) Amphitheatre of the Botanical Gardens, (27) Hothouse of the Botanical Gardens, (28) Rag Market, (29) Church of Ste-Geneviève (Panthéon), (30) Church of the Sorbonne, (31) Place de la Sorbonne, (32) Church of St-Gervais, (33) Collège de France, (34) School of Medicine, (35) Théâtre Italien, (36) Baths of Julian, (37) Palace of the Senate (Luxembourg), (38) Fountain of the Luxembourg, (39) Theatre of the Empress (Odeon), (40) Palace of the Institute, (41) the Mint, (42) Fountain of the Rue de Grenelle, (43) Palace of the Legislature, (44) Monument to General Desaix, (45) Esplanade des Invalides, (46) Dome of the church of the Invalides, (47) Cours des Invalides, (48) Palace of Versailles, (49) Versailles, Grove of the Colonnade, (50) Versailles, view of the Orangery.
    The original of this album, bound in real morocco leather, decorated in fine gold, is a museum piece preserved at the château of Malmaison. Various reproductions have been issued with an introduction and notes by M. Pierre Shonner, Curator-in-Chief of the National Museums, and in charge of the museum at Malmaison (Editions Rombaldi, February 1961). One of these copies is in the Archives of the Municipal Council of Paris (office of the syndic).

'The old dynasty and the new share pride of place in conversations about the Emperor's marriage to an Austrian Archduchess. Political coteries think only of politics and intrigues while the populace of Paris worries only about the rise in food prices, although it is highly suspicious of an Austrian princess.'

That part of the Faubourg St-Germain which had not rallied to Napoleon hovered between consternation and recrimination. Former revolutionaries might momentarily think themselves endangered by the accession to the throne of a descendant of Louis XIV. Rumours were current of a revision of Louis XVI's trial and the deportation of regicides. Attempts were even made to

'sow distrust among workers and artists by allegations that strict inquiries were being made into the gossip of the sections. This agitation was, in fact, of short duration.'

The past was banished in favour of the present.

'Everyone shows great interest in the festivities for the Empress's entry into France and her journey through its main cities.'

Stocks continued to show an upward tendency; from 79·50 at the beginning of February they rose by the 28th to 82·70 frs.

A section of the report submitted by Frochot, Réal and Pasquier on 6 March, seeking official sanction for the loan to supply water in Paris, reads as follows:

'The revenues of the City of Paris are large, but so are its needs which have grown with the glory of the French name. Paris has not been able to keep pace with this rapid progress or, rather, the astonishing impetus which has raised France to the highest pinnacle of prosperity. Her buildings and monuments are still far from suggesting the grandeur and majesty of the first city in the world, in spite of her having made every effort consonant with her means. Recently the City was authorized to borrow the sums necessary for the early completion of improvements within her boundaries to benefit its large population. The loan of seven millions proposed today is for a purpose on a grander scale, but not less useful than the earlier loan; its object is to ensure that the citizens of Paris enjoy the advantages accruing from the distribution of the waters of the Ourcq canal.

'These works,' the report continued, 'are nearing the end. The water accumulated in a vast reservoir on the outskirts of Paris is to be available to the poorest lodging and, by its freshness and purity, wipe out disease in this populous city. Without a loan the work would take several more years. The Emperor's bounty has aided his good city of Paris but his benefactions are restricted by the wide area they must cover.'

The report ended by paying homage to Napoleon and his act of
making Paris take precedence over Rome.

On 12 March Napoleon approved an interest-free loan to the
municipal budget of 10,000,000 millions granted by the Canal Fund,
and authorized the city to create additional centimes as well as to
borrow a sum of seven millions at 8 per cent (specially allocated to
compensation for requisitions).

At 9 p.m. on 27 March Napoleon, who had left Paris on 20 March,
met Marie-Louise at Compiègne where they spent three days, then
left on the 30th with a brilliant suite for Paris. The civil marriage was
performed on Sunday, 1 April at 2 p.m. in the grand gallery at St-
Cloud by Cambacérès, assisted by Regnault de St-Jean d'Angély, in
the presence of members of the Imperial family and the Emperor's
household only. On 2 April the sovereigns made their 'public entry'
into Paris by the Porte du Bois de Boulogne, the Avenue de Neuilly
and the Champs-Elysées. No triumphal highway more spacious or
more fitting could be imagined, far superior to the tortuous streets of
the centre of Paris traversed at the coronation by the Imperial coach.
The Parisians seized every opportunity of gazing at the magnificent
procession as it passed down the Champs-Elysées, the route chosen
by the Emperor to dazzle the Empress with the capital's grandeur.
By 11 a.m. the crowd from the Tuileries to the Porte Maillot was so
thick that it was straining at the cordon of troops lining the streets,
along which twelve bands were playing. The Lancers of the Guard
opened the procession, followed by glittering military bands and the
Chasseurs and Dragoons of the Guard. After the mounted heralds
came the carriages and the cortège was closed by mounted Grenadiers
of the Guard and the élite constabulary.

The coronation coach, in which were seated Napoleon in state
costume and the young Empress glittering with jewels, halted
beneath an improvised Arc de Triomphe where they were received
by both Prefects and the civic authorities to the sound of 'salvoes of
artillery, bells and thousands of cheers of "Long live the Emperor!
Long live the Empress!" ' Fouché's reports indicate that the frenzied
cheers for the Imperial couple were directed principally at Napoleon
as Marie-Louise did not make a very good impression. Nevertheless,
according to a report of 3 April, the public saw her as 'a happy augury
for the Nation's hopes of an heir to Napoleon's throne'.

On arrival at the Tuileries the Emperor and Empress mounted the grand staircase to go in procession through the Galerie de Diane and a temporary building to the Museum where Fesch as Grand Almoner solemnized the marriage in the Salon Carré converted into a chapel.

It has been suggested that the decision not to hold the wedding in Notre Dame was due to mistrust of the Parisians, who were thus deprived of an opportunity of demonstrating their feelings in the wider area offered by the situation of the church, but in fact the processional route gave them plenty of scope for full expression of their rejoicing. The strained relations between the Pope and the Emperor may also have been a contributory factor in rejecting Notre Dame since the Court of Rome did not admit the validity of the annulment by the Paris clergy of Napoleon's marriage.

To please an impatient public Napoleon and Marie-Louise had to appear after the wedding ceremony on the balcony of the Salle des Maréchaux where they received a prolonged ovation. At this moment all the regiments of the Guard marched past, officers and men waving their caps and glittering plumes on their sabres, while the massed crowd tirelessly repeated their shouts of 'Long live the Emperor! Long live the Empress!' This was one of the highlights of the occasion.

Two hours after the procession had passed, fountains gushed wine in the Champs-Elysées, the Avenue des Princes and Cours la Reine. Foodstuffs were distributed from buffets in each arrondissement to winning tickets drawn the previous evening in a lottery—4,800 pâtés, 1,200 tongues, 3,000 sausages, 140 turkeys, 360 capons, 360 chickens, 1,000 legs and 1,000 shoulders of mutton.

At the Imperial banquet Metternich proposed his celebrated toast to 'The King of Rome' and the sovereigns had to make a second appearance on the balcony. A superb concert and firework display followed, set off by a signal from the Tuileries. Immediately the whole of Paris was illuminated, monuments, squares and avenues, as well as church spires. Fouché's bulletin, written the same evening, describes the general impression of the capital's inhabitants:

'All Paris is overflowing with admiration of the brilliant festivity which has just taken place . . .'

For nearly three months there was in Paris a round of fêtes, balls, fireworks and suppers, all splendid and glittering, taking place side by side with town-planning enterprises. Among them was a decree which finally resolved one of the problems connected with the Louvre; a transversal gallery was to be built. The first clause of this decree of 1 April read:

> 'The Galerie Napoléon and the transversal gallery, to be known as the Imperial Gallery, will be completely finished at the end of 1812.'

On 12 April Frochot gave a great banquet at the Hôtel de Ville to the mayors of all the good cities of the Empire who had been invited to the wedding. Specially noted among the decorations was a ship representing the city of Paris, triumphal columns linked by garlands of flowers and laurel and allegorical figures.

The Emperor and Empress returned to St-Cloud on 1 June from a state visit to the Belgian provinces and Holland begun on 27 April. Napoleon now dismissed Fouché who was appointed governor-general of Rome. Since Marie-Louise's arrival and the 'reaction' to his impulsive behaviour over the Walcheren landing he had become undesirable, particularly because of his guilt in opening direct negotiations with England. This Napoleon angrily learned from Louis when the Emperor forced him to abdicate from the Dutch throne. To succeed Fouché the Emperor next day appointed General Savary, Duc de Rovigo, a man of proven loyalty, decision, courage and in favour of using force. As the husband of an aristocratic relative of Josephine's he prided himself on his connection with the Faubourg St-Germain and showed great eagerness to rally to the Imperial régime the reluctant remnant of the nobility.

On Sunday, 10 June, the city entertained the Emperor and Empress, a festivity which repeated the features of their wedding day; plays, sports and various games, orchestral music, distribution of foodstuffs by lottery, fountains of wine, and so on. Once again the capital was illuminated, especially the Champs-Elysées and the quays from the Louvre to the Hôtel de Ville. Napoleon and Marie-Louise were welcomed on arrival by Frochot, the Corps of Mayors and twelve ladies appointed to wait on the Empress. They stayed until midnight when they left the Hôtel de Ville to the accompaniment of enthusiastic cheers. After their departure the ball continued.

On 12 June Napoleon took Marie-Louise to the Opéra which gave him a further opportunity of presenting his wife to the Parisians.

The splendid procession down the Champs-Elysées had necessitated a temporary construction of the Arc de l'Etoile which, in spite of its taste and ingenuity, underlined the need for the completion of the arch. Napoleon was better aware of this than anyone. On 15 June he sent Montalivet this memorandum:

> 'Let me have a report on the Arc de Triomphe and what funds have been allocated to it for this year; I want to finish it. If necessary, I will give you a supplementary credit from 5,000,000 to 6,000,000 francs.'

He wrote a second note on the 15th to Montalivet, with the provisioning of the capital in mind.

> 'Check carefully that my reserves in Paris are intact and keep an eye on them. . . . I have been sacrificing nearly a million for this reserve for eight years. . . . I shan't be happy about this important matter unless I am convinced that you are making it your special province to see that the provisioning of Paris is there. No action taken by a government can influence the people's happiness and the good functioning of the administration more than certainty of the existence of this reserve.'

Napoleon's Austrian marriage made him concentrate on the immediate building of a new palace, similar to the one to be built at Lyons on the heights of Ste-Foy. Fontaine had planned it for 'a lofty situation'. David had suggested to him that this site might be on top of a hill, 'like Chaillot for instance'. Napoleon looked up but said nothing; the idea soon took root in his mind.

> 'Paris was very gay,' wrote the Duchesse d'Abrantès, recalling this period of the year 1810. 'Everyone danced a lot . . . and the future seemed to be rosier than it had ever appeared before. Everyone therefore hoped for better times.'

Festivities had continued in Paris until the beginning of July, when the terrible fire took place at the Austrian Embassy at the Hôtel de Thélusson in the Rue de Provence in which Mme Schwarzenberg, wife of the Austrian Ambassador, lost her life; this fire was to be the cause of Dubois' dismissal.

Napoleon was now certain of Marie-Louise's pregnancy and that the child must be a boy with a brilliant future. Already a decree of February 1810 had hailed him as King of Rome. As Napoleon wanted his wife to rest and relax, most of their time was spent outside the city in various châteaux, but they made several visits to the theatre in Paris where Napoleon, whose popularity was enormous, was the object of special ovations.

In addition to his public appearances at the theatre, Napoleon liked to stroll with the Empress incognito in Paris in the evening. Las Cases relates that,

'on public holidays the Emperor liked occasionally to go out late at night to mingle with the crowd, see the illuminations and hear what people were saying. He would promenade with Marie-Louise on his arm and, on the boulevards, for a small sum they amused themselves at a magic lantern show of Their Majesties the Emperor and Empress of the French, all the court, and so on.'

Napoleon's obsessive desire to give Paris notable monuments and public utility works again led him to ply Montalivet with questions:

'Let me have a report on the Temple of Victory. Where did the first instalment of money come from and how is the work going? Let me also know what monies I allocated to the Arc de Triomphe, what has been done, the balance of funds left, and what could be spent this year if I made the necessary sums available. I am anxious that this monument should be finished with the shortest possible delay as it is interfering with one of the greatest avenues in Paris. Let me know what has been done and what could be done this year at the various slaughterhouses in Paris.'

The Emperor also kept an eye on the Louvre and the Tuileries where work was proceeding apace. Although he had not been in favour of the lateral gallery he asked Fontaine what the width of the rooms would be. Told that they would be 45 feet Napoleon retorted, 'Too narrow; the dimensions must be imposing. I want this building to be as remarkable in size and shape as the Temple of Minerva at Athens or the National Library in Vienna.'

As he spoke he went to a window with a view of the Pont des Arts which looked fragile to him. 'I admit that in England iron may be used for large arches because of the scarcity of stone, but in France where there is a plentitude of everything . . .'

Under supervision so constant and energetic other public works progressed. At the Pont Neuf the ground had been cleared for the erection of the obelisk. The façade of the Legislature already wore its modern appearance—thirty wide steps flanked by two allegorical figures of Minerva and Themis and four famous legislators, Michel de l'Hôpital, Sully, Colbert and d'Aguesseau. Behind them rose twelve Corinthian columns. The 'antique and majestic' design of the façade was impressive but the pediment, showing Napoleon at the head of his army, presenting to the Legislature the flags taken at Austerlitz, and the statues did not please the public. In particular they thought the Emperor was shown to disadvantage.

The outer walls of the Bourse were rising; the houses opposite and the old church of the Filles St-Thomas had been demolished. The Arc de Triomphe de l'Etoile was being decorated. Road-works were also proceeding satisfactorily opposite Val de Grâce and in the congested area of the City. At La Villette the water-tower to supply water to Mousseaux was being completed;[1] the ports of St Nicolas and La Rapée and the aqueducts were almost ready. To the north of Paris the cemeteries were being improved. The Pont d'Iéna was ready for its arches and the Quais Bonaparte and de la Cité were being extended.

As part of the traditional birthday celebrations of 15 August the Vendôme column and Desaix' statue on the Place des Victoires were unveiled and much admired by the crowds which passed by all day. On show at the Hôtel de Ville was the City's gift to Marie-Louise of a toilet-set in silver gilt encrusted with lapis lazuli. It included a table with an oval mirror wreathed in garlands, a footstool shaped like a basket of flowers and a cheval glass nine feet high, resting on two ships representing the arms of the City supported by dolphins.

A new Prefect and a new Archbishop of Paris

From 2 June Napoleon was in residence at St-Cloud where, on 13 September, he presided over an administrative council when the credits for 1811 were submitted to him. He complained to Montalivet about the defective state of the ledgers and advised early control of the city's affairs.

> 'It seems advisable that a man of taste and a good executive should relieve the Minister of the Interior of these details. For want of such a man a lot of money has been wasted. Much more was spent at St-Denis, for instance, than necessary and still more would have been spent if His Majesty had not inspected this enterprise.'

Napoleon's suggestion was for two Masters of Requests from the Council of State to assume responsibility, one for monuments, public

[1] Four underground branches would take water from this aqueduct to the lower parts of Paris, to the Tuileries, the Palais Royal and the Louvre; it was also to feed the fountains on the Right Bank of the Seine up to St-Denis and some on the other bank as well as the abattoir then being built near the Barrière de Rochechouart.

buildings and statues, and the other for roads and bridges being built in Paris.

A cautious reply was sent in reply to Montalivet's reminder about the plan for a road from the Louvre to the Faubourg St-Antoine:

> 'This great project must be decreed only when ready to be put in hand . . . it will probably cost over 20 millions which must be available when required. . . . When so much has been undertaken for giving Paris water, sewers, slaughterhouses and public granaries it is not the time to start so large an enterprise. . . .'

Napoleon, nevertheless, had great plans in mind for the future such as building the Hôtel de Ville, laying out the Place and Gare de la Bastille and forming an open space in front of the Louvre, but only when work in hand was finished.

The Emperor attached great importance to the building of a new city centre.

> 'Entertainment of the sovereign at the Hôtel de Ville is too popular a function for expense to be considered. He can go only to the Hôtel de Ville, the Senate or Guards' headquarters at the Ecole Militaire. For receptions of this kind wooden annexes are ruinous, hazardous and absurd.'

With so much work in progress, an accumulation of materials in the streets impeded traffic and spoilt the city's appearance. When the Grand Duke of Württemberg, who knew Paris well, was on a visit he replied to the Emperor's question as to what he thought of the city, 'I think it looks very well for a city taken by assault by the architects.'

Napoleon's reaction was lively and prompt. The Minister of the Interior was ordered to clear the streets by setting up special dumps for building materials.

The execution of this order no longer fell to Dubois as Prefect. Since Fouché's disgrace and his replacement by Savary Dubois' own position had become shaky, especially as he was held responsible for the disaster at the Austrian Ambassador's ball.

Napoleon relieved Dubois of his post on 14 October and appointed in his place Councillor Pasquier, a former member of Parliament and a man of energy and probity who enjoyed a great reputation in Paris. A simultaneous appointment was of a new Archbishop of Paris, necessitated by the death of Cardinal de Belloy. Fesch had refused the nomination as he preferred to continue as Primate of the Gauls. The Emperor decided to appoint Cardinal Maury, whose joviality made him a great favourite with the people.

On 12 November Napoleon proudly sent the President of the Senate a letter, officially informing him of the happy pregnancy of the Empress, news which spread like wildfire, stimulated business at the Bourse and a rise in stocks. The Emperor was able to assess the people's happiness when he returned on 16 November to Paris and paid several visits to the Museum, the Mint and other public institutions.

Napoleon was more than ever absorbed in his great plans for beautifying Paris, among them the building of a palace commensurate with his eminence.

'The idea of a palace on the heights of Chaillot,' writes Bausset, 'fermented in the Emperor's mind which had a natural bent towards everything great and beautiful. He talked about it often. . . .'

As Napoleon was also anxious to give Paris more gardens he gave orders on 29 November for a plan to improve the Bois de Boulogne by 'a pleasure-garden on the heights of Chaillot'. Bausset adds with a touch of humour that 'Napoleon went by byways to arrive at an idea suggested to him and which he had unconsciously adopted'.

A note written by Napoleon on 31 December shows his eagerness to increase the number of buildings along the Rue de Rivoli and encourage the owners. He asked for a plan to be worked out for a twenty-year tax exemption to indemnify housebuilders for the extra cost of preserving the plan of external arcades which would add to the beauty of the city. To get quick action a time-limit was set to this immunity.

A Palace on the Heights of Chaillot

'The period between the end of 1810 and the middle of 1812,' wrote Pasquier in his *Mémoires*, 'was the quietest we had known since the Consulate.' Absent were the 'formidable hazards' of a European campaign when the Empire's fate was at the mercy of a cannon ball. Napoleon spent most of a year and a half in France, ten months of the time in Paris, which enabled him to pay close attention to the affairs of his good city. His zeal was the greater because his son would soon be born on the capital's soil.

During January Napoleon presided over a number of councils devoted to civic works. At one was discussed the future of the Palais Royal, unoccupied since the abolition of the Tribunate. Napoleon readily fell in with the suggestion that it should be used for visiting monarchs because recent visits had made him realize that Paris was short of palaces, which brought the project for the Chaillot palace into greater favour. An overall estimate provided by Fontaine for the palace totalled over 51,000,000 francs, of which 20,000,000 would be the cost of the Palais de Chaillot.

Although Napoleon had decided on the Quartier St-Bernard for the Wine Market he now changed his mind and chose Bercy as it gave greater latitude to the trade and also an economy of several millions was made. He was still undecided where to house the Archives and asked Fontaine for a further report. Approval was given to a number of projects, but the proposals for the Ecole des Beaux Arts and the Hôtel de Ville were referred for further study. The plan for the Botanical Gardens also came under fire, and the Emperor asked for something comprehensive and imaginative. He fell in, however, with a new plan for raising revenue to build the slaughterhouses.

Many of the Emperor's suggestions for increasing revenue were ingenious. One was to raise the tax on property which had increased in value, another was the sale of the markets. His suggestions were the more valuable because the city's budget showed a deficit of over a million, incurred mainly by the charitable institutions and due, according to Napoleon, to bad administration. He decided that, in future, foundling infants should be maintained by the State.

To satisfy himself about its suitability Napoleon visited the Chaillot site on the morning of 23 January; he decided definitely that the palace should be built and called the Palace of the King of Rome. The choice of locale reflected the development in the Emperor's ideas about Paris. He foresaw that it would expand westwards away from the decrepit centre and, therefore, had already built the Pont d'Iéna. The gentle slopes of Chaillot, commanding the Champ de Mars, connected by the new bridge with the Seine and sparsely populated, offered an admirable site for the magnificent structure of his dreams. To fulfil his wishes and be associated with an exceptional building his architects had devised an ambitious edifice as large as Versailles, with a host of dependencies, rising above three rows of terraces with a massive colonnade. The Palace was to have a small park and be connected by a broad tree-lined avenue (the present Avenue Kléber) with the Arc de l'Etoile.

This digression about a building which never saw the light of day must not make us forget the Emperor's concern with what had been accomplished. He told Fontaine of his conception of the palace of the Legislature:

> 'It must be spacious, comfortable and magnificent, away from noise and hubbub, in fact completely isolated. It must have a spacious courtyard, wide and beautiful avenues, be imposing in its mass and majestic in its arrangements. It must have a temple where the deputies can pray to the Eternal, a large number of rooms for the various committees, offices, archives and a library, accommodation for the staff and private apartments for the guards, and president, the quaestors, secretaries and so on. In a word this palace should be worthy of a great nation and its fame should arouse the interest of strangers. The Hôtel des Invalides would fulfil all these conditions.'

The Emperor reiterated his poor impression of the new façade and inveighed against the architects, saying that 'their accounts are scrawls which they themselves do not understand'. Fontaine sprang to his colleagues' defence without upsetting the Emperor who was never irritated by the truth; he continued discussing at length 'calmly and without anger' the plan for the Louvre and the Tuileries and reverted to his original idea that he did not want anything built between them.

Finance was again discussed at a council on the 26th; Napoleon immediately thereafter dictated a note, underlining the advantage of redeeming the bridge tolls, which he regarded as an imposition in a city like Paris. He asked for some suggestions for the purchase by the city of these bridges.

It is a fact which gives much food for thought that the Emperor now told Fontaine that he had decided to abandon the plan for the Temple of Glory. In his diary Fontaine notes:

> 'The Temple of Glory on the site of the Madeleine has lost much of its charm. The Emperor regrets spending 16,000,000 to 18,000,000 for a purely idealistic monument. He has asked what might be done about it and thinks of installing an Appeal Tribunal, a Ministry or a Palace of Fine Arts in the building. In all this I see only alarming signs of indecision and changeability.'

I myself see the mark of a realistic genius whose plans were always adapted to circumstances.

Napoleon's personal visits to sites and observation of progress made were largely responsible for his knowledge and preoccupation with detail. At this time he paid many visits in the capital, to the Printing Press, the Archives, the Cornmarket and other markets. The story goes that he climbed up to the dome of the Cornmarket and pointed to the site he wanted for the new Central Markets which were then inconvenient and inadequate.

Both the Central Markets and the Cornmarket were under consideration at a council of the Highways Department held on 9 February. Napoleon's recent visit led him to declare that the site proposed was too 'circumscribed' and to ask for a plan for the Central Markets on a scale proportionate to the capital's premier market. Frochot submitted various plans for an extension, particularly one to open the Halles from the Place des Innocents to the dome of the Cornmarket. This plan Napoleon adopted and instructed Montalivet to prepare a decree. (The plan was picked up by Baltard and approved in 1851 by the Municipal Council of Paris and Napoleon III, but it retained none of Napoleon's decorative ideas, gushing fountains, belfries, a lighthouse 'and other embellishments suitable for the capital of the French Empire'.) The Emperor ordered the necessary demolitions to be carried out in the course of the year. Two million francs were allocated from the 1811 credits for the estimated total of 6,000,000 francs.

Napoleon sent a long memorandum to his Minister of the Interior, informing him that, by means of a repayment he had ordered, the City of Paris would be liable only for seven out of the eight millions borrowed; he continued:

'The sale of the markets to the hospices will make seven millions available. I don't think this sum should be used to repay the loan since the City can make this repayment from its annual revenues, but this seven millions can be used for an extension of the market to enlarge the Central Markets from the Innocents to the dome of the Cornmarket.'

He showed the great importance he attached to this operation by declaring,

'The City of Paris can very well afford to make some sacrifice of its revenues for a few years for such important advantages, for which I realized the need and which, ever since I have known anything about it, I have considered to be vital to the city's interests. . . . I am especially interested in this scheme because it concerns the people's convenience as well as the health and beauty of the city.'

Always eager for prompt action Napoleon gave peremptory orders for a start to be made on the market as early as possible. He concluded by summing up his great visions of civic undertakings in Paris:

'For me the four most important projects for the City of Paris are the waters of the Ourcq, the new buildings for the Central Markets, the slaughterhouses and the Wine Market.'

The direction Napoleon's ideas was taking is proof that he was tired of glory and turning increasingly towards works of public utility for the people's welfare. Monuments dedicated to glory must now give way to markets, slaughterhouses and the Central Markets.

Two new decrees of 24 February provided that the Central Markets should occupy 'the whole site of the present market from the Marché des Innocents to the Flour Market', and for the Bastille elephant to be cast in bronze melted down from the guns taken at the battle of Friedland. In the meantime a temporary wooden model, covered in plaster coloured to represent bronze, should be erected. Thus winter ended on a workaday note.

VI

King of Rome and Child of Paris

---

20 *March* 1811, *in Paris*

'Today, 20 March, at 9.20 a.m. the hopes of France were realized. Her Majesty the Empress was happily delivered of a prince. The King of Rome and his august mother are in excellent health.'

Thus the *Moniteur* announced the birth of the Emperor's child. Salvoes of artillery were fired from the Invalides and the château of Vincennes.

'Napoleon, knowing how impatiently the French people were awaiting the moment to share his rejoicing, had ordered the firing of a salute of 101 guns.'[1]

As soon as the salvoes began the Parisians counted the shots with breathless interest. The effect of the decisive shot was indescribable.

'One single cry, one alone,' relates the *Gazette de France*, 'rose in Paris and made the walls tremble of that old palace where the hero's son had just been born and round which the crowd was so thick that there was no room even for a fly. And flags waved in the air, handkerchiefs fluttered— people ran hither and thither, embraced one another—announced the news with laughter and yet with tears, but the tears were of joy. . . .'

About 10 a.m. Madame Blanchard, the famous aeronaut, rose in a balloon from the Ecole Militaire to spread the good tidings in the towns and villages over which she sailed.

This was assuredly a day of rejoicing for Napoleon and for Paris. All the court went to the Tuileries and by midday the Cour du Carrousel was full of people. The windows of the château shook with the sound of the people's cheers. As the Emperor, deeply moved, watched the delirious crowd he wept silently, but he was all happiness

[1] The royal tradition was that the birth of a princess was announced by a salute of 21 guns and that of a prince by 101 guns. The 22nd shot signalled the birth of a prince.

when, after the child's birth had been registered, he took the baby
king in his arms and proudly showed him to the brilliant assemblage
of courtiers in the neighbouring rooms, then to the troops and the
crowd massed in the courtyard and on the Carrousel. Enthusiasm
became delirium when the troops marched past the Emperor. The
King of Rome, followed by the Colonel General of the Guard on duty,
and preceded by the officers of his household, was carried to his
apartments by the Comtesse de Montesquiou, governor of the
Children of France, and laid in the cradle presented by the City of
Paris.

Napoleon sent two pages, one to the Senate and the other to the
Corps of Mayors, to inform them of the happy birth of the King of
Rome. He then received the congratulations of the Princes, the
princely grand dignitaries, the ministers, the grand officers of the
Crown and of the Empire. Frochot and Pasquier told the Emperor
that 'the happiness they felt was shared by the inhabitants of the city
of Paris'.

The child was baptized with great ceremony at 9 p.m. in the
Tuileries chapel while the whole city gave itself over to rejoicing, a
happiness only temporarily reflected in the price of stocks. A police
bulletin reports that business did not improve and shares were
weakening daily. The causes of this depression were many—the
stagnation of business and the scarcity of money, the Roman question
and rumours of war with Russia. How heavy were Napoleon's cares
can easily be imagined. Although he longed passionately for peace
perhaps he felt that a new campaign was imminent.

'It seems,' wrote Bainville, 'that he no longer dared leave France,
scarcely dared leave Paris, as if he feared a recall by bad news.'

For a few more months the Emperor remained in his good city
where his presence was essential to consolidate the great empire he
was desirous of leaving to his son. If he allowed himself to be shaken
it was only momentarily and the inspiring prospect quickly restored
his equilibrium. He continued to believe in the protection of his star
which always led him to final victory; he was still the idol of the
people and the army.

On the afternoon of the 22nd a crowd of charcoal-burners and
market-porters of Paris marched into the Tuileries, headed by a band
carrying bouquets of flowers and uttering vivats and shouts of

rejoicing. Napoleon received a deputation from these good folk in the Galerie de Diane and graciously accepted the complimentary address spoken by the leader of their association. As for the young men, they continued to report enthusiastically for military service.

'The conscipts of the 2nd arrondissement,' says a police bulletin, 'drew lots on the 26th calmly and gaily. They then traversed the city with drums, shouting, "Long live the Emperor!" '

Napoleon's happiness at his son's birth made him impatient to see the Palace of Rome begun. On 12 April he went to the salon in the Pavillon de l'Horloge where the relief model of this palace was exhibited, made to Fontaine's design by the famous cabinet-maker, Jacob, attached to the Louvre. The Emperor did not find it satisfactory and made some criticisms. On his return to the Tuileries, while he was having lunch, he sent for Fontaine, whom he asked, 'Is there anything remaining in Rome of the homes of the Roman emperors? What is the most beautiful palace known?'

Obviously he was seeking great models for a palace to be greater than any yet built.

After a few minutes' silence he informed Fontaine of the poor impression made on him by his visit to the Ministry of External Relations on the Quai Bonaparte. As he rose from table to go to his study the Emperor, says Bausset, wanted to know the cost of a summer-house and its dependencies to be built in the Tuileries gardens at the end of the terrace beside the river, where he might sometimes take his midday meal. Clearly he was thinking of the leisure moments he would like to spend with his wife and son.

'Well, Sire,' answered Fontaine, 'it would cost about 500,000 francs.'

'Half a million francs!' exclaimed Napoleon. 'Twenty thousand is what I can spend and not a penny more. Architects ruined Louis XIV.'

On 13 April Napoleon wrote to Montalivet:

'I have chosen 9 June for the baptism of the King of Rome in the metropolitan church of Paris. . . . After the ceremony I shall dine at the Hôtel de Ville of my good city of Paris and I will witness a firework display. It is my wish that you should summon the mayors of the good cities to the baptism of the King of Rome.'

Thus, this ceremony was to put the seal on Paris as the supreme

capital of Europe in the presence of representatives of Italy, Germany
and Holland, with the mayors of Rome, Alexandria, Hamburg and
Amsterdam ranged alongside Frochot. Rome, the eternal city, would
be the fief of the Emperor's son whose throne was in Paris.

The conflict between Napoleon and Pius VII was further embittered
by the bestowal on his heir of the title of King of Rome. Many
bishoprics were vacant and Cardinal Maury, the Archbishop of Paris,
indicated his intention to make his own authority felt. The whole
clerical situation was considered by the Emperor to be contrary to
the conditions of the Concordat and he gave notice that a National
Synod would be held in Paris in June.

The reverse of the medal

The elaborate ceremonies planned for the baptism contrasted sharply
with the sluggishness of business. The blockade was responsible for
some unemployment, mainly in the luxury trades, which received
little stimulus from the end-of-year festivities or the birth of the
King of Rome. Only cloth- and cotton-mills and button-factories
prospered. The number of unemployed workers in Paris at the beginning of 1811 was 7,200, a high percentage of the total of 80,000
workers. Napoleon coped promptly and energetically with the
situation and waged a real war against unemployment.

On 2 May he wrote to Lacuée, Director of War Administration:

'Many hat- and cap-makers, shoemakers, tailors and saddlers in Paris
are lacking work. It is my wish that you take steps to see that 500 pairs
of shoes are made daily but only if you employ a thousand shoemakers and
do not take shoes ready-made; this will make 15,000 pairs of shoes a
month. . . .
'I should like 250 shakoes, about 30 saddles and various articles of clothing made daily with the proviso that new workers are constantly
employed. . . .'

A similar instruction was sent to Duroc on the 7th:

'There is a shortage of work in the Faubourg St-Antoine. I wish them to
have work, especially in this month before the festivities. You must go to
Paris to see the people in my furniture repository and my architect,
Fontaine, and commissions must be put in hand so that during May and
June the two thousand unemployed workers in the Faubourg St-Antoine
who make chairs, tables, commodes and armchairs should be given work
immediately. . . . Make your plans by tomorrow for an immediate start.

. . . Get together with Fontaine so that from tomorrow you can set up workshops at the Louvre and employ as many workers as possible on demolitions to give work to those without it. . . .'

Work began on the same day, the 7th, on excavations at the Palace of Rome.

Meanwhile the Emperor's attention was also given to the poor. On 8 May he sent these instructions to Montalivet:

'It is my wish that, during the months of May and June, the charitable committees should double their aid from tomorrow, the 9th, and that it should be tripled, if necessary, in the Faubourgs St-Antoine and St-Marcel. . . . I am putting at your disposal for this purpose 300,000 francs to be distributed to the charitable committees in Paris. . . . For Paris order a large increase in the yards at the St-Maur canal; in a few days' time 2,000 to 3,000 men can be employed there. Finally, take steps to see that, under no pretext whatsoever, the police find any worker who can't be sent to some workshop. Instruct the Prefect of Police about it all. . . .'

While Pasquier was busily engaged in carrying out the Imperial instructions the prefectoral administration continued with its civic tasks. Among decisions taken at this time was the decree of 10 May 1811, which came into force on 20 June, whereby for the old divisions of Paris were substituted the districts which are the present parliamentary boroughs.

On the 24th a decree was issued, ordering the building of a hospital at St-Lazare of twelve hundred beds, the foundation stone to be laid on the day of the baptism.

From Notre Dame to the Hôtel de Ville

On Sunday, 9 June, a day of brilliant sunshine, Napoleon received the Diplomatic Corps in solemn audience to a background noise of gun salutes and the ringing of all the city's church bells. At 11 a.m. twelve poor girls, dowered by the city of Paris, were married to soldiers with Imperial rites. By noon the crowd was massed behind a strong line of troops in streets from the Tuileries to Notre Dame decorated with handsome draperies, garlands of flowers and greenery.

At 4 p.m. the Senate set off from the Luxembourg and the Council of State from the Tuileries, followed by the great State bodies and finally the Corps of Mayors, accompanied by the mayors and their deputies of the forty-nine good cities invited to the fête at the Hôtel de Ville. At 5.30 p.m., as the guns boomed, the bells announced that the Emperor, the Empress and the King of Rome were leaving the Tuileries.

The procession reached the boulevard about 6 p.m. As it was due at 2 p.m. the large crowd had been obliged to wait for nearly four hours so that it was naturally tired and impatient, particularly as the usual dinner hour was between 5 p.m. and 6 p.m., but all the weariness and impatience were forgotten when the splendid procession passed.

Napoleon in state dress of purple and gold and Marie-Louise in satin, with a diadem of diamonds, were in the coronation coach. The King of Rome, his white robe slashed by the broad red ribbon of the Legion of Honour, made to his measure, was in the arms of Mme de Montesquiou in the Empress's carriage, drawn by eight horses and escorted by pages.

'For the first time people gazed on the august child whose royal name was about to be hallowed by the church. . . . The sight of him produced an indescribable effect. "Vive le Roi de Rome!" was the continuous cry which followed him along his whole course.'

In front of the main entrance to the church a portico, in the form of a tent, had been erected, supported by columns and decorated with garlands and draperies. The interior of the basilica was richly ornamented. When the Imperial cortège arrived towards 7 p.m. Napoleon and Marie-Louise were received by Fesch, who offered them holy water. After the baptism Mme de Montesquiou handed the King of Rome to the Empress, who showed him to the crowd as cheers of 'Long live the King of Rome!' burst out. Then the Emperor took the child in his arms and with deep emotion, which 'filled every heart to overflowing with enthusiasm', lifted him up. A German eye-witness speaks of a former count and émigré who was moved to tears and exclaimed, 'Who can resist this nonpareil? He has even won me over; he has restored my country to me . . . and I am a Frenchman once again.'

From the cathedral the Emperor and Empress proceeded to the Hôtel de Ville where, because of an accident to their carriage, they did not arrive until 9.30 p.m. Frochot, the Corps of Mayors and the twelve ladies appointed to wait on the Empress met them at the foot of the Grand Staircase. The Prefect made a speech pledging anew the city's respectful homage. Then the Emperor received all the Departmental and civic dignitaries in turn, the mayors and their deputies, the members of the Municipal Council and representatives of the Chamber of Commerce. A banquet followed at which Napoleon and Marie-Louise, wearing their crowns like the holy Roman Emperors, dined under two canopies at a table gorgeously laid on a special dais. The Salle St-Jean was decorated with the arms of the forty-nine good cities, headed by Paris, Rome and Amsterdam, with the remainder in alphabetical order. During the banquet representatives of the Parisian bourgeoisie filed past the dais, bowing as they went.

All the guests gathered for a concert in the throne-room where, after the banquet, Napoleon and Marie-Louise took their places. Napoleon strolled through the room, speaking to many of the assembly with 'touching cordiality'. Before they left the Hôtel de Ville towards 11 p.m. the Emperor and Empress walked out into the artificial garden made above the courtyard of the Hôtel de Ville on the same level as the throne-room. This garden was bright with the play of coloured lights and the jets of the 'fountain of the Tiber'.

A Synod in Paris

At the opening session of the Legislature at noon on 16 June Napoleon made a confident and arrogant speech which, nevertheless, betrayed some of his grave anxieties; the Spanish war, the Roman affair and the struggle with England. His opening sentences were designed to show that his son had been born to a great and peaceful future, but in fact he knew that, although his prestige was inviolate, Paris and the nation as a whole were afraid of war.

'The peace made with the Emperor of Austria,' he declared, 'has since been cemented by the happy alliance I contracted. The birth of the King of Rome has realized all my hopes and ensured my people's future.'

With some irritation he turned to the religious question which had its repercussions on internal tranquillity and reiterated his wish to see the Holy See established in Paris.

Next day the National Synod opened with the gathering at Notre Dame of ninety-seven prelates from France, Germany and Italy, a sight not to be missed by the Parisians but also an indication of their interest in religious matters. The Synod's first meeting ended in an atmosphere unfavourable to Napoleon; its main events were Fesch's election to the presidency, the speech of 'ultramontane' tendencies made by the Bishop of Troyes, and the swearing of a unanimous oath of loyalty to the Pope by the assembled prelates who, although asserting their devotion to the Emperor and their recognition of the Synod's authority, gave clear proof of their attachment to the Sovereign Pontiff.

At the final session of the Synod the suggestion of going in a body to St-Cloud to demand Pope Pius VII's liberation was unanimously approved. Napoleon's alarm at the publicity given to these discussions is evident from the categorical instructions sent to his Minister of Religions on 20 June.

'. . . Let nothing be printed without my approval and make certain that no stranger or suspicious person attends this meeting.'

Nevertheless, the public always knew what was being said at the Synod. 'It seemed, in fact,' writes Madelin, 'as if a new wind was blowing in Paris.'

Although Napoleon was affronted by this opposition to his religious policy, he could not refrain from admiring the courage shown by the clergy. An echo is heard in the *Mémorial de Ste-Hélène:*

'The determination and resistance shown by the Synod,' writes Las Cases, 'pleased the Emperor; only the spirit of opposition could lend dignity to gatherings so out of tune with the spirit of the age.'

On 11 July from Trianon,[1] where he had arrived the previous evening, Napoleon dissolved the Synod and ordered the bishops of Tournai, Ghent and Troyes to be imprisoned, decisions which darkened the atmosphere in Paris with unfortunate effects on the people, but Napoleon had had enough. He had a decree drafted that, as provided by the Concordat, he would make appointments to all the episcopal sees vacant and that the nominees should be canonically invested by the Pope within six months. Should he fail to do so the bishops would be installed. The Synod refused to commit itself without Papal approval but Napoleon could not wait. On 5 August he had his decree approved by a general congregation. Although it was accepted by the majority of the Paris chapter, a great uneasiness

[1] The Emperor made a second stay here until 22 July when he decided to restore Trianon and arrange its reception rooms to suit himself.

prevailed and thenceforward a number of clergy began to dissociate themselves from the Emperor and his government.

The great public works

Montalivet had presented his report on the state of the Empire on 29 June, with the usual special references to public works in Paris, which were proceeding satisfactorily. Out of a total sum of 138,141,727 francs devoted to public works those in Paris accounted for 22,621,785 francs and the estimate for 1811 was in roughly the same proportion.

Napoleon sent Montalivet a memorandum about public works in Paris on 5 August from St-Cloud to which he had returned from Trianon. He complained at the slight progress with the slaughter-houses and that the allocated credits had not been used.

'Only 200 workers are employed at the Montmartre abattoir; out of the 1,000,000 francs I allocated by 1 August only 50,000 francs has been spent. All this delay in getting work started means that what should have been done last year will only be done this.'

He made a similar complaint about the public granaries, the Bourse, the dome of the Cornmarket and the Panthéon. On the 9th he returned to the charge, this time censuring delays at the markets although, in fact, work was progressing here and on the aqueducts and quays. A new quay, the Quai Montebello, was ordered. Finishing touches were being put to works at the Louvre and adjustments made to the Palais de Justice. The Invalides dome was to be re-gilded 'as in the reign of the Great King' for which the scaffolding had already been erected. As well as restoring Mansart's masterpiece the huge open space in front of the Invalides, as yet undeveloped, was to be partially turfed and surrounded by ornamental fountains.

Since 7 May a substantial number of workers were busy excavating and clearing land for the foundations of the Palace of the King of Rome at Chaillot. A sum of about 2,000,000 francs had been set aside for the purchase of land from the private owners who were dispossessed. Because of his liberal ideas and desire to deal justly, Napoleon had voluntarily refused to resort to compulsion; he wanted these purchases to be made amicably. When he was told that a couple named Gaignin refused to sell their little house on the Chaillot hill, say Percier and Fontaine, he ordered that their refusal be respected, saying not without pride, 'Thanks to our laws everyone knows that in France the least landlord is more master in his own home than I.'

His order was carried out; the Gaignin house remained standing alone in the demolition area.

St-Napoleon's day and the Emperor's birthday were celebrated with the usual dignified ceremonies. The special inaugurations were the laying of foundation stones at the Wine Market, a new market at St-Martin's abbey and the water-tower on the Boulevard de Bondy. As the civic procession moved from one inaugural ceremony to another the public made the welkin ring with their cheers.

The Minister of the Interior and the Corps of Mayors then proceeded to the Tuileries to be received in solemn audience by the Emperor. After the Te Deum, jousting on the Seine, various sports and games and the usual illuminations, a concert was given at 8 p.m. on the palace terrace. Napoleon and Marie-Louise appeared on the balcony to 'show themselves to a huge crowd of people who cheered them to the echo'. At 9 p.m. a splendid display of fireworks was let off in the Place de la Concorde. As the Parisians strolled about, danced and amused themselves until late in the night they momentarily forgot their troubles.

VII

The Battle for Wheat

Bread for the Parisians

Although at his birthday reception Napoleon was all smiles it was obvious that he was gravely preoccupied; clearly this was due to the increasingly disturbing attitude of Russia, and he made a violent attack on the Russian ambassador, Prince Kourakine.

A serious internal problem had developed at the same time. In Paris the bread situation 'was daily deteriorating'; bad weather had ruined the prospects for an excellent harvest. As Napoleon attached supreme importance to the feeding of the capital he reacted energetically. As his own youth had been poor and troubled he felt an affinity with the working classes, whom he held in some affection, but he was fully aware that shortages often lead to mass revolt. Economical as he was, it irked him, in spite of his sympathies with the Parisians, that whatever their income, they absolutely refused to eat any bread but the whitest and freshest.

Although it was his birthday, the Emperor called an administrative provision council for 3 p.m. He listened, grave and anxious, to the Minister of the Interior, who affirmed that the harvest was going to be excellent, an opinion in which the others present concurred. The Emperor intervened abruptly, 'And I, gentlemen, tell you that the harvest will be bad. This is a serious matter as you all know how vital it is for the peace of mind of France, and especially of Paris, that bread supplies should be safeguarded. . . . I have seen ten riots which would not have taken place if the people had had anything to eat. This situation must be tackled urgently.'

While he was determining what should be done Napoleon initiated new enterprises in Paris. One, to build barracks round the Champ de Mars, led to the mad rumour that he was going to build a fortress on the top of the hill of Chaillot where, in case of a rebellion, he could

shut himself up and train his guns on the city. He gave up the project
of building barracks, however, when Fontaine told him that the cost
would be enormous and would spoil the appearance of the Champ de
Mars.

A decree of 26 August did prescribe the building of the General
Post Office in the Rue de Rivoli, thus adding to its imposing
buildings.

Before leaving Trianon for Compiègne, where he stayed until
18 September, Napoleon on 28 August ordered a complete overhaul
of the provision services and the setting up of a provision council
under the chairmanship of the Minister of the Interior in the event of
his own absence. He also ordered that food stocks in Paris, which
had fallen to a third of the prescribed amount, should be built up
again as a matter of urgency. The new council was to meet twice a
week.

Napoleon himself presided on 9 September, when he ordered that
enough wheat should be purchased to make distribution in Paris
normal.

At the end of the meeting Montalivet concluded his report by
assuring the Emperor that he need have no further worries.

'Bread will be dear but it will be available.'

'What does that mean, gentlemen?' Napoleon retorted. 'Bread
will be dear but it will be available?' And about whom do you think
we have been agitating for the last two months? The rich? That's not
very likely. What do I care, sir, whether you do or do not have
bread? With money it can be found, just as everything in this world
is found with money. What I want, sir, is that the people should have
bread, should have a lot of it, good and cheap, and that a man will be
able to feed his family out of his daily wage.'

His tone became more and more emphatic and finally reached a
pitch of violence, but he finally added with greater calm, 'Gentlemen,
when I am far away from France, remember that the first duty of the
government that I shall leave behind is to ensure public tranquillity
and welfare and that food, especially the people's food, is at the
heart of this tranquillity.'

Permission was refused on the 16th to the bakers' syndics to
increase bread prices above 14 sous.

On the 17th the Emperor and Empress left at 3.30 a.m. for Belgium
and Holland and were away for two months. Naturally Napoleon

kept in touch with the situation during his absence and made several personal interventions but, after his departure, bread became scarce and there were signs of panic. Nevertheless, the Emperor refused to increase prices which would be burdensome for the people. He did, however, agree to a temporary premium to bakers of five francs per sack of flour which would obviate a rise in price and tide matters over until the new wheat came on the market at the end of November.

This generous gesture, however, had little effect as people continued to buy large quantities of bread in the morning so that by evening the shops were empty. Bakers went on demanding a rise in prices; bread substitutes, particularly rice and vegetables, were rising in price. In spite of Pasquier's urging the bakers to keep their shops stocked 'in gratitude for the Emperor's goodness', they continued to ask for price increases.

From Wesel on 1 November Napoleon sent fresh instructions to Montalivet, but Pasquier and Savary began to feel that the situation was getting out of hand in spite of a further allocation by the Emperor of two millions for premiums. Napoleon dealt with their alarmist reports from Düsseldorf on 3 November. He wrote to Savary,

'You are children in Paris. Fear makes you lose your heads; fear serves no purpose. What will happen when bread costs 18 sous, when the bakers have used up their stocks and only 2,000 to 3,000 sacks of flour remain in the reserve and 800 or 900 in the Central Markets? I think a simple premium solves the problem and this premium the Provision Council has power to continue. The whole matter reduces itself to waiting five or six days for my orders. Therefore there is no need either to fear a crisis or to be afraid.'

Nevertheless Napoleon was obliged to consent to a rise in price to 15 sous. Bread, which was of poorer quality than before, was put on sale at this figure on 7 November. Stocks were withdrawn from the reserve and sales held at the Central Markets to help the bakers, but prices continued high.

Bread and games

When Napoleon returned to St-Cloud on 11 November at 6 a.m. he found a fresh problem awaiting him. This concerned the capital's fourteen gaming-houses, at the Palais Royal, in the faubourgs, the markets and the squares. He had tried several times to suppress them but finally tolerated their existence because of the large sums of money they produced for the city's budget, although Frochot had pointed out the evil consequences of gambling, 'business quarrels, bankruptcies, failures, theft, forgery, domestic discord, poverty and suicide.'

Napoleon's disgust at the immorality of gambling was tempered by his belief that in Paris it was an inevitable evil and he was concerned mainly with its financial aspect; he felt that the profits might be turned to good account, either for stocking reserves of wheat or for the benefit of hospitals.

The Emperor ordered inquiries to be made about the possibility of instituting a company to control gambling establishments for these purposes but insisted that inquiries be made with the greatest discretion and not by the official police services which he had good cause to suspect. In addition he appointed a commission to investigate the facts and give a definite ruling on two points: (1) Is it proper to allow gaming in Paris, or should it be prohibited and Paris put on the same footing as other French cities? (2) Have the steps taken elsewhere to suppress gaming been successful?

Although Pasquier, with unanimous support, opted for total suppression this was too sweeping to be possible. Three of the most dangerous houses were closed but Pasquier wrote in his Memoirs:

> 'I have no doubt that Napoleon's first reaction was to agree to total suppression, but he changed his mind because he was loath to lose substantial revenue.'

An important decree of 15 November 1811 concerned the organization of the Imperial university with a professorial body under a sole chief, acting independently of the administration. Four new lycées were set up.

Napoleon wants Paris to be gay

Napoleon and Marie-Louise with the King of Rome returned to the Tuileries from their last triumphal journey on the eve of the celebrations of Austerlitz and the coronation; the great Imperial traditions remained unshakeable. Together the Emperor and Empress paid various visits in the city, among them a visit to the catacombs of

Ste-Geneviève, where Napoleon read the inscriptions on the tombs with curiosity. He also inspected a four-hour parade of troops.

The Parisians were truly delighted to have the Imperial family with them again; since the birth of his son their devotion to the Emperor seemed to have increased. At the upper end of the social scale there were signs of fatigue and even of anxiety, not only in the salons which had been stifled and in the traditional centres of opposition, but also among the Marshals and senators. Although not yet apparent, the malaise was latent in the highest ranks and Talleyrand[1] and Fouché were discreetly emerging from the shadows of their disgrace to prepare their return to power and their ultimate revenge.

The words 'rumours of war with Russia' constantly recur in the police reports for the end of the year 1811. Times were bad. Of this the Emperor was aware but, in the war now inevitable, he knew he had a formidable hand to play and to win and he was uplifted by excitement. His activity during the four months he spent in Paris was tireless; daily he presided over councils, dictated memoranda, reviewed troops and gave audiences. His battle for the Parisians' bread was, unlike his usual campaigns, patient and prolonged but he was again obliged to acquiesce in a further price rise of a sou. His main preoccupation, however, was his military preparations. On the 15th he arranged for a levy of conscripts and on the 19th asked his librarian for 'some good books in which to study Russian topography'; he intended to prepare his planned expedition with the greatest care.

After a very gay New Year's Day Napoleon, bent as always on encouraging industry, visited Delessert's sugar-beet factory in Paris. He was so pleased with what he saw that he made Delessert the immediate award of the Legion of Honour and bestowed a week's wages on the cheering workpeople. Extraction of sugar from beet was a triumph for the Emperor's economic policy and, by striking a blow at English commerce, one of the beneficial consequences of the blockade.

To help solve the bakers' difficulties which, in spite of price rises, continued to increase, Napoleon decided on 10 January to set up a ministry of commerce and manufactures. Once again, at the insistence of the Provision Council, he was obliged to authorize an increase in the price of bread to 17 sous on 15 January.

[1] Talleyrand gave back the Hôtel Matignon in which he had been living since 1808 to the Emperor and on 11 December 1811 went to live in the Rue St-Florentin.

On 2 February from the Tuileries Napoleon issued the historic decree which gave the Parisians a free water supply, an appreciable benefit which compensated for the difficulties of food supply. Next day there was a meeting of an administrative council, devoted solely to food, which had not taken place for several months. Napoleon was in favour of controlling the price of cereals and instituting a general tax on grains but, in face of the unanimous opposition of the Council, he deferred a final decision and contented himself with temporary palliatives.

At an administrative council of the Highways Department also held on the same day to deal with public works in the city of Paris eleven questions were considered:

—Ceding the Temple of Glory to the Catholic religion.
—Purchase of several houses in the Rue du Pont de Lodi to round off the Poultry Market.
—Setting up factories and warehouses at St-Maur to improve food supply for the city of Paris.
—Restoration of the Palais du Temple to house the Ministry of Religions.
—Work at the Legislature.
—Siting of the Palace of the University, the Ecole Normale and houses for emeritus professors. (The Emperor asked that Fontaine be consulted to see whether the Palais Cardinal might not be suitable for the Grand Master of the University.)
—Arrangements of the monuments in the church of St-Denis.
—Suppression of the Hôtel Dieu necessitated by the building of the quay and construction of a hospital for incurables and convalescents.
—Siting of the Ecole des Beaux Arts. (Napoleon suggested the Rue de Rivoli.)
—Opening of a new credit of 300,000 francs to pay for buildings completed or to be erected and to house the Imperial Printing Press.
—Purchase of the Parent house in the Rue de Rivoli to extend the site intended for the building of the Hôtel des Postes.

In spite of all Napoleon's endeavours to maintain Parisian morale, the difficulties of the food situation and the rise in prices, coupled with rumours of war with Russia, were beginning to cause depression. Napoleon knew war to be inevitable; he had already raised 100,000 conscripts and ordered a first movement of troops through Germany towards the Vistula. These movements, however, he wanted to keep secret as he was still negotiating with the Czar and was not without hope of a new Tilsit.

Knowing the Parisians' fondness for spectacles and amusements and their predilection for glory, and perhaps to ward off the gathering clouds, he cloaked under balls and entertainments 'his silent preparations for the most formidable expedition ever undertaken', as Queen Hortense wrote. 'Never was carnival so brilliant as in the winter of 1812.'

Dress and masked balls, quadrilles danced by the most beautiful women in Paris, including a great masked ball attended by the Emperor and Empress, helped to make the Imperial court supreme in luxury and magnificence, but Napoleon was as closely concerned with the welfare of his people as with instigating brilliant entertainments.

On 8 February he wrote to his ministers:

'We must extricate ourselves from this vicious circle. If the distribution of 30,000 pounds of bread and 30,000 cheap soups I ordered for the poor is insufficient I will increase the amounts. As the needs of the poorest will have been taken care of, on Tuesday I shall increase the price of bread to 18 sous and reserve flour to 85 francs. The millers have to sell their flour and we need not panic as large quantities of wheat are on the way.'

Other Parisian business did not escape the Emperor. When, on 10 February, he presided over an administrative council dealing with Paris, the municipal budget presented to him showed a deficit in the neighbourhood of five million francs. The Municipal Council had decided that no reduction could be made in the cost of public works in full activity. Economies could be made only in the hospices, the military guard, the prefecture of police or the lycées. The Council asked once again that the costs of these latter enterprises should be divided between the Treasury and the City. The remedy was to be found only in 'the sovereign's munificence'.

Napoleon ordered the budget to be reconsidered. As one of the chief reasons for the deficit was the building of new lycées and the extensions to the Lycée Bonaparte and the Lycée Charlemagne the Emperor had an opportunity to expound a scheme for the lycée buildings and to suggest that the library of Ste-Geneviève should be transferred to the Senate.

From the palace of the Elysée to the château of St-Cloud

On 15 February Napoleon left the Tuileries, where he had been in

residence since 1 December, for the Elysée[1] as he thought his continued presence in Paris necessary. He had given up all idea of living
in the Louvre, which could never be made comfortable, and thought
it should remain as the show-place and museum it is today. More than
ever he was determined to build the palace of Chaillot.

A tour of the city he made at the end of February showed Napoleon
that neither fears of war nor the food crisis had impaired his prestige;
he continued to enjoy the nation's entire confidence and to be the
fount of all its aspirations.

That evening during his dinner he sent for Fontaine. He was highly
critical of the site of the Bondy fountain. Fontaine justified the choice
on technical grounds but was brushed aside by Napoleon, who interrupted him with, 'Rubbish! Now we shall have to buy and demolish
the houses to make an open space.'

This foreshadowed the present Place de la République.

Napoleon then turned to the elephant on the Bastille fountain; he
thought it was placed too high. Fontaine spoke disparagingly of its
'huge mass'.

Bausset, who was present at this interview, writes:

> 'Napoleon took no exception to his architect's expressing an opinion
> contrary to his own. In this case particularly it showed great moderation
> on his part as the elephant had some connection with his Asian and
> African campaigns.'

The conversation then turned to the Guards' barracks on the Quai
Bonaparte; Napoleon was horrified by the banality of the new façade.
'I know very well that it's the façade of a barracks and not of a
palace, but one can have architecture even in a charcoal-burner's
hut.'

Then the Emperor dilated on his vision of transforming Paris and
especially of creating a new city to the west. In anticipation of
modern town-planners, who foresee the city's division into specialized
zones, he enlarged on a plan to build a vast administrative district
in the Champ de Mars.

'We must have an area with new buildings which, in size and
grandeur, will dwarf those in existence. The Gros Caillou, under the
nose so to speak of the palace of the little King, is a suitable site for a

---

[1] By an arrangement made with Josephine on 13 February she exchanged the Elysée for
the château of Laeken.

great building to house the Archives, the University and the Palace of the Arts. Have you seen the plans shown me by the Minister of the Interior? I am not partisan of housing everything separately; it should all be under one roof.'

Fontaine agreed that, at a pinch, the Palace of the Arts and the University might be in one building, but the Archives must be isolated with no wood in the structure.

Napoleon ended the discussion by asking for plans for cemeteries to be built at the four cardinal points of Paris; he had been shocked on a visit to the cemetery of Montmartre to see the prevailing disorder and lack of decency.

The proper disposal of the archives was always one of Napoleon's problems, but it depended on what was done with the National Library and the final arrangements for the Louvre. Once again he asked for an opinion within a week on a location for what he called 'the archives of Europe'.

Only temporary alleviation had resulted from raising the price of bread to 18 sous which was beyond the means of the working classes nor could they afford the better quality bread the bakers found it more profitable to bake. Manipulations in wholesale prices defeated their own ends since they opened the way to swindles. In the event scarcity increased and the distribution of bread and cheap soups as ordered by the Emperor had little effect.

Paris had even more serious worries as it was obvious now that war with Russia was inevitable. Even the high price of bread caused less unrest than the senatus consultum prescribing the levy of the National Guards in case of necessity. Stocks fell progressively from the 82.00 francs at which they had stood for several months to 79.65 francs by the end of March.

After further visits of inspection in the city and issuing a decree to implement the suggestions made to Fontaine about the buildings for the Archives and the University, Napoleon left the Elysée for St-Cloud on 31 March, there to devote himself largely to the most colossal undertaking of his career, the war with Russia. Napoleonic Europe in arms was already advancing in powerful waves towards the east. The forty days spent by the Emperor at St-Cloud were full of anxieties with only an occasional concert to relieve the tension.

While he was at St-Cloud, the plans for the four Paris cemeteries were submitted to Napoleon; they were to be in addition to Père Lachaise, which was to be the main establishment. The Emperor agreed· in principle to the arrangements for burials and funeral services, but thought one of the chapels looked too frivolous for its purpose. He asked Fontaine a question which shows his Christian principles, 'Why is there no cross in any of your plans?'

Fontaine's answer was that as the cemeteries would be for the dead of all faiths a special symbol was unnecessary.

'You are wrong,' retorted the Emperor. 'Everyone today accepts the sign of the cross, except the Jews who have their own cemeteries.'

At another interview with Fontaine and Percier about the Palace of the King of Rome Napoleon was shown a plan of the Mikhailovsky castle, the favourite residence of Paul I of Russia where he was assassinated. The Emperor rejected it with disgust, 'For all its bastions, its dungeons and secret doors death managed to enter the Imperial bedchamber.'

Duroc, who was present, agreed with the Emperor and, alluding to the rumours current in Paris, said that it would be wise to avoid any suggestion of forts and moats: 'Too much has already been said about the Emperor's plan to rebuild the Bastille on the site of the Palace of the King of Rome.'

'Duroc is right,' said the Emperor. 'And tell me, please, of what use these fortifications would be? Gentlemen, these are flimsy, if any, safeguards at all against treason. The trust, the love and the loyalty of our peoples are our best protection—and the only one. My son shall learn from me how to govern the Parisians without fortresses or cannon and, I hope, make himself beloved by the people.'

At that moment the King of Rome was announced. He ran to his father and threw himself into his arms. The Emperor took him on his knee and said,

'We were talking about you, Sire. We were building you a beautiful palace . . .'

He fell into a reverie, musing,

'Yes, we were building you a beautiful palace . . . and if we are beaten you will not even have a hut.'

This prophecy was unhappily destined to be fulfilled.

The majority of the Provision Council was against Napoleon's wish

to impose a general tax on the price of cereals. Pasquier writes in his
Memoirs:

> 'Although these views did not correspond with the Emperor's fundamen-
> tal beliefs, to give him his due he never showed the least anger in
> rejecting them.'

The price of flour and grain continued to soar and, to quote
Pasquier again,

> 'Anxiety became panic . . . the crowds besieged the grocers' shops for
> rice and vermicelli; vegetables and tailings were at an astronomical price.
> In addition bread was being taken out of Paris to the country . . .'

At a Provision Council on 14 April Napoleon decided that the
export of bread from Paris, the distribution of flour in the suburbs
and speculation of all kinds should be prohibited and suppressed.
The principal farmers of the Department of the Seine were to send
to the market the amount of wheat necessary to feed the Department.
Next day, at a further session of the Council, Napoleon was given a
report on the first measures taken and gave additional instructions.

> 'The Emperor's wish to be fully informed and to alleviate the situation,'
> says Pasquier, 'was generally known and had a soothing effect on the
> people, but the calm did not last long. At the end of April there were
> again long queues at local bakers' shops and stocks at the Central Markets
> disappeared rapidly.'

On 27 April Napoleon received the Czar's ultimatum but he was
determined to settle the food crisis before joining the army. Decrees
were issued to ensure the free circulation of flour and wheat and to
prevent hoarding or speculation.

In a serious conversation with Pasquier on 8 May about food
supply the Emperor showed himself a determined optimist about
scarcities: 'It's over now; the harvest is being gathered and in a few
weeks' time you will be out of the wood.'

The Prefect of Police thought that reserve stocks should be issued
and pointed out that the Emperor's absence would make for a more
dangerous situation. 'Should there happen to be an unfortunate insur-
rectional movement of some dimensions have we not to fear fatal
repercussions here and abroad?'

Napoleon walked silently up and down from the window to the
hearth, his arms crossed behind his back, in deep thought, then he
spoke:

'Yes, there is indeed some truth in what you say—it's just one more hazard added to all those I shall meet in the greatest and most difficult enterprise which I have yet undertaken, but what has been begun must be finished . . . Farewell, Monsieur le Préfet.'

VIII

From the Château of St-Cloud to the Palace of the Kremlin

Public works continue

In a berline drawn by four horses Napoleon and Marie-Louise left St-Cloud at 5 a.m. on 9 May for Châlons-sur-Marne, en route for Dresden. To avoid drawing attention to the opening of the Russian campaign the journey was announced as one to inspect the Grande Armée on the Vistula. For the benefit of the Parisians especially the press made a point of mentioning that the King of Rome would spend the summer at Meudon, that he was in excellent health and would be weaned at the end of the month.

No one doubted that the Grande Armée would be victorious but the Parisians were, as always, dismayed by the Emperor's departure; knowing his contempt for danger, they feared for his safety. On 15 May a police bulletin reported that:

'On the day His Majesty left, the 5 per cents stood at 80.05 frs and are standing at 81.15 frs. Speculators, used to seeing His Majesty's campaigns end victoriously, were in a way discounting his success. Today shares are rising because news is imminently expected which will cause them to improve.'

The decree of 8 May, imposing taxation of cereals, had been kept secret for several days but on the 12th it was published in the *Moniteur* and posted up in the city. This measure did not reduce scarcity; on the contrary farmers were loath to sell their wheat to the millers which caused an alarming decline in flour supplies and led to black-market sales at inflated prices. In addition the daily illegal export of bread from Paris increased the scarcity. Threats and persuasion were used by the government to palliate the situation but the Provision Council, at its regular meetings, was obliged to make more and more inroads on the reserves, which could be restocked only by means of subsidies ruinous to the Treasury. To prevent a breakdown in supplies flour was adulterated with beans, peas and vetch.

The fair prospects for the 1812 harvest somewhat relaxed tension, aided by the publication on 8 and 9 July of two bulletins announcing the Grande Armée's advance. In the first bulletin Napoleon, who had arrived at Posen on 1 June after two weeks in Dresden, threw responsibility for the outbreak of war on the Russians and allowed it to be inferred that a speedy peace would result from a victorious campaign.

The bulletin on 22 June, dictated from Napoleon's headquarters near the Niemen, ended:

> 'Soldiers, the second Polish war will be as glorious as the first to the French armies, but the peace we shall make will carry its own guarantee and put an end to the dominion of arrogance which for fifty years Russia has exercised over Europe.'

From Gloubokojé on 19 July the Emperor sent the Minister of Manufactures a memorandum demonstrating his unshakeable optimism.

> 'I am pleased to see that our troubles are over; it was a cruel test we had to live through. Had I listened to the officials of the Minister of the Interior, whose inadequate information was partially responsible, we should never have weathered the crisis and I should have delayed still further prohibiting the export of cereals.
> 'It is all the more reassuring that you are taking steps to see that you are fully informed of what is available so that you will know when to permit or prohibit exports. This concerns the future. Another subject which merits your attention is maintaining the reserve intact. Crass ignorance has dictated all these matters so that I was faced with a crisis with my granaries empty. The time has come to bring some order to everything and to see that nothing is lacking to keep the reserves at 50 tons.'

Showing that he had not forgotten his visit on 11 December, the Emperor recalled his decision to build a huge provision warehouse in Paris to ensure that, whatever happened, Paris would be fed, but the building of this warehouse seemed to him deathly slow.

> 'Money is not lacking because the funds allocated for this year have always lasted for two years. I want you to see the Minister of the Interior and urge that work is expedited and that I am informed as to whether it is not possible to finish the building in a year from now.'

He showed his declining interest in prestige monuments by going so far as to say that the Arc de Triomphe, the Pont d'Iéna and the Temple of Glory could wait three or four years with no difficulty, but that the completion of the public granary was vital.

In conclusion he mentioned the arrangements already made for building other institutions of public utility around the capital:

'I ordered the Intendant-General of the Crown to have built at St-Maur mills and warehouses on the special account. These buildings are not to be castles in Spain; plenty of money will be forthcoming. . . . It is useless to pretend that there is sufficient accommodation available in the neighbourhood of Paris for the large quantities of food which must be stocked.'

That the Russian campaign caused no delays to Napoleon's building programme is evident from the list of achievements during his absence. Work was being actively pursued at the slaughterhouses, markets, public granaries and the wine and spirits entrepôt. Conduits and aqueducts were under construction and the navigation canal was making good progress. Wharves, quays and ports, the Pont d'Iéna, the new gallery at the Louvre, the church of St-Napoléon, the Arc de l'Etoile, the obelisk at the Pont Neuf and the Palais de la Bourse were all advancing, in common with all the other enterprises he had decreed.

Marie-Louise in Paris

The gap made by Napoleon's absence could not be filled by Marie-Louise, who had left the Emperor at Dresden and returned to St-Cloud on 18 July. Her return was welcomed by the Parisians with greater joy because it coincided with the 5th bulletin announcing the Grande Armée's entry into Vilna without a shot fired and that the Emperor's health was excellent.

Napoleon wanted the Empress to be active in court life and official ceremonies, to go to the theatres, the panoramas and visit various public places, in a word to 'be seen' by the Parisians. He also wished her to keep him informed of public opinion in Paris. In fact Marie-Louise spent most of her time at St-Cloud and rarely appeared in Paris. Used to her husband's presence and attentions she was unhappy without him.

Paris in the ensuing months was, to use Talleyrand's phrase, 'drearily calm', a state corroborated by many contemporaries. Bourrienne writes:

> 'Although Paris was in general sad and many families, made wise by experience, were looking anxiously into the future, the capital remained quiet.'

This apparent tranquillity hid a certain amount of fear. Many Parisians were deeply dismayed as the army penetrated ever farther into the immense territory of Russia and they began to realize that the Russian army was voluntarily avoiding a clash with the Grand Armée.

Napoleon's confidence was enhanced by his having been victorious in all his battles against the Russians; to propagate his own optimism, he used striking terms for the bulletins, always read with enthusiasm to tireless cheers of 'Long live the Emperor!'

Leaving Vitebsk at 1 a.m. on 13 August, Napoleon crossed the Dnieper with the army on the 14th and set off in pursuit of an elusive enemy. When he reached Smolensk on the 15th he believed that he could fight the battle for which he was longing. Destiny herself took a hand in offering him this exhilarating prospect.

Paris meanwhile was celebrating St-Napoleon's day in the usual way, but a special feature was the publication of the 10th bulletin, which told of the victory of Ostrovno and the delivery of Smolensk to the Emperor. The city paid particular attention to the story of two hundred light infantrymen who, unsupported, had attacked the right wing of the enemy's cavalry. The Emperor was impressed by their courage and asked to what Corps they belonged. 'To the ninth, and three-quarters of us sons of Paris.' 'Tell them,' said the Emperor, 'that they are heroes and they all deserve the cross.'

The special inaugural ceremonies on the 15th were the laying of the foundation stones of the Palaces of the University and Fine Arts and the Archives while the Ourcq waters were released to the wash-houses near the Meat and Fish Markets, previously without water. Marie Louise came to Paris for the celebrations but returned immediately thereafter to St-Cloud, having docilely obeyed the Emperor and made herself pleasant to the Parisians.

As the press announced that the price of wheat was likely to fall faster than it had risen the citizens read the 11th bulletin in the

Moniteur of 4 September with even greater pleasure. Under a date line, 11 August, the entry of French troops into Smolensk was announced and the bulletin concluded, 'Never has the French army shown greater bravery than in this campaign.'

Letters arriving in Paris from the army told of alarm at its height in Moscow, news which produced a rise in stocks but also some speculation which the Prefect Pasquier did his best to check. The optimism engendered lasted until the end of the month.

Now almost daily communiqués gave official news of the 'ardour and good health' of the troops. On 26 September the guns thundered in Paris in honour of 'the memorable victory' of Mojaisk on the 7th. The truth was somewhat less brilliant, as the Parisians learnt from the 17th bulletin, recounting the battle of the Moskowa, fought 'under the walls of Moscow'.

Both sides suffered enormous losses, the Russians 50,000 killed or wounded but the Grande Armée 10,000.

> 'The Emperor was never exposed to danger. Neither the foot nor mounted Guard took part nor lost a single man. Victory was never in doubt.'

This conclusion, determinedly triumphant, did not succeed in calming spirits beginning to show signs of agitation. Couriers from the front helped to corroborate the bloodiness of these battles, not denied by the official bulletin. The loss of many officers was particularly mourned. Stocks fell to 81.00 frs.

News of the army's entry into Moscow came in letters from the front and had a tremendous psychological effect. Official confirmation was received on 3 October in the 19th bulletin which aroused universal rejoicing.

On Sunday, the 4th, salvoes of artillery were heard in the capital whose citizens, waking early, had already read the 20th bulletin dated 17 September announcing the fire of Moscow, 'an incalculable loss to Russia'.

Marie-Louise returned from St-Cloud to the Tuileries to hear a Te Deum in celebration of 'the victory of His Majesty the Emperor and King'. This was followed by the usual ceremonial, after which the Empress returned to St-Cloud.

At 2.30 in the afternoon a further Te Deum was sung at Notre Dame 'in thanksgiving for the crossing of the Niemen, the Dvina, the Borysthenes (the Dnieper), the battles of Mohilov, Dvina, Poltovsk, Ostrovno, Smolensk and the Moskowa'. Cambacérès, with a brilliant entourage which included both Prefects and the Corps of Mayors, was present with a huge crowd in the cathedral. According to the *Moniteur*:

> 'The large attendance of citizens of all classes proved by the lively expression of their happiness and admiration what great share they take in the memorable events which will ever redound to the glory of the French Empire.'

Bulletins and communiqués continued to flow in from Moscow, reporting the 'absolute quiet' prevailing in the city and stressing the Emperor's perfect health but, on 15 October, Napoleon, after days spent in deep thought, prepared to quit the holy city where for two days the first flakes of snow had been falling. Calculating the possible psychological effect on Paris of the retreat and to show that his freedom of action was unaffected he signed the famous decree which in 101 articles regulated the organization of the Comédie Française.

It had long been in the Emperor's mind to settle the actors' perennial dissensions by a special charter and he found it piquant to sign the document in Moscow. In the evening he marched up and down in his Kremlin salon, talking easily about the decree as an innovation for Paris, apparently seizing on the most trivial subject to distract his mind from his anguished thoughts. Bourrienne saw the measure as part of the Emperor's cleverness in deceiving the Parisians about the true state of affairs. People would say, 'If the Emperor has leisure to think about the theatre then things are going well and his star is in the ascendant.'

On 19 October Napoleon left Moscow in command of Mortier. The memorable retreat had started.

The Malet affair

General Malet's conspiracy, which disturbed Paris on the night of 22/23 October, arose from the prospect of a Russian disaster coupled with Napoleon's absence. Malet, a republican in politics and a former brigadier-general, was arrogant, bold, embittered and malicious but without political influence. He allowed his fundamental admiration for Napoleon's genius to be swamped by his envy of the Emperor's power and by fierce hatred.

After the 1808 plot Malet had been transferred for health reasons from the prison of La Force to a clinic where he made common cause with the Abbé Lafon. News of the Grande Armée's difficulties in the Russian steppes led Malet to believe that the time had come for action; the Emperor's prestige stood too high in France for his overthrow but, if he was believed dead, a surprise attack had a chance of success. It might produce a shock sufficient to cause the Senate to appoint a provisional government with General Malet in command of Paris. Then, supported by the troops, he would arrest the military leaders and install the new government.

Malet carried out the first phase of this plan with speed and mastery but he then became confused and lost control. The deception was discovered and the plot collapsed; the General was imprisoned. Paris had remained undisturbed and its first reaction to the conspiracy was to laugh and mock at the men who had so easily allowed themselves to be duped by someone escaped from a mental home. The Imperial government earned nothing but ridicule for its conduct, while the Emperor continued to inspire veneration and prayers for the safety of his person.

Cambacérès, the only man who had kept calm, took the situation in hand and called an immediate council with Clarke, Minister of War, Savary and Pasquier, each of whom tried to minimize his own responsibilities to lay the blame at his neighbour's door.

At 11 a.m. Cambacérès left for St-Cloud to pay his devoted respects and homage to Marie-Louise and the King of Rome. Marie-Louise had been unconscious of danger and, when told about what was described as 'a brigands' riot' quickly suppressed, she asked Cambacérès, 'What could they have done to me?'

Cambacérès' initiative had come rather late. During the night's disturbances no one had given a thought either to the Empress or the King of Rome, which was one of the most alarming inferences of the plot.

Official circles were apprehensive about Napoleon's reactions and tried, by unseasonable zeal, to compensate for their supine and mistaken conduct. Those inculpated in the plot were tried before a summary military court and executed on the day after.

It was at Dorogoboujé on 5 November, ten days after the bloody battle of Malojaroslavetz, that Napoleon learned from a Paris courier of the Malet affair. What astounded him was that, during the ephemeral moments of the conspiracy's success, no one had remembered that the Empire was hereditary, that to Napoleon I constitutionally succeeded Napoleon II. He realized bitterly the fragility of his régime and its institutions to which he had devoted his whole genius and life. When he was informed of the bloody repression which followed the plot he cried, 'What a misfortune! What kind of effect is this going to have in Paris!'

Only a few intimates were made parties to his fears. Deeply concerned though he was with the gravity of events in Russia, he had one idea only; to return to the Tuileries. 'I cannot be everywhere but I must return to my capital where my presence is vital to retrieve the situation.'

Meanwhile Paris was anxiously awaiting news from the army. In the 24th bulletin dated from Moscow on 14 October, published on 1 November, several victorious engagements against the Russians were announced and also the damage done by fire to the city. The first fall of snow was also mentioned and the people, who began to realize that the coming of winter would intensify the dangers of the campaign, increasingly longed for news from the front.

Their anxiety was somewhat dissipated by the opening at the Louvre of an exhibition by living artists; it was to be the last Salon of the Empire and one of the final evidences of the prosperity of Napoleon's reign.

The 25th bulletin, published on 9 November, announced that the retreat and evacuation of Moscow had begun.

'The burnt city has no further political importance and is ruined for a hundred years.'

The final phrases struck an optimistic note:

'The weather is very fine, like France in October, but perhaps a little warmer.'

Business circles, sniffing disaster in the air, grew anxious.

'There was a crowd at the Bourse on the 9th and 10th,' says a police report, 'and the sharp fall in stocks is ascribed to the 25th bulletin.'

Stocks fell from 80.50 to 79.40 frs and the public clamoured for more news of the progress of the Grande Armée.

A report of the 14th drew attention to the fact that:

'Scarcity of news daily draws huge crowds to the Bourse, mainly of small *rentiers* who go to sell their holdings. which caused the progressive fall in shares.'

On 16 November the papers devoted almost all their space to the new bulletin published in the *Moniteur*, describing the army's departure from Moscow with details of the explosion in the Kremlin. As a postscript it mentioned 'the sun and fine weather' with which Russia was still blessed.

Although still anxious, people's anxieties were somewhat soothed because the bulletins had announced only victories—nor, indeed, had Napoleon suffered any defeat. According to Caulaincourt,

'The continued confidence in the Emperor's genius, which people were accustomed to see triumph over the greatest obstacles, was such that opinion now tended to diminish rather than exaggerate what had transpired about our disasters.'

The 28th bulletin, dated 11 November from Smolensk, and published in the *Moniteur* on the 29th, began to reveal 'difficulties due to cold and fatigue', but it ended with the intentionally soothing words, now customary, 'The Emperor's health has never been better.'

Napoleon, in spite of the severity of the winter, was, in fact, in excellent physical shape, but he complained of lack of news from Paris. When writing to Maret on 30 November about army supplies, he added:

'You don't tell me about Paris, about which I have had no news for three weeks. Where are the missing eighteen dispatch riders? How is the Empress?'

On 2 December, after the memorable crossing of the Beresina, he dictated from Molodetschno the 29th bulletin (published in the *Moniteur* of 17 December), which was taken to Paris by Montesquiou, Berthier's aide-de-camp. Anticipating the effect that the disastrous crossing would have on the capital, the Emperor told the unpalatable truth revealed by the high figure of the losses.

And now the moment had come to leave the Grande Armée. After long consultations about his route he decided to return the way he had come. At Bennitsa on 5 December he handed over command of the Grande Armée to Murat then, entirely in his own hand, wrote Cambacérès a brief note:

'You will have learnt from the bulletin about our situation and what has happened. You must have been very anxious.'

Referring to the Malet affair which had affected him severely, he said:

'The quarrels of the Ministers of Police and War are absurd. I'm afraid that the Minister of Police was in the wrong. Why is he angry with the General Staff which saved the situation?'

He made his stand clear to Savary personally:

'Your quarrels with the General Staff in Paris seem to me to be lamentable, unjust and ill-advised.'

At 8 p.m. in the greatest secrecy Napoleon, followed by his most faithful adherents, plunged with Caulaincourt into his carriage sleigh which bore him through a blizzard towards Paris.

The Return from Russia

Joy and astonishment in Paris

Marie-Louise returned to Paris from St-Cloud on Saturday, 5 December, to preside over the traditional anniversary celebrations of the coronation which particularly attracted 'many soldiers who had been decorated for valour and citizens of Paris', according to a bulletin of the 7th.

Stocks felt the influence of the prevailing depression due to absence of news of the Grande Armée. At last on 17 December the 29th bulletin was published in the *Moniteur*; the city was struck dumb. 'Everyone,' writes Montesquiou, 'searched for an explanation' as large crowds gathered at the Bourse and government shares fell from 78 to 77.20 frs. All thoughts turned to Napoleon whose return was impatiently awaited.

The Emperor had left Smorgoni in feverish haste, knowing that only his presence in Paris could magic away any panic. During a headlong course of thirteen days he began to forget the nightmare days through which he had lived and, as he neared the capital at breakneck speed, so his optimism and his courage grew.

A few miles from the Rhine he received reassuring news of his wife and son and was also informed that morale in Paris remained high, although no communiqué since that of 29 November had yet been published. It was while he was dining at Château-Thierry on 18 December that he saw the *Moniteur* of the 17th. Obsessed as always by the mocking Faubourg he exclaimed, 'They're going to make a great to-do about all this. For the Faubourg St-Germain it will be a victory—these are their successes. They will crack up our losses to the hilt and do you know what will affect them most? The death of Alfred de Noailles. The loss of my guns and my cavalry will be a bagatelle for the Faubourgs St-Germain and

St-Honoré, but the loss of one of their own people means everything.'

The Emperor was in such haste to reach Paris that at Meaux his
worn-out carriage fell to pieces. With Caulaincourt he hurled himself
into a post-chaise and drove like a whirlwind to Paris which he
reached at 11.45 p.m. on 18 December. While Napoleon rushed to
the Empress's apartments Caulaincourt went to see Cambacérès,
who was extremely surprised by this unexpected nocturnal visit, but
absolutely delighted to learn of the Emperor's presence in Paris.

Napoleon spent the whole day at the Tuileries, giving audiences,
first to Cambacérès, then to each of his ministers in turn. General
Malet's plot was mentioned even before the Russian disaster and the
Emperor's first words were, 'You believed me dead? But the King
of Rome? Your oaths? You make me tremble for the future!'

He talked freely and frankly about the terrible campaign and
admitted his mistakes, avowing to Decrès and Cassac, 'Well,
gentlemen, I was dazzled by fortune . . . I was in Moscow. I thought
I could sign a peace. I stayed there too long. I made a very big
mistake but it is one I shall be able to repair.'

He then, with Parisian reactions in mind, asked for every detail of
the Malet affair. Everyone gave his own version, attempting to
exonerate himself rather than give a clear explanation of what had
actually occurred. Frochot, who had foolishly put the Hôtel de Ville
at the disposal of the conspirators, was made the scapegoat but
Napoleon, who had a high regard for his Prefect whose loyalty he
prized, declared, 'Well, what would you? This poor Prefect of Paris,
Frochot, was unfortunately deceived by Malet's escapade. I'm not
angry with him; he is an honest and able magistrate.'

About 2 p.m. Napoleon appeared on the balcony of the Tuileries
to a huge crowd which cheered him to the echo. This warm welcome
had a particularly emotional character. Napoleon had not returned
wreathed in laurels; he had been hard hit by misfortune and his army
was virtually decimated, but the miracles he had performed and the
courage he had shown inflamed the imagination and inspired
admiration. Paris showed its surprise and joy at his lightning return.
The city had its hero again and loved him more in defeat than in
triumph.

'The effect of his return,' wrote Caulaincourt, 'was remarkable.
All previous grudges against him were immediately forgotten' and

the mere expression, 'He is an extraordinary man' was enough to raise the spirits of the Parisians.

The Emperor himself was much encouraged by the capital's high morale and his own continuing great prestige. He wrote to Murat, 'I have arrived in Paris and am extremely pleased with the national spirit.'

That the mere sight of the city seemed a comfort to him was the opinion of his travelling companion, Caulaincourt, to whom he remarked, 'The terrible communiqué has had its effect but I see that my being here gives greater pleasure than the grief aroused by our misfortunes. People are distressed rather than discouraged, a state of mind which will be learnt in Vienna and in three months all will again be well.'

After mass on Sunday, 20 December, Napoleon received the Senate and the Council of State in audience. The Presidents, speaking for the nation as a whole, denounced the Malet affair and reiterated the nation's unshakeable devotion to the Emperor and his hereditary throne. Napoleon in his reply insisted on the vital importance of the stability of the government and referred to the magistrates' 'strict duty to defend with their lives if necessary "the sovereign, the throne and the laws" '.

Frochot was the unfortunate who bore the brunt of attacks in these speeches on 'cowardly magistrates'; on the 23rd he was dismissed from his functions as Councillor of State and Prefect of the Department of the Seine. Chabrol, Prefect of Savona and Lebrun's son-in-law, was appointed in his stead. And so one of the Emperor's most devoted servants, whose achievements in Paris were considerable, withdrew from the scene to Napoleon's secret regret.

'I have had to make an example,' he said, 'for which I am sorry,' but time was lacking to dwell on this sad affair; he had now to think of all Europe shaken by the Russian disaster, Europe now at last eluding him and already preparing to strike the death blow.

Throughout December the food situation worsened; queues of the poor were again seen outside bakers' shops while the price of flour continued to rise and reserve stocks were becoming exhausted. When everyone was in despair an unexpected fall in prices at the Marché de Montlhéry on 28 December produced the long-awaited alleviation. in which one may perhaps see one of fortune's last gifts to Napoleon

He had fought a real if bloodless campaign for the public weal, presiding in person over many councils, concerned only with the Parisians' welfare, particularly that of the working classes, rejecting any suggestion of rationing and avoiding recourse to compulsion.

During January 1813 and the following months Napoleon's activity was prodigious; he presided over daily councils, reviewed troops, annotated reports, took decisions of all kinds, even found time to appear in public at the Salon des Arts and in his box at the theatre. According to Bausset,

> 'The effect on him of the disasters of this fateful campaign did not diminish his eagerness to know how buildings and improvements in Paris were proceeding.'

On the 2nd he visited the Wine Market, the Fountain of the Elephant and again the Bourse. 'The Emperor's eyes were everywhere,' wrote Bourrienne.

Napoleon's most urgent concern was to raise a new army, considerably larger than he had originally thought necessary. After the Russian disaster the situation had deteriorated; the Grande Armée was reduced to mere details and had been abandoned by Murat, who returned to Naples. General Yorck, serving under Macdonald, had defected, taking the whole of Prussia with him. The Russians had entered Königsberg and in Metternich Austria had a first-class negotiator who, while hypocritically offering to mediate, was already plotting Napoleon's fall and trying to wring concessions from him which would sap his power.

On 11 January a senatus consultum put at the War Minister's disposal 350,000 men—100,000 members of the National Guard and 100,000 anticipated from the 1814 conscription. The country was asked for an all-out effort. Some complaints there were; many homes had suffered the loss of their sons and more mothers still were already trembling at the dangers their children must run, yet there was no increase in desertions.

> 'Every family was in mourning,' writes Caulaincourt, 'but the Emperor's presence and actions inspired so much assurance that hope and even confidence were widespread. Paris and the Court were in a grave mood.'

Contrary to what has often been written the Bourse remained firm;

stocks, which fell to 76.90 when the 29th bulletin was published, stood at 80.20 frs on 9 January and 79.15 on the 11th. The people as a whole remained loyal to Napoleon, especially the workers of Paris, who were kept employed on the great public works, which continued despite the situation. The middle classes, however, whose sons had hitherto escaped military service by payment of substitutes, were now involved in enrolment for the National Guard, which diminished their sympathy with the Imperial régime. The Faubourg St-Germain indulged in its usual pointed witticisms, mocking at the 'balls for wooden legs' given by the Emperor.

Paris offers horsemen to the Emperor

As Europe began to mobilize against France, Paris took the lead in 'a general national movement', inundating the Emperor with loyal addresses. On 12 January the Municipal Council and Corps of Mayors met at the Hôtel de Ville where one speaker referred to the cavalry losses in the Russian winter and suggested, 'Let us offer our august sovereign the means to reconstitute his cavalry. Let the City of Paris offer an example which others will follow so that when History shall speak of these remarkable times the City will rank as the first to take the road of honour.'

This speech met with universal approval and an address to the Emperor was enthusiastically adopted:

'Sire, your good city of Paris is fortunate in being the first to express those feelings which France as a whole will share within a few hours. . . . Your good city of Paris, priding itself on taking the initiative, begs you to accept the offer of a regiment of five hundred cavalrymen and its assurance that no sacrifice will be too great to preserve the honour of the nation.'

On the 16th Chabrol published a notice to the citizens of Paris, 'inviting them to participate in public acts of generosity'. A register was opened in all town halls and offers flooded in as leading citizens, senior officials and all classes of Parisians rivalled one another's zeal in paying their debt to the monarch and the nation.

The example set by Paris was soon followed. On the 16th and for weeks thereafter the *Moniteur* published loyal addresses from every Imperial city and all the National Guards, claiming, 'the honour of sharing the dangers and glory of their brothers in arms of the Grande

Armée', and offering to equip and mount cavalry at their own
expense.

On 17 January the Mayoral Corps of the City of Paris, with a
delegation from the General Council of Seine Inférieure, delivered to
the Tuileries addresses voted to the Emperor, who next day wrote to
the Minister of War,

> 'As a sign of my gratitude to the City of Paris it is my desire that these
> five hundred men should form part of the Third Regiment of the Lancers
> of my Guard.'

And this was done.

As a contribution to his colossal task of reconstruction and pacification, Napoleon decided to meet Pius VII at Fontainebleau with two
objectives; to obtain the Sovereign Pontiff's agreement to the transfer
of the Holy See to Paris and to the coronation of Marie-Louise and
the King of Rome. Using a hunting-party at Berthier's property at
Grosbois on 19 January as a pretext, Napoleon surprised the Pope
whom he had not seen for eight years. The sovereigns embraced each
other and, after talks lasting several days, the Emperor succeeded in
persuading the Pope to sign a provisional concordat on the 25th.
Napoleon returned the same evening to the Tuileries.

On 28 January, after a ministerial council, the Emperor at 4 p.m.
presided over an administrative council for home affairs with
Chabrol and Girard, the water-engineer. The main Parisian subject
reviewed was that of water. The progress of the Ourcq canal (which
to date had cost over 12 millions) and of the water supply in Paris
were reported to the Emperor, who approved the decisions taken and
went on to discuss the revenues of the Paris internal customs.

Napoleon's desire to see the fruits of his skilful financial 'system' is
evident in a memorandum he dictated after examining the special
budget for 1812.

> 'This budget is not in its usual form. As the Prefect of Paris will not yet
> have familiarized himself in detail with his functions, the Minister of the
> Interior will, at the next council, furnish me with the account of the sale of
> the hospice buildings. I ordered a sale which should bring in 9 millions.
> What was sold up to 21 December 1812? How much money has come in?
> What must still be sold to reach the amount fixed? How much has been
> spent? How much remains to be spent? What will be sold in 1813 and to
> what use will the money be put? This whole complex of sales, loans and

work done or to be done out of these receipts must be submitted to me in detail.'

The Emperor used his rare moments of leisure to continue his inspection of works in Paris. On 5 February, as the Russians were occupying Warsaw, he instigated a senatus consultum, providing for Marie-Louise's regency and announced that the Empress would be crowned at Notre Dame by Pius VII, a measure designed as insurance against any conspiracy during his absence and as a gesture to Austria.

The text of the Fontainebleau concordat appeared in the *Moniteur* on Sunday 14 February, and at 1 p.m. Napoleon left the Tuileries in state to open the session of the Legislature, where he made an arrogant speech, stressing the continued strength of the Empire and his intention to preserve it intact. He announced the signature of the new concordat then made a solemn declaration, 'My wish is for peace, but I shall never make any but an honourable peace and one which satisfies the interests and greatness of my Empire.'

This assertion foreshadowed the tragic sequence of events.

To lend a cheerful note, Napoleon further announced that his Minister of the Interior would shortly make public a report about the Empire's prosperity; this was done impressively by Montalivet on the 25th when he dwelt on the increased population, the flourishing state of agriculture and the advances in industry. As usual, prominence was given to public works in Paris, revealing that, over a ten-year period, 102 millions had been devoted to them.[1]

This resumé was intended by Napoleon both to impress his enemies and as a formidable retort to some of the scepticism expressed in Paris, although he was not unduly disturbed by certain 'gossip' reported to him. He regarded it as normal in opposition circles and remained rightly convinced that he could trust the people of Paris. He said to Bubna, the new envoy of his father-in-law, the Emperor of Austria, 'You must not judge what Paris thinks by what you hear because Paris adores gossip, making epigrams and enjoying itself above all.'

Carnival time had now arrived, which offered some distraction even if it was not particularly gay. On 28 and 29 February the fatted calf was led with a large and brilliant escort through Paris and round the courtyard of the Tuileries, followed by a 'mass of people'. In the evening a masked ball at the Opéra drew 'a good class attendance',

[1] See Appendix IV.

evidenced by the 'numbers of brilliant carriages' outside the theatre.

Despite his overwhelming cares the Emperor continued to watch over the affairs of his good city, continuing his early morning tours with the faithful Duroc, who took notes of Napoleon's remarks to pass on to Fontaine. Napoleon always wore his legendary grey greatcoat with his round hat pulled down over his eyes to avoid recognition.

The city's finances also occupied his attention. A session of the Council of State on the 4th was followed by an administrative council for home affairs at which the city's budget for 1813 was considered. Napoleon reiterated his wish 'that expenditure should be restricted and new methods sought to increase revenue'. At the end of the meeting he gave orders for the putting in hand of various measures, which are particularly interesting as being the last directions he gave at an administrative council for Paris.

'(1) No further loans from the special domain, costly both to the city and the domain which requires the use of its own funds.

(2) In 1813 houses belonging to the hospices to be sold for a sum of 6,600,000 frs, with 325,000 revenues mortgaged on the Wine Market in lieu.

(3) A credit of 1,300,000 frs to be opened for the Wine Market which, with 1,600,000 frs from 1813, should yield 2,900,000 frs to be spent in 1813.

(4) A credit of one million to be opened for the slaughterhouses which, with 1,500,000 frs from the Poissy Fund and the 460,000 frs balance of the 1812 credit, should provide 2,900,000 frs.

(5) A credit of one million to be opened for the Central Markets, bringing the total funds to 2,300,000 frs, apart from the balance of the 1812 credit, estimated at 1,860,000 frs.

The Minister of the Interior to add receipts from demolitions to increase the credit of the Central Markets and the Wine Market, which should provide revenue for 1814 without need for recourse to the special funds.'

The Emperor's predominant need now was for large sums to rebuild his army; he wanted to economize his resources but without interrupting the great Paris public works.

The King of Rome and his Palace

After a military parade on the Carrousel on 5 March Napoleon took the King of Rome in his arms to a window to the great delight of the troops on parade whose cheers were echoed by the many spectators present. The little King was now one of Napoleon's most precious hopes and he never missed an opportunity of attracting to his son the affection of the Parisians. Was the child not the child of Paris? On his frequent outings on the boulevards, to the Luxembourg and to Mousseaux the people of Paris were always touched by the sight of the King of Rome driving his little cart, drawn by two young does trained by the famous circus-rider, Franconi—a gift from the Queen of Naples.

It was now that Napoleon, after hunting in the Bois de Boulogne and lunching at Bagatelle, revisited the yards at Chaillot. According to Percier and Fontaine the Russian campaign had not influenced the scale and magnitude of his plans.

'The work he ordered at the palace had not been suspended, although progress was slower, but this slackening, which might have seemed the worst possible omen was, on the contrary, proof of the Emperor's determination to proceed with the palace in spite of the difficulties involved.'

During dinner Napoleon sent for Duroc, the Grand Marshal, Baron Costaz and Fontaine for a 'discussion about the buildings which was long and somewhat inconclusive'. On his return to his apartments the Emperor dictated this memorandum to the Grand Marshal:

'The moment is now ripe to discuss the plans for building the palace of the King of Rome. I do not want to be led to spend too much. I want a palace smaller than St-Cloud, but larger than the Luxembourg. I should like to be able to live there when the 16th million has been spent so that I can have the benefit. If something grandiose is put up it will be like the Louvre, never completed. A beginning must be made on the park, its area determined and enclosed. I want the palace to be better than the Elysée, which cost less than eight millions to build and yet is one of the finest palaces in Paris. The King of Rome's palace will rank second after the Louvre which is a great palace. It won't be a kind of country house in Paris because it would always be preferable to spend the winter at the Louvre and the Tuileries. I can scarcely credit that St-Cloud cost 16 millions to build. I want the plan to be fully discussed and worked over by the Buildings Committee before I see it so that I can be assured that the amount of 16 millions will not be spent. I don't want a castle in Spain but something genuine which I am building for my own pleasure, not the architect's. Once the plan has been approved I shall go ahead with it forthwith.'

The Emperor was now more than ever insistent on economy and speed in the building of this palace. The first reverses he had met caused him to reject a large-scale plan. Although circumstances were now leading him to war his supreme objectives continued to be peace and repose so that simplicity was his primary requirement. Gradually the conqueror was making way for the man.

'I don't like the Elysée,' continued the Emperor, 'and the Tuileries is uninhabitable. Unless the new palace is very simple and built to my taste and way of living it will not satisfy me. If it is built as I want it the palace will be useful to me. I want it to be something like a larger Sans Souci, but above all a palace pleasant rather than beautiful, which are incompatibles. Like the Tuileries, it should stand between courtyard and garden so that from my apartments I can walk out into the garden and park as at St-. Cloud. . . . My own rooms should be those of a rich private individual, like those at Fontainebleau. To sum up, I need a palace where I can rest or a home for a man growing old. . . . I want a small chapel,' and so on.

The Emperor disliked English gardens and spoke disparagingly of landowners who allowed their architects to build at great expense small lakes (generally lacking water) with miniature rocks and rivers. 'These are bankers' whims. *My* English garden is the forest of Fontainebleau and I want no other.'

Conversation then turned to the Opéra, which Fontaine suggested should be built on the site of the Palais Royal fountain, necessitating the demolition of the houses between the Louvre and the Tuileries and thus furthering his cherished plan of clearing of the space between the two palaces and dividing it by a transverse building.

'You're always coming back to your own ideas,' the Emperor told Fontaine. 'Only architects agree with you; the division you want to make will destroy the grandeur; it does not matter if a large building is not wholly symmetrical. These are faults seen only by artists and a triviality which impresses the minority only. What is true is always beautiful. Small buildings, which take ten, twenty or more years to build, should be completely regular, but monuments to last for centuries should always take on the form and colour of their time.'

Napoleon expressed regret that Versailles did not reflect the periods when it was built. 'If I ever build a façade on the side looking towards Paris I should want it to be of my own architecture and not to harmonize with the rest.'

Fontaine's reply to this preoccupation with size was: 'In the arts as well as in much else the true is not always beautiful, and without order and symmetry there is no architecture.'

When, one afternoon early in March, the Emperor received the Duchesse d'Abrantès, he asked questions about the finest palaces in Europe and had laid out numbers of plans of royal and imperial residences in his study. When the Duchesse observed that Versailles was not among them, Napoleon replied: 'Although I don't like Versailles it is very beautiful. If a magic wand could transport it to the heights of Chaillot it would make a fine sight, wouldn't it?'

The Duchesse remarked that Paris had ceased to gossip about a citadel being built under the pretence of a palace for the King of Rome, to which the Emperor retorted, 'The asses!'

The Vigil

Next day the sovereigns left for Trianon where they stayed until the 23rd with one visit to Paris by the Emperor on the 15th to review regiments on the Champ de Mars.

During his absence there was some 'vague anxiety about the real condition of the Grande Armée' and the movement of Russo-Prussian troops. A police report of 18 March mentions this feeling:

'For the last two days there has been a rumour in Paris of an early second enrolment of the National Guard which has caused some disquiet.'

Stocks, standing at 78 frs at the beginning of January, fell on the 24th to 72 frs and on the 27th to 70 frs. Business was at a standstill.

On the 24th, the day after his return to Paris, Napoleon received a deputation from the Legislature, summoned to an extraordinary session which closed on the 25th. He reiterated his plan for the coronation of the Empress and the King of Rome 'as soon as his military preparations left him a free moment'. His speech ended with this lapidary sentence: 'Soon I shall leave to take command of my troops. The integrity of the Empire is not nor will be in question in any negotiation.'

It was also his intention that, come what might, public works in Paris should continue.

The Pope was literally besieged after the signature of the concordat by the Cardinals, who rushed to Fontainebleau to reproach him for

making concessions to Napoleon, a démarche which revived his
scruples and he retracted, an unpleasant shock for the Emperor who
feared the effects of this reversal on Paris. Despite his orders that the
Pope's change of heart should be kept secret it did leak out and produced its effect. Nevertheless, Napoleon insisted on imposing the
concordat on the French clergy.

As he could no longer count on the coronation of the Empress and
the King of Rome at Notre Dame, Napoleon took out letters patent,
conferring the regency on Marie-Louise. On 28 March he took up
residence at the Elysée where, in the ground-floor reception rooms,
he held a Cabinet Council on the 30th, composed of the grand
dignitaries and ministers, whom he informed of this decision, but
in fact the Empress's authority was purely nominal and he continued
to govern the country from his headquarters.

This first fortnight in April saw a redoubled effort on the Emperor's
part to stimulate the nation, especially Paris, where the last levy had
caused some uneasiness. This was most obvious in the great State
bodies, the Senate, the Legislature and even the Council of State
although they had not yet reached the point of leaving him in the
lurch. To his weary Marshals Napoleon had said, 'You want to
enjoy your handsome fortunes in Paris! Am I myself taking any rest?'

In less than three months he had raised more than three hundred
thousand men and organized a cavalry; the National Guards had
rapidly developed into an active corps; the sale of communal properties was proceeding profitably and, perhaps more encouraging, even
though the old nobility which had remained aloof from him was still
hostile, the majority of young aristocrats burned to serve him and
share his glory. The press announced that,

'the city of Paris, anxious always to give fresh proofs of attachment to
His Majesty, has already produced many voluntary enrolments to the
first regiment of the guards of honour.'

Among the volunteers registering at the Prefecture were many sons
of the nobility.

It was in the mass of the people, however, that the Emperor met
the greatest courage and most indomitable faith, evidenced by the
welcome he received in his tours through the faubourgs.

'If he was in doubt,' says Duroc, 'as to what people felt he must have
been gratified. One morning in the Faubourg St-Antoine even I did not

believe him to be loved as he is; you have no idea how wild they are about him. He wanted to stop in front of a large house being built Charonne way. His hat was pulled down well over his eyes, but the two hundred masons working there recognized him easily and shouted at the tops of their voices, "Long live the Emperor! Long live the Emperor!" They clustered round him immediately, throwing aside their tools and spades, wanting to kiss his hands . . .'

In this frank and rough ardour which moved him deeply Napoleon found some recompense for his exertions and was stimulated to feel himself to be yet the man of Austerlitz. His confidence in his own destiny was infectious and revived everyone's good spirits; even the enemy was impressed. The Russian and Prussian troops descending the Elbe were filled with a lively fear of encountering the man whose strategy had always outwitted them.

The Carrousel review on Sunday, 4 April, has been immortalized by Balzac.[1] Thousands of spectators were present 'to gaze in open-mouthed admiration'. Drums beat the general salute when the Emperor appeared and silence fell on the multitude, 'a silence so deep that a child could have been heard speaking', then 'everything trembled, moved and shook', and cries of 'Long live the Emperor!' sprang from every throat, making the walls of the old palace quiver.

'There was about it all something unearthly, something magical, some reflection of divine power, or perhaps a fleeting microcosm of this reign itself so fleeting. The man surrounded by so much love, enthusiasm, loyalty and so many prayers, for whom the sun had chased the clouds from the sky, remained seated on his horse. . . . To all the emotion he had aroused he seemed impassive.'

Before leaving the Elysée on the 6th, Napoleon toured the city, inspecting work at the Louvre, the Hôtel des Postes, the obelisk at the Pont Neuf, the Arc de Triomphe and then rode on to Neuilly, greeted everywhere by shouts of 'Long live the Emperor!' That evening he went with Marie-Louise to see *L'Abencérage*. The sovereigns were acclaimed with rousing cheers, renewed when they left the theatre. For the Parisians it was a way of saying farewell to the Emperor who yet again was going to war, to hazard the Nation's destiny on the battlefield.

Next day Napoleon returned to St-Cloud, where he spent a week before joining the army. He enjoyed its pleasant situation but continued to exert remorseless energy and settled various financial and

[1] *La Femme de Trente Ans.*

military problems. On 10 April he issued a decree creating a Corps of
Imperial Gendarmerie for Paris while the Paris Guard, previously
under the Minister of War, now was to be under the jurisdiction of
the Prefect of Police. On 11 April a further decree was issued concerning the finances of the City of Paris, including approval of the
city's budget of 20,890,105 frs.

'To give the citizens of Paris as well as those in the Departments
and abroad' an idea of the changes wrought in the capital during the
last twelve years the *Gazette de France* published an article on the 12th
about improvements in Paris. The conclusion was full of hope and
encouragement.

> 'The moment is opportune, the building season is beginning; larger
> funds have been allocated for this year despite the heavy demands of war.
> Public works will soon be in full activity. More than four thousand
> workers are already employed and there will be twice as many within a
> fortnight.'

There was no better way of raising morale or complying with the
Emperor's wishes.

Book III

Napoleon and the People of Paris

I

The Last Public Works in Paris

Paris wants peace

The Empire is tottering and will soon collapse. Gradually around Napoleon a vacuum will develop; only the working classes, the troops and a few of the faithful will never despair and will to the end remain devoted to him. This will be especially true of Paris where, in spite of their critical, turbulent and fickle temperament, his people will prove an attachment and confidence that no misfortune will succeed in shaking.

On 15 April at 4 a.m. Napoleon, accompanied by Caulaincourt, left incognito for Mainz, which he reached on the 17th, while for the Parisians a new period of separation began, heavy with anxiety.

> 'His departure made a deep impression on the city of Paris,' says the Duchesse d'Abrantès. 'No anxiety had been felt about any of his previous absences—victory came so easily to him—but the luck had changed and now disquiet was as keen as once confidence had been deep. News was awaited with impatience tinged with fear.'

The Emperor's determination was nevertheless approved; and it was hoped that early victory would wipe out the stain of the Russian disaster. When the *Moniteur* announced Napoleon's departure, to maintain morale it published an encouraging article on the state of the Army of the North and a fortnight later reported the first French troop movements and the Emperor's dispositions.

The victory of Weissenfels on 2 May was announced on 5 May. Here the infantry had marched at the double, their shakoes on the point of their muskets, crying 'Long live the Emperor!'

> 'Business at the Bourse was brisk since victory definitely strengthens and promotes the upward trend of stocks.'

Consols rose to 76.90 frs. The Empress was informed on the 7th that:

'His Majesty the Emperor has won a conclusive victory at Lützen over
the Russian and Prussian armies, commanded in person by the Emperor
Alexander and the King of Prussia.'

The cannon in Paris were still booming at midday and rejoicing
was general.

The news in Paris on the 13th, which caused 'general satisfaction',
was that Napoleon had entered Dresden on the 8th. Even at the
Wine Market it was noticed that 'news of the army has already
affected dealings in wines and spirits'.

As Napoleon continued his victorious advance, triumphing anew
at Bautzen near Hochkirch and at Würschen on 20 and 21 May, the
French army mourned two deaths, that of Marshal Bessières at
Lützen and of the Grand Marshal, Duroc, the Emperor's faithful
friend, at Würschen.

The Emperor himself had laid down the ceremonial for the official
celebration of the victory of Lützen (on Sunday, the 23rd). Mass
enthusiasm made a deep impression on Marie-Louise, aware that the
people's explosion of devotion was intended for Napoleon himself,
to whom she wrote next day:

'I was much touched by the evidence of the great love the people have
for the Emperor. The French have never worshipped him as they do
today . . .'

Reports of the victory celebrations for Lützen in the *Moniteur* of
the 24th were accompanied by an announcement that Napoleon had
suggested the holding of a congress at Prague, 'well received by
everyone'. Paris, which was in a permanent fever of impatience,
heard on the 26th of the victories of Bautzen and Würschen, announced in the newspapers on the following day, when Montesquiou
brought the Empress details of the battles.

Napoleon now found himself in a great dilemma; he was victorious,
but should he pursue the Allies in full retreat? Metternich, too, was
stupefied and had thought the moment opportune to make peace
overtures to the Emperor. Should he accept them? He was strongly
urged to sign an armistice, especially by his entire staff, headed by
Berthier, while Caulaincourt practically implored him to do so.
Echoes of an active peace campaign came from Paris, where people
were overwhelmed with grief at the deaths during the Russian
retreat, to which were now added the losses sustained in Germany.

This state of depression was calculated to undermine resolution and open the way to intrigues. When Maret arrived in Dresden from Paris he made himself the mouthpiece of the universal French desire for peace. Victory had delighted the Parisians but to them victory offered a definite opportunity, not to be let slip, for making peace. Parisian pressure won the day and Napoleon finally yielded. On 4 June at 2 p.m. he signed the armistice of Plesswitz, to expire on 20 July.

The Emperor's interest in the capital's affairs continued to be keen; he thought that the Empress's intention of attending a Te Deum at Notre Dame in honour of the battle of Bautzen an excess of zeal and that such ceremonies ought to be restricted. He reproved Cambacérès in a letter on 7 June:

'I am not in favour of the Empress's going to Notre Dame. Great state occasions should be of rare occurrence, otherwise they become commonplace. If the Empress goes for the victory of Würschen she would be obliged to attend for all the other victories.' The victory of Lützen had justified a Te Deum, but 'on this occasion it serves no purpose. With a people like ours one must keep one's distance.'

Before returning to Dresden, where he intended to stay in great state during the armistice, he wrote again to Cambacérès on 8 June:

'Caulaincourt should have written to the Comte de Rémusat to ask for actors to come to Dresden. I should rather like this request to make some stir in Paris as it can only do good in London and Spain to know that we are amusing ourselves in Dresden.' He recommended that the actors should travel 'without fuss and without cluttering the roads', but he made it clear that 'nevertheless the journey should be organized to appear as if the whole troupe of tragedy actors was leaving so that people in Paris can gossip about it.'

Napoleon took up residence in the Palais Marcolini on the 10th. Next day the *Moniteur* reported the signature of the armistice and published the programme for the Te Deum for Würschen. Large crowds cheered the cortège on its way and on the 16th there was a big review on the Place Vendôme, attended by many soldiers who showed their eagerness to rejoin the Grande Armée, an attitude in vivid contrast to that of the 'governing classes' and the great military leaders who longed only for rest and a definite term to war.

Savary, whose reports to the Emperor were full of this state of mind, brought down on his head this rude reply on 13 June:

'The tone of your letters displeases me; you are always boring me with the need for peace. I know better than you the state of my Empire. . . . I want peace and it concerns me more than anyone else. . . . Your speeches about it are therefore superfluous; I shall not make a dishonourable peace nor one which will lead us to a more savage war in six months' time. . . .'

He used the same kind of language to Cambacérès on 18 June:

'All the ministers' chatter about peace is doing me the greatest disservice. I have seen more than twenty letters from foreign ministers in Paris who write home that we want peace at any price . . . this is just the way to make peace unattainable. . . . Paris is barking up the wrong tree if it thinks peace depends on me. . . .'

Napoleon was right; a general coalition was massing against him. Prussia, Russia and England, which had concluded an alliance at Reichenbach, were soon joined by Austria whose minister, Metternich, was implacably pursuing his aim of overthrowing the Emperor and reducing France to the frontiers of 1789.

On 26 June at noon took place the celebrated interview between Emperor and diplomat, which was inconclusive; the only decision reached was for an extension of the truce until 10 August. In reality both sides sought a breathing-space to regroup their forces.

At a further interview on the 30th, which lasted four hours, Napoleon and Metternich agreed to hold a congress at Prague on 5 July, but Napoleon's need for a decisive victory became acute when he heard of the defeat at Vitoria, which would lead to the final loss of Spain.

Paris, meanwhile, was living only in the hope of peace but publication of the news from Spain increased anxiety. The working population continued unshakeably attached to the Emperor; hope was reborn when it was learned that Marie-Louise was going to meet him at Mainz and that the armistice was definitely extended until 10 August.

While the congress was 'apparently' holding its meetings, the capital was busy preparing to celebrate the Emperor's birthday, but deep anxiety persisted.

'Paris was then in a state of febrility,' wrote the Duchesse d'Abrantès, 'which recalled the stormy days of the revolution. People were nervous and no illumination came to lighten our darkness. The armistice of Plesswitz was about to expire with no sign of the longed-for peace.'

The communiqué of the 13th, giving news of Napoleon's return to Dresden, did nothing to relieve anxiety.

'As the armistice may be denounced before 15 August, the armies are preparing to celebrate the Emperor's birthday on 10 August.'

To keep up the city's spirits the government ordered the traditional free performances on Saturday, the 14th, at the Opéra, the Théâtre Français, the Opéra Comique and the Odéon.

Napoleon cheers Paris dismayed by the first reverses

Napoleon himself said that the Prague congress never had any 'real' existence; it was the cloak behind which the Allies perfected their military preparations. Metternich declared the congress dissolved on 11 August at noon, at the very moment when the Emperor let it be known that he was ready to accept his enemies' equivocal proposals. Next day Austria denounced the armistice and informed Napoleon that hostilities would begin again after midnight on the 17th. A new campaign was opening.

Although without official confirmation, Paris soon learned with great alarm of the rupture of the armistice. On the 18th the fall in stocks was

'attributed to the rumour going round the Bourse that Austria was making common cause with the coalition and that she had already received substantial subsidies from England.'

On the 23rd consols fell to 72.40 frs.

Napoleon remained unmoved; his morale was the more steely because his many reviews had demonstrated the army's sense of dedication, in which veterans and young recruits were keen rivals. 'The Emperor was unchanged, always the fabulous and extraordinary man at the head of his army.' He took the initiative at Dresden where bitter engagements were fought on 26 and 27 August when, despite his numerical inferiority, the Emperor in the mud, defying shot and shell, repulsed attacks from the Russian, Austrian and Prussian armies which were forced to retreat. It was here that Moreau (who had returned to Europe in July and was fighting as the

Czar's adjutant-general in the ranks of the enemy) was killed by
French bullets. When Napoleon commanded in person he was
victorious but elsewhere victory proved elusive. Vandamme was
beaten at Kulm, Macdonald at Katzbach, Oudinot at Grosbeeren,
Ney at Dennewitz.

After a silence of seventeen days the *Moniteur* published a letter
on 1 September from Maret to Cambacérès, giving the first news of
the battle of Dresden. More detailed information appeared in a
communiqué of the 6th, referring to the rupture of the armistice and
recent battles. These were the closing lines: 'The brilliant opening of
the campaign has given rise to great hopes.' Stocks rose to 74.50 frs.

Marie-Louise had a Te Deum sung in the chapel at St-Cloud on
Sunday, the 19th, followed by a grand reception, a theatrical performance in the evening and a Court. 'The palace and public buildings
were illuminated' but the *Moniteur*'s notice was curt, with reference
neither to the large crowd nor the enthusiastic cheers. The Te
Deum at the Tuileries and St-Cloud began to sound like *misereres*
and things looked serious. 'The great hopes began to fade.' The
government did its best to sustain morale by publishing reassuring
bulletins, with frequent repetitions of 'His Majesty has never been
better in health'.

Napoleon for his part gave instructions that the Parisians should
be fully informed and prepared for the fresh sacrifices to be demanded
of the nation. He ordered publication in the *Moniteur* of 5 October of
the weighty series of documents about the war with Austria and
Sweden, preceded by a report of the previous day's session of the
Senate and one from Maret, castigating Sweden's treachery which
had resulted in 'a continuation of the war which the Emperor did not
desire'. The Emperor also laid down the ceremonial procedure for the
session at the Senate at which he wished the Empress to make a
solemn proclamation, inviting the country to rally to the defence of
the national territory.

On 7 October Marie-Louise, who had returned early in the
morning from St-Cloud, left the Tuileries at 1 p.m. for the Senate
in the coronation coach 'with all suitable pomp', as Napoleon had
prescribed to impress the people and so that during his absence the
Empress should in her own person incarnate the Empire.

Marie-Louise ended the speech written for her by the Emperor
with the appeal, 'Frenchmen, your Emperor, the fatherland and

honour call to you.' Then followed the proposal to raise 280,000 men.

On departure as on arrival the Empress was loudly cheered.

A senatus consultum published on the 10th ordered the new conscription, from which married men were exempt. Stocks continued to deteriorate; from 74.50 on 22 September they had now tumbled to 58.00 frs, but if there was increasing depression there was no sign of revolt. No one could as yet conceive the fall of the régime. Although gradually the clergy, the bourgeoisie and the business world were detaching themselves from the Emperor and treachery was latent in the higher military and political echelons, the masses, especially the workers, were unwavering in their devotion to Napoleon, from whose genius they awaited miracles.

The city of Paris, as after the Russian campaign, took the initiative in demonstrations of patriotism and loyalty to the Emperor. At an audience granted by Marie-Louise to the Prefect Chabrol and the Corps of Mayors in the Salon de Mars at St-Cloud on 17 October she was presented with an address which enshrined these words:

'What Frenchman could remain deaf to the voice of the Emperor, to the cries of the fatherland and to honour? Never did the cords which bind and unite his subjects to the sovereign need to be drawn tighter.'

Bernadotte's conduct was severely criticized.

'A prince who owes his fame only to the honour of fighting with our armies ... he is compromising his throne to which the kindness of his Emperor had raised him ... he is no longer French. . . . Madame, by intensifying our zeal and affection, by fixing our eyes on this august throne to which Your Majesty has with all her own virtues brought the noble courage of her ancestress,[1] the inhabitants of the good city of Paris will, as faithful subjects, be conscious of all they owe to their prince and their fatherland.'

Meanwhile Napoleon had been trying, but in vain, to initiate negotiations through a Prussian general taken prisoner, while preparing to meet the furious assault of Blücher's and Schwarzenberg's armies, now joined by the Swedish army of Bernadotte. The fate of the Empire was fought out on the plain of Leipzig on 16, 17, 18 and 19 October. After bitter fighting and a great victory won at

---

[1] The Empress Maria Theresa. Ed.

Wachau French troops were forced to fall back because of the betrayal of the Saxon corps, but the Allies were too battered to pursue them.

The Emperor reached Erfurt on 24 October at 4 a.m. where he regrouped his army, weakened still further by Jerome's departure. On the 30th Napoleon repulsed the Austrians and Bavarians who were attempting to bar his road at Hanau, a victory which enabled him to continue his march towards Frankfurt which he reached on the 31st.

Both at Paris and St-Cloud, where Marie-Louise and the Court were residing, anxiety persisted. Nothing had been heard of the army since 4 October and the government was demoralized. News came at last on the 29th and the *Moniteur* of the 30th carried a long report of the military situation on 4, 15, 16 and 24 October, of which the last few lines made painful reading:

> 'By the battles of the 16th and 18th the enemy was thrown into disorder, but the disaster on the 19th revived his courage and he emerged victorious. After such brilliant successes the French army has lost its victorious ascendancy.'

Napoleon had insisted that nothing should be concealed from the nation and wrote to Cambacérès,

> 'I have told the whole truth because of my regard for the nation, but you must know that accurate communiqués exaggerate rather than minimize the extent of the losses. . . .'

At the Bourse shares suffered severely; stocks weakened to 52.50 frs. Paris command headquarters reported that people

> 'were seen to weep bitterly as they read the accounts in the papers that the battle on the 19th had wiped out the great achievements of the previous day.'

The Saxons' treachery affronted the Parisians.

> 'Fury against our treacherous allies is at its height, but there is great determination in all sections of society that, should it become necessary, every hand will bear arms to aid His Majesty to conquer peace and to repel our enemies should they dare to approach our hallowed soil.'

In spite of overwhelming demonstrations of loyalty misfortune continued to dog the Emperor. Wellington's entry into Pamplona on 31 October provoked Suchet's flight. Joseph made blundering attempts to keep himself on the throne but Spain was lost while Murat, urged on by Caroline, opened the Neapolitan ports to British ships and Italy in its turn was lost.

Napoleon was as deeply concerned about the repercussions of these fresh reverses as he had been after the Russian débâcle. From Frankfurt he wrote to Marie-Louise on 1 November that he was 'sending twenty flags taken by his armies at the battles of Wachau, Leipzig and Hanau . . .' then on the 3rd from Mainz, to revive patriotic enthusiasm in the capital, he sent orders to General Clarke for the formal presentation of the flags to the Empress before they were laid up in the Invalides.

'You have long known my feelings about these military ceremonies, but as things now stand I believe they may have their use.'

On the same day he soundly berated the Minister of Police for his defeatist reports and also wrote in the same vein to Cambacérès:

'Have a word with the Councillors of State and those poltroons of senators. Everyone tells me that they are terrified and show little resolution. You must rest assured that my infantry, my artillery and my cavalry are so much better than those of the enemy that there is nothing to fear . . . I am sorry I am not in Paris; they would see that never in my life have I been calmer or more at ease.'

On 5 November the *Moniteur* reported the 'total victory' at Hanau and that 'the flags taken at that battle and at the battles of Wachau and Leipzig are on their way to Paris', news which had a stimulating effect; stocks rose three points to 55.00 frs. Although morale had been shaken by the defeat and defections at Leipzig the people's trust in 'Napoleon's genius' and their confidence that fortune would change and there would be a further victory kept their equilibrium steady.

A final progress report

To cheer up the Parisians the newspapers stressed the progress made in public works in Paris. The year 1813, destined to be the last of the Empire in civic enterprise, had been a full one and the total achievement was impressive.

Among the palaces and great public buildings the interior of the
Cour Carrée of the Louvre was now restored, which had involved the
renewal of the Doric entablature and a prolongation of the sculptured
frieze of the old Louvre right round the buildings. Marble columns
were being installed at the entrance to the Colonnade and a low wall
supporting a grille replaced the wooden fence.

Little decoration was needed at the Tuileries but, to make the
entrance more imposing, four huge statues had been set on top of
each of the small lodges at the side doors, and a grand grille erected
at the entrance to the Grand Courtyard near the Arc du Carrousel.
On the garden side a gentle ramp to replace the flight of steps had
been built for the direct access of carriages to the foot of the grand
staircase.

The junction of both palaces on the north had been the largest
task. Part of the gallery, including several arcades, had been constructed between the Place du Carrousel and the Rue de Rohan in
addition to a section facing it.

Demolition of dilapidated buildings and remodelling of the parterre
had disengaged the Luxembourg of its encumbrances and it now
directly faced the Observatory. The gardens, too, had been much
improved and their beauty increased by marble vases and statues.

Although much excavation was still necessary a start had been
made on the foundations of the Palais de Rome.

Large-scale repairs and improvements were in progress at the
Invalides where, in the centre of the Cour d'Honneur, the white
marble plinth had been placed for the statue of the Duc de Montebello
(Marshal Lannes), sculpted by Cartellier. The boulevards leading
to the Invalides had all recently been renovated and gravelled and the
esplanade from the forecourt to the new quay divided into six
sections to make an elegant promenade.

Four hundred workers were completing the excavations at the
Palais des Archives which would have been 600 feet square enclosing
four courtyards; the principal façade on the north would have run
parallel with the Quai des Invalides (Quai Branly) and the remainder
with the Avenue de la Bourdonnais, a new avenue to be built and a
garden to be reclaimed from marshland.

The barracks on the Quai Bonaparte needed only a roof on the left
wing. Over the entrance a bas-relief, the work of Tannay, featured
Imperial crowns between a figure of Fame with her trumpet to her

lips and Victory holding a flag of the Imperial Guard. Near the barracks the Ministry of External Affairs had reached ground-floor level.

Work on the Palais du Temple, to house the Ministry of Religions, was going steadily forward. The General Post Office was taking shape, its frontages built in harmony with Fontaine's designs for houses along the Rues de Rivoli and Castiglione. Forty-seven of the arcades on the Rue de Rivoli and eighteen on the Rue de Castaglione had reached first-storey level.

The restoration and ornamentation, the stables and coachhouses of the Archbishop's palace were finished; all that had yet to be done was the laying out of an ornamental basin to be fed by a small cascade flowing over a rock in the garden which was to be enlarged.

Work had begun on a lycée for four hundred pupils at the Collège d'Harcourt.

Erection of the Arc de Triomphe de l'Etoile continued; the cofferings and rosettes for the two arches facing the outer boulevard were being sculpted, but this work, under Goust's direction since Chalgrin's death, had been slowed down because of the difficulty of quarrying the stone and transporting it from Château Landon. On 6 August 1813, the *Moniteur* would write, 'The monument so built will survive into centuries far distant.'

The obelisk on the Pont Neuf was rising steadily. The model of the elephant for the Fountain of the Elephant was already covered in plaster and sculptors were modelling the legs in one of which a spiral stairway was to be built. Four columns had been erected at the Bourse, indicating by their proportions the size of the building.

Demolition of the eastern side of the Grand Châtelet was enlarging the Place de Gesvres; the western side was maintained intact for use as an assembly room for the notaries of Paris. The cast-iron dome of the Cornmarket, an innovation for a building of this size, aroused great interest and discussion.

The grand design of enclosing the Seine between quays throughout the length of the city was being actively pursued, particularly the continuation of the Quai des Invalides section on the Left Bank between the Ponts de la Concorde and d'Iéna, near which a double ramp had been made for the use of vehicles coming to the port. Stonemasons were still busy sculpturing eagles over each of the piers of the western parapet of the Pont d'Iéna which was nearing completion.

Facing the Quai du Gros Caillou work was in progress on extending the quays along the verge parallel to the Champs-Elysées (Port de la Conférence and Avenue de New York) so that, in the space of a few years, the Seine was flowing between quays from the Pont d'Austerlitz to a point beyond the Pont d'Iéna and all danger to Paris from even the severest floods was eliminated. Two and a half miles of quay had been built.

Near the Luxembourg the new boulevard (Avenue de l'Observatoire) was being embanked. This would prolong the grand avenue of the Luxembourg through the garden of the former abbey of Port Royal (at that time the Hospice des Orphelins). Finally the principal barriers of Paris were to be renovated and completed.

Much had been accomplished in works of public utility. The unsavoury markets sited in narrow and dirty streets were soon to give way in all districts to large, airy and hygienic market buildings with fountains. Some of them had been newly built or enlarged like the Marchés du Temple and des Innocents (Jacobins).

The foundations of three further markets were being laid while the construction of slaughterhouses, particularly in Montmartre, were helping to make the streets cleaner and healthier.

Both the Wine Market halls for daily business were virtually finished; each contained seven large connecting halls where business had been in progress for several months. The road through the Market was already lined with trees and the pavements nearly all in position. Wines previously housed at the Ports of St-Paul, the Tuiles and St-Bernard were now temporarily lodged in safety in the old Wine Market where they were protected from the weather. Surveying had been carried out for the large thoroughfare to run to the Rue St-Denis and to fix the total area to be occupied by various markets.

The public granary had not as yet been finished but the vaulted cellars and part of the ground floor were complete.

An underground conduit was planned along the Rue de Hauteville to carry the waters of the Ourcq canal to the esplanade of the Boulevard Bonne Nouvelle where a water-tower was to be built and the navigation canal of St-Maur was being cut at the same time. Finally good progress was being made with laying the pipe-junctions of the Ourcq canal, from the eastern end of the 'village' of La Villette to the Seine below St-Denis.

In spite of the gravity of the hour there was no slackening in public works in Paris.[1]

---

[1] See Appendix II for a resumé of works carried out during the Consulate and Empire.

II

Devotion and Distress of the Paris Populace

Napoleon's last tours

After three days at Mainz Napoleon decided to return to Paris where he was impatient to be. When, at 5 p.m. on the afternoon of 9 November, he reached St-Cloud he learnt of the total liberation of Spain. Next morning he held a finance council at 11 a.m. before attending the Council of Ministers. In the afternoon he sent for Fontaine to give him a progress report on building works in Paris. On the 11th it was the Council of State he received in audience at noon to tell them of his vital need of subsidies but he realized the bitter truth that his distracted councillors' 'sole objective was peace at any price'. He would have to put fresh heart into them and his dejected government.

To impress the Parisians and arouse their patriotism Napoleon arranged a special ceremony. On the morning of the 14th a troop of horse, led by a band, entered by the Porte St-Martin, with the flags taken from the Austro-Bavarians at Hanau and Frankfurt, and escorting the Minister of War to the Tuileries, there to present them to the Empress.

Clarke and the official cortège, after their reception by Marie-Louise, proceeded to the Invalides to lay up the glorious standards. After mass the Emperor received the senators in audience at noon; they came to assure him in fawning language of their attachment to 'the fatherland, to honour and to the sovereign' but the President's grandiloquent speech was a flimsy cloak barely hiding the Senate's demoralization to which the great military leaders and the 'governing classes' as a whole were equally subject.

The headquarters report of 16 November emphasizes the contrast between this demoralization and the enthusiasm shown by the large crowds which pressed round the troops.

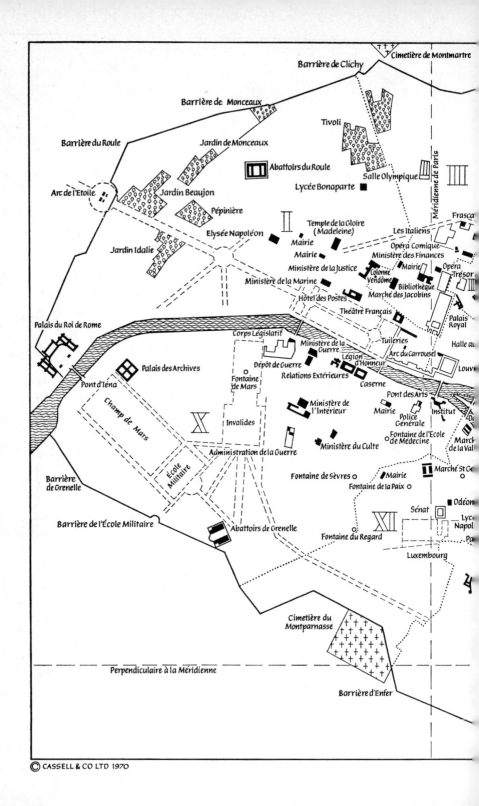

Cimetière de Montmartre

Barrière de Clichy

Barrière de Monceaux

Barrière du Roule

Tivoli

Jardin de Monceaux

Méridienne de Paris

Abattoirs du Roule

Salle Olympique

Arc de l'Etoile

Jardin Beaujon

Lycée Bonaparte

Pépinière

Frasca

Elysée Napoléon

Temple de la Gloire
(Madeleine)

Les Italiens

Jardin Idalie

Mairie

Opéra Comique

Mairie

Ministère des Finances

Mairie

Opéra

Ministère de la Justice

Trésor

Colonne
Vendôme

Ministère de la Marine

Bibliothèque

Marché des Jacobins

Hôtel des Postes

Théâtre Français

Palais du Roi de Rome

Palais des Archives

Corps Législatif

Ministère de la
Guerre

Tuileries

Palais
Royal

Halle au

Pont d'Iéna

Dépôt de Guerre

Arc du Carrousel

Légion
d'Honneur

Louvr

Fontaine
de Mars

Relations Extérieures

Caserne

Champ de Mars

Pont des Arts

Invalides

Ministère de
l'Intérieur

Mairie

Institut

Police
Générale

D

X

Marché
de la Val

Fontaine de l'Ecole
de Médecine

Administration de la Guerre

Ministère du Culte

Barrière
de Grenelle

École
Militaire

Fontaine de Sèvres

Mairie

Marché St Ge

Fontaine de la Paix

Barrière de l'École Militaire

Odéon

Fontaine du Regard

Sénat

Lyc
Napol

Abattoirs de Grenelle

XII

Pa

Luxembourg

Cimetière du
Montparnasse

Perpendiculaire à la Méridienne

Barrière d'Enfer

© CASSELL & CO LTD 1970

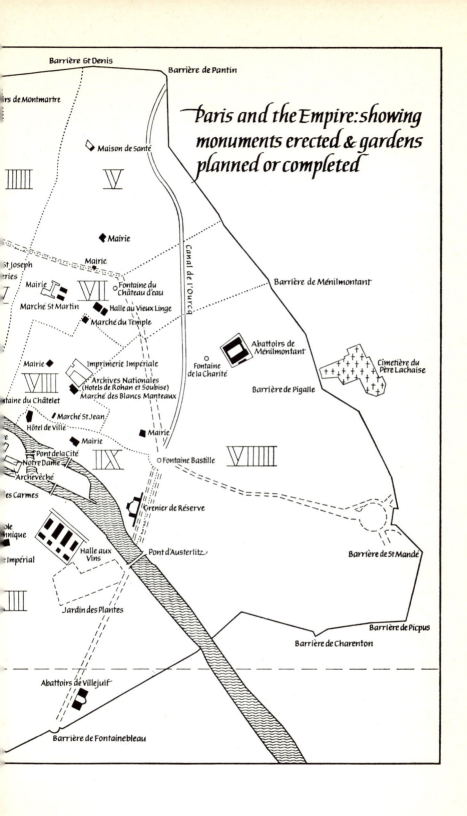

Paris and the Empire: showing monuments erected & gardens planned or completed

Barrière St Denis

Barrière de Pantin

rs de Montmartre

Maison de Santé

V

Mairie

Mairie

St Joseph
eries

Mairie

Mairie

VII

Fontaine du
Château d'eau

Marché St Martin

Halle au Vieux Linge

Marché du Temple

Canal de l'Ourcq

Barrière de Ménilmontant

Abattoirs de
Ménilmontant

Fontaine
de la Charité

Cimetière du
Père Lachaise

Mairie

VIII

Imprimerie Impériale

Archives Nationales
(Hotels de Rohan et Soubise)
Marché des Blancs Manteaux

taine du Châtelet

Barrière de Pigalle

Marché St Jean

Hôtel de Ville

Mairie

Mairie

Pont de la Cité

IX

Fontaine Bastille

VIII

Notre Dame

Archevêché

es Carmes

Grenier de Réserve

ole
nnique

Impérial

Halle aux
Vins

Pont d'Austerlitz

Barrière de St Mandé

III

Jardin des Plantes

Barrière de Picpus

Barrière de Charenton

Abattoirs de Villejuif

Barrière de Fontainebleau

'The sight of the flags taken through vast crowds to the Invalides confounded that malevolence which doubted our victories and still seeks every means of undermining morale. There is no doubt that government circles are not as active as they should be in keeping spirits high. This may not be true of the Councillors of State, but it is a fact that the people have nicknamed them "the tremblers" and accused or suspected them of being the first to unload their government stocks and bank shares while their speeches fail to show the firmness of tone expected of them.'

In his mansion in the Rue St-Florentin Talleyrand was at the heart of intrigues fostered by royalist agitators, the salons of the Faubourg St-Germain, the opponents of the régime or the merely discontented, among them important officials like Fontanes and Pasquier. Savary's ineptitude made him an unwilling accomplice in this subversive activity although he was wholly devoted to the Emperor.

The Bourbon cause, long neglected, began to gain ground and in Chateaubriand, who had finished his pamphlet, *De Bonaparte et des Bourbons*, found an enthusiastic propagandist.

'The former dynasty' says a contemporary report, 'had long been forgotten and it was reasonable to assume that it had no supporters, but those émigrés who had lived in London are making the great mistake of showing some kind of interest in the Bourbons while others barely conceal their regrets and guilty aspirations.'

At St-Cloud on 19 November Napoleon presided over a session of the Council of State when it was decided to raise two armies, each of one hundred thousand men. Next day, accompanied by the Empress and the King of Rome, he returned to the Tuileries for a stay of two months. Court ceremonies, with unrelaxed etiquette, Court balls and command performances continued as in his happiest days. The 'Marseillaise', never actually banned, was restored to its honourable place and sung in the Emperor's presence.

As a conciliatory measure to one political group Napoleon dismissed Maret, regarded as narrow and uncompromising, from the Ministry of External Affairs, which was given to Caulaincourt but, when approached by the Emperor, Talleyrand refused to act as his plenipotentiary to the Allies. The Emperor would have liked to dismiss him but a further demonstration of weakness allowed Talleyrand to continue with impunity in office as Vice-Grand Elector and to work in the shadows to demoralize political circles in Paris. His task was made easier because of the cordial relations he maintained with

Caulaincourt, who kept him informed of the progress of the delicate mission with which he had been entrusted, negotiation with the Allies.

The support Napoleon failed to find in his own disorientated and even hostile entourage he sought from the people of Paris who gave it him wholeheartedly. At the daily lengthy parades on the Carrousel they cheered the soldiers and their great leader and gave him a tumultuous welcome on his frequent visits to the theatre, which he used to test the public temperature.

Napoleon's favourite occupation was touring the works in progress in Paris which brought him into direct touch with the people and gave him the opportunity of speeding up the work involving the employment of more workers. When on the 24th he visited the gallery of the Museum and the Louvre he thought little had been done since he last went away but Bausset says that he was wrong.

'It was his outlook which had changed. He felt the need to ingratiate himself with the people and made this remark only because he was afraid that the workers in Paris had insufficient work and pay.'

This was one of the Emperor's obsessions.

From the Louvre he went on to the Cornmarket at 12.30 and was enthusiastic about its metal dome.

'It was market time,' reports the *Gazette de France*, 'and the many people about showed their delight at seeing him. Those who could not reach a point of vantage to gaze at him clustered round his horse which seemed borne on a tidal wave of heads.'

Still surrounded by people, the Emperor rode at a walking pace to inspect the Marché des Innocents, then returned via the quays to the Tuileries.

After his usual quick midday meal he drove to the Rue de Rivoli to inspect the building of the new Hôtel des Postes where he was again quickly recognized and surrounded by people who cheered him with shouts of 'Long live the Emperor!' On the 26th it was the turn of the west of Paris; the Emperor went to the Quai du Gros Caillou (Quai Branly) where he examined the foundations of the Palais des Archives and crossed the Pont d'Iéna to have a look at the yards at the Palais de Chaillot before returning to the Tuileries. Bausset, who accompanied him, writes sadly in his Memoirs,

'It was obvious to those with him that, although he tried to hide it, he was thinking of matters other than great building projects.'

On the morning of the 27th Napoleon went by way of the Quai Voltaire, through the courtyards of the Palais des Quatre Nations, to the new Marché St-Germain, thence via the Rue de Tournon to see the alterations made to the Palais du Luxembourg and its gardens. He stayed here for some time, then rode slowly on to see the new boulevard leading from the Luxembourg to the Observatory. His next visit was to the new Wine Market where he expressed great satisfaction with the way the entrepôt was working and had long talks with the tradespeople.

All along his return route by the Archbishop's palace, the Flower Market and the quays he was cheered by large numbers of people who had gathered to see him. Napoleon spoke graciously to those who sought his favours and made money gifts to some of those begging for alms.

Laplace notes in a report:

'The populace has never been quieter. His Majesty's ease in conversation and the reception he deigned to accord those who spoke to him have made a great impression in Paris. He is the sole topic of conversation in all the districts he visited.'

The report alludes finally to the underlying current of hostility:

'His Majesty's tours and rides give the lie to the disgraceful slander that he would make no public appearances.'

Popular enthusiasm was the more remarkable because the new conscription measures were coming into force. Calling up of conscripts had begun on 3 December at the Hôtel de Ville and was proceeding normally. The day's report mentions that the raising of three hundred thousand men was the universal subject of discussion and observations of varying wisdom. The many detachments of conscripts about to leave Paris showed themselves to be in excellent heart.

Napoleon continued his cherished tours. On the morning of the 7th he visited in turn the Palais de la Bourse, the Marché St-Martin, the public granary, the Madeleine, and so on. At noon he reviewed several infantry regiments on the Carrousel.

Fontaine writes, when Montalivet raised the question of the Temple of Glory (now the Madeleine):

'we observed that it pained the Emperor, who had fallen into a pensive mood, to hear the name of a deity he had worshipped so ardently and who had turned her face away from him.'

He broke a few minutes' silence to say, 'What shall we do with the Temple of Glory? Our grandiose ideas about it all have altered considerably. As things are today the only belief possible is in the Catholic faith. We must hand over our shrines to the clergy to hold since their knowledge of rites and the preservation of a cult is greater than our own. Let the Temple of Glory be henceforward a church; thus it can be completed and preserved—and mass must also be said in the Panthéon.'[1]

During dinner that evening Napoleon sent for Fontaine and asked him several trivial questions in a melancholy and abstracted way. From the Emperor's expression Fontaine could see 'how deeply preoccupied he was and how little was his interest at that moment in monuments ancient or modern'. This was probably their last conversation about building in Paris. Napoleon expressed approval of the Bourse and hoped that the interior, particularly the great hall, would be as magnificent as the exterior, but he was critical of the material used for the Marché St-Martin which he thought insubstantial. He ended the interview by giving orders that work should be found for the city's poor.

There was an appreciable downturn in trade and industry with a consequent large increase in the numbers of unemployed and needy workers. A report of 6 December echoes one of 30 November:

'Work in the factories, particularly the cotton-mills, is much reduced; several in the Faubourgs St-Antoine, St-Marcel and Gros Caillou have virtually shut down; the plight of those workers who have been dismissed gives rise to anxiety.'

And, in the report of 13 December,

'The cabinet-makers, joiners and locksmiths of the Faubourg St-Antoine, the Marais and other districts have paid off nearly all their employees, most of whom say they will have to beg.'

Every day distress made perceptible progress among the workers, who besieged the cheap soup centres in the Faubourg St-Marcel. These developments disturbed the Emperor who ordered the

---

[1] An allegorical fresco by Ziegler on the choir vault above the present high altar shows Napoleon receiving his crown from Pius VII. This is of special interest because the Madeleine is the only church in Paris to bear on its walls a likeness of Napoleon.

charitable committees to distribute soup vouchers and the price of
bread reduced by a sou from 13 December. He also wrote to Daru,
Minister of State and Administrative Director of the War Office:

> 'You have ordered carts for the army to be made at Metz but, as the
> Paris cartwrights are now short of work, you must order two hundred
> carts to be made here which will be done to time and give employment
> in Paris.'

When, on the 17th, Pasquier told Napoleon that some twenty-one
thousand workers were unemployed he sent Montalivet this note:

> '. . . It is my wish that work be found for them. It is scarcely credible that
> in Paris 350 trimmers, 700 hatters, 1,200 locksmiths, 500 carpenters, 200
> joiners, 2,000 coachbuilders, 300 bootmakers, in all some 6,000 to 7,000
> people are workless when there are complaints of insufficient men for
> war work and administration and for the Guard. Rather than leave these
> men unemployed jobs must be doubled or tripled. Please inform me of
> the precise number of workless and what steps must be taken to find
> them employment. . . . The cotton-spinners can be put to making cloth-
> ing, shirts, greatcoats, gaiters, etc. I have given orders to the Duc de
> Cadore (Champagny) to see how work for the Crown can be increased to
> keep goldsmiths, clockmakers, jewellers, tapestry workers, etc., busy.
> When I have your suggestions about increasing orders to these trades to
> keep the workers fully employed you can then set in hand either the
> demolition of houses round the Halles or excavation and embanking in
> various parts of Paris.' Finally he called for information within forty-
> eight hours so that 'everyone can be kept at work'.

The Emperor also instructed Pasquier to stop the large influx of
wounded from the front which threatened to overwhelm the hospitals
in Paris but, in spite of this interdiction, military convoys to the
city continued to increase.

As he wished the constituted bodies to participate in his great
work for national defence Napoleon summoned the Legislature, the
Senate and the Council of State for 19 December. He went in state
to the Palais Bourbon where, in a firm and lucid speech, he vigorously
called upon the country's representatives to show the courage needed
if France were to be saved.

'There is no opposition on my side,' he declared, 'to the restoration
of peace. The feelings of the French are known to and are shared by
me—I say the French because there is not one Frenchman who desires
eace at the expense of honour.'

Excellent order prevailed as the official procession passed through

the Tuileries garden and the Place de la Concorde. A police report of
22 December noted that

> 'His Majesty's speech, by silencing the false rumours current, reassured
> everyone and made a most favourable impression; his desire to make an
> honourable peace was obvious.'

Nevertheless this official optimism could not stem an upsurge of
anxiety. It was rumoured that coins were to be withdrawn from
circulation; news from the front was bad. The announcement on 26
December of the Allies' entry into Basle created much fright and

> 'large numbers went to the money-changers. Exchange of thousand-
> franc notes against gold began at 16 frs, closing at 24 frs and by 5 p.m.
> the gold had run out.'

Government stocks dropped in two days from 54·60 to 50·75 frs.
Midnight mass on Christmas Eve attracted 'a considerable attendance
in the capital's churches. Perfect order continues to prevail'. Paris
prayed silently.

The Allies tried, as they began their mass invasion of France, to
ease their task by causing alarm and despondency in Paris. Copies
of the declaration of Frankfurt were broadcast throughout the city.
This declaration, deceptively moderate in tone, insidiously pinned
responsibility for the misfortunes afflicting France on Napoleon and
his ambition. The enemy was attempting by undermining the
Parisians' loyalty to bring them to agree to a peace whose dishonourable terms would be concealed from them. In fact Metternich,
the moving spirit of the coalition, knew the deep devotion of the
people of Paris to the Emperor so his plan was to work on the capital's
political circles.

Napoleon's desire to defend Paris

Napoleon's reaction to the depression gradually gaining on the
people was to show unexampled coolness and activity. On 26
December he ordered the National Guard in Paris to be set on a
proper footing and counted on raising thirty thousand men.

> 'A National Guard is needed in Paris,' says one of Laplace's bulletins on
> 29 December, 'either because people of substance fear for their own
> security or because they have come to realize that the fatherland must be
> defended.'

The Emperor had sent the documents relating to the Frankfurt negotiations to the committees of the Legislature and the Senate which on 29 December, after studying them, voted a loyal address to the Emperor which ended with these words:

'Sire, by a supreme effort worthy of you and the French people, make peace. And, when you have signed the repose of the world, let the sword fall from the hand which has so often carried it to victory.'

The Senate's loyalty to Napoleon was not shared by the Legislature which thought the time ripe to reveal its hostility to the Imperial régime by composing an insulting address which had most unfortunate psychological repercussions. The Emperor replied to this address next day in a brief and moving speech. 'You are aware, from the documents sent you, of what I am doing in the cause of peace. I have accepted the sacrifices called for in the preliminaries but Béarn, Alsace, Franche-Comté and Brabant have been invaded. I call upon Frenchmen to come to the aid of Frenchmen. I call upon the French of Paris . . . and of the other Departments to help their brothers . . .'

On the 31st he ordered the Legislature to adjourn.

The ritual ceremonial of the last Imperial celebration of the New Year took place in an atmosphere of sadness and anxiety. Nevertheless 'the Court was present in large numbers at the Tuileries . . . never had so many people attended,' wrote the Duchesse d'Abrantès. Before mass the Emperor received the final homage of the great bodies of state and the Mayoral Corps of Paris in the throne-room. To rouse everyone's patriotism he used manly language, but his words to the deputies were violent and reproachful. 'What do you want? To seize power? It is I who can save France and not you . . .'

The decree proroguing the Legislature and the text of the Emperor's angry speech were published in next day's *Moniteur*, to be severely criticized by the opposition. People began, and with cause, to fear the worst. Theatres were empty and few people went to the Opéra Ball on 26 January. Commerce was, in fact, at a complete standstill and stocks had fallen to 50 frs.

The three Allied armies had already crossed the Rhine and were marching towards the valley of the Seine in the direction of Paris. Only a battle, supported by the mobilization of the nation's vital resources, could retrieve the situation. The nation and its leader were justified in believing that this could be done as the people continued to be sanguine and the young men were wildly eager to fight.

On 8 January 1814, Napoleon signed a decree, putting into service under his direct command the National Guard of 'his good city of Paris'. This was a popular measure.

'The Parisians are very pleased with the National Guard and are impatient for its reorganization.'

The newspapers paid fulsome homage to the Emperor's act on behalf of his good city.

'The capital,' wrote the *Gazette de France*, 'has ever been dear to our princes, to whom it was a kind of touchstone. . . . Who among the most famous of our royal benefactors has devoted so much treasure to the beautifying and prosperity of this valiant city, and then has bestowed upon it such a mark of honour. . . !'

Alas, this Guard, which should have played a vital part in the defence of France and Paris, was tainted by the presence in its ranks of men of suspect loyalty alongside officers devoted and resolute. The Guard, as Bourrienne wrote pertinently,

'soon became the home of dark intrigues where, when the hour struck, the defence of Paris was of less moment than profiting by Napoleon's overthrow.'

The Emperor's original idea was to make the capital a fortress. He wrote to Clarke on 11 January,

'My plan is to make Paris a fortified city. Should the enemy succeed in his avowed design of reaching it I intend to wait for him here and in no circumstances to leave Paris.'

This intention he formally confirmed on the 15th by dictating these orders:

'(1) No preparations whatsoever to be made for abandoning Paris and, if needs must, to be buried in its ruins.
(2) Large quantities of muskets to be brought up with all speed for storage in the Ecole Militaire, the Invalides and at Vincennes.
(3) Units stationed in fortresses to be brought up to Paris, etc.'

When, on the 13th, he reviewed an impressive parade of thirty infantry battalions, forty squadrons of cavalry and a large artillery train at the Tuileries, many veterans from the Invalides asked to be presented to him, and offered him their services. Touched by their gallantry and spirit the Emperor accepted the offers of several hundreds, aged between 25 and 40, who had completely recovered from

their wounds and were able to give a good account of themselves.
The *Moniteur* of the 14th remarked that:

> 'there were soldiers over 60 who, forgetting their age and the effects
> of their honourable wounds, insisted on being allowed to fight until the
> enemy was driven back from our frontiers, but eagerness alone was not
> enough to make them fit to fight again.'

The importance attached by the Parisians to military parades was
shown by the crowds they attracted but, says a report by Laplace,

> 'what really restores the confidence and hope of the citizens is the extra-
> ordinary energy and industry shown by the government.'

As hostility to the régime increasingly found its focus in Talleyrand the opposition sought to make capital out of the invasion to
spread despondency and undermine patriotism. Already by the 14th
royalist posters had appeared on the walls of Paris and the Faubourg
St-Germain had openly declared war on the Emperor. One morning
a placard was seen on the plinth of the Vendôme column with these
words: 'Pass by quickly, he is going to fall.'

But the Emperor was still erect and facing the storm although he
was fully aware of the subversive intrigues to bring him down.

At a Council of Ministers he shouted at Talleyrand, 'I know very
well that in Paris I am leaving enemies other than those I am going
to fight.'

His battle indeed was one which had to be fought out on the
field and on this battle rested all his hopes. To Queen Hortense he
said with a point of malice, 'So they've got the wind up in Paris?
They already see the Cossacks there? Well, they're not here yet nor
have we forgotten how to do our job—don't worry.'

Napoleon multiplied his efforts, encouraging the levies, speeding
the manufacture of arms and munitions, the making of equipment,
and so on. His prestige and supremacy were as great as ever both
among the veterans of bronze who had conquered Europe and the
young conscripts, those 'Marie-Louises'[1] who in the previous year
had wrought such miracles.

Houssaye says that in three months, out of fifty thousand recruits
who reported at the Courbevoie barracks, only 1 per cent had
deserted and

---

[1] The conscripts raised by the proclamation made in the Emperor's name by the Empress
were nicknamed the 'Marie-Louises'. Ed.

'when at a review or on a day of battle the Emperor passed in front of his men they succumbed to his fascination'.

As a whole the people rallied round the Emperor who was always highly gratified when he rode through the Faubourgs of St-Antoine and St-Marcel. Some members of his entourage advised him to take advantage of this popularity to range himself alongside the Jacobins, whom they believed alone to be capable of rousing the masses, but Napoleon refused, as he had done after 18 Brumaire, to become the man of a faction. He valued the people's affection but he meant to continue to be a man of order and legality, declaring, 'The demagogic principles of 1793 and the monarchy are incompatible; there can be no point of contact between the extremist clubs and a properly constituted ministry, between a committee of public safety and an emperor nor between revolutionary tribunals and the rule of law. . . .'

To suggestions that he would do better to appeal to the higher nobility he retorted, 'Gentlemen, you may say what you please, but in my present position I see nobility only in the rabble of the faubourgs and rabble only in the nobility I created.' In this he was not mistaken.

Paris now knew of the Allies' astonishing advance on to the soil of France.

'For the last few days,' notes a report of 20 January, 'news of the enemy's progress in several sectors has caused considerable anxiety in Paris.'

On the 19th many people went to the Banque de France and next day 500,000 francs' worth of notes were exchanged. To anticipate trouble, Pasquier arranged for the Governor of the Banque to send each of the Paris mayors tickets for distribution to people going to change money, but informed them that it would be paid out only to those genuinely in need. Stocks fell from 50.50 on the 8th to 46.50 frs. on the 19th.

The Emperor decided on 21 January that twelve regiments should be raised and an office opened in the Quartier Napoléon in addition to the offices permanently open in each Paris town hall for the enrolment and reception of volunteers. Next day he made his last tour. Towards 2 p.m., attended by his aide-de-camp, a groom and a page, he rode to the Faubourg St-Antoine where he was at once surrounded by a crowd which showed its pleasure at this mark of his confidence by hailing him with shouts of 'Long live the Emperor!' and offering him their services. 'No, Sire, let the enemy flatter himself, but he will not reach Paris any more than he did in 1792. We've thrown him out of Champagne and we'll chase him farther still. We all beg to be of service to you and to enter your Guard.'

The Emperor, touched by the evidence of such great loyalty, permitted the crowd to escort him as he rode back at a walking pace to the Tuileries.

Napoleon's tours of the city made a great impression on its citizens. According to a report of 22 January,

'Everyone is talking about His Majesty and the great pleasure given by his visits to different parts of the capital. Every detail of what was said to him is repeated and his fatherly kindness to those who accosted him is discussed, while his serene expression did much to cheer even the most apprehensive.'

A proclamation to the people of Paris was also issued on 22 January by the Municipal Council from the Hôtel de Ville:

'Parisians, His Majesty the Emperor and King in his speech to the Senate called on the French of Paris, of Brittany, etc. . . . to fly to the aid of those of our provinces which have been invaded.

'The city of Paris will not linger behind Normandy, Brittany and the rest of France; it will not remain in the rear when devotion to the fatherland and to honour must be shown, together with the unshakeable loyalty of the French to the sovereign who re-established the monarchy . . .

'The people of Paris, who have ever set the example by being the first to provide their quota for the conscriptions, will once again prove their attachment to the sovereign to whom both as Frenchmen and Parisians they owe everything.

'What Frenchman can remain deaf to the groans of the Francs-Comtois, the Lorrainers and the voice of the Lyonnais threatened by the enemy? Who would not shed his blood to preserve inviolate the honour we hold from our ancestors and to keep France within our natural boundaries . . . ?

'May recognition of these great and cherished benefits lead those men able to fight, and those who were obliged to relinquish the profession of arms, to join the valorous ranks which will do battle under the eyes of the sovereign and under the standards of the world's greatest captain.'

The first farewells to Paris

Napoleon determined to leave Paris as he was anxious about the enemy's advance which his marshals were powerless to stem. On

Sunday, 23 January he signed the letters patent conferring the regency on Marie-Louise and likewise took a series of measures for the capital's defence, among them the formation of artillery companies of the National Guard to be stationed at the barriers.

After mass he received the nine hundred officers of the Paris Guard in the Salle des Maréchaux, which he entered with the Empress holding the King of Rome by the hand. Bourrienne gives an eye-witness account of this scene memorable in the history of Paris and of France.

> 'In part portentous, in part solemn and in part sad, this ceremony took place in a silence deeper than any I have observed in so large a gathering, nor have I ever known one pervaded by such latent anxiety and tacit desire to hear Napoleon's voice . . . then that voice was heard.'

'I am setting out tonight to take command of the army. As I quit the capital it is with confidence that I leave my wife and son on whom rest so many hopes. . . . My future operations might result in the enemy's advance towards Paris. If this should occur remember that it can be for a few days only and that I shall soon come to your aid.'

The tumultuous and prolonged cheers of 'Long live the Emperor!' were taken up and swelled by the National Guard gathered on the Place du Carrousel.

During the night Napoleon dictated a long list of instructions to Joseph, now his Lieutenant-General and commander of the Paris National Guard.

Everyone waited impatiently for the departure for the front of the Emperor, the repository of their hopes. In general people were 'calmer and more reassured'; bank notes and shares regained a little popularity and the rush on the Banque de France relaxed, but there was now some anxiety about food stocks and crowds at grocers' shops. Pleasure also staked its claim and the evening's masked ball 'attracted more people than its predecessors'. *Panem et circenses.*

The orders left by the Emperor show his deep concern about the defence of Paris.

> 'One of my orders,' he wrote, 'was for the making of wire entanglements and stockades to close the barriers. Two pieces of artillery at each of the thirty principal barriers would protect them from any assault by light troops. Unless the enemy has considerable forces at his command only a few of these thirty barriers are liable to attack, as Paris is too large for a simultaneous assault by light troops on all its barriers. . . . The skeleton

units of the thirty battalions of the Guard in Paris are to be strengthened
by eighteen thousand conscripts. Four of these battalions should be
retained at the Eugène and Napoleon barracks. . . . These battalions will
be brought up to strength when they leave for the front, but in such a way
as to leave four full-strength battalions for the defence of Paris. . . .
Facilities exist for raising three thousand men in Paris for the cavalry of
the Guard. By uniting all these elements the government will continue
to be master of Paris.'

Napoleon embraced his wife and son for the last time and on 25
January at 4 a.m. left the Tuileries, which he would not see again
for a whole year. He was determined to take fate by the throat and
cut its jugular vein. Once again his martial spirit inspired his entourage while the people, seemingly unaware that the Allies' major
force had reached the area between the Marne and the source of the
Seine and were threatening Paris, firmly believed that they were on
the eve of another Austerlitz. When lots were drawn on the 27th for
the 1815 conscription, there were very few rejections. 'All the young
men appear to be in excellent heart.' The demand at town halls for
tickets to exchange bank notes declined appreciably.

This was the day when Napoleon entered St-Dizier and on the 29th
he again defeated the enemy at Brienne where Gourgaud saved his
life threatened by a Cossack's lance thrust.

The entry into St-Dizier was enthusiastically welcomed in Paris,
but even greater rejoicing hailed the announcement of the victory at
Brienne where Napoleon with ten thousand men beat Blücher with
thirty thousand. In two days stocks rose from 49.75 to 51.50 frs.
Arms production in Paris was stepped up and, as a precautionary
measure, work begun on stout oaken palisades for the capital's
fifty-two barriers and reinforcing weak spots in the enclosing wall.
Cannon were drawn up in front of the stockades to be manned by
students of the Ecole Polytechnique and the Faculties of Law and
Medécine. Thus Paris would be defended.

The Final Victories and the Capitulation

Paris still believes in victory

The first performance on 1 February of *L'Oriflamme*, an opera by Méhul and Paër, based on the story of Charles Martel's fight against the Saracens, was a runaway success, due in some part to good news from the front. A number of National Guards in the audience showed by their applause their response to the opera's theme of courage and patriotism. The fleeting rumour that the Empress and King Joseph and even the King of Rome might be present helped to swell the audience to bursting point as the crowd's imagination was as unbridled as its excitement. Even in face of such grave events Paris continued to be gay, while hope of an early deliverance from the enemy became a sudden conviction, strengthened by the sight of the 'superb' troops who daily arrived in Paris on their way to the front.

As the combat area drew nearer to Paris news from the army came swiftly to quench the Parisian's thirst for information. The majority longed passionately for peace, but a peace arising from victory, a hope they shared with the Emperor, who scorned to enter into negotiations dishonourable to him and to the nation. The sacred bond of trust which for fifteen years had linked Napoleon and the people of Paris remained intact; he had heaped glory on his good city which in return had grudged him neither its devotion, its support nor its blood.

However, as hope was reborn in Paris, Napoleon was fighting a bitter battle at La Rothière, near Brienne, against forces three times the size of his own. He was forced on the 3rd to withdraw on Troyes, which he found given over to grief; this was his first setback on the soil of France and it delighted the Allies, who were already making appointments to meet in the gardens of the Palais Royal.

The Parisians who, after *L'Oriflamme*, had begun to dream of

peace with glory, had a rude awakening. Instead of reading in the
Moniteur of 2 February of 'the great victory of Brienne' all they saw
was a five-line communiqué which summed up the battle in these
words:

> 'The Emperor took possession of the town and the castle after a lively
> rearguard action.'

Excitement collapsed. The withdrawal from La Rothière, known on
the 4th, turned disillusion into despair with immediate results. Consternation was general at the Bourse, which was besieged by the
public; stocks tumbled to 47.75 frs. 'Anxiety was obvious at the
markets where people were buying more foodstuffs.' Shortage of
funds caused the suspension of much work ordered by the War
Administration.

The opposition busily spread alarm; they said that:

> 'His Majesty has been in the greatest danger; General Corbineau killed
> a Cossack who had taken aim at the Emperor; and our troops have
> suffered severe losses.'

The government was showing signs of panic. At Notre Dame the
Forty-Eight Hours' Prayers were being said and Marie-Louise
wanted to go into retreat at Ste-Geneviève. Denon rushed to ask
Joseph's permission to pack up the Louvre collections. The Faubourg
St-Germain was jubilant and declared that the Allies would be in
Paris by 12 February at the latest.

As desertions began in the French ranks the Emperor sent Caulaincourt to the advanced posts to proffer an armistice to the Allies about
to confer at Châtillon. Little importance was attached to this move
by Napoleon who believed that his own destiny and that of France
could be determined only by force of arms.

> 'If these bases of negotiation are rejected,' he wrote on 5 February, 'we
> may have to fight and must run the risk of losing Paris with all its
> consequences.'

Immediately on arriving at Nogent on the 7th he wrote to King
Joseph: 'Guard the barriers of Paris well.' When Cambacérès told
him of the state of anguish into which everyone had fallen, he answered
indignantly, 'Why are you losing your heads like this? What is the
meaning of all these misereres and the Forty-Eight Hours' Prayers
in the chapel? Is Paris going mad . . . ?'

On the 8th he wrote his brother this pathetic letter:

'I answered you about the fate of Paris; you have only to look up my letter. This affects more people than ourselves. Should the battle be lost and you hear of my death you will be informed before the ministers. Send the Empress and the King of Rome to Rambouillet. Order the Senate, the Council of State and the army to assemble on the Loire. Leave in Paris the Prefect, a special commissioner or a mayor. It may happen, however, that if the enemy does approach Paris I shall beat him, then none of this will happen. It may also be that, in a few days' time, I shall make peace. . . . I see that fear is driving everyone in Paris out of their minds. I would rather see my son strangled than brought up in Vienna as an Austrian prince'—a sad premonition.

Paris remained a prey to anxiety.

'All are worried,' wrote the *Gazette de France* on 12 February, 'by the enemy's approach, contradictory reports, the normal fear of disaster and misgivings of nobler origin than pure self-interest.'

The social order was deteriorating dangerously. Queues formed outside the bakeries for bread baked by the Army Commissariat and the people were stocking up with dried vegetables of all kinds. Homeless soldiers, many reduced to begging, thronged the streets; the orders of the Minister of War that these men should be assembled at the barriers and sent to reception centres outside Paris were ignored. There was a further rush to change bank notes; public vehicles disappeared from the streets. Gloomy rumours were rife; the French army had suffered total defeat; the Empress was about to leave for Tours; the Allies would sign peace only in Paris. The royalists were exultant, but public order was not disturbed.

Recruiting in the Department of the Seine for the 1815 conscription ended on 4 February and 1,151 conscripts had already been seconded to the Imperial Guard.

'Departures of conscripts have been infinitely more satisfactory than for a long time. The young men are all in excellent heart and leave as gaily as the volunteers.'

Even some of the rejected wanted to follow their comrades to the field of honour. On the 9th Chabrol advised the mayors to invite the Parisians to make voluntary gifts to equip military hospitals, to which there was a ready response. In twenty-four hours large numbers of mattresses, sheets and blankets were taken to the town halls.

Then, on the 11th, came news of Champaubert, where, on the 10th, by a brilliant piece of strategy Napoleon had beaten General Olsouvieff; fifteen thousand French had put sixty thousand Russians to flight. Joseph learned of this victory while, in the presence of the King of Rome, he was reviewing the grenadiers of the Paris Guard on the Carrousel, where the news had a 'galvanizing effect'. With unanimous and spontaneous cries of 'Long live the Emperor!' the crowd besieged the grille of the Tuileries.

'The excitement of the National Guards, who threw their caps in the air as they gave voice to their affection for the Emperor, was at its height.'

Less than an hour later the 'happy news' had spread all over Paris where strangers stopped one another in the streets to discuss it. At the Bourse the communiqué was read to thunderous applause. Stocks rose from 50.00 to 56.00 frs. At 5.30 the guns of the Invalides woke from a long silence to boom as in the glorious days. The dispatch was read in the evening at all the theatres and at the Opéra actors and audience joined in the fervent singing of 'Victory is Ours'.

The French army was indeed victorious again. On the same day Napoleon beat Yorck and Sacken at Montmirail and sent Montesquiou immediately to Paris with a message which ended:

'I am of the opinion, therefore, that these two days will ward danger off from Paris.'

And, confident now, he wrote to Maret, 'I am now in a position not to yield an inch of territory.'

Napoleon's dispatch was delivered to Joseph on the following day when he was again reviewing troops at the Tuileries. There was pandemonium as everyone rushed into the courtyard, shouting 'Long live the Emperor! Long live the King of Rome!'

On the 12th Blücher won a victory at Château-Thierry where Sacken was killed but on Sunday, the 13th, the people of Paris, still unaware of this victory of which they did not hear until evening, had reached a pinnacle of happiness. They crammed the boulevards beyond the barriers to admire the government's measures to defend them from attack; their hearts were full of gratitude as they blessed the paternal solicitude of the Emperor for his good city of Paris.

Montesquiou's dispatch had turned gloom into joy.

'Never had public opinion in Paris been healthier, never were the Parisians more united in devotion to a sovereign who cared more for glory than for his own safety and who in recent battles, it was said, had exposed himself to danger like any common soldier.'

To the amazement of all Europe Napoleon for a few days went from triumph to triumph; victorious communiqués followed hard on one another. 'Gaiety today is greater because alarms and anxieties were so great.' The sole topic of conversation was now the brilliant manœuvres which had secured Napoleon's victories and his name was everywhere cheered. Already it seemed as if the enemy had been thrown out of France. On the 14th the Emperor won another victory at Vauchamp and on the 15th the booming guns announced it to Paris.

Three Russian generals, including General Olsouvieff, who had been taken prisoner, entered Paris by the Barrière de Pantin at noon on the 16th, escorted by six constables. The city's entire population had massed from the Barrière St-Martin to the Place Vendôme in the hope of seeing the famous Cossacks of whom they had heard so much. The generals were followed to headquarters with repeated shouts of 'Long live the Emperor! Long live Marie-Louise!'; in the Place Vendôme the cry was 'Long live the column!' as a riposte to the Allies' plan to demolish the monument.

'In this display of loyalty to the Emperor not a single word was uttered to offend the prisoner generals.'

Paris knew how to treat the vanquished with respect.

Next day the first ragged column of Russian and Prussian prisoners, led by a body of the gendarmerie and followed by grenadiers of the National Guard, marched down the boulevards for nearly an hour and a half, watched by a huge crowd which had gathered from morning on the Place de la Concorde, the boulevards and the Rue du Faubourg St-Martin. This march, which flattered the national self-esteem, 'made a great impression, inspired great confidence and hope for the future'.

Meanwhile Napoleon's able tactics were successful; on the 17th it was Nangis and the 18th Montereau, where he heard of Murat's defection. To keep up the Parisians' spirit he sent Clarke ten flags taken at Montereau, together with those captured at Montmirail and Vauchamp, to be presented to the Empress before being taken to the Invalides. Paris went wild when it heard of these victories

and confidence seemed restored. Many people returned to the homes
they had left abruptly; the theatres again attracted large audiences
and 'any allusion which seemed at all applicable to current events was
seized on and applauded repeatedly'; the masked ball at the Opéra
was most successful. Paris continued to set an example; the numbers
of army enrolments went on increasing.

Napoleon was cheered as never before when he entered Troyes
on the 24th; the enemy was in full retreat along the Aube. As Houssaye
writes, '150,000 men would not give battle to 60,000.' The Allies,
assembled at Lusigny, were in a great dilemma. Schwarzenberg
sent an envoy to seek an armistice, although in reality the Allies
only wanted a breathing-space to regroup their forces and strengthen
their accord, much shaken by Napoleon's victories.

Hulin's report describes the state of mind in Paris at this moment.

> 'Rumour has it that the Prince of Liechtenstein has arrived at His
> Majesty's headquarters with full powers from the Allies to seek an
> armistice. They say that His Majesty is ready to grant it and even to sign
> peace if the Allies agree to the Treaty of Frankfurt. In Paris this news
> sustains hope and happiness. Public morale is good and improves daily.'

The great aspiration seemed on the point of being fulfilled; peace
after victory.

This may have been the general feeling in Paris but plots were
still being woven by the experienced hands of Talleyrand, of which
Napoleon was well aware. He also knew that certain individuals,
particularly rich bourgeois or nobles, so far from rejoicing at his
victories, saw 'enemy occupation as liberation'. To counteract this
belief and prevent its spreading to the loyal populace he decided that
Paris should be informed of the atrocities committed in the invaded
area. On 23 February he sent Joseph instructions on how to deal with
the delegations sent to Paris from the towns which had suffered:

> 'It is perfectly in order for the General Council of the Paris commune
> to receive and hear these deputations. The addresses they submit must be
> highly factual and should afterwards by posted up in the city so that the
> people of Paris will see that they are threatened with plunder, rape and
> fire. . . . If intelligent use is made of these reports from the invaded
> communes they will, I repeat, create an enormous effect. . . . Everyone
> will be profoundly indignant and, as a consequence, fear will dictate their
> duty to the Parisians.'

The Emperor knew full well how feckless and timid was the

government he had left in Paris. On the 24th in the full flush of
excitement at his victories he wrote to Joseph:

> 'I am writing to the Empress to have thirty salvoes of artillery fired . . .
> the enemy ranks are terrified . . . a few days ago they thought that I was
> defenceless; today their imagination knows no limits. . . . The newspapers
> in Paris must make full use of this fear. I do not approve of the comments
> made on the communes' reports to Paris; they are to be made in accor-
> dance with what I ordered. The Minister of the Interior is a weakling; he
> has mad ideas about people. This is not a state ceremony nor a ruse. . . .'

To Savary he wrote on the same day:

> 'It would be hard to find greater inertia than in Paris. You're all asleep
> and talking rubbish.'

The Corps of Mayors met on Sunday, the 27th, at the Hôtel de
Ville in extraordinary session to welcome the deputations from
Montereau, Sézanne, Nogent-sur-Seine, Provins and Château-
Thierry. An address was read, giving details of the grievous state of
these towns, to which the Prefect Chabrol made a reply demonstrative
of his patriotic feelings:

'Gentlemen, we have been deeply moved by what you have told
us. . . . The enemy has disclosed his plans against the inhabitants of
this city which once extended a generous welcome to travellers. The
Allies rally to the war-cry of "Paris!" which is to be plundered. . . .
This disclosure of their intentions has strengthened the will of the
capital's inhabitants to resist and their hopes and prayers will unite
to form a single shield around the sovereign. . . . No, never will this
famous city, this centre of culture and civilization, the common property of the Empire, be the enemy's prey and subject to his fury.'

Before the session ended it was decided that the reports of the
delegations should be billposted in Paris for the information of its
citizens.

This, one of the last 'glorious days' of the Empire, began with the
flag ceremony ordered by the Emperor. At 11 a.m. a splendid procession left the Ministry of War for the Tuileries where the Carrousel
was filled with troops. The procession passed through the Arc de
Triomphe to the Grand Entrance of the Cour de l'Horloge. As the
flags were borne through the courtyards the drums beat the general
salute and the troops presented arms as a single cry rang out, 'Long
live the Emperor!' At noon Clarke and the Staff presented the flags

to the Empress in the throne-room, glorious trophies indeed but it
was hard to forget that they had been captured only fifty miles from
the capital.

Paris followed with feverish attention the drama being played so
near the city and of which the effects were more intimately and
speedily felt than those of any previous campaign. Daily, people came
in from country districts with their wives and children and dragging
carts filled with their most precious possessions. Hospitals were
literally inundated with sick and wounded. Gold vanished from the
money-changers. Shops began to limit their displays but no anxiety
diminished loyalty to Napoleon.

> 'Public morale,' wrote Pasquier on 5 March, 'is in the main good
> although affected by the desires for peace, but confidence in the Emperor's
> genius is boundless.'

In spite of the numerical inferiority of his armies the Emperor
had held the whole of allied Europe in check, beating Russsians,
Prussians and Austrians in turn and proving the truth of the proud
words he had uttered at the opening of the campaign, 'I and 50,000
men make 150,000 men.'

He refused to entertain acceptance of the pre-1792 frontiers, however, but the Allies, having got their second wind and consolidated
their alliance, concluded at Chaumont on 9 March a twenty-year
treaty, expressing complete unity of views and barring any separate
peace.

Neither Napoleon nor his opponents were in truth ready to sign
a peace treaty, or rather the peace one side would have signed was
not acceptable to the other and the terms proposed varied with each
army's fortunes. Napoleon did not despair of crushing the Allies
who, although recognizing his genius and belligerence, were determined to reach Paris come what might. Between the Prussians and
the Russians it was a point of honour to be the first to arrive in the
city.

The Allies threaten Paris

March was to be Napoleon's fatal month when he was deserted or
betrayed by his lieutenants and the wiles of the 'fifth column' laid
Paris open to the Allies and restored the Bourbons to the throne.

During the night of 27/28 February Blücher crossed the Seine at

La Ferté-sous-Jouarre and advanced to the left bank of the Ourcq, pressing on towards Paris. Napoleon therefore hurled himself on the Prussian rear which was saved on 3 March from encirclement by the shameful capitulation of General Moreau at Soissons.[1]

The Emperor, always anxious about public opinion in Paris, wrote on the 3rd to Hulin, 'Anyone would think you're asleep in Paris' and to Cambacérès:

'I see that you have a genius in Paris for being afraid. Be satisfied that today the capital is no longer seriously threatened. That is quite enough with all the bad spirit abroad in everyone connected with government, from the Prince of Benevento to I do not know whom; it is they who since November have upset public opinion.'

The city's loyalty contrasted with the confusion in official circles. An article in the *Gazette de Santé* on 2 March underlines the many examples of devotion shown by 'all the doctors and surgeons in Paris together with the students of the faculties'.

Napoleon was tirelessly pursuing the retreating enemy. On the 5th he attacked Rheims which fell to General Corbineau. From Fismes the Emperor himself dictated the wording of a communiqué for the *Moniteur* and told Marie-Louise to have salutes fired. After a further victory at Berry-au-Bac on the 7th he repulsed Blücher at Craonne and obliged him to retire on Laon, but he could not, in spite of fierce attacks, force him out of the town and had himself to fall back to Soissons. His troops had covered themselves with glory in the recent battles but at a cost of enormous losses, which rendered their situation highly vulnerable in face of an enemy whose ranks were swelling daily.

From 4 March, when stocks fell from 55.00 frs to 53.75, the situation in Paris began to worsen.

'Although the Bourse was crowded, little business was done,' says a bulletin of Pasquier's. 'The cry for peace seems to be on everyone's lips and anxiety is expressed about the commercial and administrative future of France if a speedy peace does not crown the new victories won by the armies commanded by His Majesty.'

In spite of the guns saluting the victory at Berry-au-Bac on 6

---

[1] Commandant of Soissons, not to be confused with General Moreau, victor of Hohenlinden, killed at Dresden. Ed.

March stocks dropped slightly to 53.50 frs. On the 9th salvoes again hailed the battle of Craonne, but it was significant that, although this victory was greeted as 'most glorious for the French armies', stocks which in three days had fallen to 51.00 frs rose only to 51.25. People were now more attentive to the guns thundering near Paris, than to those at the Invalides. The victories of Champaubert, Montmirail, Berry-au-Bac and Craonne were not on the scale of Austerlitz and Wagram. Bourrienne writes,

> 'They were accompanied by convoys of wounded, whose sufferings were seen close at hand, as the hospitals were choked with these sad cases . . . and all over Paris, in mansions as in shops, women were busy making lint, so great were the numbers of wounded. . . .'

Nevertheless the people admirably continued to believe unshakeably in Napoleon, bent on snatching victory from his enemy with whom he disputed the territory yard by yard.

To make defence truly national he increased the number of companies of men 'dressed in regional dress or blue overalls' so that every worker, every bourgeois, who donned his overall found himself in uniform. The torpidity of the government in Paris enraged the Emperor who wrote to Joseph,

> 'Nobody could be worse supported than I am; I left a fine army and cavalry at Troyes but the stuffing had gone out of it. . . .'

Joseph and the government in Paris saw salvation only in peace, even if it meant a return to the frontiers of 1792. At a council Joseph had approved this standpoint, but Napoleon ignored his letter proposing it as too humiliating. The fervour Napoleon had hoped to find in his army he thought he had found in these bands of partisans, 'these blue overalls', whose numbers increased as the countryside rose against the invader. He also knew that it existed in the people of Paris, who clamoured in vain for arms and seemed determined to fight at the barriers, but there was no longer the same spirit abroad as in 1792. In the hope of getting Joseph and his ministers to shake themselves out of their torpor and take energetic measures for the public safety, Napoleon sent letter after letter to his brother. On 10 March he again urged mass mobilization:

> '. . . I think you should call a ministerial meeting to decide how to raise thirty thousand men out of those taking refuge in Paris and from the unemployed workers. This levy should be called "mass mobilization of

the National Guards"; as you have muskets it should be simple and all those workers who don't know what to do will be well placed. If the National Guard takes part then the rich will no longer fear a proletarian rising but, on the contrary, will join in the city's defence.'

Reproaches have been levelled at Napoleon that his tardy decision to arm the Parisians was due to distrust, but the real reason is that he did not believe that the enemy would ever threaten the capital.

The Emperor laid down the measures to be taken to fortify Paris in a memorandum on the 11th:

'Give orders for certain necessary works in Paris, such as charity workshops, to be set in hand. I think that the moral effects of some redoubts on the heights would be useful. You must give orders for redoubts to be started at Montmartre.'

He was embittered by the defections taking place even among his own entourage and declared:

'On all sides I hear complaints from the people that they are prevented from defending themselves by the mayors and the middle class. I see the same thing happening in Paris; the people are determined and honourable —I am much afraid that certain leaders do not want to fight. . . .'

After regrouping his army Napoleon inflicted a sharp defeat on the Russo-Prussians, who had recaptured Rheims; he drove them out of the city which he entered in triumph on 13 March.

While Napoleon was trying, and even meeting with some success, to put fresh heart into everyone, the internal collapse was worsening. The English, supported by the royalists, entered Bordeaux on the 12th, quickly followed by the Duc d'Angoulême. When Joseph heard the news that evening he and his government were stunned. With certain members of the Council of State and the Senate, and inspired no doubt by Talleyrand, they determined to make a formal and public request to the Emperor to force him to agree to a cease-fire and to make peace. Marie-Louise in fright instructed Méneval to warn Napoleon who was still at Rheims. His reply was excoriating:

'The first petition presented to me asking for peace I shall consider in the same light as a revolt.'

On 14 March he sent Savary this haughty and angry message:

'You tell me nothing of what is happening in Paris. They are talking about a petition, about a regency and a thousand and one intrigues as commonplace as they are foolish. . . . None of these people know that,

like Alexander, I am cutting the Gordian knot. Let them take it to their
hearts that I am the same man I was at Wagram and Austerlitz. . . .
Either you are inefficient or you are no longer serving my interests.
Realize that if an address with no basis in authority had been sent me I
should have had the King [Joseph], my ministers and the signatories
arrested. . . . I want no tribune of the people. Let it not be forgotten
that it is I who am the great tribune.'

To a despairing capital the news on the 16th of the victory at
Rheims brought fresh hope, but it was short-lived. Until 23 March the
Moniteur was silent and anxiety rose to new heights as Napoleon
was known to be far from Paris. Groups were seen on the boulevards,
the squares and streets, waiting for the publication of communiqués, while the royalists, stimulated by events at Bordeaux, plastered
the walls of Paris with seditious posters. Although the theatres were
still staging attractive plays they remained empty. Most distressing
of all was the continued influx of wounded, some of them stricken
with typhus and filling the Hôpital de la Pitié to capacity.

Savary, in an attempt to obey the Emperor's orders, tried but
without success to arm the faubourgs. Pasquier in particular declared
that picks (since no more muskets were available) ought not to be
handed over 'to a mass no one can lead, for whom no one would be
responsible and who could as easily turn against the government as
fight for it'.

In this he was mistaken.

Will Napoleon save Paris?

Napoleon's plan to save the capital was one of genius. He would turn
aside from Paris to march towards Lorraine via St-Dizier, there to
raise the garrisons of the eastern fortress towns. This move would put
the enemy's communications in hazard and they would set off in
pursuit of him, leaving the capital behind them.

Knowing the ineptitude and confusion of Joseph and his associates,
he sent his brother orders on the 16th before he took the offensive
that, in case of danger, Marie-Louise and his son should leave Paris:

'In conformity with the verbal instructions I gave you, and the spirit
of all my letters, in no case must you permit the Empress to fall into the
hands of the enemy. . . . Should the enemy advance on Paris with such
forces as to render all resistance impossible, send off towards the Loire

the Regent, my son, the grand dignitaries, the ministers and officers of the Senate. . . . Do not leave my son and remember that I should prefer to see him in the Seine than in the hands of France's enemies.'

With only twenty-three thousand men he did not hesitate to attack Schwarzenberg with one hundred thousand and left Rheims at noon on the 17th for Epernay. On the 18th he was at La-Fère-Champenoise where he heard quite unruffled of the fall of Bordeaux and the break-up of the Congress of Châtillon at the same time as couriers brought him news of the panic which had seized Paris and Marie-Louise's desperate appeals.

His energy nevertheless was indefatigable. He ordered Marmont and Mortier to contain the Russo-Prussian thrust behind the Aisne and, if need be, to fall back on the Marne to bar the way to Paris, then himself set forward to Arcis-sur-Aube. After two days' fighting against forces three times the size of his own Napoleon was master of the town on 22 March but, unable to pursue the enemy, had to fall back towards Vitry. On the same day Augereau, incredibly supine, allowed the enemy to enter Lyons.

Napoleon's decision to march on St-Dizier was of capital importance and determined his own future and that of the Empire; he knew that the numerical inferiority of his troops made a prolonged struggle difficult, but were he able to reach the eastern garrisons his army could be reinforced. The Emperor was aware that this plan would expose Paris and that he risked its falling into enemy hands if he wished to preserve it intact. Whichever course he took was a gamble. Everything, his own fate, the fate of France, and the fate of the Allies, depended on the fate of the capital.

When the campaign opened he had deemed it impossible that Paris, the brightest jewel of his great empire, should be taken. He had written to Joseph, 'If the enemy advances on Paris then there is no more Empire.' It was the Emperor who spoke. He believed Paris to be adequately defended by Marmont's and Mortier's corps, the National Guard and the remaining garrison troops. He also thought that the enemy, knowing his communications to be threatened, would not dare risk a thrust on the city where failure would be fatal. As the battles multiplied the ruler gave way to the conqueror who, although he thought the possibility remote, conceded that Paris might fall. For him it was only 'a painful moment' and one essential to his military operations. He was sure of recovering by force the treasure stolen from him, which was why on 16 March he had made arrangements for the departure of the Empress and the government.

Two conditions were vital for the success of his plan; first of all, secrecy about his intentions and their execution to fox the enemy who would be in the dark about his strategy; second was the continued loyalty of Paris, which meant the elimination of traitors. Neither of these conditions was to be realized.

Napoleon, still full of confidence, entered St-Dizier on 23 March. Champagne had risen against the invader, the 'blue overalls' were on the warpath, the fortresses of Metz and Thionville had released their garrisons. Numbers were reinforcing genius but the Emperor's aides were far from sharing his optimism. In Caulaincourt's check at Châtillon they saw the last straw. Now fickle Fortune turned against her favourite child; she allowed the leakage of the brilliant plan which would yet again have ensured the great captain's victory.

On 22 and 23 March the enemy intercepted two letters; in one Berthier asked Macdonald to hasten his march, specifying that the Emperor was between Vitry and St-Dizier, in the rear of the Grande Armée; in the other Napoleon had written to Marie-Louise:

'I have decided to make for the Marne to divert the enemy from Paris and to make closer contact with his forces. I shall be at St-Dizier this evening.'

Without information about the Emperor's movements the Allies had been worried. What was his object in leaving Paris vulnerable? Now they knew, and on the night of the 23rd a council of war met at Pougy, attended by the Czar, the King of Prussia and the Chiefs of the Allied Staffs. The Allies, disconcerted by Napoleon's rapid advance, decided that the Austrian troops, instead of advancing towards the Seine and the Aube, should march on Châlons, but the interception of another letter struck a decisive blow at Napoleon. This was from Savary, saying that,

'many influential people in Paris are openly hostile to the Emperor and would be a source of trouble if the enemy approached the capital.'

This was the signal for Alexander, urged on by Pozzo di Borgo, who loathed Napoleon, to decide on the 24th to march on Paris. The Prussians and Austrians agreed with greater alacrity because they had just heard that Marmont and Mortier had been pushed back by Blücher after bloody battles.

On the 25th the enemy armies of a hundred and fifty thousand men set off in two parallel columns towards Meaux where they joined up to open their offensive on Paris, with the same lifting of the heart as the Napoleonic cohorts had felt marching on Moscow . . .

The *Moniteur* of the 22nd mentioned only that the Emperor had arrived at Arcis-sur-Aube on the morning of the 20th, but no mention was made of the battle fought there. It was learned on the 24th that the Emperor was making for Vitry, but, says Pasquier:

> 'Little definite information was given about the battles from the 20th to the 24th. Personally I was certain that the 21st had been a very bad day for us, and the movement towards Vitry seemed at the least to be fraught with danger.'

This opinion was shared by Joseph who, during the night of the 22nd/23rd, had received a message written by Napoleon to Clarke:

> 'My advance posts are at Vitry. . . . I shall march on St-Dizier. . . . The Duc de Raguse (Marmont) and the Duc de Trévise (Mortier) have orders to make towards Châlons.'

This movement, which would expose the roads to Soissons and Coulommiers, caused some anxiety but the public were still full of hope. On the 24th a long column of Russian and Prussian prisoners marched down the boulevards towards Headquarters, watched by a huge crowd of sightseers. Reinforcements of men and horses were seen daily going in the direction of Meaux. Nothing, therefore, was yet lost.

> 'It is obvious,' wrote the *Gazette de France* on the 27th, 'that highly important movements are being carried out by the whole French army which are causing great confusion to the enemy's operations. . . .'

Disillusion was not slow in coming. An article in *The Times* became known, calculated to demoralize.

> 'If the Cossacks and Blücher reach Paris, the principal seat of French wealth and industry, what mercy will they show her and why should they be merciful? Will they spare the chief monuments of the arts? Oh, no. This is the day of vengeance and destruction.'

Marmont's defeat at La-Fère-Champenoise was learned in the evening; stocks dropped a point and continued to do so on the days following which were barren of news from the army.

Napoleon, who believed that the enemy was pursuing him,

pinned all his hopes on a last battle. At Doulevant on the 25th he
came up against the Allied cavalry sent out as a feint to mask the
large-scale attack against Paris which had just opened. Napoleon
crushed the Allies in his final victory. Momentarily he had faith in
his ultimate success until he heard from a prisoner the horrifying
news that the enemy's main force was advancing towards the capital.

Paris now knew that Napoleon was at some distance and that the
enemy's advance made communication with him impossible. Country
people, fleeing from the invader, flocked to the barriers. When King
Joseph realized that further instructions would not be forthcoming
and that he must rely only on himself he began to appreciate the
nature of his responsibilities. He tried, with the aid of Clarke and
Savary, to organize resistance but this tardy effort in an atmosphere
of disarray and demoralization produced only trivial and ineffectual
results. Without fortifications, all that could be done was to man the
bridges at Charenton, St-Maur and Neuilly and station the available
troops of the line at the barriers.

To hearten the people, King Joseph reviewed a great parade of
troops, lasting for four hours, on the Carrousel on 27 March. A burst
of cheering greeted Marie-Louise's appearance at a ground-floor
window, holding in her arms the King of Rome, wearing a military
hat and his chest slashed by the Grand Cordon of the Legion of
Honour. Throughout the review constant and resounding cheers were
uttered by the people who continued to trust in the Emperor, but
disquieting news of the allied advance leaked out, while in the
shadows treachery was rearing its head.

The vital question whether the Empress and the child-King should
remain in Paris or leave the capital was settled at a Council held the
following evening at 8.30. Under Marie-Louise's presidency with
Joseph beside her were the three grand dignitaries, Cambacérès,
Talleyrand and Lebrun, all the ministers except Maret and Caulaincourt, and the President of the Senate. The prevailing opinion
throughout the discussion which lasted until 2 a.m. was that the
Empress should remain in Paris. Savary was one of those who was
strongly in favour of her staying and went bail for the loyalty of the
popular quarters. Boulay de la Meurthe, the former Jacobin, declared
himself in favour of a call to arms and suggested that the Empress,
with her son in her arms, should go to the Hôtel de Ville and then
tour the faubourgs.

Joseph then thought it his duty to read Napoleon's letter of 16 February, which proved decisive. The Emperor's wishes must be respected; Marie-Louise and the government must go. The night was spent in feverish preparations but in the morning the officers of the National Guard on duty at the Palace, who had been informed of her departure, came to beg Marie-Louise not to abandon Paris, and promised to defend her to the death. The words spoken to them by Napoleon on 23 January were still echoing in their ears; the Empress was moved to tears.

While on the morning of the 29th the Prussian troops were approaching Villeparisis, Marie-Louise, utterly at a loss, left the Tuileries with Cambacérès, never to see the palace again. She had until the last moment awaited a counter-order from the Emperor, bidding her stay, but the Cossacks' imminent arrival forced her to go.

Under a sombre sky the procession of ten heavy green berlines, emblazoned with the Imperial arms, the coronation coach hidden under grey canvas, a long line of waggons and an escort of fifteen hundred horse and foot wound its way slowly towards Blois through the dull and deserted Place du Carrousel, once the scene of brilliant parades. At the Pont Royal a handful of people gazed blankly at the cortège, so like a funeral procession.

The final battle communiqué was published that same day in the *Moniteur*:

'On the 26th of this month at St-Dizier the Emperor defeated General Wintzingerode, took two thousand prisoners, guns and many vehicles and baggage trains. This corps was pursued for some distance.'

The Empress's departure was a shock to Paris. Stocks fell to their lowest ever, 45.00 frs.

'The people who early in the day were clamouring only for arms now found themselves at a loss; the National Guards, who had been ready to fight, were now utterly discouraged,' writes Queen Hortense.

The presence of Marie-Louise and the King of Rome had been a guarantee and a safeguard for Paris which was now both ashamed and frightened. The Cossacks were going to smirch the soil of the great city. All over Paris people gathered to give vent to their disgust. Joseph, in a sudden access of energy, had the happy thought of posting up this proclamation, signalling the arrival of Napoleon.

'Citizens of Paris, an enemy column is advancing on the road from

Germany, hotly pursued by the Emperor at the head of a victorious army. The Council of Regency has taken steps to ensure the safety of the Empress and the King of Rome. I remain here with you. Let us arm ourselves to defend this city. . . . The Emperor is marching to our aid. Let us support him by a short and sharp resistance and preserve the honour of France.'

Savary also preached resistance 'to allow the Emperor time to come to the capital's help'. A patriotic movement was forming. All might yet be saved by 'holding firm' until the return of the Emperor whose genius might still avert misfortune.

It was precisely the city's resistance which the Allied chiefs feared. As the sun was setting, their troops, intoxicated with victory, descried Paris in the distance and cheered wildly, but Alexander and the King of Prussia were anxious; they had munitions and provisions for only two days and their rear was vulnerable to a surprise attack by the embattled peasantry. Their predominant fear, however, was the return of the Emperor, of whom they had no news, but they knew that the sound of his artillery would galvanize his men. As Houssaye writes, 'Alexander's eyes were strained not towards Paris but on the Troyes road along which Napoleon was advancing.'

Could Paris resist for several days? Her defence was assured by the troops of Marmont, Mortier, Compans, the National Guard commanded by Moncey, the garrison, the pupils of the Ecoles Polytechnique and Alfort, volunteers, veterans and pensioners, in all some forty-two thousand men against a hundred and twenty thousand of the enemy. This numerical inferiority might have been decisive but for the people, that indomitable populace which had toppled the monarchy and shaken the thrones of ancient Europe, who could raise barricades and make each house a bastion. Victory demanded a civil and military leadership both able and resolute to give the example of resistance to the death, a resistance strengthened by loyalty to the Emperor. There is no question but that had Napoleon reached Paris and taken command of operations the enemy would have been beaten. Queen Hortense wrote:

'Each citizen at the approach of danger would have become a soldier burning to defend his home. Only one man was missing and the Emperor could not be everywhere.'

After lunch on 28 March, as Napoleon was leaving St-Dizier for Troyes, a distinguished prisoner, the Comte de Weissemberg, Austrian Ambassador in London, was brought to him and entrusted with an urgent and confidential mission to negotiate with the Emperor Alexander for Austria. By evening Napoleon was at Doulevant where, while he was still hesitating about his next move, he received his first news for ten days of Paris from a messenger sent by Lavalette. The message read:

'The partisans of the foreigner, encouraged by events in Bordeaux, are rearing their heads. Napoleon's presence is essential if he wants to prevent his capital falling to the enemy; there is not a moment to lose.'

At first light next day the Emperor left Doulevant abruptly, learning little by little on his way of the Allies' heartrending advance. He at once sent his aide-de-camp to Joseph to confirm his arrival to the Parisians and to ensure the city's defence. Towards midnight he reached Troyes which he left to Berthier's command and set off at dawn at top speed for Paris. As on his return from Moscow, to make faster progress he abandoned his exhausted horse and with Caulaincourt hurled himself into a worn-out wicker cabriolet, lent him by a butcher, and ordered the postilion to scorch.

The Battle of Paris

Paris was awakened at 4 a.m. by an almost simultaneous cannonade and roll of drums as the call to arms was sounded and the faubourgs rose. The workers, followed by the militia men, overran the city, calling for arms. Belligerent citizens eagerly joined the fighting troops and picked up the rifles of the dead to fire a shot. The Place Vendôme, dominated by the Emperor's statue, was the rallying point for the crowd and their spirits. The Café Tortoni was the miserable headquarters of the young dandies, monarchists sick for the Bourbons, who vehemently discussed whether 'it would not be absurd to fight'. Two opposing tendencies were apparent, that of the people of the streets and the faubourgs, still wholly Bonapartist, and the ladies and gentlemen of the salons and the Faubourg St-Germain who sought Napoleon's overthrow and allied victory. The great misfortune was the betrayal of the Emperor by those in authority who went over to the enemy camp.

In the early part of the morning the Parisian troops showed magnificent fighting spirit and held back the enemy masses all along the eastern and north-eastern front from Vincennes to Clichy but, if

Paris was 'holding on', its supreme head, Joseph, who stood for the Emperor and who had remained in the capital, was about to commit an unpardonable act of weakness which proved fatal.

After the negotiations opened the previous day by Alexander, whose apprehensions have already been mentioned, Joseph went to the Hill of the Four Mills at Montmartre to supervise operations. At 10.30 a.m. when battle had been re-engaged after a lull he was met by Peyre, the architect, of whom circumstances had made an emissary, accompanied by Count Orloff, the Czar's aide-de-camp. This emissary had been received during the night by Alexander, who had handed him copies of Schwarzenberg's royalist proclamation to the people of Paris and told him that, if talks failed, the fight would be carried on to the end, with this threatening valediction, 'In palaces or in streets, Europe will sleep tonight in Paris.'

Joseph, in the depths of despair, at once called a defence council, which unanimously agreed that capitulation was inevitable. Instructions in this sense were immediately sent to Marmont and Mortier:

> 'If the Duc de Raguse and the Duc de Trévise can no longer hold their positions, they are authorized to enter into negotiations with Prince von Schwarzenberg and the Emperor of Russia who face them. They will retire to the Loire.'

Just as he had abandoned Madrid so Joseph left Paris, forgetting in his scurry to delegate his powers. At 12.30 he took the road to Rambouillet. The only constitutional authorities in Paris were the two Prefects and the General Council, who held their authority directly from the Emperor.

Battle was raging at Pantin and on the plain of Romainville. Marmont, although wounded, was fighting bravely and withstanding furious attacks. He received Joseph's note at 1.30 but seemed impervious to it and continued the battle with the same fury. At 2 p.m. the enemy launched a general offensive on the front and on the flank and overran the French. The Marshal saw himself overwhelmed on all sides and thought that he could no longer hold his position. It was 4 p.m. He then remembered Joseph's order, withdrew to Belleville and sent three emissaries to seek an armistice. Moncey, however, was still resisting heroically at the Clichy barrier. Time was passing. Paris had not yet yielded.

The people of Paris had recovered from their early fear of the Cossacks and, while a bloody battle was being fought round their walls, they filled the streets and public places and the cafés were black with their numbers. The sound of cannon did not interfere with impassioned discussions among the groups gathered everywhere but especially in the Faubourgs St-Marcel, St-Antoine, St-Denis, Poissonière and Montmartre. Those who had waited in vain to fire a shot were indignant; the consensus of opinion was for fighting and resisting, not for capitulation.

'The Faubourg St-Antoine was ready for anything except to give in,' wrote Savary. 'There was a willing belief that the enemy had been repulsed. Above all it was believed that the Emperor would soon return.'

There was even a rumour current that he had been seen on a white horse, surrounded by a group of officers, and when this proved false,

'the working people,' says Béranger, 'counted all day long on the Emperor's arrival and were preparing to witness a victory.'

When Joseph left Montmartre he issued orders for the immediate departure from Paris of all personages in authority but these tardy and hurried orders were only partially carried out; this was another of Joseph's errors. Certain persons, who believed it to be in their own interest to remain, failed to obey. The most influential of them all, Talleyrand, feinted a departure, was turned away at the barrier and shortly afterwards was back in his mansion in the Rue St-Florentin.

Savary, firmly believing that Talleyrand had gone, had left Paris and thus the Prince of Benevento had a free hand. The success of the trick played by Talleyrand was to be fatal to the Emperor whose intentions and formal orders could not have been more rudely ignored. In a letter written on 7 February to Joseph he, in fact, had said,

'If Talleyrand opts for letting the Empress stay in Paris if our forces have to evacuate it, he will be plotting treachery. I repeat, beware of that man. I have known him for sixteen years; I even had a partiality for him, but he is beyond the shadow of doubt the greatest enemy of our house now that luck has for some time forsaken me.'

If Napoleon had been the tyrant his enemies believed him to be he would have imprisoned Talleyrand at Vincennes, which might perhaps have altered much.

Marmont's envoy with the request for an armistice was received during the afternoon by Alexander, who appointed his aide-de-camp, Orloff, to continue the negotiations. As he thought capitulation a foregone conclusion the negotiations were merely to determine the

conditions. Meanwhile, Napoleon's aide-de-camp, who had been
searching in vain for Joseph, came to tell Mortier that the Emperor
was making for Paris at top speed and had ordered that his arrival
should be awaited. The only influence this news had on the negotiations was to hasten their painful conclusion.

Marmont, Mortier and the Czar's representatives met at an inn at
the Barrière St-Denis for long and laborious discussions which
lasted until evening. It is to the honour of the Marshals that they
opposed the humiliating ultimatum which the Allies tried to force
on them. Their continued opposition would have gained precious
time, which would have allowed Napoleon to arrive, but they did not
resist further. While Nesselrode was to seek fresh instructions from
the Czar, Orloff was to remain with Marmont as a hostage, but
capitulation had practically been conceded. Marmont felt his part
as a soldier was ended and with Orloff went home to the Hôtel de
Raguse in the Faubourg Poissonière.

While the people of Paris slept in ignorance of what had happened
after the day's battle, the politicians, who had flouted Joseph's orders
and remained in Paris to take care of their own future, were meeting
at Marmont's house. Most were hostile to the Emperor whom they
were ready to abandon or betray. Present were Chabrol, Pasquier,
Bourrienne, the banker Laffite, and his satellite Perrégaux (Marmont's
father-in-law), Baron Louis (Talleyrand's trusted ally), members of
the Senate, the Legislature and the Corps of Mayors.

When Marmont entered his drawing-room he was unrecognizable;
he had a week's beard, the greatcoat over his uniform was in tatters
and from head to foot he was blackened by gunpowder. His entry
caused a sensation as he was admiringly hailed as a victor by those
present. They were in fact acclaiming the man who was about to sign
the surrender of Paris, but it was believed this capitulation would
spare its citizens the 'horrors of plunder'.

The Marshal, so far from expecting the honours of a triumph,
had feared reproaches for delivering the capital to the enemy. He
was more astonished still to hear hostile voices rising in a crescendo
of accusation against the Emperor as one and all, throwing off the
mask, pinned responsibility for the country's plight on Napoleon.
Bourrienne says that 'the name of the Bourbons was mentioned for
the first time'.

These recriminations were interrupted by the arrival of an emissary from the Emperor, Gérardin, who had just heard of the imminent capitulation and came to announce his master's return. Supported by Lavalette, he rightly insisted that the Emperor's return nullified any agreement with the enemy, or at the least was a reason for suspending negotiations. For a moment the great shadow of the absent Emperor passed over the heads of the men present, causing a brief shudder of fear.

Marmont's attitude was still one of reserve although his pride was flattered to be the hero of the evening, nor was he privately displeased to take his revenge on the man whose devoted lieutenant and companion in arms he had been, but who had so often humiliated him.

At this moment arrived the man who was to be the real *deus ex machina*, Talleyrand, whom Marmont received in the neighbouring dining-room. In his own inimitable way the Prince sounded out the Marshal, trying to make him disclose his intentions while carefully concealing his own. Talleyrand then went into the drawing-room, where his appearance created some surprise since he was believed to be far from Paris. In no wise disconcerted he went up to Orloff, sitting in a corner of the room, and asked him, 'to take to the feet of His Majesty the Emperor of Russia the expression of the profound respect of the Prince of Benevento'. Talleyrand, his trump-card played, then bowed and left the room.

This short scene had a decisive effect on the sequence of events. It put Talleyrand in the forefront, detached Marmont from the Emperor and facilitated the return of the Bourbons. A political revolution was in being, sparked off by the politicians and bankers of Paris, supported by enemy bayonets. It was not the work of the faubourgs but was directed against the man who was still their idol.

Shortly after his arrival Marmont told Pasquier that it was a usage of war and essential that the Municipal Council should go that night to Bondy to make its submission to the Czar Alexander 'and discuss everything pertaining to the interests of the city'. After a short discussion at the Hôtel de Ville, Pasquier and Chabrol settled the procedure with greater political opportunism than professional conscience; they then awaited a message from Marmont. The Municipal Council, in session in the Great Chamber, was deeply perturbed.

'It must be recalled that in this crisis not a single voice had yet been raised against the man who had provoked it,' writes Pasquier, known however for his scant affection for Napoleon. 'We heard not one murmur. It seemed as though we had to shoulder a burden which had to be borne.'

Nevertheless, in the heart of one member, Bellart, revolt was simmering; he had sworn to bring about Napoleon's downfall and he intended to keep his word.

At 2 a.m. Schwarzenberg's aide-de-camp arrived at Marmont's house with the Allies' acceptance of the Marshal's terms and an hour later, led by Orloff, a delegation consisting of Pasquier, Chabrol, eight members of the Municipal Council and three officers of the National Guard, left for Bondy to take the city's capitulation to the Czar.

The second phase opened at 4 a.m. This was the signature of the capitulation by Colonels Denys and Fabvier, the Marshals' aides-de-camp, and the representatives of the Allied staff. It was read aloud by the Marshal in a deathly silence. The articles included the evacuation of the city of Paris by the troops at 7 a.m. on the 31st and their departure. The capital's interests were covered by the curt phrase, 'The city of Paris is recommended to the generosity of the Allied Powers.'

The city's delegates arrived at dawn at Bondy. What was said to them can be summed up in this one sentence, 'Get rid of Napoleon and we will agree to anything you put in his place.' At 7 a.m. the Czar welcomed the delegation in a most friendly way and ended the audience with these words, 'In France I have one enemy only. All other Frenchmen I view with a kindly eye. . . . Tell the Parisians I do not enter their city as an enemy and it depends on them if they want me as a friend.'

The delegates then left Bondy. At the Barrière de Pantin they were stopped at a sentry-post manned by grenadiers of the Imperial Guard. The officer in command recognized Pasquier, to whom he made this touching little speech, 'Monsieur le Préfet, I have seen you sometimes when I was on guard at the palace. So there can be no further doubt! Paris has been abandoned to the enemy; our capital is taken and this is the result of twenty years of fighting, of so many battles and victories in which I took part. . . .'

He hid his face in his hands to hide the tears which flowed also from the eyes of all the soldiers who remained loyal to the Little Corporal.

At the barrier the delegation met Caulaincourt on his way to see the Czar with the full powers entrusted to him by Napoleon. Caulaincourt was able to exchange only a few words with Pasquier who, like his companions and their Cossack escort, was impatient to get back to Paris. At Bondy Caulaincourt registered Alexander's implacable hatred of Napoleon and, although he eloquently pleaded the Emperor's cause, it was too late.

'This is a fine time to come,' said the Czar, 'when nothing can be altered. I cannot talk to you now; we will meet in Paris and I will see you there. . . .'

Faubourg St-Germain and Faubourg St-Antoine

At 10 p.m. on 30 March while in Paris Marmont was being acclaimed and everyone was waiting for the Czar's acceptance of the surrender terms, Napoleon arrived like a whirlwind at the staging-post of the Cour de France at Fromenteau-Juvisy. He intended only to make a brief halt, hoping to reach Paris in time to take command of the army. As he strode feverishly up and down, mulling over his plans, he saw General Belliard, who was carrying out Marmont's orders to look for billets for the troops about to evacuate the capital.

Napoleon fired off questions at Belliard, burning for immediate news and the most minute details of what had been happening. 'Why are you here? Where is the army? Who is defending Paris? Where is the Empress? The King of Rome?'

When the General had given him a brief account he burst out angrily, 'What cowardice. . . . Capitulate! Joseph has ruined everything. . . . Four hours too late! . . . If I had arrived four hours earlier all would have been saved.'

He continued to repeat similar phrases with deepest sorrow but then regained his equilibrium and, with the citizens of his good city in mind, cried, 'Four hours have put everything in hazard but in a few hours the courage and loyalty of my good Parisians can yet save the situation. My carriage, Caulaincourt! We will go to Paris.'

While fierily asserting his resolve to be off 'to retrieve the situation' he noticed a general commanding one of Mortier's corps who had arrived from Paris. It was true then that the army was evacuating the city! He was overwhelmed; the plan of coming to the capital's aid must be abandoned.

'Everyone has lost their heads. There is some dirty work afoot. . . .
Did they but know I was in Paris the people would rise against the
Cossacks.'

He again reviled his brother.

'Joseph lost Spain. He is losing Paris.'

General Flahaut was at once sent off for news, followed by
Caulaincourt with this order:

> 'We command the Duc de Vicence to go to the Allied sovereigns . . .
> to recommend to them the faithful subjects of Our capital. By these presents
> We invest him with full power to negotiate and make peace. . . . If need be
> We likewise invest him with military powers as governor and commander
> of this good city side by side with the commanding general of the Allies.'

Napoleon did not know that the Municipal Council was turning
against him and the Prefects had assumed responsibility for carrying
out the Allied orders although they both held their office directly
from him.

While impatiently awaiting his messengers' return the Emperor
shut himself up in a small room at the inn and pored over his maps.

At 4 a.m. a courier arrived from Caulaincourt with news of the
capitulation. Hard on his heels came Flahaut with a letter from
Marmont which included this scarifying sentence,

> 'Not only is there no inclination for self-defence; there is a definite resolve
> against it.'

About the army the Marshal was silent. Napoleon was shattered by
these letters.

'Paris, the capital of civilization,' he mourned, 'to be occupied by
the Barbarians! This great city will be their tomb. Who knows what
will happen tomorrow?'

Blindly and exhausted he took the road to Fontainebleau. The time
was 4 a.m., when a few miles away the Czar was receiving the city's
envoys.

On the morning of 31 March gunfire had ceased in Paris whose
citizens were still unaware that their fate had been decided. What
would their reaction be to the surrender? How would they show their
loyalty to Napoleon? These were questions of vital importance. True,
the capitulation had been signed but it had been accepted only by a
political and opportunist minority, hostile to the Emperor, which

could hardly be regarded as representing the feelings of the Parisians, whose hearts, cold to the name of Bourbon, beat fiercely at that of Napoleon, who was nearing the ramparts of the capital.

Astonished by the silence, the crowd from early morning poured all over the city, seeking news. At 9 a.m. they learned simultaneously that the capitulation had been signed, that Alexander had given a cordial reception to the civic deputation and that the entry of enemy troops was imminent. Faces grew grave and the atmosphere heavy with anxiety; only the royalists expressed their glee, noisily and shamelessly. They were aware that the Allied sovereigns were hesitating about what form of government was most suitable for France and tried all means of propagating their own opinions to make it appear that the population of Paris was royalist and wishful for Napoleon's fall. In general they met few people of like mind and then only in some of the fashionable districts.

In the popular quarters, however, they met lively hostility, which increased with the distance from the city's centre. The royalists' attempts to distribute white armlets were unsuccessful; their brashness only drew insults from the crowd. Beyond the Rue de Richelieu popular reaction was more violent still. Near the Porte St-Denis the people's attitude was threatening. Groups of workers and the poorer people from the Faubourgs St-Denis, St-Antoine and St-Marcel made for the centre of the city intending to fight.

At 11 a.m. Alexander, preceded by Cossacks of his Guard, with Schwarzenberg at his right and the King of Prussia on his left, arrived at the Barrière de Pantin. The sovereigns were followed by a brilliant staff and by soldiers of all arms who marched past for some hours. Their white brassard was worn as a sign of victory, not at all as a royalist emblem, but this white armlet impressed the public and created confusion of incalculable consequences. The Allies were believed to be coming out openly for the Bourbons, whose emblem was the white brassard with the fleur-de-lys.

In the Faubourg St-Antoine the enemy columns were met by faces 'angry rather than distressed'. Many people vehemently uttered their conviction that Napoleon would arrive soon to hound out the invader. Patriotic Paris was in mourning.

In that part of the city, however, between the Boulevard des Italiens, the Place de la Concorde and the Rue de Richelieu up to the Palais Royal, the royalists were in full spate, their numbers swollen by many bourgeois who were now assured of having nothing to fear from Napoleon.

> 'From the Boulevard des Italiens,' wrote Caulaincourt, 'there was a complete reversal of attitude, almost another race, other feelings. Here shouts were heard of "Long live Alexander! Long live the Bourbons!" The abrupt change from extreme anxiety to unexpected calm and security, which entailed no alteration in daily habits, had turned all heads and brought about this spiritual revolution.'

Royalists and their sympathizers crowded round the Allied chiefs whom they hailed as liberators.

Towards evening a few noblemen, to crown a day which for them had been one of triumph, thought they would topple the Emperor's statue from the column in the Place Vendôme, the quintessential symbol of the glorious French army and whose lofty presence now seemed to proffer an insolent challenge but, try as they would, their paid hirelings could not budge the statue. The Emperor remained unshakeable.

At some distance from this scene, as Colonel Fabvier, Marmont's aide-de-camp, wrote,

> 'The men of the people, who owned a fatherland but no mansion, bore on their faces the grief which overflowed from their hearts. The fatal white armlet had led the mob to believe that these cries of "Long live the Bourbons!" expressed the desire of the enemy sovereigns so that, in relief at being spared the rape of the city, those who knew least about the former dynasty, in their turn took up the cry of "Long live the Bourbons!" '

These fervent demonstrations, in which women were particularly noticeable, were more vociferous on the Champs-Elysées, where the Faubourg St-Germain had arranged to meet and where the troops were marching past their commanders.

It must be admitted that the Czar had a great prestige success; his face, his height and his elegance were calculated to attract the Parisians. 'How handsome the Emperor Alexander is! How graciously he bows!' they said. The shame of Moscow had been wiped out for him and so, his graciousness, the confusion created by the white armlet and the deliverance from a nightmare, combined to make the people of Paris resigned to the Allies' presence. And what could they attempt with eighty thousand men encamped on their soil?

Nevertheless, writes Houssaye:

> 'No Parisian could forget that, however glittering their appearance,

these soldiers' bayonets were stained with French blood and yesterday's corpses of "Marie-Louises" and National Guards were still unburied. The Parisians could not but feel that in enemy-occupied Paris even the air was no longer theirs.'

When the review ended about 6 p.m. Alexander went to Talleyrand's house in the Rue St-Florentin which seemed to show on his part a certain inclination towards the Bourbons. During the day Talleyrand had received a visit from Nesselrode, who appeared to be in favour of a restoration, which he thought would ensue and to whose realization he promised his full aid. The Czar as yet had come to no decision, sincerely believing that he should support only what he thought was the people's wish. As Pasquier writes:

'He had noticed that the royalist cheers he had heard in the morning had begun tardily nor were they uttered by the populace at large . . . but his main concern was with the army. Could he succeed in divorcing it from a leader under whom it had fought so heroically and to whom it was still devotedly loyal? He could not forget the heroism of the National Guards at La-Fère-Champenoise who, as they died, shouted, "Long live the Emperor!", a scene he recounted with deep feeling.'

Talleyrand opened the attack with the statement that peace with Napoleon held out no guarantees. He believed the only acceptable formula was the restoration of the Bourbons who represented a 'principle' and he guaranteed the Senate's adhesion. The enemies of Napoleon were raising a real hue and cry! The Czar hesitated momentarily and took counsel of the representatives of the other Powers, who concurred with Talleyrand's proposals. Unhappily the voluntary absence of the Emperor of Austria, Napoleon's father-in-law, ruled out the solution of the Empress's regency. The Czar allowed himself to be persuaded and came down in favour of banishing Napoleon and his whole family. A declaration, whose terms had already been prepared by Talleyrand, was immediately finalized and signed by Alexander. To blight the ambition of 'Bonaparte' the Allied sovereigns declared that they would no longer treat with him nor with any member of his family, that they guaranteed the constitution the French nation would choose for itself and they invited the Senate to appoint a provisional government. Once this proclamation was signed no time was lost in publishing it and an hour later it was billposted next to Schwarzenberg's declaration.

During the evening Talleyrand and his henchmen lobbied the

Senators to persuade them to come out publicly against Napoleon and to secure their approval of the provisional government of which Talleyrand reserved the presidency for himself with the right to nominate its members. He had little difficulty in getting the Senate's support; all that was needed was the assurance that they would preserve the honours and benefits bestowed on them by Napoleon. That evening Talleyrand proceeded to appoint his government.

At 10 p.m. Caulaincourt had a further audience of the Czar when he pressed Napoleon's claims but he felt that Alexander had made an irrevocable decision. The Czar spoke only in general terms, recalling that the Allies had no intention of imposing a sovereign on France. The Duc de Vicence, refusing to be discouraged, continued to plead his brief which concluded with the telling words, 'France is not Paris and what Paris wants is not what is said in the antechambers of this house'—indicating the mansion in the Rue St-Florentin. His words found no echo in the Czar who even implied that his presence was no longer desirable. The senators whom Caulaincourt visited showed him even scanter attention; they had already become partners in Talleyrand's game.

Next day in the *Moniteur* the Parisians had their first official news of Schwarzenberg's proclamation to them. In general the city was calm but there was a marked difference between the central districts which paraded gaiety of a kind and the silent and even menacing faubourgs.

As he had pledged himself to do, Talleyrand summoned the Senate to approve his government. How ironic it was that the fate of Napoleon and his empire was now at the mercy of this obsequious assembly, which owed its existence and its supremacy only to the Emperor's will, and for ten years had given blind support to everything he proposed, even exceeding his wishes.

Ninety senators out of a total of a hundred and forty were present in Paris and at 3.30 p.m. sixty of them, all hostile to Napoleon, met at the Luxembourg. Although Vice-Grand Elector, Talleyrand had no authority to convene the Senate which, by virtue of the senatus consultum of 28 May 1804, could meet only by order of the Emperor. Legality had now gone by the board. The Senate was summoned 'at the request of the Allied sovereigns'. Talleyrand, with his habitual prudence, now asked only for the Senate's approval of the government he had just formed.

The Senate had not yet avowed the true aim of its discussions, which was the outlawing of Napoleon, but the Municipal Council did not hesitate to deal the Emperor the cruellest blow which, however, involved only fourteen of its twenty-four members. All owed their appointment to him and all were equally hostile. If they were prejudiced they were non-elective so that there was small justification for their claim to represent the people of Paris. The Councillors had kept silent, waiting for the Allies' public proclamation of Napoleon's overthrow, but they now showed more boldness than the Senate. True, for fifteen years they had proven their submission to the Emperor, but without allowing him to encroach on their prerogatives, although he had acted as Grand Master of Paris. It may be that they now saw their opportunity for revenge. Bellart proposed the resolution to be adopted by the Council with an insulting diatribe against the man so recently his master. This resolution was approved during the afternoon of the 31st by thirteen of his colleagues out of fourteen. Pasquier, shocked by 'the insulting tone' of the proclamation refused to sign it as being 'neither in the general interest nor in accordance with my own feelings'.

This is part of the text:

'Citizens of Paris, your magistrates would be traitors to you and the nation if base personal considerations any longer stifled the voice of their conscience, which cries aloud that all your overwhelming misfortunes are attributable to one man alone. It is he whose conscriptions annually decimate our families. Who among you has not lost a son, a brother, relatives or friends? For whom did these brave men die? For him alone, not for the nation. There is not one of us who, in the secret places of his heart, does not loathe him as a public enemy; not one who, in his inmost thoughts, has not yearned to see an end to so many fruitless and cruel deeds.

'Parisians, even Europe in arms could not influence your magistrates were it not their duty. Consequently, the members present of the General Council of the Department of the Seine, assembled spontaneously, decide unanimously to make a formal abjuration of all obedience to Napoleon Bonaparte and express their heartfelt desire that monarchical government be restored in the person of Louis XVIII and his legitimate heirs.'

Thus, the Council was the first to demand the banishment of Napoleon and to launch an appeal to the King.

Although, like Pasquier, Chabrol had scruples about signing it he did, in the course of the evening, authorize the printing and billposting of the resolution, which was done that night.

Talleyrand, however, who thought the resolution too precipitate and showed excess of zeal, ordered the posters to be removed and publication prohibited. Nevertheless the text was published in the *Journal des Débats* and made considerable stir.

'So much publicity given to such an act,' wrote Pasquier, 'and one emanating from the body with the greatest right to express the feelings of the city of Paris, created a great sensation.'

On 2 April the *Moniteur* published the Czar's proclamation and a solemn undertaking by the Allies that soldiers of all ranks in Paris should be at liberty. A note from Pasquier informed the public of the opening of the Paris barriers and of freedom to come and go. Public opinion had to be mollified and any demonstration scotched which might serve the Emperor's cause.

To help achieve this end another communiqué was published, revealing Caulaincourt's failure to obtain a hearing from the Allied sovereigns since his proposals were not those,

'that the Powers had a right to expect, particularly after the outstanding demonstration of the feeling of Paris and France as a whole.'

The Senate, emboldened by the Municipal Council's resolution, voted Napoleon's overthrow in the evening and forthwith sent a message to the Provisional Government, ordering the publicizing of this decree on the 4th and stating that, by reason thereof, the French people and the army were released from their oath of loyalty.

Still nothing final could be achieved without the army's consent. An effort was therefore made to secure Marmont's adhesion. A bulky file of newspapers, together with the Czar's and Schwarzenberg's proclamations, and the Czar's address to the army was sent to him. A former aide-de-camp was also sent with instructions to persuade the Marshal to put his troops at the disposal of the Provisional Government.

The Allies' entry into Paris and the fall of Napoleon

When Napoleon arrived at Fontainebleau on 31 March at 6 a.m. he shut himself up alone in a small room where he spent the day in deep thought. Next day he began to regroup his forces and plan the attack which would liberate Paris. The concentration of his troops went well and in less than three days he had sixty thousand men available. In the morning he informed his Marshals and Maret of his decision to march on Paris and in the afternoon went to Essonnes to ascertain the position taken up by Marmont's and Mortier's Corps. He was cordial to the Duc de Raguse, showing his friendship and confidence, with no reproaches about the fall of Paris for which he held Joseph responsible.

While talking to Marmont he was told that his messengers had returned from Paris. Avid for news of the city, he received them on the spot, but his brow darkened when he heard of the triumphal entry of the Allied troops, of royalist provocations and Alexander's declaration.

On his return to Fontainebleau he spent part of the night alone in his room, studying his maps. Next day he told his aides what he had heard from Paris but asked them not to repeat it so as not to upset his soldiers' morale. At noon he attended a review of the Guard in the Cour du Cheval Blanc, where he was cheered loud and long as in the days of the great reviews on the Carrousel.

Caulaincourt returned to Fontainebleau in the evening to tell Napoleon of the impression he had gathered from the Czar that, if the Emperor abdicated, the solution of a regency might be reconsidered. Napoleon listened to his envoy impassively and his first reaction was, 'I set no store by the throne,' but he spoke of his wish to fight, not for his crown, but for 'the honour of France'.

Caulaincourt then told him of what had been happening in Paris during the last few days, but he seemed unaffected by the royalists' attempt to overthrow his statue from the column in the Place Vendôme. He dismissed Caulaincourt to give himself up entirely to his battle plans and sent for Ney and his other Marshals, to whom he gave his first orders for the attack, orders received in silence.

Next day, 3 April, at noon Napoleon, with his staff, gathered his infantry and cavalry in the Cour du Cheval Blanc where he called together the officers and non-commissioned officers and, from a position in the centre of the square formed by his Guard, addressed them in a resonant voice, castigating the action of the enemy and the royalists.

'Because of treachery by those émigrés whose life I spared and whom I loaded with favours, the enemy allows them to wear the white cockade which soon they will substitute for our national

cockade. In a few days I shall attack Paris. I place my reliance on
you. . . .'

Thunderous shouts of 'Long live the Emperor!' and 'To Paris!'
was the army's response as the troops enthusiastically and with one
voice took the oath to attack the city, but there was a devastating
contrast between the soldiers' fervour and the icy and reproachful
silence of the Marshals. Influenced by their families, weary of war,
their resolution sapped by appeals from intriguers in Paris, they
longed for tranquillity.

While this affecting scene was in progress Marmont, outstripping
all the other Marshals, had taken the first step on the road to betrayal.
The 'saviour of Paris' was implored to range himself under 'the
standard of the just French cause'. Pride spurred his reply to
Schwarzenberg that he and his troops were ready to quit Napoleon's
army, with the proviso of guarantees for the person and freedom of
the Emperor.

Napoleon at Fontainebleau was still unaware that he was being
stabbed in the back and urged on the concentration of his troops,
whom he again reviewed on 4 April and again provoked a storm of
cries, 'To Paris! To Paris!' In the afternoon he had several discussions
with his aides, to whom he repeated his decision to continue the fight
before Paris, but said that he was ready to renounce his crown in
favour of the King of Rome. The Marshals, by no means anxious for
the Bourbons' return, were in favour of the regency, but still strongly
opposed a resumption of hostilities. After a scene less stormy than
has often been described Napoleon ended by signing his act of
abdication.

When the Marshals had left he sent for Caulaincourt, to whom he
emphatically denied the reproach levelled at him that he was inspired
by the desire to avenge himself on Paris, reiterated that traitors were
responsible for this rumour and asked how he could be angry with, 'a
population which had always been well disposed and wholly devoted
to him, or make it responsible for the treachery of a handful of
intriguers in English pay'.

Reverting to what had happened in Paris, he expressed bitter
contempt for the part played by the Parisian authorities. The
proclamation of the Municipal Council was perhaps what most
offended him, 'first of all because it was the first' and then because
he saw it as 'a spontaneous act which revealed hatreds which he had

never suspected'. Chabrol's behaviour in particular outraged him. 'The Prefect of the Seine is a scoundrel. I have loaded him and his family with favours—there is no family in France for which I have done so much.'

To Pasquier he was kinder. 'He is the only one who has behaved decently. I always thought a lot of him and as a man of worth. I knew I could rely on him. He has also abandoned me, but at least he was frank about it and knew what he wanted while danger still persisted. That excuses a lot and he at least warned me of what he was going to do.'

He then exclaimed passionately, 'I am going to fight the Russians and not the Parisians who will assuredly support me. Maret's last reports leave me in no doubt as to their kindly feelings towards me. What is happening is only the work of fifty traitors. . . .'

While waiting for hostilities to begin he ordered Ney, Macdonald and Caulaincourt to take his abdication act to the Allied sovereigns. Still putting his trust in the man who was betraying him, he thought of making Marmont his plenipotentiary but then decided it was better for the Marshal to remain at Essonnes with the choice of accompanying his other envoys to Paris. The Emperor revised his declaration several times and it was now phrased only that 'he was ready to leave the throne'. His decision was purposely conditional, if not equivocal; to be final it needed the Allies' acceptance, nor was there any indication that he had relinquished the idea of settling the situation by force of arms, which in fact he had not. On the contrary he said, 'What glory for the Parisians and for the National Guard if it throws out the Cossacks and sweeps away all those foreigners. . . .'

As the Emperor's messengers left Fontainebleau the Guard began to move off and the army took up its position. It was the cannon's turn to speak.

In Paris the situation continued strained and doubtful as the Provisional Government piled decree on decree and published proclamations and articles. The influence of the royalist groups in the centre of the city remained static while Napoleon's supporters gained ground. Debates in the assemblies aroused no reaction from the populace, which was impervious to political questions but whose ears were pricked for news from Fontainebleau.

'The people were quiet,' wrote Caulaincourt, 'because foreign bayonets prevented them from acting.' The workers, badly hit by unemployment, looked back with regret to the time when they worked with a will on building projects which the Emperor had so often honoured with visits of encouragement.

Despite official amnesties many patriotic officers and men were hiding in the faubourgs, ready to rise when the Emperor's cannon thundered. Although the people as a whole were not equally fanatical and longed to see the end of fighting they did believe that the Allies should make peace with Napoleon, but by their clumsy handling of the people the Powers only made matters worse, nor did Talleyrand's Provisional Government fare better. In spite of all he could do, the people felt that the government owed its existence to enemy support; they believed that Napoleon had been betrayed and knew how he longed to throw the invaders out.

Nesselrode wanted the National Guards to adopt the white cockade but, faced with the refusal of at least half their officers, had to postpone this plan, while the National Guards continued to wear the tricolour cockade, an ostentatious reminder of the glories of the revolution and empire.

Marmont, who on the morning of the 4th had received from Schwarzenberg the guarantees for which he had asked, planned to move his Army Corps off in the evening, hoping that darkness would facilitate the departure of his troops whom he intended to leave in ignorance of their destination. His generals were very astonished but he secured their secrecy. When Napoleon's three emissaries arrived at 4 p.m. he was greatly embarrassed to be told of their mission and revealed his undertakings to Schwarzenberg. Under pressure from Caulaincourt and the other Marshals he agreed to do his utmost to secure his release from these obligations and to accompany them to Paris. Before he left he handed over command to General Souhan, ordering him to defer any troop movements until his return, but he made the grave mistake of instructing Souhan to tell the troops of the Emperor's abdication.

The four envoys left Essonnes at 6 p.m. and proceeded to Petit-Bourg, near Chevilly, where Schwarzenberg had his headquarters. Later Marmont claimed that the Austrian Field Marshal had freely released him from his obligations but, in fact, it seems he did nothing of the kind since next day the Press published a note from him, disclosing Marmont's adhesion and the departure of the Sixth Army Corps.

Talleyrand and the members of the Provisional Government were staggered to hear during the evening of the Marshals' arrival with the Emperor's act of abdication and the mission with which they were entrusted. All Talleyrand's work seemed to be in jeopardy and with a single gesture 'more than two thousand white cockades fell from hats', Macdonald would write.

While waiting for an audience with the Czar, the Emperor's envoys gathered at Ney's house where Marmont was stupefied to learn that during the night his Army Corps had crossed the Austrian advanced posts and were marching towards Versailles. It was disaster! He left at once to see what could be done to retrieve the situation but was informed that, when the troops realized that they had been tricked, they had mutinied on reaching Versailles occupied by the Cossacks. They had raised the cry of 'Long live the Emperor!' and declared that they wanted to join him. About a hundred Polish lancers had ridden hell for leather for Fontainebleau. When Marmont arrived the generals had not yet succeeded in pacifying their men and he himself did so only with great difficulty.

> 'It is certain,' wrote Pasquier, 'that if, when everyone was at fever pitch, a bold leader devoted to the Emperor had seized command, all the enlisted men and almost all the junior officers would, at whatever peril and risk, have taken the road with him to Fontainebleau, even if they had had to cut their way through.'

But no leader emerged.

The Marshals were received by the Czar at the time appointed and sturdily informed him of Napoleon's abdication, dwelling insistently on the solution of the regency. For the first time Alexander was shaken, but an aide-de-camp entered with the unfortunate news of the defection of Marmont's Corps. This ended all discussion. The Czar demanded unconditional abdication; the Bourbon cause was won and Talleyrand had triumphed anew. Marmont's 'heroic deed' had saved France.

Napoleon at Fontainebleau was in a fever of impatience, 'wholly absorbed by the need to march on Paris and confident still in his messengers' mission'. It was during the night of the 4th/5th that with angry stupefaction he heard of Marmont's betrayal and the movement of his Corps, but still he did not give up. On the morning of the 5th he composed his magnificent proclamation to the army, branding the part played by the Senate, and telling his troops of the negotiations with which he had entrusted his Marshals. At noon he again inspected his soldiers in the Cour du Cheval Blanc where he was wildly cheered. He then gave orders for the army's withdrawal to the Loire; he would reach Blois and Marie-Louise; he would give battle; a miracle was still on the cards.

When Caulaincourt and the Marshals returned during the night of the 5th/6th Napoleon heard of the failure of their interview with the Czar, of Alexander's demand for unconditional surrender to be announced forthwith by the Senate and the choice of the island of Elba or some other place for exile. Although with no illusions left as to the outcome of further negotiations after Marmont's betrayal, he reacted violently, declaring that 'he would still find brave men to die with him'. Alone with the faithful Caulaincourt, recovering his calm, he listened to an account of the latest developments then gave free rein to his bitterness.

'That Marmont, that the Duc de Raguse, should desert with his Corps in face of the enemy. . . . And when? . . . At a moment when almost certain victory could have crowned an all-out effort, when we would have made Europe repent of having occupied our capital with our army at his back. . . . Believe me, Caulaincourt, we would have made every French heart in Paris leap . . . the foreigners and traitors would have found there only enemies. . . . Marmont's Corps certainly did not know where it was being led.'

Continuing his sad monologue he made this prophecy, 'Even Paris will quickly tire of Alexander's affability; it will become bored with the sight only of foreign uniforms; in the end Parisians will remember that they are French . . . at the end of a year they will be sick of the Bourbons.'

He ended with these words, 'What's to be done? . . . If I resist there will be civil war in France. They want me to abdicate? Very well, I will abdicate.'

Napoleon sent for his Marshals and again signed his act of abdication.

This document, together with his final instructions, he gave to Caulaincourt, who with Ney and Macdonald left Fontainebleau for Paris which they reached towards midnight. They were received immediately by the Czar whom they informed of Napoleon's final renunciation. Detailed negotiations proceeded for several days to decide the final terms of the treaty governing the Emperor's future

and Caulaincourt had to fight inch by inch to limit the Allies' demands.
Opposition to Napoleon had in fact increased during the last few days
while the Provisional Government exerted itself to pass measures for
the permanent destruction of the Empire and to vilify the Emperor
whom they now, in an address to the French people, qualified as 'an
adventurer who seeks fame, a king of barbarians'.

The same vengeful spirit animated the capital's civic authorities.
On 4 April Chabrol presided over an extraordinary session of the
Corps of Mayors which in the name of the City of Paris 'rendered
solemn thanks to the Senate for having fulfilled the general desire' by
pronouncing the fall of Napoleon. During the day Colonel de
Rochechouart, the Czar's aide-de-camp, gave Launay, who had
cast the bronze for the Vendôme column, orders to pull the statue
down before noon on the 6th. Next day a deputation from the Corps
of Mayors waited on Marmont to congratulate him 'on his noble and
generous conduct in recent events'.

Chabrol had told Marmont of

'the great gratitude felt by the inhabitants of the City of Paris whom he
had saved from grave misfortunes by ignoring the sacrilegious orders he
had received.'

On the same day the royalist press took pleasure in announcing the
publication of Chateaubriand's pamphlet, *De Bonaparte et des
Bourbons* which did more for the Restoration 'than an army of
Vendéens could have done at any time'. On 8 April Pasquier published
a notice that the statue on the Vendôme column could not be allowed
to remain in its place and must give way to a statue of peace. Launay
had, in fact, done his work by the stated time and the statue was now
back in his studio.

Paris without Napoleon

The Bourbons in Paris

On the morning of 6 April the Senate voted a constitution of which the second clause stated that the French people 'freely' called to the throne of France Louis-Stanislas-Xavier de France, brother of the late King, thus giving the signal for adhesions to the Bourbon cause. Daily the columns of the *Moniteur* were filled with reports of acts of submission by the constituted bodies, civil, military and religious. The Emperor's former ministers, headed by Cambacérès, also rallied to the Bourbons and even the Marshals offered their swords in the Princes' service, notably Marshal Jourdan, military governor of Rouen, who had made his troops swear allegiance to Louis XVIII and in consequence wear the white cockade. The Provisional Government decided on the morning of the 9th that General Dessolles, commander of the National Guard, should copy 'this lofty example' and order his troops to change their emblem. On the 13th the white flag and the white cockade were adopted.

This climate of abandonment did little to help Caulaincourt's efforts to obtain a treaty favourable to Napoleon's interests, but his persistence was rewarded when on 11 April the representatives of the Allied Powers signed the final agreement, known as the Treaty of Fontainebleau, which governed the Emperor's status and decreed that he should reside on the island of Elba. Next day the act of abdication was published in the *Moniteur*.

These happenings may have rejoiced the capital's politicians but the people merely endured them.

'No one had become more inclined towards the monarchy, but everyone was in favour of the government which was supposed to have restored peace.'

The citizens of the faubourgs, however, where there was **great** poverty, continued their hostility to the new régime. The Faubourg St-Antoine, 'where the greatest hotheads were to be found', wrote Pasquier, 'was still rebellious' and, as the Prefect of Police admitted, 'needed particular supervision'. If the great army leaders had betrayed their master the soldiers and junior officers, the major part of the army, continued loyal to the Emperor. Broken-hearted, they had been obliged to wear the white cockade.

> 'What had to be guarded against,' says Pasquier, 'was the army's knowledge that their Emperor was still alive and that, from one moment to the next, he could reappear to put himself again at their head. This hope was strengthened by their grief in having to change their cockade, which they did with the greatest reluctance.'

At noon on 12 April the Comte d'Artois, the King's brother, made his entry into Paris to be welcomed by Talleyrand in the name of the Provisional Government and by Chabrol, representing the Municipal Council. Many shouts of 'Long live the King! Long live Monsieur!' were heard but, says Bourrienne, who was nevertheless a fanatical royalist,

> 'Enthusiasm was greater in the procession and among those who seemed to belong to the upper classes than among those who are called "the people".'

Caulaincourt and Macdonald had left Paris for Fontainebleau that morning and were received immediately on arrival by the Emperor, who made them tell him in detail of their negotiations and the state of mind in Paris. He was desolated to hear that most of those who only recently had obeyed him slavishly had deserted him. Feeling himself totally abandoned and suffering from the humiliations that foreigners had imposed on France, he tried during the night of the 13th to commit suicide but, when the attempt failed, he regained his composure and began his preparations to leave for the island of Elba.

On 20 April as Louis XVIII was making his entry as King of France into London, Napoleon wrote a last letter to Marie-Louise. At noon he took a touching farewell of his Old Guard in a voice as strong and resonant as in the days of his glory then, his eyes full of tears and walking jerkily, he got into the cabriolet in which General Bertrand had already taken his seat and which was to carry him on the road to his first exile.

On 2 May Louis XVIII arrived at St-Ouen where he was welcomed in great state by the representatives of the constituted bodies. Chabrol, accompanied by the twelve mayors of the Mayoral Corps, laid at the King's feet a golden salver on which were the keys of the City of Paris.

Next day the King made his solemn entry into Paris. The enormous crowd which had gathered to see the royal procession pass showed no enthusiasm. Bourrienne indeed noted 'some surprise followed by indifference'. The hearts of the public went out to the Imperial Guard which, with solemn faces, led Louis XVIII's escort. As the procession passed loud cheers rang out of 'Long live the Guard', which was one way of cheering the Emperor. Chateaubriand wrote an unforgettable eye-witness account of this scene:

> 'I do not believe that human faces have ever worn expressions at once so menacing and so terrible. These grenadiers, covered in wounds, victors of Europe, were compelled by the watchful eyes of an army of Russians, Prussians and Austrians in Napoleon's invaded capital to honour an old king, disabled by time not by wounds. . . . The fury with which they presented arms and the clash of their weapons made one tremble. Never, it must be admitted, have men been forced to submit to such a trial nor suffered such torture. . . .'

These valorous soldiers, loaded with glory by their indefatigable leader, whose sinewy figure in his plain grey uniform was still present in their minds, could not but gaze with bitterness on the poor gouty and helpless man in a blue coat frogged with gold lace who was their new master. They were only at the beginning of their humiliations.

Next day they had to endure the distasteful sight on the Carrousel of Louis XVIII, accompanied by Alexander, Francis II of Austria, Frederick William of Prussia, the Comte d'Artois, the Duc de Berry and the Duchesse d'Angoulême attending a march of enemy columns past the Louvre and the Tuileries, those grand and silent witnesses of yesterday's Imperial parades.

On 6 May the Grenadiers of the Guard, rendered suspect by their uncompromising attitude, were withdrawn from duty at the Tuileries and banished from Paris, where they had their homes and where their families lived, to Fontainebleau, prior to being shut up in the eastern garrison towns.

Further measures of extreme clumsiness were taken under the

pretext of army reorganization. Some two hundred thousand other ranks and twenty thousand officers on half-pay (most of whom remained in Paris) were sent on indefinite leave and their pay reduced by a third. Those officers who, by length of service, wounds or poor health, had the right to retire were pensioned, but their place in the officer corps was taken by many émigré soldiers whose seniority was reckoned by campaigns fought against France since 1792 in Condé's army or in foreign armies. At the same time the Princes reinstated the Maison du Roi, the Household Troops, as it had been brilliantly constituted in the reign of Louis XIV. Military circles were affronted by the revival of this privileged body for men who for twenty-five years had neither carried a sword nor handled a musket.

By the Treaty of Paris, signed on 31 May, France was reduced to her frontiers of 1792, the monarchy accepting 'the humiliating terms' consistently rejected by Napoleon. The eclipse of the conquests of the revolution and Empire struck a deep blow to French hearts and was bitterly resented in Paris, the home of many soldiers.

In the political sphere the long-awaited Constitution, adopted on 4 June, raised discontent to boiling point. Louis XVIII rejected the Senate's draft as too liberal and 'granted to his subjects' voluntarily and by the free exercise of his authority a Charter dated 'in the nineteenth year of his reign'. The Imperial Senate and Legislature became simply a royal Chamber of Peers and Chamber of Deputies.

The calm prevailing in Paris was illusory since it was here that latent hostility to the new rulers was greatest; the royalists were indeed in command, their numbers swollen by 'reinforcements' of émigrés who flooded the Faubourg St-Germain. These émigrés, who 'had learnt nothing and forgotten nothing' showed an arrogance and spirit of vengeance which demanded no less than the restoration of the privileges for whose abolition the people had revolted in 1789. This people was enraged by the insolence of the officers of Condé's army, swaggering on the boulevards in their pale blue uniforms, apparently forgetting that only recently they had fought alongside the enemy.

He will return

The populace, especially the workers, continued to be attached to the Emperor, to whom they were deeply grateful for abolishing class distinctions. To answer the attacks of the royalist party the old Jacobin party revived.

> 'Every day,' wrote Pasquier, 'there was some incident in the taverns, especially in those near the Central Markets or the barriers, where Napoleon's supporters were greatest in numbers and strength.'

The Parisian middle class, which had turned its back on the Emperor to rally to the monarchy, wavered; it was offended by the measures, inept to say the least, taken by Beugnot, appointed Director-General of Police (*vice* Pasquier who, at his own request, became Director-General of the Highways Department).

Beugnot, wanting to make his presence felt, issued a decree on 7 June, ordering a cessation of work on Sundays and feast days, which was a source of great annoyance to tradespeople and much of the public. A further decree on 10 June increased their indignation by forbidding traffic to circulate or to park on Corpus Christi (12 June). The immediate reaction was that the government was 'led by the nose' by the Church and the wave of anti-clericalism which Napoleon had checked revived with greater intensity.

The Legion of Honour was another source of grievance since the government replaced Napoleon's head on the medal by that of Henri IV. Of the rumour current in Paris that the Order would henceforward be only a civil order the government was obliged to issue a denial. The scattering of the Legion cross far and wide provoked more irritation; it was awarded to all the staffs of the ministries, even the most humble employees, while the Princes in their tours bestowed it to curry favour as a reward 'for the servilities and assiduities of worthless people'.

The government showed no more acumen in the political sphere. It met lively opposition from the liberal element in both assemblies during debates on bills on the liberty of the press and the restoration of censorship, the restitution to émigrés of national property which remained unsold, the right of petition and Sunday and feast day observance.

> 'However wisely,' wrote Pasquier, 'the Chamber might have handled the decisions it took, it was unable to obviate unfortunate repercussions among the public. So far from diminishing, the number of discontented and hostile people increased. . . .'

On 30 December Louis XVIII, who had had enough, dismissed both Chambers.

The new rulers' problems were cleverly and violently exploited by the régime's enemies who rained on the capital pamphlets, leaflets and caricatures holding the government up to ridicule. The press naturally let fly, firing off pithy epigrams and pointed sallies at the personalities of the old monarchy.

In the realm of foreign affairs the meeting of the Congress, which would refashion Europe shattered by Napoleon's fall, was eagerly awaited. Although France's own fate had been settled by the Treaty of Paris she could not be unaffected by the Allies' new territorial arrangements for the countries conquered by the Grande Armée.

Talleyrand, the King's representative, arrived at Vienna at the end of September and the Congress held its opening session on 1 November, where he supported the cause of the Bourbons rather than that of France. 'He played a fine diplomatic hand,' is Madelin's assessment, 'less national than dynastic.' Above all he worked desperately to smash Napoleon, suggesting that the Emperor be sent to a distant island, the Azores or St Helena, that the Duchy of Parma should be given to Marie-Louise and that the King of Rome, reduced to the rank of an Austrian archduke, should be deprived of all his hereditary rights. On 3 January 1815, a secret treaty was signed by Austria, England and France from which France not only did not draw any territorial advantages but on the contrary was considerably weakened. The victors grew fat on the corpse of the vanquished.

Although in ignorance of what was being negotiated at Vienna, the nation instinctively suspected that the Allied spirit of vengeance would result in the humiliation of France—which they now saw as linked with the Emperor—and to make her pay for fourteen years of victory. In Paris the course of events was followed more closely still by the numbers of 'demobilized' soldiers who lived there in spite of the keen watch kept on them by the royal police. 'This horde of officers and men who since the recent events have inundated Paris' and the faubourgs lived over and over again the agonizing moments of the battle which had led to the total surrender, today severely judged as humiliating. The feeling prevalent was that the city had been handed over on a plate to the attacker and had succumbed only beneath the weight of abandonment and treachery. A mere four hours of resistance would have enabled Napoleon to liberate his capital! In people's hearts the spirit of revenge germinated and the thoughts of many Parisians as of many Frenchmen groped their way towards the Emperor, fallen but still alive, who was only a few hours' distance from France. He will come back. . . .

From Porto-Ferraio to the towers of Notre Dame

Napoleon had disembarked on 4 May at Porto-Ferraio where, once in possession of his small domain, he had immediately set energetically to work, in the manner of the monarch of the great Empire from which he had been expelled, but by the end of the year he had exhausted all possibilities of activity and was beginning to be bored. Many causes contributed to increase his hardships; the chances of seeing his wife and son again were vanishing, his income was no longer paid and he had wind of threats of deportation and even of assassination. Finally he had news from France of the decreasing popularity of the Bourbons and the increasing number of Frenchmen who secretly longed for him.

On 12 February he received a visit from Fleury de Chaboulon, a former auditor of the Council of State, sent by Maret. The news he brought from Paris confirmed that his return would be welcome. From that time his mind was made up to return to Paris without delay.

'I shall reach Paris so quickly,' he said, 'that the Bourbons and their supporters will not know which way to turn. . . . The army will certainly not hesitate between the white flag and the tricolour.' He composed his proclamation to the army, declaring with passion, 'The eagle with the national colours will fly from steeple to steeple to the towers of Notre Dame.' On Sunday evening, 26 February, he embarked full of confidence on the *Inconstant*—destination, the mainland.

At 1 p.m. on 1 March he landed with twelve hundred faithful followers at Golfe Juan. Everywhere astonishment rapidly gave way to delight and cries of 'Long live the Emperor!' sprang from every mouth as soldiers and peasants formed little groups to escort him. By Sunday, the 5th, the day the capital heard of his disembarkation, Napoleon was at Sisteron. 'The first effect of this news,' wrote Pasquier, 'was stupefaction.'

'The city,' reports the son of Lazare Carnot, 'heard the news silently and tardily; the scant details of the Emperor's progress were whispered by one to another. Everyone seemed overcome by the anxieties of waiting. Would Napoleon succeed in his daring march? There were crowds, but silent crowds, on the boulevards, gloomy faces, drooping shoulders but

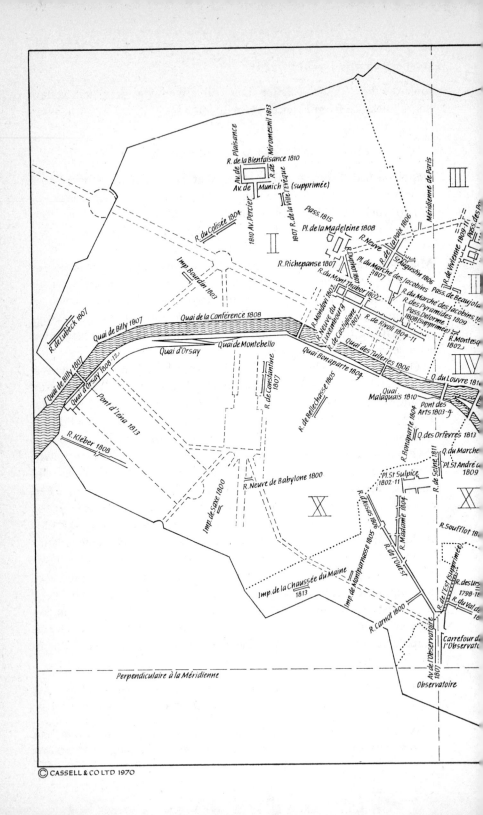

R. de Plaisance

R. de Miromesnil 1813

R. de la Bienfaisance 1810

Av. de

Av. de Munich (supprimée)

1810 Av. Percier

1807 R. de la Ville l'Évêque

Pass. 1815

Pl. de la Madeleine 1808

R. du Colisée 1804

II

R. Neuve

R. de la Paix 1806

Méridienne de Paris

III

R. de Vivienne 1809-11

Pass. des P...

Imp. Bourtin 1803

R. Richepanse 1807

R. du Mont Thabor 1802

St. Augustin 1806

Pl. du Marché des Jacobins

Pass. de Beaujola...

R. du Marché des Jacobins 18...

R. Dumont 1807

R. des Pyramides 1809

Pass. Delorme

R. de Lübeck 1807

Quai de Billy 1807

Quai de la Conférence 1808

Quai d'Orsay

Quai de Montebello

R. Moidon 1802

R. Neuve du Luxembourg

R. de Castiglione 1802

R. de Rivoli 1804-11

Quai Bonaparte 1804

Quai des Tuileries 1806

Pass.Delorme 1808 (supprimée)

R. Montesq. 1802.

IV

R. de Belléchasse 1805

R. de Constantine 1807

Quai Malaquais 1810

Q. du Louvre 181...

Quai de Billy 1807

Quai d'Orsay 1808-12...

Pont d'Iéna 1813

R. Kléber 1808

Imp. de Saxe 1800

R. Neuve de Babylone 1800

R. de Bellechasse 1805

Pont des Arts 1803-4

R. Bonaparte 1804

Q. des Orfèvres 1813

Q. du Marché

Pl. St André ...

1809

Pl. St Sulpice 1802-11

R. d'Assas 1806

R. de Seine 1811

R. Madame 1804

X

R. Soufflot 18...

R. de l'Ouest

Imp. de Montparnasse 1805

R. de l'Est (supprimée) 1798-18...

R. des Urs... 1798-18...

R. du Val de...

Imp. de la Chaussée du Maine 1813

R. Carnot 1800

Av. de l'Observatoire 1807

Carrefour de l'Observato...

Observatoire

Perpendiculaire à la Méridienne

© CASSELL & CO LTD 1970

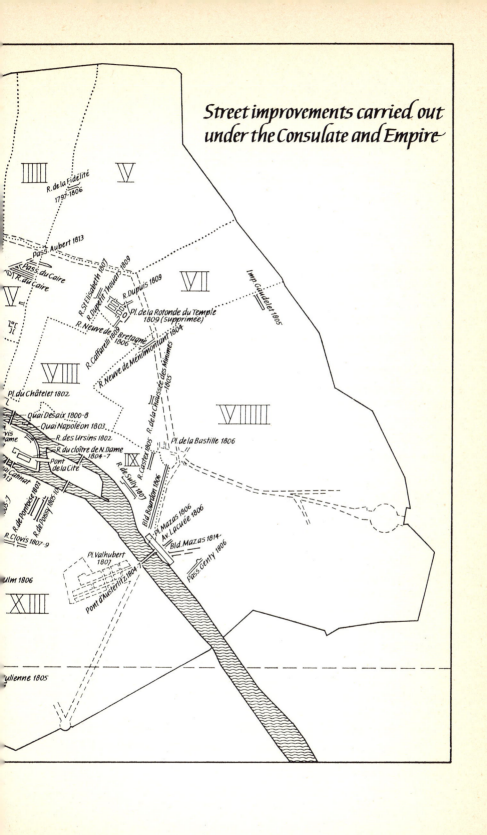

Street improvements carried out
under the Consulate and Empire

eyes shone with a ray of hope. As people talked they looked about them suspiciously; shopkeepers seemed to have lost the voices with which they called to shoppers and were absorbed only in gazing at the passers-by.'

The King may not have been worried, but all those about him either 'reassured one another wildly' or 'fell into a profound state of alarm', recounts Molé. Cried Mme de Staël, 'So he's back. . . . Oh, my God, then freedom has vanished. . . !'

In the first instance Louis XVIII ascribed no importance to the landing; he saw it as a mad adventure which would be Napoleon's ruin. The King decided to halt 'the usurper' by sending to Lyons the Comte d'Artois and the Duc d'Orléans but the Duc, who knew better than other members of the Bourbon family the people of Paris and their devotion to the Emperor, was considerably less optimistic. The decree summoning both Chambers, which Louis' entourage had urged him to recall, appeared in the *Moniteur* of the 7th, followed by a decree declaring Napoleon an outlaw.

The Municipal Council of Paris again raised its battle cry against the 'tyrant'. Under the presidency of the enraged Bellart the Council met at the Hôtel de Ville to vote a loyal address to Louis XVIII in which they violently attacked the 'foreigner' who defiled the capital's soil with 'his hateful presence'. The address continued:

'Already steeped in so much blood, it is more blood he seeks, it is civil war that he wants to impose on the children of France.'

Seventeen councillors, two thirds of the whole, among them the signatories of the resolution of 1 April 1814, signed this address. Almost at the same time in the Laffrey gorge Napoleon was triumphant, wildly cheered by the soldiers ordered to fire on him.

'In ten days we shall be at the Tuileries,' he cried.

He entered Grenoble that evening.

Louis XVIII and his ministers struggled hard to stem Napoleon's irresistible advance. Every day saw pitiable communiqués in the *Moniteur* and other papers, monotonously reviling the 'brigand' and the 'adventurer' whose landing was described as a miserable failure, but the people were not deceived. Nothing could halt the Emperor who would reach Paris in a few days.

One man, but for entirely different reasons, was following the course of events as avidly as were the people; that man was Fouché, whose duplicity and cunning were to make him master of the situation. After Louis XVIII's advent he had made an unobtrusive return to Paris and was now collecting his trumps to play every hand in the game.

At Lyons, which Napoleon entered on the evening of 10 March, he was borne in triumph by a people screaming with joy. On the 13th he issued his decree abolishing feudal rights, dissolving both Chambers and calling the electoral colleges to meet in Paris, but his order of general amnesty excluded thirteen people, among them Bellart, Bourrienne, Marmont and Talleyrand. All these measures were enthusiastically welcomed by the nation and the Jacobins. Napoleon had become the man of the people and the revolution.

When Paris heard on the 11th of the fall of Lyons the position of the royal government became hazardous and Louis XVIII at last took action. Proclamations and patriotic orders of the day followed one another, even the voting of a law providing for compensation to those garrisons which had taken part in the struggle against Napoleon, and instituting a special pension for those wounded in it. As often happens during troublous times the first step taken was the appointment of a Prefect of Police. While Napoleon was already leaving Lyons behind him on the evening of the 13th the King sent for Bourrienne to appoint him to the revived Prefecture of Police.

That same evening the new Prefect was present at a Council of Ministers held in the Pavillon de Flore when his advice was sought on the probable sequence of events.

'Defections are inevitable,' he answered. 'The soldiers are enjoying themselves and drinking in their barracks with the money you recently gave them as a sop. Do you know what they are saying? "Louis XVIII's a jolly decent chap but long live the Little Corporal!"'

These truths were unpalatable to the ministers who, in their disarray, proposed steps to be taken to ensure public safety. Chateaubriand, Benjamin Constant and Lafayette were among those who thought a change of government would put new heart into officialdom and an end to Napoleon's success. The army was entrusted to Ney.

While on the 16th Louis XVIII was addressing both Chambers and urging on them the necessity of rallying to the Charter, the Municipal Council in extraordinary session under Chabrol composed a proclamation to the citizens of Paris:

'It is your duty to defend your King, your fatherland and the honour of
the Capital. Your magistrates call upon you to carry out this sacred duty.
. . . The struggle cannot be long; the cause is that of the entire nation
against the enemy of Europe. . . . Parisians! support the efforts of your
magistrates. Long live the king!

These vivats would soon cease and be stilled. 'In the interval,'
wrote Chateaubriand, 'people seemed to hear Napoleon's footsteps
in the distance.' The Emperor in fact was making better progress
with his deeds than the politicians with their speeches. It was at
Auxerre, which he reached on 17 April, that Ney, who had distributed
the tricolour cockade to his troops, was 'carried away by the tide' to
fall into Napoleon's arms.

Ney's defection, known in Paris on the evening of the 17th,
caused the government to lose its head and Louis XVIII to make
hasty arrangements to leave Paris. The Bonapartists and the Jacobins
were jubilant; the people remained quiet, showing as yet no sign
of their happiness, but the soldiers gave themselves up to noisy
explosions of rejoicing.

Since humour is always present a placard was found stuck up on the
Vendôme column, carrying this message from Napoleon to Louis
XVIII: 'My good brother, don't send me any more soldiers. I have
enough.'

On the 19th Paris knew that Napoleon was marching on Fontainebleau and that night, under driving rain, Louis XVIII secretly left the
Tuileries. He had not grasped that Napoleon's bed in which he had
slept 'was made of laurels and its sheets were of flags'.

V

The Final Effort

Napoleon resumes building

At 10 a.m. on Monday, 20 March, the King of Rome's fourth birthday, Napoleon reached Fountainebleau again where he heard from the faithful Lavalette, reinstated as Minister of Posts, that the King had left Paris during the night. At once Napoleon decided to make for the capital.

At dawn on this spring day Paris was calm and empty. 'No one in the Tuileries, its courtyards, the neighbouring barracks, the ministries nor in many mansions in the Faubourg St-Germain,' writes Pasquier, but news of the nocturnal flight of King and Court spread rapidly, to be the butt of rude jests by workers and soldiery. Little by little Napoleon's supporters issued into the streets where large crowds began to assemble. Tightly packed groups of workers came down between 10 and 11 a.m. from the faubourgs, making for the Carrousel where they mingled with soldiers of all ranks, mostly 'half-pay officers', sporting the tricolour cockade.

At 2 p.m. many reserve army units assembled at the barriers to march into the Carrousel, led by General Exelmans, all wearing the tricolour cockade which, after its enforced absence for so many months, produced a magical effect. The tricolour was hoisted in place of the royal ensign on the dome of the Tuileries as cries of 'Long live the Emperor!' rose from thousands of throats, mingled with shouts of 'Down with the clergy!'

Soon the tricolour floated over the Hôtel de Ville, then over the column of the Grande Armée. Rejoicing in the Place Vendôme, crammed with people, baffles description. 'Everyone embraced everyone else, everyone cheered; it was pandemonium,' wrote Hippolyte Carnot, who witnessed the scene in his room at the Lycée Louis-le-Grand from which he could see the top of the column.

Thousands of copies of Napoleon's proclamation to the army were distributed and, as they were snatched from hand to hand, the soldiers' excitement reached a new peak. Soon the walls of Paris were thick with people. Stocks maintained their high figure of 81.40 frs.

In the course of the day several former ministers or associates of Napoleon met to discuss the formation of the future government while members of the revived Imperial court and notabilities in Paris rushed to the Tuileries. By the light of innumerable torches the crowd which had formed round the Tuileries, in the Rue de Rivoli and on the quays waited eagerly for the Master's arrival. No theatres were open and the time of waiting seemed endless.

Most impatient of all were the soldiers gaunt in face and thread-bare in dress who had emerged from their retirement, with new hope, to cheer their idol. At last, about 9 p.m., by the Louvre entrance opposite the Seine, a small barouche surrounded by a knot of horsemen drove in like a whirlwind and stopped in front of the stair next to the Pavillon de Flore. Out stepped a man dressed in a grey greatcoat and wearing a small hat. It was Napoleon. At once the cheers broke out, 'Long live the Emperor!' There was a wild stampede towards Napoleon. The Emperor was literally lifted off the ground and hoisted on the shoulders of his admirers who, pushed forward by a human tide, carried him up to the first floor of the palace while those fortunate enough to get near him covered his hands with kisses.

After delirium had to come practicality. During the night, Napoleon received in turn most of his former ministers, Lavalette, Caulaincourt, Cambacérès, Maret, Savary, Davout and Fouché, each man applauded as at the theatre as he threaded his way through the dense groups of courtiers filling the salons. To each of them the Emperor spoke of the conclusions he had reached along his route, especially from Grenoble onwards. The people had indeed literally carried him to Paris and reinstated him on the throne, but this was a populace beside itself, violent and ready to unleash its revolutionary fury against the aristocracy and the clergy.

'Nothing astonished me more,' Napoleon told Molé, 'on my return to France than this hatred of the priests and the nobility which I find as violent and immutable as it was at the beginning of the revolution.'

This hatred was particularly obvious in Paris where hostility to the aristocracy was great, but the Emperor had no intention of being outstripped by the extremists.

'The Jacobins must be used at this moment to meet the most urgent dangers, but do not worry, I am here to hold them in check.'

Part of the night was spent in discussions about the future composition of the government. Maret was appointed Secretary of State, Fouché Minister of Police; two new prefects were nominated, Comte Bondy to the Seine and Councillor of State Réal to the Police.

The Emperor's return was officially notified to Paris by the *Moniteur* (which had again become Napoleon's own paper) on the 21st:

'His Majesty the Emperor arrived at 8 p.m. at his palace of the Tuileries. He entered Paris at the head of those troops who had left the city in the morning to prevent his arrival.'

This announcement was a brilliant riposte to that of 1 April. The Parisians could again lift their heads; they were purged of the insult to the capital.

At the end of the morning the Emperor sent for Carnot, who was invited to take office as Minister of the Interior. Napoleon was anxious to resume contact with the Paris garrison and his decision to review the troops would give the people a further opportunity of expressing the warmth of their feelings. Huge crowds gathered round the Tuileries and some eager spirits had even climbed on the roofs of houses overlooking the Carrousel. Cheers rang out as detachments of all arms debouched on to the Place, but the loudest applause was reserved for the heroic battalion from Elba, their faces blackened with gunpowder and their uniforms in tatters; it was they who had accompanied the Emperor from the island of Elba to the towers of Notre Dame. 'Never have I seen such enthusiasm,' wrote Queen Hortense.

The account in the *Moniteur* was as follows:

'The whole capital was witness to the spirit of devotion and affection which inspired these brave soldiers. All had again found their country, had escaped from persecution and, in the national colours, recovered the memory of all that generosity of feeling which has always characterized the French nation.'

When the Emperor had passed down the ranks he made a stirring speech to the troops drawn up in a hollow square: 'Soldiers! I came to France with six hundred men because I relied on the love of the people and the memories of the veterans. . . . Soldiers! only the Imperial throne can ensure the people's rights. The French nation and I count on you.'

These words were greeted with frenzied cheers both from the public and the soldiery who swore to defend the sacred soil of the fatherland while the band played, 'Veillons au salut de l'Empire'.

In the days which followed, Napoleon inspected the regiments of the Guard of his good city of which he had resumed command. Many soldiers came to Paris by forced marches, 'spontaneously impelled by a burning desire to see the Emperor again'. Houssaye tells the story of some Dragoons of the Guard from Tours who on the quays heard that Napoleon was inspecting a parade. Taking their officers with them, they rode at the trot through the entrance to the Louvre and, spurring their tired horses on to the Place du Carrousel, arrived covered in dust and shouting, 'Long live the Emperor!' On another occasion, says Houssaye again, during a parade in open order the Dragoons of the line lifted their sabres and crossed them over the Emperor's head which he laughingly bowed and ended his inspection under this arch of steel.

Napoleon's task was colossal; everything must be started afresh. While his first efforts had to be directed to reorganizing his army and his finances he intended to resume the public works of his good city which, during his absence, had slackened considerably. His first note to Carnot on this subject was sent on 25 March.

'Work must begin in Paris on Monday, the 27th. Let me have a report tomorrow, Sunday, on what should be resumed first, giving priority to works of public utility. It is my plan that works undertaken on behalf of the City of Paris from funds received from the sale of houses and hospices or from special funds should be regulated at 20,000 frs a month, which for the remainder of the year will amount to 1,800,000 frs; that works chargeable to the special funds deposited at the Caisse d'Amortissement should be paid at the rate of 100,000 frs. a month; and as, in addition, I have allocated a sum of 100,000 frs monthly from the Civil List of the Crown, this will make a gross sum of 400,000 frs a month, which will produce the means for an adequate resumption of public works in Paris.'

In another letter to Montalivet, now Intendant General of the Crown, he said:

'Please let me have tomorrow, Sunday, a report on the orders to be given to stop work at Versailles and to start disbursements for work on the Louvre and other Crown property, at the rate of 100,000 frs a month, starting from April. Work will be resumed as of Monday next.'

Work began again immediately in the yards; one thousand workers were employed on the slaughterhouses, markets, wine entrepôt, and the Lycée d'Harcourt, another three hundred at the Ourcq canal and several hundreds at the Bourse, the Bastille fountain, the Palais du Temple and several additional thousands for the defence of Paris. An official report in the *Moniteur* announced:

> 'Work at all buildings in Paris was resumed last week and several thousand workers are busily employed in completing the monuments left standing idle eleven months ago. His Majesty's orders are that the number of workers should be doubled next week.'

Napoleon had planned a great obelisk and a high tower for use both as a clock for the city and as a master milestone for the Empire to be built at the approaches to the Pont Neuf. When he heard that royalists had raised a subscription to erect a bronze statue of Henri IV on this spot in place of the obelisk he showed his great political liberalism by announcing his resolve to continue with the project to honour the memory of a monarch whom he held in great esteem.

'I am flattered to see Henri IV thus honoured and I wish to associate myself with the homage paid to a monarch whom France remembers and who, by his courage alone, won the right to command the French and thereafter to make them happy. I myself will add the sum necessary to finish the work which has been begun.'

Fontaine, reinstated in his appointment, was ordered to speed this project and was likewise told to allocate a certain number of workers to the Palais de Chaillot where work had been resumed, but it was little more than a gesture. 'It had become impossible,' Napoleon was to write, 'to recapture the illusions of the dream which had faded.'

Paris acclaims Napoleon

On Sunday, 26 March, Napoleon resumed his old practice of receiving the ministers and constituted bodies at the Tuileries before mass. The restoration of the Empire had to be solemnized and he himself assured of everyone's loyalty. Bondy, the Prefect of the Seine, in the name of the Municipal Council read a loyal address voted the previous day at the Hôtel de Ville:

'Your Majesty was raised to the throne of the French people by the unanimous will of the nation and for twenty-seven years one principle has weathered with us all the storms of the revolution. There is not, nor can there be in France, a legitimate power other than that freely and legally bestowed and recognized by her. . . .

'What legality has ever been sanctioned more forcefully than your own by the universal good wishes and feelings which marked your progress fron Golfe Juan to the château of the Tuileries. . . . ?

'Sire, the City of Paris lays at your feet renewed declarations of its respect, its admiration, its love and its loyalty. . . . Where is the city which owes you more? Where is there one which has more to hope from your love and your genius?'

In his reply Napoleon recalled the birthday of the King of Rome, which had been acclaimed by the whole capital.

'I accept the expression of the feelings of my good city of Paris. I made a point of entering the city on the anniversary of the day four years ago when the entire population of this capital offered me such touching signs of the interest it takes in the affections nearest my heart.'

Napoleon was also bent on making an official announcement of his wish to proceed with the great public undertakings in his good city:

'I have ordered the suspension of the great public works in Versailles in order to do everything circumstances permit to complete what has been started in Paris, which will ever be my home and the capital of the Empire. Thank the people of Paris on my behalf for all the signs of affection they show me.'

The Emperor had realized on his return that the nation was veering in two opposite directions which rapidly rivalled each other; one, of which Carnot was the most distinguished representative, was revolutionary and Jacobin, supported by the people and the army; the other, liberal and constitutional, was led by Lafayette and based on the middle class and high official circles.

Strong Jacobin feelings were expressed in the faubourgs of Paris where the 'Marseillaise' and the 'Ça ira' of the sans-culottes were fervently sung. They were also noisily apparent in the resuscitated clubs and at the theatre, particularly the Théâtre Montansier, and even at the Opéra where performances frequently ended with songs in the style of 1792.

'Men of a certain age,' wrote Caulaincourt, 'heard with emotion those patriotic airs which had electrified their youth while the youth of today, to whom they were new, listened attentively and with astonishment. The "Marseillaise" was sung in the streets, at theatres and at the head of battalions. If the "Marseillaise" was not heard it was because the people were absent. . . .'

All these patriots were ardent Bonapartists who in Napoleon saw the 'generalissimo of the nation'. The Emperor was touched by these spontaneous demonstrations of a veritable cult for his person. He lent himself eagerly to maintaining this atmosphere of enthusiasm by incognito visits to workshops and yards where he spoke familiarly to the people and workmen as in the days when, weighted down with glory, he returned to Paris. Those men who had already found work again showed their great gratitude.

'We rely on him,' they said, 'but he can rely on us. Last year they would not give us weapons, but if the enemy returns to Paris we shall have them and he will see whether we can use them!'

In sharp contrast to the Emperor's popularity was the fierce hatred shown towards the aristocracy. On a visit to the Faubourg St-Antoine, Napoleon was enthusiastically greeted by the populace which followed him on his tour but, says Las Cases:

'As they traversed the Faubourg St-Germain the crowd spewed out its anger at the fine houses and pointed with furious gestures to the windows. The Emperor said that rarely had he found himself in so delicate a situation and remarked, "What disasters might have ensued from one single stone thrown into that crowd or one impetuous word or even a reproving look from me. The malicious Faubourg might have disappeared completely and I do believe that it was only because of my own sangfroid and the people's respect for me that it survived." '

Napoleon was struck by the strength of the revolutionary current of feeling and also by the rapid growth of liberal ideas.

'They have recaptured,' he confessed, 'the ground I had won for the government but one cannot take up arms against a nation; it is the earthenware pot against the iron pot.'

At the time of the landing the bourgeoisie had adopted an attitude of 'wait and see', but it showed no hostility towards the Emperor and welcomed his pronouncements in favour of the restitution of their liberties and the promulgation of a constitution to guarantee them. Jacobin excesses, however, alarmed them and still more the imminence of a new campaign which they believed might be disastrous.

Trade was even more disturbed. Stocks weakened progressively and on April 10 fell to 66.25 frs. Business was languishing and theatre receipts declining.

The bourgeois elements, mainly business people, who made up the large part of the Paris National Guard, were far from sharing the army's enthusiasm for the Emperor who, on the 16th, to overcome this hostility, reviewed the forty-eight battalions of this Guard on the Place du Carrousel, going down all the ranks and halting before each battalion. He then addressed the officers, who had formed a circle:

'Soldiers of the National Guard of Paris, I am happy to see you. Fifteen months ago I set up your Guard to keep the capital safe and to maintain order. You have fulfilled my expectations. You have spilt your blood in the defence of Paris and, if enemy troops did penetrate your walls, yours is not the fault but treachery.

'The royal throne was not suitable for France as it gave no security to the people's most vital interests. It was forced on you by the foreigner. . . .

'Soldiers! you were made to wear colours banned by the nation but in your hearts you wore the national colours. You swear to see them always as a rallying-point and to defend the Imperial throne, the only and natural guarantee of our rights.'

'We swear it,' cried every member of the National Guard who then for two hours marched past Napoleon standing in front of the Pavillon de l'Horloge.

Although deeply involved in his military preparations, the Emperor had to cope with the mutually antagonistic and powerful forces with which he was faced, without disappointing either. The gravity of the French situation, which demanded total mobilization of the nation's forces, militated towards the dictatorship which the Jacobins were urging on him.

'If tomorrow,' he said, 'I donned the Phrygian cap the kings of the coalition would be done for.'

But he feared the incalculable consequences of possible disorders, nor would he be the Emperor of the Jacobins. He, who so lately had been sovereign of Europe, scorned today the dictatorship of a faubourg, but he also hesitated to become a constitutional monarch, hemmed in by the restrictions of a Charter, obliged to make no decisions without the approval of Chambers whose endless and ineffectual speeches he despised.

To escape from the people's warm demonstrations of affection at all hours of the day, when he was cheered even under the windows of the Tuileries, Napoleon, who was very lonely in the château, went to the Elysée on the 17th, but he still wanted to keep in touch with the Parisian public. He went twice to the theatre, on 18 April to the Opéra to *La Vestale* and the ballet, *Psyche*, and to see Talma and Mlle Duchesnois in *Hector*. He received a tumultuous welcome from the audience which made the actors repeat any verses applicable to the present, in particular the lines:

'A warrior appears—it is he. It is Achilles who at last returns . . .'

Hobhouse, who witnessed the scene, wrote:

'The Emperor paid great attention to the play, not talking to anyone with him and apparently ignored the cheers. He left so quickly at the end of the performance that the public had no opportunity to cheer him.'

He did not forget, however, to express his pleasure to the actors for their acting.

Napoleon's eagerness to keep his promises decided him to follow the liberal course urged on him by his entourage. He made conciliatory gestures to Lafayette and Mme de Staël and invited Benjamin Constant to prepare a draft constitution. This was the Additional Act of 22 April to the Imperial constitutions. Legislative power was to be exercised by the Emperor and both Chambers; the Chamber of Peers was to be hereditary and the Chamber of Representatives elective. The Additional Act guaranteed the freedom of the Press, individual liberty and the abolition of censorship. Alluding to the many pamphlets with which his enemies had peppered him during the Restoration, Napoleon declared philosophically, 'I am not afraid to give liberty to the Press. For a year they've been saying everything and anything about me.'

The Act was a compromise between the ideas of the Emperor, reluctant to break with his past, and the liberal conceptions of Benjamin Constant. Apparently a return to revolutionary principles, the Act gave the impression of 'having carved liberty on the tree of despotism' and pleased neither republicans nor liberals, nor naturally the royalists who saw in it a pale imitation of the constitutional Charter.

Napoleon wanted the new constitution to be ratified by the people and a ceremonial return made to him of the results of the referendum in the presence of the Assembly at the Champ de Mai, when the constitutional charter accepted by the people should be proclaimed.

In this vast popular assemblage the Emperor saw a device for postponing the meeting of the Chambers and leaving him the absolute authority he needed to mobilize an army strong enough to withstand the eight hundred thousand men of the enemy coalition, but the liberals, at Lafayette's instigation, urged him to convene the assemblies. Napoleon once again bowed to what he was told was the nation's wish and summoned the electoral colleges. This move was distasteful to the old revolutionary party and the masses who opened their arms to their sovereign; it displeased them to see him embarking on the stultifying course of parliamentary debates.

Then came the spontaneous formation of the Federations as the capital was one of the first cities to mobilize patriotism round the Emperor. The Paris Federation soon numbered twenty thousand members. In the meantime Napoleon was reorganizing the National Guard of Paris.

Napoleon's heavy preoccupations did not interfere with his tours in the city. On 6 May he went at 6 a.m. with his aides-de-camp via the boulevards to the Faubourg St-Antoine to visit the newly established munitions factory; armament and arms manufacture were now of crucial importance. He next visited the cotton-mills of Richard Lenoir, with whom he had a long conversation.

'Almost the entire population of the faubourgs and streets through which he passed crowded round him. It was a most impressive sight to see this prince, almost alone, among a huge crowd which offered him such moving proofs of its affection, speaking to him, pressing against his horse and touching his garments.'

Many struck up revolutionary songs, with menacing cries and threatening gestures against the aristocrats. The Emperor was worried about the possible effect of this demonstration on the Faubourg St-Germain and he was vexed to hear that the noble Faubourg called him 'the Emperor of the mob'. He, therefore, had a report published in the *Journal de l'Empire* that he regretted the association of his name with songs 'which recalled too notorious a period'.

The revival of patriotism

Napoleon agreed to receive the Federates of the Faubourgs St-Antoine and St-Marcel in audience on Sunday, 14 May; they were all workers or artisans and most zealous in showing their devotion to nation and Emperor. At noon some twenty-five thousand of them, marshalled in battalions, marched through the Arc de Triomphe on to the Place du Carrousel to be met by Napoleon.

An address to the Emperor was read on behalf of all the Paris Federates:

'Sire! we received the Bourbons, who had become strangers to France, with coldness and indifference because we do not care to have kings foisted on us by the enemy. You we welcomed with enthusiasm because you are the Man of the Nation, the defender of the fatherland, from whom we await glorious independence and reasoned liberty. . . . We have come here to offer you our services, our courage and our blood for the Capital's benefit. Oh, Sire, why were we defenceless when foreign kings, emboldened by treachery, advanced to the very walls of Paris! . . . Our united resistance would have given you time to arrive, to liberate the capital and destroy the enemy. . . .

'Then, as now, our sole ambition is to maintain the honour of the Nation and prevent the enemy from entering this Capital should it again be threatened. . . . Long live the Nation! Long live Liberty! Long live the Emperor!'

To this speech Napoleon replied:

'Federated soldiers of the Faubourgs St-Antoine and St-Marcel, I returned alone because I relied on the people of the cities, the countrymen and the soldiers of the army, of whose devotion to the nation's honour I am aware. You have justified my confidence and I accept your offer. I will give you weapons. . . . You shall be the scouts for the National Guard. With the capital's defence in their hands and yours I shall be relieved of anxiety. . . . I trust in you. Long live the Nation!'

He then moved along the ranks and talked familiarly to any old soldier whom he recognized, recalling glorious memories of past campaigns. Some of them were moved to tears of joy.

Next day Napoleon issued a decree instituting twenty-four battalions of Federated sharpshooters, to be made up of volunteers, citizens and workers of Paris and its suburbs.

The Emperor was particularly pleased that men of such obvious bravery had offered themselves for the defence of Paris, one of his chief anxieties; he wanted the capital to play an important part in national resistance. Sensitive always to public opinion in Paris, he had not since his return, nor during the month of April, given any specific orders to fortify the city. It was on 1 May that he instructed Davout to build earthworks on the heights of Montmartre, Ménilmontant, the Butte Chaumont, the Couronne de Belleville and the heights of Charonne where, by the 15th, more than two thousand workers were employed, a number which soon rose to four thousand. Montmartre then became the popular place for sightseers whose presence encouraged the workers while 'everyone was satisfied with works so well planned and so quickly put in hand'.

The Imperial Guard also wanted some part in the capital's patriotic exertions. When Napoleon received the Guard on 18 May, he was presented with this address:

'The Grenadiers of your Old Guard have not forgotten how enthusiastically they were welcomed in such unhappy circumstances by the honest citizens of Paris. Their shouts of "Long live the Old Guard" still echo in our hearts. . . . For this reason, Sire, we beg Your Majesty for permission to use that time when you can spare us to join in the defensive works for the capital . . . were it but to rid the enemy armies of the mere thought of entering our gates a second time. . . .'

This request was granted by the Emperor and, on the very same day, five hundred Grenadiers went to work on the fortifications of Charonne and five hundred Chasseurs on the Butte Chaumont which, like Montmartre, became a centre for sightseers. Meanwhile the popular movement was spreading and the Faubourgs St-Denis and St-Martin amalgamated with the Federation of St-Antoine and St-Marcel.

To give his personal encouragement to this fervent patriotism Napoleon made a long tour of inspection on 25 May from 6 a.m. to 2 p.m. He inspected the armament works and armouries and spent a considerable time at Vincennes.

Napoleon decided to open factories for making guns in Paris where more than two thousand workers, among them locksmiths and cabinet-makers, found work. The same thing was done for clothing; one and a quarter thousand uniforms were manufactured daily. The capital showed its patriotic feelings in many ways. As all classes of citizens had several times announced that they would make voluntary contributions towards equipping the National Guard, Bondy had registers opened for their reception at the Hôtel de Ville and the town halls. These registers filled daily with the names of many donors who in one way or another were taking part in the national effort; the employees of the Prefecture of the Seine donated a tenth of their salaries and those in the Prefecture of Police 20,000 frs. The Imperial Court of Paris gave 50,000 frs, the factors of the Corn-market 3,700 frs and the Comédie Française 1,500 frs.

The Champ de Mai

Many abstentions were noted in France when votes on the Additional Act were counted at the end of May. The provinces were comparatively indifferent to constitutional changes but in Paris, more politically minded, there were fewer abstentions, although revision of the constitution was demanded by a number of electors. The nation as a whole approved the new constitution as only 4,206 noes were registered.

This result was announced on Thursday, 1 June, at the Champ de Mai, a demonstration to which Napoleon attached supreme importance. As it preceded the meeting of the Chambers it was intended to show the new members that the multitude of citizens gathered together on that day were better representatives and mouthpieces of the sovereign nation than deputies or senators.

The ceremony held on the Champ de Mars was popular, military and religious; it more than gratified the Parisian appetite for the spectacular. Fontaine had put up large wooden buildings to house the Emperor and his guests and had erected an altar and a throne.

At 6 a.m. a salute of one hundred guns, echoed by batteries all over the city, announced the opening of the proceedings, and from 9 a.m. onwards all that Paris owned of official and distinguished people made their way to their appointed seats. The field was lined with two hundred standard-bearers of the regiments and eighty-seven officers of the National Guard of Paris with their flags, and the parade-ground covered by troops with glittering weapons, drawn up in battle array. In a small box behind the throne sat Queen Hortense and her two sons, one of them the future Napoleon III.

A real human sea surged along the whole route to be taken by the

Imperial procession, whose departure from the Tuileries was announced at 11 a.m. by salvoes of artillery. Through a guard of honour of the Imperial Guard the magnificent cortège moved off, led by the Red Lancers and Chasseurs of the Guard, followed by Comte de Lobau, Governor of Paris, riding with his staff and followed by the heralds.

Surrounded by the carriages of the Princes and the great officers of the Crown the crystal coronation coach, drawn by eight white horses with white plumes, proceeded slowly with the Emperor, four Marshals, Soult, Ney, Jourdan and Grouchy, aides-de-camp, equerries, staff officers and pages in green, red and gold uniforms. Napoleon was wearing a theatrical state costume consisting of a scarlet tunic and mantle, white satin breeches, pumps tied with ribbons and a black velvet toque with white feathers. He wore this costume to underline his role as monarch as he had been seen at his coronation and to impress the European sovereigns. His aim was not to dazzle the people of Paris whose simplicity he understood and who, he well knew, would have been still more thrilled to see him in his legendary uniform. However, the Parisians, always enamoured of shows and ceremonies, cheered and loudly applauded him and his troops as they passed by.

At noon further salvoes rang out while drums beat and troops presented arms as the cortège crossed the Pont d'Iéna and cries of 'Long live the Emperor! Long live the Nation!' burst from every throat.

When Napoleon, in his showy costume, got out of his carriage, followed by his brothers dressed in satin, surprise for a moment suspended the people's rejoicing but, when he reached his throne and took his seat, surrounded by all his Marshals, applause broke out again. The Emperor listened attentively to the mass said by the Archbishop of Tours, but the majority paid scant attention and even manifested some displeasure. After this brief moment devoted to religion came the turn of democracy, the address to the sovereign by the nation's delegates:

'Sire, the French people bestowed on you the Crown which you laid aside contrary to their desire. The duty of wearing it again is imposed on you by our votes and a new contract has been entered into between Nation and Your Majesty. . . . We spurn the leader our enemies want for us and we want him whom they do not want.

They dare to outlaw you personally, you, Sire, who, so frequently Master of their capitals, generously strengthened their hold on their tottering thrones! ... Is it possible that your march in triumph from Cannes to Paris has not opened their eyes?

'Has there ever, in the history of all peoples and all ages, been a scene more national, more heroic and more impressive? ... The entire Nation girds itself for war. ... Every Frenchman is a soldier; victory will follow your eagles. ...'

'Long live the Nation! Long live the Emperor!' was the response to the end of this speech from all those present on the Champ de Mars. Then Cambacérès announced that the Additional Act had been accepted almost unanimously by the voters, whereupon Napoleon, seated and with his head covered, signed the act promulgating the constitution and replied to the address of the electoral colleges:

'As Emperor, Consul, Soldier, I owe everything to the people. In prosperity or in adversity, on the battlefield, in the council chamber, on the throne or in exile, France has been the constant and only subject of my thoughts and my deeds.

'Frenchmen! my will is the people's will; my rights are its rights; my honour, my glory and my happiness can only be the honour, the glory and the happiness of France.'

This moving speech met with tumultuous and prolonged cheers. The Emperor then on bended knee took the oath on the Holy Scriptures to obey and have obeyed the constitutions of the Empire.

To the beating of drums as the regimental flags of the National Guard were being carried to the Imperial dais, the Emperor advanced to the first steps of his throne and in a resonant voice invited the troops to join in the oath to defend with their lives the Imperial eagle with the national colours. This was the most emotional moment of all. Prolonged shouts of 'We swear it!' rang round the Champ de Mars as, in the midst of these cheers and surrounded by the eagles of all the fighting corps of France and his entourage, Napoleon took his seat on the throne raised in the middle of the Champ de Mars to begin the distribution of the eagles.

As the mass of troops marched past in battalions or squadrons the Emperor uttered these words: 'Soldiers of the National Guard of Paris! Soldiers of the Imperial Guard! I entrust to you the Imperial eagle with the national colours. You swear to die if it is necessary in its defence against the enemies of the fatherland and the Throne.'

The Emperor's words were continually interrupted by repeated shouts of 'We swear it!' It was, says an eye-witness, a scene of indescribable grandeur.

Next, some fifty thousand soldiers marched past Napoleon, shouting, 'Long live the Emperor!', their cheers echoed by the vast crowd which covered the slopes of the Champ de Mars as far as the Seine.

Although the ceremony of the Champ de Mai lasted for nearly seven hours it was still not long enough for distribution of eagles to all the troops of the Paris army, so the Emperor summoned the electoral colleges and military deputations to the Tuileries on Sunday, 4 June, to complete the award.

After mass he went with a brilliant escort to the gallery of the Louvre Museum, magnificently decorated for the occasion, where the members of the electoral colleges were lined up in alphabetical order of the Departments they represented. Some ten thousand people were present and cheered the Emperor warmly.

'The eagle for each Department and corps had been placed next to the President of the Departmental electoral college or the leader of the military deputation and no more magnificent sight could be imagined than this huge assemblage of Frenchmen in a gallery so rich in works of art where everyone crowded round the symbol which would rally them to the defence of their homes.'

The distribution of eagles was made personally by the Emperor, who afterwards chatted familiarly with many people and graciously received the numerous petitions handed to him. The ceremony ended at 7.0 p.m. when Napoleon returned to his own apartments accompanied 'by most lively cheers'.

The afternoon saw the traditional dancing in the Champs-Elysées to the music of many bands and lavish distribution of food; poultry, pâtés and sausages were handed out from vast buffets while the fountains gushed wine in profusion. This was the last time Paris enjoyed the Imperial bounty.

At 8 p.m. the Tuileries was brilliantly illuminated and a huge crowd on its way back from the Champs-Elysées gathered round the main block to hear the concert.

The Emperor with his brothers and Queen Hortense appeared on the balcony at 9 p.m. to be greeted by repeated cheers. After the concert there was a splendid fireworks display in the Place de la Concorde.

Napoleon leaves the Tuileries

The newly elected Chamber of Representatives was not favourably inclined towards Napoleon; five hundred of its six hundred and twenty-nine members were liberals, the reason being that the majority of electors belonged to the middle class which had been won over to liberalism and moreover feared Imperial autocracy above all. The total number of electors in the electoral colleges was ninety-eight thousand but, had France enjoyed universal suffrage, it is certain that the Chamber would have been Bonapartist. More serious still was the fact that there were only seventeen Departments in which, as the law required, half the electors plus one had voted; in the other sixty-seven the election was therefore definitely void.

Be that as it may, it seems that this Assembly was honestly anxious to make a constitutional monarchy work, but unfortunately its good intentions were expressed spasmodically and Fouché, shamelessly betraying Napoleon, managed to impose his own will through the members whom he had helped to get elected.

The distrust rather than hostility felt by the members towards Napoleon showed itself in the election of their president. Lucien was set aside and Lanjuinais, who had composed the act of deposition in 1814, was elected. Although the one hundred and seventeen members of the Chamber of Peers had been appointed by the Emperor himself they took up a completely independent stance.

As head of state Napoleon opened the session of both Chambers in a ceremony which took place on Wednesday, 7 June. He went in procession at 4 p.m. to the palace of the Legislature where on the steps of the new frontage he was received by Lanjuinais and twenty-five deputies, followed by the Peers and a guard of honour. As the Emperor entered the Chamber the members, standing and bare-headed, cheered him unanimously. Peers and representatives took the formal oath of obedience to the constitutions and loyalty to the Emperor.

Napoleon, wearing his hat, made a speech which, says Pasquier, was 'remarkable mainly for the difference in temper from the one to which we were accustomed'. He confirmed most emphatically his new dispositions and constitutional ideas:

'For the last three months I have been endowed with unlimited powers by the force of circumstances and the people's trust. Today

I am fulfilling the dearest wish of my heart by initiating constitutional monarchy. Men alone are not strong enought to underwrite the future; only institutions can insure a nation's destiny. France needs a monarchy to guarantee liberty, freedom and the rights of the nation. . . . My aim is that France should enjoy the greatest possible liberty, I say possible since anarchy always brings absolutism in its train. . . .'

He then struck an emotional chord, 'It may be that a prince's first duty will shortly call me to lead the children of the nation to fight for the fatherland. Both the army and I will do our duty. You, Peers and Representatives, will set an example to the nation of confidence, energy and patriotism. . . . The sacred cause of the fatherland will triumph. . . .'

This speech, which fulfilled everyone's hopes, drew loud cheers from every part of the Chamber and continued after Napoleon's departure.

Great solemnity had distinguished this occasion. The Emperor had been acclaimed not as the glorious captain but as the constitutional monarch who was now to share his sovereign powers with the Chambers. Napoleon, fully aware of what he was doing, felt it deeply.

'His own distress and the iron constraint enforced on him by this new development,' said Lafayette, 'could be read on his face.'

Once again he considered the city's defence, and gave Davout definite instructions to fortify the Left Bank, about which nothing had so far been done.

'I don't think the plan for the defence of Paris has been fully worked out,' he wrote to his Minister in reply to a report which Davout had sent him. 'The line of defence should lie on St-Denis not on Clichy.

'The Left Bank must be fortified before work is started on the second line between Clichy and Montmartre. No army would ever attack between Montmartre and St-Denis even if the canal and the redoubts which should cover them did not exist. . . .

'Give orders that from tomorrow, the 8th, work is begun at the four main points of the Left Bank of the Seine as it is essential that there should be some balance. Let me know when this has been sketched out and I will ride over the sites.'

Before replying to the speech from the throne the Chamber of Representatives held several meetings at which the majority acrimoniously showed their mistrust of Napoleon. A proposal to bestow on him the title of 'Saviour of the Nation' was ironically received; a similar attitude was evident in the Chamber of Peers. Finally both assemblies voted addresses in language respectful but indicative of their intention to assert their independence and dignity.

After mass on Sunday, 11 June, the Emperor with his brothers, the Princes, grand dignitaries and his ministers received in turn the parliamentary delegations presenting their addresses: to the Peers' representatives Napoleon said:

'The struggle in which we are engaged is grave. . . . The justice of our cause, the public spirit of the nation and the courage of the army give solid grounds for hope of victory but, should we experience reverses, that would be the moment when I would wish to see this great people expend its forces; it would be then that I should find in the Chamber of Peers proofs of devotion to the nation and to me . . . .'

To Lanjuinais the Emperor replied,

'I am pleased to hear the echo of my own feelings in those which you express. At this time of stress my own thoughts are filled with the imminence of war, whose outcome will determine the independence and honour of France.

'Tonight I shall leave to take command of my armies.'

The Emperor left the Tuileries on the afternoon of 11 June, never again to live there, and took up residence at the Elysée.

VI

Napoleon King of Paris

Napoleon's meetings with the Assemblies had caused him great bitterness. To concessions freely made both Chambers had responded with signs of often petty mistrust, hard for him to endure when he was putting out superhuman efforts to restore his Empire to good order and preparing to face united Europe.

He had a long interview with Carnot, to whom he confided his plan of campaign, saying, 'I need a striking success but do not worry, victory will be mine—it is my internal policy which needs a striking success.'

The conversation turned to the defence of Paris. Carnot was of the opinion that the fortifications had not made sufficient progress and that the opening of the campaign should be postponed. Napoleon did not agree. He had put Paris into a perfect state of defence but he did not believe that the enemy would get as far as the city's ramparts; all his hopes were set on a great and decisive battle.

On Sunday evening as usual Napoleon had those members of his family who were in Paris to dinner at the Elysée, and afterwards received Cambacérès, Lanjuinais, his ministers and a few faithful friends. He seemed relaxed, even gay, and talked about literature and art but, when the time came to say goodbye, the few words he said to Mme Bertrand revealed that he was not without apprehension, 'I hope we don't regret the island of Elba.'

On 12 June at 3.30 a.m. he left the Elysée in his carriage and took the road to Brussels, a route which proved fatal.

Everything now depended on Napoleon's sword.

In Paris the atmosphere was charged with anxiety, particularly among the bourgeoisie, as people realized the gravity of the situation.

Business was virtually at a standstill; stocks continued their down-
ward trend, from 60.00 frs on 13 May to 54.75 frs on 12 June.
Financiers were gambling on a defeat which must result in an improvement in the market. Given the numerical superiority of the Allies
it was calculated in government and political circles that the Emperor
might win some victories early in the campaign but that disaster
was inevitable. The Chamber of Deputies, convinced that it could
face any storm, put on a show of courage but Fouché used his creatures
in the lobbies to make the Chamber a centre of disaffection. Within
the government itself Carnot, alongside Fouché's intrigues, dedicated himself to ensuring the nation's safety. On 13 June he presented
to both Chambers an accurate report on the state of the Empire
which, to raise morale, he had printed in the *Moniteur*.

In his preamble Carnot scourged the enemies of France:

> 'Since yet again we must defend our homes against this barbarous
> coalition of envious Powers, yet again they will learn how intense an
> effort a great nation can make when fighting for its independence.'

For the benefit of Paris he had inserted a section concerning the
building in the city, which was the last official report:

> 'The Emperor has always taken a special interest in the public works
> being carried out in Paris, intended not only to beautify the city but
> inspired also by a generous concept of public utility.
> 'The building of a huge reserve granary has reached an advanced
> stage.
> 'Paris had no Bourse but now the Palais de la Bourse will be one of the
> finest buildings in the city and till 1814 work had proceeded actively.
> 'The restoration of the metropolitan church (Notre Dame) is finished
> and excellent progress has been made at St-Denis. When the Madeleine,
> started again with an improved plan, is finished in a few years' time the
> capital will have a building which will be a credit to French architecture.
> 'Under way are several buildings such as the Hôtel des Postes and the
> Ministry of Foreign Affairs.
> 'Other great monuments have been begun in various parts of the city,
> some intended to hand down to future generations the glory of our
> armies—work on these has been interrupted for a year. Let us hope that
> peace will soon permit their resumption and that on them will be inscribed
> further names of the brave men who are going to fight for our indepen-
> dence.'

Additional interest was aroused in this report because a strong
wave of patriotic feeling had swept over the people, who remained

immutably attached to Napoleon and until the last moment had come in large numbers to the Elysée to shout their loyalty. An increasing part in building defences for the capital was taken by the Federates who were constantly gaining new recruits; the twelve legions of the National Guard and the battalions of Federate sharpshooters offered their services free for making earthworks. The battalion of the legion of the Faubourgs St-Victor, St-Jacques and St-Marcel had built a little shelter at Charonne with this incription:

'Liberty, Fatherland, Napoleon. The 12th Legion, which has raised this earthwork, swears to die in its defence.'

Thus, ranged solidly behind the Emperor, the armed men of Paris rose fiercely against the enemy. The Parisians had not forgotten the humiliation of 1814; the hour of vengeance had struck.

Waterloo

By 14 June Napoleon had grouped his forces. On the 15th he was at Charleroi, on the 16th he beat the Prussians in a surprise attack. Soult, the Chief of Staff, at once sent a telegraphic dispatch to Paris announcing the victory. The front on the 17th was comparatively quiet and Napoleon strongly hoped that the next day would be decisive. Although deep in his last military preparations, he still thought of Paris and was avid for news of the city where his enemies were on the watch, eager to pounce on his slightest mistake, to bring about his downfall and where the assemblies also were prepared to strip him of power. During the evening he sent letters to Paris which, according to Davout, 'he was obliged to do because of the difficulties made for him and the obstacles put in his way by the intrigues in the Chamber'.

From early morning on the 18th, which was a Sunday, the cannon of the Invalides boomed out the victory of Ligny as the public crowded for news to the Tuileries and the Place Vendôme. On the 16th at 8.30 p.m. the *Moniteur* had published the following communiqué:

'The Emperor has just won a sweeping victory over the English and Prussian armies under the command of Lord Wellington and Marshal Blücher. The army is now entering the village of Ligny beyond Fleurus in pursuit of the enemy.'

A crowd bubbling with happiness spread over the boulevards and squares, to hear the reading of the communiqué. Lanjuinais, in the name of the Chamber, much impressed by this victory, hastened to send congratulations to the Emperor. Stocks rose to 57 frs. Imperial Paris knew its final hours of triumph and rejoicing, the more poignant because it was on this very day that the drama of Waterloo was being played out which culminated in the total defeat of Napoleon and the Grande Armée. As the capital, once again quietly confident, was putting out its lights the Emperor sadly left the last square of the Grenadiers of his Guard.

On the 19th Napoleon reached Charleroi at 5 a.m. Four hours later he was at Philippeville. After much deep thought he decided that his presence in Paris was essential and he would return there, fearing the consequences of the announcement of Waterloo, an outbreak of plots, the collapse of morale and Fouché's stab in the back. He might still retrieve the reins of power and be invested by the Chamber with absolute powers to ensure public safety, regroup his forces and show a bold face to the enemy. When he had dictated the bulletin for the fatal battle he wrote two letters to Joseph, one intended to be read to the Council, which admitted the defeat but in moderate language, 'mentioning neither what had caused the loss of the battle nor what might ensue'; the other, a personal letter, baldly told the horrible truth and announced his immediate return.

A dispatch dated from Fleurus on the 17th was published in the *Moniteur* of the 19th. This announced the pursuit of the enemy and ended:

> 'Never have I seen such ardour among my soldiers. Among the columns marching up to the battle and the wounded returning from the dressing-stations there was one continuous shout of "Long live the Emperor!" '

Followed a copy of a letter from Soult to Davout, giving further details about the battle of Ligny but nothing about subsequent operations. In the absence of a full bulletin the silence about the battle was causing anxiety. Apparently, however, Fouché was, through his many spies, better informed than the government; he had got wind of the disaster about which he kept quiet.

It was not until 9 a.m. on 20 June that Joseph received Napoleon's two letters. He immediately called the ministers to the Tuileries where there was general consternation. Molé says that the 'Assembly preserved a melancholy silence'. In view of Napoleon's imminent arrival no action was taken. Although nothing had been released about the defeat the sudden meeting at the Tuileries caused some anxiety as it seemed to indicate bad news. Faces everywhere were grave; crowds forsook the Palais Royal. There was a sinister presentiment abroad.

During the night a dispatch rider brought the bulletin Napoleon had dictated for publication in a supplement to the *Moniteur* next day. News of the disaster, spreading quickly to political and parliamentary circles, caused great consternation and distress. The Emperor's sudden return greatly annoyed Fouché, actively engaged in fomenting opposition to him, waving in front of the deputies the bogey of dissolution and frightening Napoleon's supporters with a vote of deposition. His true aim was to force the Emperor to abdicate and deprive him of power, for which he had to move fast.

The final return

Three months after his return from the island of Elba, Napoleon, at 8 a.m. on the following day, reached the Elysée with Drouot after a gruelling journey, the last of his hellish dashes to his capital to raise morale. He entered his palace, his face drawn and in greater anxiety than on his return from Russia. The first person to greet him was Caulaincourt, who had been awaiting him since early morning.

'The army performed miracles,' said the Emperor, 'but it panicked. All is lost . . . I can do no more. . . . Three times I saw victory elude me. . . . But no, all is not lost. I will make a report to the Chambers on what happened. . . . I shall ask them for the means to save the country . . . and then I shall go away again.'

When Caulaincourt told him of the deputies' hostility he answered, 'I think you are not giving them their due. The majority are well-intentioned and French. Against me are only Lafayette and a few others. . . . My presence here will hold them in check . . . I am in their way; they would like to work for themselves.'

At 10 a.m. Napoleon presided over the Council of all the ministers, summoned by Joseph, the last to be held at the Elysée. 'With a calm which his face belied,' he gave an account of the battle and an estimate of the resources still at the nation's disposal. 'To save the fatherland I need to be invested with full powers, a temporary dictatorship. I

could seize this power in the public interest but it would be better if
it were accorded me by the Chambers on a national plane.'

The Additional Act empowered the Emperor to dissolve the
Chambers, a right he was reluctant to use, just as a little earlier he
had refused to rouse the masses against the nobility. Imperial Caesar
scorned the high hand. Napoleon was not the bloody autocrat he
has often been painted . . . he believed in legality, in law and in
justice. Only because circumstances compelled him to do so on 18
Brumaire did he decide to use his grenadiers.

At the Council meeting Lucien, Carnot, Davout and Decrès came
out in favour of dictatorship. So did Fouché, but he treacherously
suggested seeking the Chambers' consent, well knowing their
hostility. Regnault de St-Jean d'Angély, loyal to the Emperor and
conversant with Fouché's intrigues, thought he was doing the right
thing in suggesting that the Emperor abdicate in favour of the King
of Rome to ensure the continuity of the Imperial dynasty.

Napoleon listened in silence to the various suggestions made by
his ministers. Meanwhile crowds began to gather round the palace.
Las Cases would thus describe the first signs of the people's wild joy
at Napoleon's return to Paris:

> 'His return caused enormous activity round the Elysée with surging
> crowds showing the liveliest interest in what was going on. Many
> individuals got inside the palace, some of the populace even climbing the
> walls. Some were in tears, others in frenzy had come with every kind of
> offer to the Emperor, who was quietly strolling in the garden. He was
> the only one to keep calm and bade the people reserve this ardour and
> love for the country's safety.'

Napoleon believed that he could trust the Chambers' patriotism:
'The enemy's presence on the soil of the fatherland will, I hope,
revive a sense of their duty among the deputies. The nation elected
them not to overthrow me but to support me. . . .'

Calling to witness the public which continued to cheer him, he
exclaimed, 'I'm not afraid of the deputies. Whatever they do I shall
always be the idol of the people and the army. I have but to say the
word and they would all be killed but, if I fear nothing for myself, I
fear everything for France. . . .'

He then forcefully explained the plan he had devised to defend the
country and overwhelm the enemy, only his enemy now was not the
coalition armies but the Chamber of Representatives.

Meanwhile political and financial circles in the capital were in a great state of agitation and large crowds gathered at the Bourse. Stocks from 57 frs on the 19th had fallen on the 20th to 53 frs but the jobbers, who had gambled on Napoleon's defeat, were preparing to reap the maximum profit from the situation. Both the salons of the Faubourg St-Germain and middle class business circles showed their pleasure at the Emperor's defeat. At the Palais de Justice the lawyers held endless conversations and at the palace of the Legislature the lobbies from eight in the morning onwards were in a great state of bustle. Gradually a large crowd, mostly silent and serious, assembled outside the Palais Bourbon and along the quays in search of news and to see what was going on.

The session of the Chamber opened at 12.15 p.m. while the meeting at the Elysée went on endlessly. Lafayette was the dominant factor who secured a vote that the nation's independence was threatened and that the Chamber would remain in session, treating any attempt to dissolve it as criminal treason. It was a parliamentary coup d'état. The Chamber of Peers adopted a similar resolution about 1.30 p.m.

The Emperor was extremely angry when informed of these votes but, recovering himself, he merely sent a message to the Assemblies, asking that measures for the public safety should be concerted, but this was not what the Chambers wanted. What they meant to have was the Emperor's abdication and demanded that he appoint ministers to bring them his confirmation. Napoleon, who had already rejected the idea of using force, did not long delay in acceding to their demand.

The working population did not hear of the Chambers' intransigence until the middle of the afternoon. There was then an immediate explosion of anger and determination to show their loyalty to Napoleon. Workers from the faubourgs, waving tricolour flags, Federates in their blue uniforms faced with yellow and the citizens of the outer districts came down in a body to the Palais Bourbon and the Elysée, calling for arms and shouting, 'Long live the Emperor!'

'If this crowd,' writes Madelin, 'massing and nearly in revolt around the Elysée, seemed to growl, it was not against but on behalf of the sovereign.'

But this crowd was the people of Paris, the people of the revolution who had thrown out Louis XVI and who soon would do the same to

Charles X and Louis-Philippe. It hailed the man who was its own king.

Napoleon had again left his study and with Lucien gone out into the Elysée gardens, where the people in the Avenue de Marigny caught sight of him and burst into frenzied cheers and shouts.

'Well,' said Napoleon to his brother, 'you hear these people? One word and the Emperor's enemies would lie dead.' Then, waving his hand to the delirious crowd, he added with emotion, 'Am I more than a man to win a misguided Chamber over to the union which alone can save us? Or am I a poor partisan chief who would set a spark to civil war? No! never! In Brumaire we could draw our sword for France's benefit. Today for her benefit we must throw this sword far away. Try to win the Chambers over. With them I can do anything. Without them I can do much for myself but I could not save the country. Go, and I forbid you as you go to address these people who are asking me for arms. For France I will dare all; for myself nothing.'

During popular demonstrations, ever more noisy and more excited, Napoleon received Benjamin Constant about 5 p.m. in the garden. He called him to witness the homage he paid to the people of Paris.

'Look at them, it is not they I have loaded with honours and gorged with money. What do they owe me? I found them as I leave them, poor, but in them speaks the voice of the country. If I would have it so, in an hour the rebellious Chamber would have ceased to be, but a man's life is not worth the price. I do not want to be King of the Mob. I did not come back from Elba for Paris to be bathed in blood.'

Lucien, appointed by Napoleon as the government's representative, went to the palace of the Legislature at 6 p.m. but his brilliant eloquence was nullified by Jay, one of Fouché's men, who virtually ordered him to ask the Emperor to take 'a decision which in the future will bring him more credit than his many victories'. It was then resolved that each Chamber should send a committee of five members to the discussions of the Council of Ministers. The Assembly at once chose its representatives, chief among them being Lafayette. Lucien then went to the Chamber of Peers which, after a short debate, elected its representatives.

Farewell to the Elysée

After a night of anguished thought Napoleon was informed by his ministers on the morning of the 22nd of the conclusions they had reached during the night. They made it clear to him that he must abdicate, a decision he accepted and a sacrifice he was already prepared to make.

The Chamber met at 8.30 for a stormy and impassioned session which lasted until noon. Only one thing mattered to the deputies; that Napoleon should give up the crown. At 12.30 p.m. their wishes were granted. Napoleon signed his act of abdication[1] in favour of his son whom he proclaimed Emperor of the French as Napoleon II. This decision was at once made known by Carnot to the Senate and by Fouché to the deputies. During the afternoon the Assemblies held further stormy meetings which ended with the voting of a motion avoiding any mention of recognizing Napoleon II.

'The fraternization of the Federates with the army,' wrote Molé, 'fanned the soldiers' anger and belief that the nation shared its feelings.'

The people, increasingly realizing how illusory and deceptive was the proclamation of Napoleon II and foreseeing the Bourbons' return and the ensuing upheavals, went wild. All over the centre of Paris groups of men, their ranks swelling hourly, paraded waving the tricolour; many half-pay old soldiers joined with the workers and artisans of the faubourgs. The National Guard was obliged to intervene at the Palais Royal to disperse rallies of exuberant Federates. Noisily, to cries of 'Long live Napoleon II! Long live the Emperor! Death to the royalists', the crowd shouted for arms. Their focus was the palace of the Elysée which harboured their idol.

'Never did the people which pays and does the fighting,' said an eye-witness, 'show him more devotion.'

Napoleon was deeply touched by the rough tenderness of the Parisians. In these dark days his good city of Paris, which he had loaded with so many benefactions, spoke its gratitude in the voices of its humblest but also its most courageous sons. The market porters and the charcoal-burners, his most faithful adherents, came to talk to him familiarly in the afternoon, entreating him to assume the crown again. He answered by a gesture pointing to his heart and stooped to hold out his hand to them. While he was meditating in a corner of the garden in the evening he was surprised to see a young officer, who

[1] This act was signed at the Elysée on a pedestal table in the Salon d'Argent, which has been carefully preserved.

had climbed over the fence, drop to his knees to kiss the hem of the Emperor's uniform. This fervent patriot had come in the name of all his regimental comrades to entreat the Emperor to resume command of the army. Napoleon raised him up and, pinching the officer's ear as was his wont, said, 'Go, and rejoin your post.'

All these demonstrations and noisy gatherings inspired Fouché with the liveliest fears, increased by Napoleon's habit of occasionally going out during the day without a guard, to be at once surrounded by the crowd which cheered him lustily.

By 24 June Fouché could no longer restrain his impatience and asked Davout to invite the Emperor to hasten his departure, a move which was ill received by Napoleon.

'You hear these cries?' he said. 'If I wanted to put myself at the head of this people, who understand instinctively what the country really needs, I should soon have done with all those men who showed themselves brave only when they saw me defenceless. . . . They want me to go. That will cost me no more than the rest.'

He had in fact made up his mind to go to Malmaison. On the 25th it was Carnot, also urged by Fouché, who came to tell the Emperor how important it was that he should leave. Napoleon, who knew how faithful his minister was, received him kindly and said, 'I am no longer anything more than a private individual, in fact I am less.'

He confirmed his decision to leave that day for America.

Napoleon, who wished his departure to be unremarked, had fixed the time for noon. The populace, however, could not tear themselves away from the neighbourhood of the Elysée, like a lover who cannot leave the place inhabited by his loved one for whose presence he clamours. By 11 a.m. several thousand people had gathered in the Rue du Faubourg St-Honoré, shouting at the tops of their voices, 'Long live the Emperor! Long live the Emperor! Do not abandon us!'

The Emperor was afraid of being unable to control his feelings when faced with these last demonstrations of affection, and may also have feared lest some embarrassing though well-meant obstacle be put in his way. He, therefore, ordered his escort and the Imperial coach drawn by six horses to leave with Montholon, Gourgaud and Las Cases by the principal entrance in the Rue du Faubourg St-Honoré. He then had the Grand Marshal's carriage sent round to the little garden door giving on to the Champs-Elysées, into which he got with Bertrand. The berline carrying Napoleon and Bertrand rattled off quickly by the Barrière de Chaillot towards Neuilly. It was half-past twelve.

Such was Napoleon's final farewell to Paris.

Fate would have it that the last road taken by Napoleon was the Avenue des Champs-Elysées and that, as he left his capital, he should pass in front of the Arc de Triomphe. He left not in triumph but without a sound, without an escort and as a fallen monarch, yet the colossal monument which he had raised became forever, like his victories, identified with triumph.

The romance was ended. Never again while he lived would Napoleon see Paris.

Epilogue

St Helena

Often at St Helena Napoleon mused on the great plans he had made for his capital. To Gourgaud he said, 'Paris is superior to the other cities in France. I wanted this capital to be so magnificent that no other city in the universe could approach it. I did and wanted to do everything for Paris. I quarrelled with the Pope because I wanted him to live in Paris and I had the Archbishop's palace set in order for him.' He talked to Las Cases in the same vein, foreseeing the expansion of the great city: 'It was always my dream to make Paris the real capital of Europe; I wanted it to be a city of two, three or four million inhabitants, in brief something fabulous, colossal and as yet unknown, with institutions comparable to the size of the population. . . . If providence had granted me only twenty years and a little leisure, Paris as it had been would have been sought in vain; not a trace would have remained and I should have changed the face of France.'

He also liked to recall his enormous achievement in public works, many of which unfortunately had not been finished. To the English press which accused him of having accumulated a vast fortune he retorted, 'Do you want to know what are Napoleon's treasures?'

And, to the impressive list of great enterprises he had carried out all over Europe he added, 'The building of the Louvre, the public granaries, the Banque de France, the Ourcq canal, the water supply of Paris, innumerable sewers, the quays, the beautifying of the city and the monuments of this great capital.'

He also stressed that these operations he had been able to finance without burdening Paris with the cost, and told Bertrand, 'Nearly everything I did in Paris cost the city nothing.'

Napoleon freely praised Parisian wit: 'Men of wit are found at every street corner in Paris.'

Las Cases says that 'he paid homage to the capital's exquisite tact', remarking, 'Nowhere probably is there so much wit and good taste as in Paris.'

In 1821, the year of his death, Marchand relates that on 11 February the Emperor recited these lines by Lusignan which he was fond of quoting,

> But to see Paris again,
> I can no longer hope . . .

and added sadly, 'I shall not see the year out.'

On 15 April he made his will, expressing his last wishes. The second clause is historic, 'I desire that my ashes may rest on the banks of the Seine in the midst of the French people whom I loved so well.'

In the course of a conversation with Dr Arnott on 24 April he asked him various questions about Paris and its institutions, 'Have you seen the School of Medicine in Paris? . . . Have you see the Jardin des Plantes? . . . Have you visited the Paris hospitals? . . . What seemed to you most beautiful in Paris? . . . Is London more beautiful?'

These were the last thoughts of the dying Emperor for his good city which he had dreamed of making the most beautiful in the world.

Death

Paris learned of the Emperor's death on 5 July 1821. The *Moniteur* published this report on the 7th:

'A special delivery of English newspapers of the 4th has arrived in which Bonaparte's death is officially announced. This is the official text:

'Bonaparte is dead; he died on Saturday, 5 May, at six o'clock in the evening of a lingering illness which had kept him confined to his bed for more than forty days.

'He expressed the wish that, after his death, his body should be opened to discover whether his illness was the same which had killed his father, that is cancer of the stomach. The opening of the corpse showed that his beliefs were well founded. He kept his faculties until the last day and died without pain. . . .'

This icily cynical official report only sharpened the grief and sorrow which overwhelmed the Emperor's old associates. Louis XVIII showed both tact and greatness when he said to General Rapp, who was trying to restrain his tears, 'General, weep freely. The loyalty you show to the memory of him who led you on so many battlefields does you credit in my eyes and is proof to me of your integrity.'

Many among the people refused to believe the news; the masses could not bring themselves to accept the fact that the man who was still their god had drawn his last breath.

The return of the ashes

Years went by. The *Mémorial de Ste-Hélène* was read all over Paris and France. The veterans of the Grande Armée never tired of recounting their stories of the Emperor's battles. Napoleon became a legend. In 1833 the Imperial statue was restored to the Vendôme column to the accompaniment of tumultuous cheers from the people. He was glorified by poets, writers and songsters; Balzac, Béranger, Hugo, Musset and Vigny made the immortal epic live again. As Rostand would write, 'the soldiers were his no longer but he had the poets'. The capital was flooded with engravings of the great man and events in his life.

In his angry poem, *Cavale*, Auguste Barbier used his own words to express the ardour of the Parisians:

> *En veste d'ouvrier dans son ivresse folle,*
> *Au bruit du fifre et du clairon,*
> *Paris d'un pied joyeux dansait la Carmagnole*
> *Autour du Grand Napoléon!*[1]

The body of the great man could no longer rest silently on the rock of St Helena. Paris in thousands upon thousands of petitions demanded the return of the Hero's remains. Victor Hugo made the solemn promise:

> *Sire, vous reviendrez dans votre capitale,*
> *Sans tocsin, sans combat, sans fureur,*
> *Traîné par huit chevaux sous l'arche triomphale.*
> *En habit d'Empereur!*[2]

On 7 July 1840, the Prince de Joinville (one of the sons of Louis-Philippe), with Bertrand, Las Cases and four of Napoleon's old servants, embarked on the *Belle Poule* for St Helena where they

---

[1] In working blouses and mad with joy Paris to the sound of bugle and fife dances the Carmagnole gaily around the Great Napoleon.
[2] Dressed as an emperor, Sire, you will return to your capital, drawn by eight horses through the arch of triumph, with neither tocsin, nor battle nor fury.

dropped anchor on 8 October. Ten days later the frigate bearing the
Emperor's remains set sail at sunset for France.

On 14 December the catafalque ship, *La Dorade*, brought the coffin
up the Seine seeming, in the words of the Prince de Joinville, 'to take
possession of the river as it sailed', while the bells tolled and the
people of Paris, massed since morning along the river banks, bowed
their heads in solemn silence.

The unforgettable ceremony of handing over the mortal remains
of the Emperor took place on 15 December in the presence of the
King (Louis-Philippe) and the most distinguished representatives of
the nation and the capital. The richly decorated Champs-Elysées and
the Avenue de Neuilly as far as the bridge were 'filled to capacity
with a crowd of several hundred thousand whose numbers swelled as
the procession passed'. Under the Arc de Triomphe the impressive
cortège made a brief halt while a salvo of twenty-one guns was fired.
The hearse arrived at the grille of the Invalides at 1.30 p.m.; the bier
was carried into the church and blessed by the Cardinal Archbishop
of Paris, attended by all his clergy.

'Those who witnessed this ceremony,' said the *Moniteur* of 16 December,
'will never forget the sudden sight of the Imperial coffin passing draped
in purple velvet, that coffin in which fancy might see Napoleon the Great
calm and asleep in his soldier's uniform.'

By four o'clock the service was over. The guns signalled the
departure of Louis-Philippe and the crowd withdrew in silence, taking
with them their 'imperishable memories'.

Conclusion

By making Paris the heart of the Grand Empire and the seat of his
greatness and power, Napoleon, more than all the kings of France,
ensured the city's pre-eminence in France and its influence in the
world.

Paris, as city and capital, in its government and administration,
still bears the imprint of Napoleonic principles. In many cases
national authorities and great institutions are today housed in the
palaces or mansions where Napoleon installed them. The most
famous instance is that of the Elysée where the Emperor took up
residence for the first time on 28 February 1809.

In spite of war and perpetual foreign tensions Napoleon's municipal achievement in Paris was extensive; the number of monuments he left behind is impressive. The capital's most majestic buildings, the Arc de Triomphe, the Bourse and the Madeleine all bear the stamp of his powerful mind. Few, even among those buildings for which he was not responsible, do not show the influence of his fertile ideas. The Louvre, where the great courtyard is still called the Cour Napoléon and the entrance to the Colonnade still wears the Imperial cypher, 'N', owes numbers of its art treasures to the great man, who continually added to the Museum's riches with the aim of making Paris the world centre of culture.

His record in works of public utility is equally valuable, although many of them have now vanished because new needs demanded other developments. Those which persist, particularly in road works, are noteworthy; the Rue de Rivoli by its width and the delicacy of its arcades; the Rue Soufflot and the Rue de la Paix because the majestic prospects they opened up have shown the way to modern town-planning.

As Consul and Emperor Napoleon's method was always to avoid excessive expenditure which would have borne too heavily on future generations. The captain who threw his cavalry into furious attacks always set his face against mortgaging the public treasure in what Zola called 'the infernal gallop of millions'. At St Helena he recalled with satisfaction that his improvements were achieved 'at no cost to the Parisian taxpayer'. Imperial monuments were paid for by taxes levied on conquered countries (the special account) and from his privy purse (Civil List). However glorious and profitable this method was it could not constitute a precedent for the future, but it did demonstrate the sovereign's desire to honour and embellish his capital. This desire was also surprisingly shown by the Emperor's insistence on his personal right to direct the great public works in Paris and to determine how they should be paid for, just as he himself drew up the city's budget which he instituted in 1800. The Municipal Assembly's powers may have been diminished thereby, but in the long run the capital and its inhabitants benefited.

Napoleon did not have the time to do the further building in Paris he would have liked to do. Many of his great plans never saw the light of day or, if they did, they rose no more than a few feet above the ground and soon disappeared. Other plans were taken in hand by his successors; on the site of the Palace of the King of Rome rose the Palais de Chaillot and the residences round about it, which the Emperor dreamed would house kings, became a diplomatic enclave.

In fact Paris, through Napoleon, took a decisive step in its historic development. Here, as in his political policy and like Alexander the Great, Napoleon was the link between yesterday's city, whose appearance he preserved, and the city of tomorrow which he inspired and helped to build. It is because he brought water to the city, because he built the port of Paris, developed canals and sewers, widened pavements and paved the streets—humble and inglorious task— that Napoleon III, who inherited from his uncle the desire to beautify the capital, could make of it the City we admire. Today, however, our admiration is increasingly giving way to anxiety in face of the vast and complex problems with which we are faced. Paris has reached a turning-point and must seek a new direction. Both Napoleons await a successor.

A study of Napoleon's achievements in Paris, in addition to its historic interest, sheds light on his characteristics. He is revealed as enthusiastic and indefatigable, but also as almost obsessed with the desire to build solidly and rapidly; this is shown most clearly by the visits to yards and building-sites which he liked to make and even regarded as part of his duty.

Moreover the strategist showed himself possessed of a lively 'business' sense which he utilized to increase and scrutinize the great city's assets as if they were part of his personal fortune. Anticipating modern legislation, he suggested to his Council of State that owners of land required for a given operation should participate in the cost estimated by themselves in proportion to their capital gains there-from. In an ancillary domain he gave proof of a large spirit of equity and great vision by showing himself categorically opposed to public compulsory purchase, declaring that the least of landowners was more his own master than was the Emperor. It is striking to observe how the development of his ideas followed the graph of his successes. Reverses purged his ambitions and allowed freer play to his humanitarian ideas. Buildings of public utility became of greater significance to him than prestige monuments.

In addition to her Imperial monuments and some of her streets Paris still wears a Napoleonic air if only in the street names which call the great epic to mind—from Rivoli to Austerlitz, from the

Pyramids to Jena, from Campo-Formio to Tilsit, from the Grande Armée to the Marshals.

The historic links which bind Napoleon and Paris are made immortal by two monuments, the Arc de Triomphe de l'Etoile and the Invalides. Foreigners who come from the four corners of the earth to see these pinnacles of his glory pay homage simultaneously to the Man and to the City.

Appendix I

*Table of Time Spent by Napoleon in Paris
and the Paris Region*
(21 October 1784—25 June 1815)

PARIS	8 years	4 months	4 days
St-Cloud	2 years	3 months	21 days
Malmaison		10 months	12 days
Fontainebleau		5 months	15 days
Trianon		1 month	13 days
Compiègne		1 month	21 days
Rambouillet		1 months	14 days
Total length of stay:	12 years	4 months	27 days

Appendix I

Schedule of time spent by Napoleon in Paris and its neighbourhood
(21 October 1784—25 June 1815)
PARIS: 8 years 4 months 4 days

Total = 12 years 4 months 27 days

Saint-Cloud	2 years 3 months 21 days	
Malmaison	10 months 12 days	
Fontainebleau	5 months 15 days	

Trianon	1 month 13 days
Compiègne	1 month 21 days
Rambouillet	1 month 14 days

Year	Jan.	Feb.	March	April	May	June	July	August	Sept.	Oct.	Nov.	Dec.	month	day
1784										21			2	11
1785										21			10	
1787													2	
1792					28				9				3	13
1795					25								7	6
1796												2	2	11
1797			11											26
1798											5		4	4
1799					4								2	16
1800								10 days at Malmaison		16			10	6
1801		5 days at Malmaison			6		2						11	27

9 days at Malmaison

3 months 25 days at Malmaison

9 12

16 days at

Year		
1804	27 days at Malmaison — 1 day at Compiègne · 2 days at Fontainebleau · 1 month 6 days at St-Cloud · 5 days at Fontainebleau	3 · 11 · 3 · 19 · 9 · 14
1805	17 days at Malmaison · 1 day at Fontainebleau · 2 days at Malmaison · 19 days at St-Cloud · 18 days at St-Cloud · 5 days at Fontainebleau	6 · 18 · 12 · 4 · 14
1806	3 months 25 days at St-Cloud — 8 days at Malmaison — 12 days at Rambouillet	4 days at Compiègne · 11 · 2 · 24 · 24 · 3 · 7 · 29
1807		27 · 4 · 3 · 21
1808	10 days at St-Cloud	28 days at St-Cloud — 9 days at Rambouillet · 1 month 24 days at Fontainebleau · 16 · 4 · 22
1809	5 days at Rambouillet — 5 days at Malmaison · 2 · 1 month 7 days at St-Cloud · 7 days at St-Cloud · 18 days at Fontainebleau · 10 days at Trianon	23 · 13 · 14 · 21 · 18 · 29 · 26 · 4 · 28
1810	3 days at St-Cloud · 1 month at Compiègne · 2 days at Rambouillet · 26 · 2 months 25 days at St-Cloud · 1 month 22 days at Fontainebleau · 8 days at Trianon · 11 days at Rambouillet	2 · 10 · 25
1811	10 days at St-Cloud · 7 days at Rambouillet · 18 days at Trianon · 24 days at Compiègne · 1 month 29 days at St-Cloud · 19 days at St-Cloud	22 · 4 · 19 · 11 · 9 · 28
1812	1 month 9 days at St-Cloud · 9 · 18	4 · 23
1813	8 days at Fontainebleau · 17 days at Trianon · 8 days at St-Cloud · 10 days at St-Cloud	14 · 9 · 4 · 6
1814	Fontainebleau	31 · 20 · 1 · 15
1815	20	24 · 11 · 21 · 25 · 2 · 27

Appendix II

Buildings undertaken in Paris during the Consulate and Empire
Principal Buildings begun, restored or completed[1]

[1] Only exterior work is included. Not included are internal arrangements in the Château des Tuileries, the Palace of the Luxembourg, the Palais Royal, the Hôtel des Invalides, the Hôtel de Ville, Notre Dame, the Château de Vincennes, and so on.

Buildings or Monuments	Architects or Sculptors	Dates	Remarks
Palais du Louvre Cour carrée North Wing	Percier and Fontaine	1806–14 1808–14	Completed Just beyond the Rue de l'Echelle
Church of St-Napoléon Beside and to the east of the Pavillon Colbert			Not completed; destroyed in 1852
Palace of the King of Rome (on the hill of Chaillot)	Percier and Fontaine	1810–15	Foundations—not built
Palace of the Archives (Quai d'Orsay)	Cellerier	1812–15	Foundations—not built
Palace of the Bourse	Brongniart	1808–15	Finished by Labarre in 1826 Enlarged in 1902–3
Palace of the University and Fine Arts (Quai d'Orsay)	Poyet and Gisors	1812–15	Foundations—not built
Palace of the Legislature (façade on the Quai d'Orsay)	Poyet	1804–10	Present façade the work of Cortot (1842)
Palace of the Temple	Delannoy and Blondel	1812	Restoration work. Demolished in 1853

Buildings or Monuments	Architects or Sculptors	Dates	Remarks
Ministries or Public Buildings			
Ministry of External Relations (Quai Anatole-France)	Bonnard, Cellerier	1810–15	Finished in 1838 under the Restoration which housed the Council of State, then the Cour des Comptes here. Burnt in 1871. Gare d'Orsay built on the site
Banque de France	—	1811–15	Restoration work. Enlarged several times since 1853
General Post Office, Rue de Rivoli	Bénard	1811–15	Occupied by the Ministry of Finance 1827–71. Burnt during the Commune. Hotel Continental built on this site[1]
Bonaparte barracks (Quai d'Orsay)	Bonnard	1808–15	Demolished in 1898 to build the Gare d'Orsay
Lycée d'Harcourt	—	1810–15	Succeeded by the Lycée St-Louis
Monuments			
Arc de l'Etoile	Chalgrin and Raymond Chalgrin, Goust	1806–08 1808–11 1811–15	Finished in 1836

[1] The main room is called the Salle Napoléon.

Buildings or Monuments	Architects or Sculptors	Dates	Remarks
Arc du Carrousel	Percier and Fontaine	1806–08	
Vendôme column	Gondoin, Lepère, Chaudet (sculptor)	1806–10	The present statue erected in 1863 is by Dumont. The column overthrown in 1871 was re-erected in 1873
Obelisk on the Pont Neuf	Chalgrin and Peyre	1809	Foundations—not built. Now statue of Henri IV
Temple of Glory (Church of the Madeleine)	Vignon	1807–15	Finished in 1842
Church of Ste-Geneviève (Panthéon)	Rondelet	1806–12	Restoration work
Bridges			
Pont d'Austerlitz	Becquet, de Beaupré Chief engineers	1802–06	Enlarged in 1854—rebuilt in 1884
Pont d'Iéna	Lamandé Chief engineer Dillon engineer	1806–13	Widened in 1937
Pont des Arts	—	1803–04	Footbridge
Pont de la Cité or St-Louis		1803	Rebuilt several times. Now a footbridge.

Buildings or Monuments	Architects or Sculptors	Dates	Remarks
Theatres			
Théâtre de l'Odéon	Chalgrin	1808	Burnt in 1818—rebuilt in 1819 by Baranguey and Prévost
Fountains			
Fontaine du Regard (at the corner of the Rue de Vaugirard and the Rue du Regard)	Bralle	1806	Removed, now at the rear of the Fontaine Médicis
Fontaine du Palmier Place du Châtelet	Bralle Boizot (sculptor)	1806–08	Removed in 1858. Decoration altered by Davioud. Column restored in 1899 by Formigé and sculpted by Blanchard
Fontaine du Fellah Rue de Sèvres	Bralle Beauvallet (sculptors)	1808–10	Copy by Gechter in 1844
Cornmarket fountain, Rue de Viarmes	Bélanger	1812	Restoration work
Fontaine de la Paix or St-Sulpice	Destournelles and Voinier	1806–10	Removed. Now alongside the Rue Bonaparte

Buildings or Monuments	Architects or Sculptors	Dates	Remarks
Fontaine de la Charité Rue Popincourt	Bralle	—	A bas-relief by Fortin remains in the Rue de Sévigné
Fontaine de Mars, Rue St-Dominique	Beauvallet	1806–09	Site altered in 1809 and small arcaded square made round the statue
Fontaine de l'Ecole de Médecine	Gondoin Voinier	1810–15	Foundations—not built
Bastille elephant	Cellerier Mouton (sculptor)	1810–15	Foundations—not built
Fontaine de Bondy or Water-Tower	Girard Engineer	1809–15	Removed when Place de la République built. Now in the courtyard of the Abattoir of la Villette
Markets and market halls			
Wine Market, Quai St-Bernard	Bélanger Gauché	1811–15	Completed in 1819. Demolished to make way for Faculty of Science
Cornmarket, Dome	Bélanger	1810–13	Burnt in 1854, demolished in 1885, the hall replaced by present Bourse du Commerce

Buildings or Monuments	Architects or Sculptors	Dates	Remarks
Marché des Jacobins or St-Honoré	Molinos	1807–10	Rebuilt in 1865. Again demolished in 1958
Marché St-Jean	Molinos	1812–15	
Marché des Carmes	Vaudoyer Rondelet	1813–15	Completed in 1829
Marché St-Germain	Molinos Blondel	1813–15	Completed in 1817. Part still remains
Marché St-Martin	Peyre	1811–15	Finished in 1816
Marché des Blancs Manteaux	Labarre Delespine	1811–15	Finished in 1819. Rebuilt in 1840. Now houses part of the Prefecture of the Seine and Laboratory of the City of Paris
Marché du Temple, Rag Market	Molinos	1809–11	Demolished in 1865
Marché St-Joseph	—	1805	Restored in 1843. Demolished in 1882
Marché des Prouvaires	—	1812–15	Demolished in 1867
Marché de la Vallée, Quai des Grands Augustins	Happe	1809–13	Demolished in 1867

Buildings or Monuments	Architects or Sculptors	Dates	Remarks
Public granaries, Boulevard Bourdon	De Lannoy	1808–15	Completed during the Restoration. Burnt in 1871
Slaughterhouses			
Abattoir de Mousseaux da Roule	Petit-Radel		
Abattoir de Rochechouart	Bélanger and Poidevin	1811–15	All completed in 1818. All have been demolished
Abattoir de Popincourt	Happe		
Abattoir de l'Hôpital	Leloir		
Abattoir de Grenelle	Gauché and Gisors		
Cemeteries			
Cemetery of Père Lachaise	Brongniart	1802–04	

Appendix III

Road Works carried out during the Consulate and Empire

Present names	Present Arrondissements	Former names	Date of Completion
Assas (rue d')	6e	Partly rue de l'Ouest	1806
Bastille (place de la)	4e, 11e, 12e		1806
Béarn (rue de)	3e	Rue de la Chaussée des Minimes	1805
Beaujolais (passage de)	1er		1812
Bellechasse (rue de)	7e		1805
Bienfaisance (rue de la)	8e		1810
Bonaparte (rue)	6e		1804
Bourdin (impasse)	8e		1809
Bourdon (boulevard)	4e		1806
Bourse (place de la)	2e		1809
Caffarelli (rue)	3e		1809
Caire (rue, place, passage)	2e		1799
Cambacérès (rue)	8e	Rue la Ville l'Evêque	1807
Cambon (rue)	1er	Rue Neuve du Luxembourg	1810
Carnot (rue)	6e	Rue Joseph-Barat	1800
Castex (rue)	4e		1805
Castiglione (rue)	1er		1802
Châtelet (place du)	1er and 4e		1802
Cloître-Notre-Dame (rue du)	4e		1804–7
Clotaire (rue)	5e		1805–7
Clotilde (rue)	5e		1805–7
Clovis (rue)	5e		1807–9
Colisée (rue du)	8e		1804
Commines (rue)	3e	Rue Neuve de Ménilmontant	1804
Constantine (rue de)	7e		1807
Daunou (rue)	2e	Rue Neuve St-Augustin	1808
Dupetit-Thouars (rue)	3e		1809
Duphot (rue)	1er		1807
Dupuis (rue)	3e		1809
Estrées (rue d')	7e	Rue Neuve de Babylone	1800
Fédération (rue de la)	15e	Rue Kléber	1808
Fidélité (rue de la)	10e		1797–1806
Froissart (rue)	3e	Rue Neuve de Bretagne	1806
Gaudelet (impasse)	11e	Impasse de Ménilmontant	1805
Genty (passage)	12e		1806
Julienne (rue)	13e		1805
Ledru-Rollin (avenue)	11e	Avenue Lacuée	1806
Lübeck (rue de)	16e		1807

Present names	Present Arrondissements	Former names	Date of Completion
Madame (rue)	5e		1804
Madeleine (place de la)	8e		1808
Madeleine (passage de la)	8e		1815
Maine (avenue du)	14e		1813
Marché St-Honoré (rue, place)	1er	Rue et Place du Marché des Jacobins	1807
Mazas (place)	12e		1806
Miromesnil (rue de)	8e		1815
Mondovi (rue de)	1er		1802
Montesquieu (rue de)	1er		1802
Mont Thabor (rue du)	1er		1802
Observatoire (avenue de l')	6e		1807
Paix (rue de la)	2e	Rue Napoléon	1806
Panoramas (passage des)	2e		1800
Parvis Notre-Dame (place du)	4e		1804
Percier (avenue)	8e		1810
Poissy (rue de)	5e		1803–10
Pontoise (rue de)	5e		1803
Pyramides (rue des)	1er		1801
Richepanse (rue)	1er		1807
Rivoli (rue de)	1er		1802
Robiquet (impasse)	6e	Impasse Montparnasse	1805
St-André-des-Arts (place)	5e		1809
St-Augustin (rue)	2e	Rue Neuve St-Augustin	1806
St-Elisabeth (rue)	3e		1807
Ste-Foy (rue)	2e	Passage Aubert	1813
St-Sulpice (place)	6e		1802–11
Saxe (villa de)	7e		c. 1800
Seine (rue de)	6e		1811
Soufflot (rue)	5e		1804
Sully (rue de)	4e		1807
Téhéran (rue de)	8e	Avenue de Plaisance	1810
Ulm (rue d')	5e		1806
Ursins (rue des)	4e		1802
Ursulines (rue des)	5e		1807
Val de Grâce (rue du)	5e		1812
Valhubert (place)	5e, 13e		1806
Vivienne (rue)	1er, 2e		1809–11

QUAYS

Quai Anatole-France	7e	Quai Bonaparte	1804
Quai Branly	7e, 15e	Quai d'Orsay	1810–12
Quai Catinat	4e	Quai de l'Archevêché	1813
Quai de la Conférence	8e		1808
Quai de Corse	4e	Quai Desaix	1803–6
Quai aux Fleurs	4e	Quai Napoléon	1803–13
Quai du Louvre	1er		1810
Quai Malaquais	6e		1810
Quai du Marché Neuf	1er		1811
Avenue de New York	16e	Quai de Billy	1807
Quai des Orfèvres	1er		1807–13

Present names	Present Arrondissements	Former names	Date of Completion
Quai d'Orsay	7e		1802–12
Quai des Tuileries	1er		1806

Length of quays built by the end of June, 1812   about 2 miles

SEWERS

Length of system built   about 3 miles

Appendix IV

Balance sheet of large Public Works carried out in Paris during the Consulate and Empire

As of 1 January 1812

	Sums disbursed (*in millions of francs*)
Water supply	19·5
Slaughterhouses	6·75
Wine Market	4
Cornmarket (dome)	0·8
Central Markets	2·6
Markets	4
Public granaries	2·3
Mills and warehouses at St-Maur	1
Bridges	8·7
Quays	4
Lycées	0·5
Churches and Archbishop's Palace	7·5
Ministry of External Relations and General Post Office	2·8
Palace of the Archives	10·2
Legislature, Vendôme column Temple of Glory—Bourse Arc de l'Etoile—Bastille Fountain and their ornamental statues	12·9
Other works	15
TOTAL	102·55

Palace of the Louvre	21·4	
Tuileries (clearing the Carrousel)	6·7	
Palace of Rome	2·5	30·6
GRAND TOTAL		133·15

Present valuation

This schedule shows a total of 135 million francs in round figures, but 'other works' total only 15 million, which could not have included all the works carried out in addition to those mentioned by name above, particularly road works, fountains, cemeteries, theatres and gardens on the one hand and on the other the Arc du Carrousel, the Obelisk on the Pont Neuf, the Luxembourg, the Palace of the Temple, the Palais Royal, the Hôtel de Ville, the Bonaparte Barracks, and so on. Works carried out after 1 January 1812 should also be added to the total of money spent.

It would be dangerous to put a figure on this supplementary expenditure. We would estimate it tentatively at 135 millions, but for an idea of what that represents today one must take two facts into account:

—the price of a cubic metre of quarried stone; 21 francs in 1804, 210 francs in 1964, that is a coefficient of 10.
—the price of a square metre of a coat of plaster which rose from 1·10 to 11·90, that is the coefficient of 10·8.

By applying an average coefficient of 10 to the sum of 135 millions one arrives at an approximate figure of 1,350 millions of new francs, that is 135 milliards of old francs, an enormous sum for expenditure which does not include road works.

Appendix V

Schedule of Paintings brought from Italy to France
from 1796 to 1814 (Louvre Museum)

Date of Removal	Number of Paintings Removed	Recovered in 1815	Remaining in France	Lost
1796–97	227	110	115	2
1798–1803	206	116	83	7
1811–14	73	23	50	
	506	249	248	9

(Bulletin of the Société d'Histoire d'Art Français) 1936

Appendix VI

L'Hôtel Bonaparte

The Hôtel Bonaparte has many claims to remembrance. It saw the planning of the coup d'état of 18 Brumaire (9 November 1799) which created the modern state; it saw the great man's hours of greatest passion and, finally, this was the only house in Paris which he owned as a private person.

The house was 6, Rue Chantereine, in the fashionable and elegant district of the Chaussée d'Antin where, in the eighteenth century, financiers and distinguished actors built charming little houses, 'follies', in this once marshy area.

Only a porte cochère, attached to iron railings decorated with lictors' fasces, was flush with the street at No. 6 (60, Rue de la Victoire). A porter's lodge of two low storeys and a single ground-floor room with two windows looking on to the street stood on the western side of the entrance doorway which gave access to a long narrow path (about 30 by 3 feet), just wide enough for a carriage, and bordered with rose bushes and a few shrubs. This path separated the two neighbouring properties, No. 5 (62) on the west and No. 7 (58) on the east, both less extensive than Bonaparte's. On a frontage of only 55 feet, and slightly set back from the road, were lodges used as kitchen or porter's quarters. The houses they served were not, as many historians think, alongside the roadway but stood behind a courtyard about 90 feet long. They belonged first to the Marquis de Saint-Chamans and then to the widow of the Marquis d'Argenson. (This house was bought by Marshal Berthier but has been demolished and no trace remains.)

The path at No. 6 opened on to a rectangular courtyard flanked by two wings, a coach-house on the right and stables on the left, with a garret and servants' rooms above. At the far end of the courtyard stood the narrow white façade, 30 feet wide by 50 feet long, of a detached stone and ashlar building. Six semi-circular stone steps led up to a terrace, arranged as a veranda and used as an ante-room, bordered by a low balustrade decorated with antique vases.

The house had three principal rooms; an oval dining-room, from which a small stairway led down to the basement consisting of a cellar, a box-room and a kitchen; a small boudoir decorated with mosaics on the left with beyond it the large drawing-room, lit by two tall french-windows leading on to the garden. This room had an elegant chimney-piece. At the far end of the house facing north was the study where, on a simple oak desk, Bonaparte no doubt made the plans which changed the destiny of France.

The low-ceilinged rooms on the first floor were similarly arranged; Josephine's bed and dressing-room, a small boudoir, then the General's bedroom, entered by a door carved with Egyptian motifs. This bedroom was connected with the ground-floor study by a staircase. A bathroom was on the half-landing. There was a second attic floor above.

The ground- and first-floor rooms, hung with mirrors and tapestries, were always filled with flowers, especially roses from the garden, tastefully arranged by Josephine's gifted hands. This garden, approximately four yards square, occupied the largest part of the site to which it lent a rural air.

Both the Hôtel Bonaparte and its neighbours had been built by Perrard de Montreuil, the Comte de Provence's architect, on marshy land bought on 30 July 1776 from a speculator, Bouret de Vezelay.

The first tenant was Louise-Julie Carreau, a rising young actress, the mistress of Vicomte Alexandre de Ségur, whom she left in 1790 to marry Talma. She took a lease on the house on 15 March 1780, and bought it, through her protector's generosity, for the sum of 55,000 francs on 6 December 1781 by a deed registered with Maître Rouen, a Parisian notary.

On 17 August 1795 she let the house to Josephine de Beauharnais who, in exchange, sold Talma her small apartment at 371, Rue de l'Université, almost opposite the Rue de Poitiers. The future Empress made a few improvements, notably turning the terrace into a veranda under a wooden tent, hung with cotton draperies and decorated with painted or carved flags and pennants.

It was now that Josephine made the acquaintance of Bonaparte, who apparently first visited the Hôtel de Chantereine on 15 October 1795. As we know, the young General was absolutely enthralled both by her fascination and the showy and rather theatrical décor in which she chose to live. From this time on and for the next five months he spent all his evenings with his *dolce amor*.

Josephine, beginning to credit her future husband's star, on 21 December 1795 extended the three-year lease originally granted by Julie Carreau to nine.

On 9 March 1796 Bonaparte married the charming Creole and took up residence in his wife's house, leaving after two days of passionate love-making to join the Army of Italy.

On 28 December 1797 the central administration of the Department of the Seine decided to change the name of the Rue Chantereine in honour of the young conqueror to Rue de la Victoire.

Bonaparte bought the house, numbered first 46, then 60, on 26 March 1798. The deed was signed in the presence of Maître Raguideau and registered by the civil tribunal on the following 2 August; the price was 52,400 livres, of which 6,400 were paid in cash and the remainder in four instalments due on 30 August, 16 September, 10 November and 4 December, 1798.

Bonaparte lived in the Rue de la Victoire from 5 December 1797, the date of his return from Italy, until 3 May 1798, when he left for Egypt. He returned on 16 October 1799 to prepare the coup d'état of 18 Brumaire (9 November) and finally left the house on 14 November to take up residence with Josephine in the Petit Luxembourg. Henceforward the house was occupied only sporadically by members of the Bonaparte family.

Here the First Consul, before his departure for the Consultum at Lyons, arranged for the religious marriage by the Papal Legate, Cardinal Caprara, of Hortense de Beauharnais and Louis Bonaparte, and the blessing of the civil marriage, which had taken place on 20 January 1800 of Murat and Caroline. For the ceremony on 4 January 1802 an altar was set up in the ground-floor drawing-room.

At the end of the Consulate various additions were made to the property. According to a deed registered by Maître Raguideau on 28 May 1803, and transmitted to the Mortgage Office on 7 June, a parcel of land of some twenty square yards was purchased, which represented the porter's lodge the property of the Marquis de Saint-Chamans. On 3 May, 1804, the garden was extended eastwards by parcels of land of a thousand square yards situated behind Nos. 56 and 56a Rue de la Victoire, which were sold by M. Jacques Brou (by a simple contract registered on the following 2 August and deposited in Maître Noël's records on 11 December 1806).

By a deed dated from St-Cloud on 1 July 1806 executed after examination of the title on 11 December by Maître Noël, his notary, Napoleon gave the property as a dowry to his cousin, Marie-Louise-Stéphanie Rolier Benielli (daughter of Jean-Charles Rolier, Treasurer to Madame Mère, and of Marie Lavinia Benielli, second cousin of Felix Baciocchi, husband of Elisa Bonaparte). Marie-Louise married Colonel Charles Lefebvre-Desnouettes, his equerry (and afterwards Jerome's), who rallied to the Emperor during the Hundred Days and fought at Waterloo. Exiled under the Restoration, he joined Joseph Bonaparte in America and his wife was obliged to sell her house. The purchaser was one Aimé Deschasaux and the deed was signed on 16 December 1815 before Maître Sencier, notary in Paris. The purchase price was 58,200 francs (plus 11,100 francs for the furniture) which suggests that this was a fictitious sale. General Desnouettes died on 22 April 1822 on his way back to France after the Emperor's death.

His widow recovered the house on 13 August 1823 (according to a deed signed before Maîtres Bauchau and Bertrand, notaries in Paris) and kept the property for more than thirty-five years. In 1830 and again in 1837 she bought further parcels of land to enlarge her garden and to make an exit on the Rue St-Lazare, where she bought a house and garden at No. 57. She welcomed to her home General Bertrand, Napoleon's old companion in arms.

In 1840 she let the house to Jules Costes, founder of *Le Temps*, then from 1846 to 1852 to the Boutet Organization. It was probably round about this time that she built a large wood and plaster annexe consisting of a ground floor and two square storeys.

According to a deed registered by Maîtres Carré and Goudchaux, Parisian notaries, she sold this annexe on 2 April 1857 to Joseph Goubie, a banker, owner of a neighbouring house at 67, Rue St-Lazare, for the sum of 625,000 francs, of which 50,000 was paid in cash and the balance in three instalments, 175,000 on 12 June 1857, 200,000 on 2 April 1859, and 200,000 on the following 7 April.

The area of the property sold, roughly just under an acre, was bounded by the Rue de la Victoire and the Rue St-Lazare, across the Rue Ollivier, which was the principal site of Bonaparte's house. Under the huge town-planning and road-works programme undertaken at the beginning of the Second Empire the Rue Ollivier was extended to become the Rue du Cardinal Fesch, then the Rue de Châteaudun; the former Hôtel de Chantereine was fated to disappear.

Following a decision by the Paris Municipal Council of 5 February 1858, and by deeds registered on 5, 6 and 7 May of that year by Maîtres Carré and Delapalme, Goubie parted with a section of his property, of about a third of an acre, for the cutting of the new street. He did not make a gift of the property as most historians claim but received from the City the sum of 273,960 francs.[1] This sale involved the demolition of the house which had harboured the love of Napoleon and Josephine.

When the Rue de Châteaudun was made between 1858 and 1862 buildings were put up along it, particularly on the site of the Hôtel Bonaparte, as far as No. 48 and from Nos. 47 to 51 on the opposite side of the street. At No. 49, site of part of the First Consul's principal house, Goubie, on an area of about a tenth of an acre, built a block of apartments, with cellar, ground floor and four square storeys, with an attic and loft.[2] The remainder, that is, about two thirds, of the site of Bonaparte's house, was taken up by the pavement and the roadway.

On 4 July 1863 M. Oscar Benazet acquired through Maître Fould the Hôtel Saint-Chamans and on 4 August, according to a contract registered by Maîtres Turquel and Carré, Goubie sold him that part of the former Hôtel Chantereine which comprised the porter's lodge and the famous path leading to the house.

When this lodge and the wall dividing the Hôtel Bonaparte and the Hôtel Saint-Chamans was demolished in 1867, a building was erected in front of the latter at No. 60, Rue de la Victoire. Thus the old path along the east of the property at 58, Rue de la Victoire was absorbed into the parcel of land comprising the new building at No. 60 and the former Hôtel Saint-Chamans.

Now let us look at the buildings at present occupying the site of the former Hôtel Chantereine. Mention has already been made of the huge block, nearly a century old, from No. 60 to No. 64 (there is no No. 62). This, together with the buildings at Nos. 64 and 66, and 53, Rue de Châteaudun, is owned by the Crédit Industriel et Commercial. Entrance is by a

[1] The area was made up thus: cutting of a street of sixty feet over the Hôtel Bonaparte, about a thousand square yards; back of the property in the rue St-Lazare about two hundred and thirty-two square yards; part of the ground to the right of 55, Rue St-Lazare, annexed to the Hôtel Bonaparte, 60, Rue de la Victoire, about sixty-eight square yards.

[2] According to a document preserved by the Plan de Paris, the building was already in existence in 1862.

porte cochère only a few yards west of the one giving access to the First Consul's house. Farther on at the rear of a courtyard is the former Hôtel de Saint-Chamans, which in the course of years has undergone only slight alterations, principally to the north. Since 13 January 1920[1] this house belongs to the Société Immobilière de Chantereine.

Beyond the mansion a well-kept lawn runs up to the southern side of 51, Rue de Châteaudun. The entire site between this frontage and that of 60, Rue de la Victoire extends along the length of the path Bonaparte used to reach his house. Except for a small piece of ground on the east of the court-yard in front of the Hôtel de Saint-Chamans this path has been built over by No 60 and some small buildings skirting the wall separating it from No. 58.

A solitary paulownia, believed to date back to the eighteenth century, stands on the west of the lawn. I have made several pilgrimages to this spot and questioned a workman who was doing restoration work to the Hôtel de Saint-Chamans. He told me unhesitatingly, 'That is Napoleon's tree,' and added that this lawn was an annual meeting-place for Bonapartists who commemorate the historic anniversary of 18 Brumaire around this tree which they consider, erroneously alas, to be a survival of Bonaparte's property.

Goubie's building at 49, Rue de Châteaudun still exists. It was sold to M. Félix-Emile Lamy by a deed registered on 15 March 1876 by Maîtres Breillaud and Pean de Saint-Gilles; a deed dating back to Napoleon Bona-parte's original property. The building now belongs to M. Lamy's heir, M. de Chillaz. Nos. 47 and 51, Rue de Châteaudun, erected about a hundred years ago, now belong to the insurance company, *La Protectrice*, and their title deeds also go back to the Emperor; their head office has been here since 1911. Nos. 46, 48, and 50 are also nineteenth-century houses. The head office of *Le Soleil* has been at No. 48 since 1894 and is owned by the Company as well as 57, Rue St-Lazare. Both the owners of these buildings and their staffs set great store by their distinguished history of which they are justly proud.

Although some of these buildings laid claim to occupy the site of the vanished Hôtel Bonaparte, no mark had as yet indicated its actual site and I fear that very few of those who walk along the Rue de la Victoire or the Rue de Châteaudun call to mind the man who lived here. Laudable efforts are made to preserve old houses of historic interest but those of which no trace remains also deserve to be remembered. The Hôtel Bonaparte, both because of the historic events it witnessed and its master's personality, figures in the front rank of buildings which deserve commemoration. I therefore took the initiative of having a commemorative plaque placed at 60, Rue de la Victoire, as authorized by the Prefect of the Seine, on 25 June 1965. The inaugural ceremony took place on 4 June 1966 in the presence of H.I.H. Prince Napoleon and was organized by M. Lebée, President of the board of directors of the Crédit Industrial et Commercial.

[1] This mansion, which has had many owners since it was first erected, once belonged to Marie Walewska.

Dramatis Personae

Abrantès, Duchesse d', 1785–1838, Laure Permon, married Junot, q.v. Early friend of Bonaparte family. Left in poverty after the collapse of the Empire, wrote famous Memoirs, with Balzac's aid, on the revolution, Empire and restoration.

Alexander I, Czar of Russia, 1777–1825, Succeeded his father, Paul I, in 1801. Joined coalition against Napoleon in 1805. Signed Treaty of Tilsit with him in 1807. After invasion of Russia in 1812 was a leader in the coalition against Napoleon.

Angoulême, Duc d', 1775–1844, Louis-Antoine de Bourbon, eldest son of Charles X of France, married Marie-Thérèse, daughter of Louis XVI and Marie-Antoinette. Went into exile with his father in 1830.

Artois, Comte d', see *Charles X.*

Augereau, Pierre François Charles, Duc de Castiglione, 1756–1816. Served with distinction in the Italian campaigns 1796–7, leader of the coup d'état of 18 Fructidor 1797, fought at Jena, Eylau and Leipzig, Marshal of France.

Austria, Emperor of, see Francis II.

Barante, Guillaume Prosper, Baron, 1782–1866, historian and politician, Prefect under the Empire, auditor at the Council of State 1806, published Memoirs.

Barbé-Marbois, François de, 1745–1837, negotiated treaty which ceded Louisiana to the U.S.A., deported to Guiana after 18 Fructidor, Minister of the Treasury and first President of the Cour des Comptes.

Barras, Comte de, Paul, 1755–1829, deputy to the Convention, voted the death of Louis XVI, then helped to overthrow Robespierre, real head of the Directory 1795–18 Brumaire, 1799.

Bassano, Duc de, *see* Maret, Hugues.

Bausset, Louis François, 1770–*c*.1830, Prefect of the Palace, 1805, accompanied Napoleon to Spain, Germany and Russia, superintendent of the Théâtre Français, 1812, wrote Memoirs.

Beauharnais, Eugène de, 1781–1824, son of Josephine de Beauharnais and adopted son of Napoleon, Arch-Chancellor of State and Viceroy of Italy from 1805, married Augusta Amelia of Bavaria, where he retired at the fall of the Empire.

Beauharnais, Hortense de, 1783–1837, daughter of Josephine de Beauharnais and adopted daughter of Napoleon, whose brother, Louis, she married, mother of Napoleon III.

Beauharnais, Josephine de, 1763–1814, born Tascher de la Pagerie, married first Vicomte de Beauharnais, guillotined, then Napoleon Bonaparte in 1796, divorced 1809.

Bélanger, François Joseph, 1745–1818, first architect of the Comte d'Artois, built Bagatelle and several mansions in Paris, including some in the Place Vendôme.

Bellart, Nicolas François, 1761–1826, magistrate, defender of General Moreau, member of the General Council of the Seine, attacked Napoleon in 1814, became an ardent Legitimist.

Belliard, Augustin Daniel, Comte, 1769–1832, General, distinguished himself at Borodino, surrendered Cairo to the British 1801.

Belloy, Cardinal du, Jean Baptiste, 1709–1808, Archbishop of Paris 1802, Cardinal 1803, much esteemed by Napoleon.

Benevento, Prince of, *see* Talleyrand-Périgord, Charles Maurice de.

Bennigsen, Levin August Théophil, Count, 1745–1836, Hanoverian general in Russian service, implicated in murder of Czar Paul I in 1801, served with distinction at Pultusk and Eylau and in the campaigns of 1812–14.

Béranger, Pierre Jean de, 1780–1857, lyric poet, author of many poems which did much to further the cult of Napoleon. Clerk in the office of the Imperial University, prosecuted for republican and Bonapartist sympathies 1821 and 1828.

Bernadotte, Jean Baptiste Jules, Prince of Pontecorvo, 1763–1844, Minister of War 1799, Marshal of France, elected Crown Prince of Sweden 1810, commanded the Army of the North against Napoleon 1813, King of Sweden and Norway 1818–44, married Désirée Clary, first fiancée of Napoleon.

Berri, Duc de, Charles Ferdinand, 1778–1820, younger son of the Comte d'Artois, emigrated with his father in 1789, assassinated in Paris 1820.

Berthier, Louis Alexandre, Prince of Wagram, sovereign Prince of Neuchâtel, Marshal of France, Chief of Staff to Napoleon, served under Lafayette in American War of Independence, signed act of overthrow of Napoleon in 1814, killed or committed suicide.

Bertrand, Comte Henri-Gratien, 1773–1844, General, took part in all the Imperial campaigns, appointed Grand Marshal of the Palace 1813, accompanied Napoleon to Elba and St Helena, sent to bring back his ashes 1840.

Bessières, Jean Baptiste, Duc d'Istrie, 1768–1813, Marshal of France, served with distinction in major Napoleonic battles, killed at Lützen 1813.

Biennais, Guillaume, 1764–1834, goldsmith, inspired by Louis David, Grand Prix at exhibitions 1806 and 1809.

Blücher, Gebhard von, 1742–1819, Prussian field-marshal and one of Napoleon's outstanding adversaries, defeated him at Laon 1814 and occupied Paris, severely defeated by Napoleon at Ligny 1815 but recovered in time to support Wellington at Waterloo, again occupied Paris 1815.

Bonaparte, Caroline, see Murat, Caroline.

Bonaparte, Jerome, 1784–1860, youngest brother of Napoleon, married Elizabeth Patterson of Baltimore, marriage annulled, married secondly Catherine of Württemberg, King of Westphalia 1807, after the fall of the Empire lived in exile in Italy, returned to France during the Second Empire.

Bonaparte, Joseph, 1768–1844, elder brother of Napoleon, King of Naples 1806, King of Spain 1808–13, Lieutenant-General of France 1814, escaped to the U.S.A. 1815, married Julie Clary.

Bonaparte, Louis, 1778–1846, younger brother of Napoleon, married Hortense de Beauharnais, q.v., King of Holland 1806, abdicated 1810, lived in exile in Italy.

Bonaparte, Lucien, Prince of Canino, 1775–1840, younger brother of Napoleon, member of the Council of Five Hundred 1798, President 1799, Minister of the Interior 1799, ambassador to Spain 1800, after quarrelling with Napoleon went into exile in Italy, reconciled with him in 1815.

Bonaparte, Maria Letitia Ramolino, 1750–1836, married Carlo Buonaparte 1764, received title of Madame Mère during the Empire, mother of Napoleon, exiled in Italy.

Bondy, Pierre-Marie Taillepied, Comte de, 1766–1847, Chamberlain, Prefect of the Rhône 1810, during the 100 Days Prefect of the Seine and Councillor of State, signed the Convention of Paris.

Boulay de la Meurthe, Antoine, 1761–1840, magistrate and politician, fought with the Army of the Rhine, member of the Council of 500, Councillor of State, played a large part in drawing up the Civil Code.

Bourrienne, Louis Antoine Fauvelet de, 1769–1834, Napoleon's schoolfellow at Brienne, became his personal secretary until 1802, then Minister Plenipotentiary in Hamburg. Became hostile to Napoleon and rallied to the Bourbons, wrote Memoirs.

Brongniart, Alexandre-Théodore, 1739–1813, Member of the French Academy, directed under Gabriel work at the Ecole Militaire, architect of the Bourse.

Brunswick, Friedrich Wilhelm, Duke of, 1771–1815, commanded the 'Black Brunswickers', killed at Quatre-Bras, 1815.

Cadore, Duc de, see Champagny, Jean Baptiste Nompère de.

Cadoudal, Georges, 1771–1804, royalist conspirator and Chouan partisan, led the Vendéen rising in 1799 against the republic, conspired to restore the Bourbons, apprehended and executed 1804.

Cafarelli, Louis Marie Joseph Maximilien, Comte, 1756–1849, General, commanded engineer corps in Egyptian campaign.

Cambacérès, Jean-Jacques-Régis, Duc de, Prince of Parma, 1753–1824, Member of the Convention and Council of 500, Minister of Justice 1799, Second Consul, Arch-Chancellor of the Empire 1804, exiled 1815, returned to France 1818. One of Napoleon's closest advisers and principal architect of the Code Napoléon, a famous gourmet.

Carnot, Lazare, 1753–1823, general and statesman, member of the Convention, voted the death of Louis XVI, organized the republican armies and given the title of 'Organizer of Victory' 1793, member of the Directory, 1795, Minister of War after Brumaire, then became opponent of the Empire, rallied to Napoleon and was Minister of the Interior during the 100 Days, exiled by Louis XVIII.

Cartellier, Pierre, 1757–1831, sculptor, collaborated in decoration of the Panthéon, Senate, Louvre, Arc du Carrousel, sculpted tomb of Josephine at Rueil, member of the Institute, one of the best sculptors of the neo-classic period.

Caulaincourt, Armand Augustin Louis de, Duc de Vicence, 1772–1827, Diplomat and general, ambassador to Russia 1807–11, Minister of Foreign Affairs 1813–14 and during the 100 Days, wrote Memoirs.

Cellerier, Jacques, 1742–1814, built several theatres in Paris, including the Ambigu and the Variétés.

Chabrol, Gilbert Joseph Gaspart, Comte de, 1773–1843, member of the Egyptian scientific commission, Prefect of Montenotte, Prefect of the Seine 1812–30.

Chalgrin, Jean-François, 1739–1811, Member of the Academy, architect, designed St-Philippe du Roule in Paris and drawings for the Arc de Triomphe de l'Etoile.

Champagny, Jean Baptiste Nompère de, Duc de Cadore, 1756–1834, politician and diplomat, ambassador at Vienna 1801–4, Minister of the Interior 1804–7, Minister of Foreign Affairs 1807–11.

Chaptal, Jean Antoine, Comte de Chanteloup, 1756–1832, chemist and politician, member of the Council of State after Brumaire, Minister of the Interior 1800, Senator and Treasurer of the Senate.

Charles X, 1757–1836, brother of Louis XVI and XVIII, King of France 1824–30, emigrated 1789, re-entered Paris 1814 with the Allies, emigrated in 1830 and died in exile.

Chateaubriand, François-René, Vicomte de, 1768–1848, author and statesman, emigrated in 1792, returned to France 1802, published a eulogy of Christianity, *Le Génie du Christianisme*, leading writer of the Romantic movement with great influence on literature, appointed to diplomatic posts by Napoleon, resigned after the execution of the Duc d'Enghien, q.v., ambassador in London 1822, Minister of Foreign Affairs 1823–4.

Chaudet, Denis Antoine, 1763–1810, sculptor, Grand Prix de Rome, one of the leading sculptors of the neo-classic period, sculptured statue of Napoleon on Vendôme column 1810–14, and seated figure of Peace in the Salon de la Paix in the Tuileries.

Clarke, Henri Jacques Guillaume, Duc de Feltre, 1765–1818, Marshal of France, Minister of War 1815–17.

Constant, Benjamin Constant de Rebecque, 1767–1830, novelist, politician, protégé and lover of Mme de Staël, member of the Tribunate 1799–1802, banished by Napoleon, returned in 1814 and accepted office during the

100 Days, member of the Chamber of Deputies 1819–30, his novel, *Adolphe*, is considered a masterpiece.

Corbineau, Jean Baptiste Juvenal, 1776–1848, instrumental in saving the Grande Armée at the Beresina, saved Napoleon's life at Brienne, 1814, aide-de-camp 1815.

Costaz, Louis, Baron, 1767–1842, engineer, member of the Egyptian expedition, member of the Tribunate, Prefect of the Manche, Intendant General of Crown Property 1809, Director of Highways Department 1813, Councillor of State.

Crétet, Emmanuel, 1747–1809, member of the Council of 500, after Brumaire Councillor of State, director of the Highways Department, governor of the Bank of France 1806, Minister of the Interior 1807.

Curée, Jean-François, Comte de la Bedissière, 1756–1836, Member of the Legislative Assembly and Council of 500, after Brumaire entered Tribunate, demanded establishment of hereditary Empire 1804, Senator 1807.

Daru, Pierre Antoine, Comte, 1767–1829, statesman and historian, Intendant General of the Army of the Danube 1795, Councillor of State 1805, Minister of State 1811, member of the Chamber of Peers 1819.

David, Jacques Louis, 1748–1825, historical painter, founder of the French classical school, member of the French Academy, 1783, Court painter to Louis XVI whose death he voted, Court painter to Napoleon, genre paintings include the *Rape of the Sabines* and *Leonidas at Thermopylæ*, painted Napoleon's Coronation.

Davout, Louis Nicolas, Duc d'Auerstädt, Prince d'Eckmühl, 1770–1823, Marshal of France, distinguished himself at Aboukir, Austerlitz, Auerstädt, Eckmühl, Wagram and the Russian campaign, Minister of War during the 100 Days.

Decrès, Denis, Duc, 1761–1820, admiral, served under de Grasse, took part in the battle of the Nile, Minister of Marine 1801–14.

Déjean, Pierre François Aimé Auguste, 1780–1845, soldier and entomologist, served with distinction at Ligny and Waterloo, general 1810, aide-de-camp to Napoleon 1813, wrote works on entomology.

Delessert, Benjamin, 1773–1847, founded first cotton spinnery at Passy 1801 and a factory for making beet sugar, regent of the Bank of France, instituted Society for the Encouragement of Industry and savings banks.

Denon, Dominique Vivant, 1747–1827, engraver, member of the Egyptian expedition about which he published a great illustrated work, appointed Director of Museums by Napoleon and first organizer of the Louvre.

Desaix, Louis Charles Antoine Desaix de Veygouz, 1768–1800, General, conquered Upper Egypt, decided the victory of Marengo where he was killed.

Dessolles, Jean Joseph Paul August 1767–1828, general and politician, served with distinction under Moreau in Italy in 1799 and Germany in 1800, Minister of Foreign Affairs 1818–19.

Drouot, Antoine, Comte, 1774–1847, colonel of artillery, served at Wagram and Moskowa, general and aide-de-camp of Napoleon in 1813, accompanied him to Elba and after Waterloo brought back the remnants of the Guard to France, acquitted at a Court Martial under Louis XVIII.

Dubois, Louis-Nicolas-Pierre-Joseph, Comte, 1758–?, lawyer, deputy for the Gironde after Brumaire, Prefect of Police.

Duroc, Géraud Christophe Michel, Duc de Frioul, 1772–1813, served with Napoleon at the siege of Toulon, took an active part in 18 Brumaire, Grand Marshal of the Palace, enjoyed Napoleon's confidence.

Enghien, Louis-Antoine, Duc d', 1772–1804, son of the Duc de Bourbon and grandson of the Prince de Condé, emigrated 1789, kidnapped by Napoleon under suspicion of implication in royalist plot, given a summary trial and executed at Vincennes.

Fain, Agathon, Baron, 1778–1837, secretary and personal archivist to Napoleon, accompanied him in all his campaigns, wrote Memoirs on the last years of the Empire.

Fesch, Joseph, 1763–1839, half-brother of Letitia Bonaparte, Archbishop of Lyons 1802, Cardinal 1803, collector of pictures which he bequeathed to Lyons.

Flahaut, Auguste Charles, 1785–1870, Comte de, son of Talleyrand and father of the Duc de Morny by Hortense de Beauharnais, general and aide-de-camp to Napoleon, ambassador to Vienna 1841–8.

Fontaine, Pierre-François-Léonard, 1762–1853, chief architect to Napoleon, later employed by Louis XVIII, responsible for stages of completion of the Louvre, the Arc du Carrousel, the Chapelle Expiatoire and laying out of Compiègne. Supervisory architect of the Louvre and Tuileries for nearly half a century, collaborated with Percier, q.v.

Fontanes, Louis de, 1757–1821, politician and poet, President of the Legislature 1804, Grand Master of the University 1808, Senator 1810.

Fouché, Joseph, Duc d'Otrante, 1759–1820, voted the death of Louis XVI, Minister of General Police under the Directory, took part in 18 Brumaire, disgraced 1802, recalled 1804, Governor of Rome, then Illyria, plotted treason and intrigue, Minister of Police under Louis XVIII, exiled 1816.

Francis II, Emperor of Austria, 1768–1835, last Holy Roman Emperor and first Emperor of Austria, joined coalitions against Napoleon but consistently defeated by him, father of Marie–Louise.

Frochot, Nicolas, 1761–1828, deputy to the States-General, imprisoned during the Terror, Prefect of the Seine 1800–12.

Gabriel, Ange-Jacques, 1698–1782, Member of the French Academy, first architect to the King, built the Ecole Militaire, the Place de la Concorde, the Versailles Opera and began the Petit Trianon, carried out important works at the Louvre, Fontainebleau and Compiègne.

Gaudin, Michel Charles, Duc de Gaète, 1756–1841, Minister of Finance

1799–1814 and again during the 100 Days, advised Napoleon to revive the Droits Réunis.

Gérard, François Pascal Gérard, 1770–1837, historical and portrait painter, among his works are the Battle of Austerlitz and portraits of the Bonaparte family.

Girodet, Anne Louis, 1767–1824, pupil of David, Grand Prix de Rome 1789, best works are *Scène du Déluge* and *Burial of Atala*, decorated Malmaison with Gérard 1801.

Gisors, Henri-Alphonse Guy de, 1796–1866, pupil of Percier.

Gondoin, Jacques, 1737–1818, Member of the French Academy, chief work the School of Surgery.

Goujon, Jean, *c*.1515–64, Renaissance sculptor, worked on the Louvre under Lescot, including the caryatides, and also the Fontaine des Innocents, completed the decoration of the Louvre, where his *Diane Chasseresse* now is.

Gourgaud, Gaspard, Baron de, 1783–1852, Napoleon's aide-de-camp from 1811, accompanied him to St Helena, returned to France 1818, among those bringing back the ashes 1840, wrote Memoirs of Napoleon.

Goust, L. *c*.1760–1829, architect, inspector of works at the Luxembourg and the Arc de l'Etoile under Chalgrin whom he succeeded as architect in 1811. In 1823 resumed work on the Arc, resigned in 1829.

Gros, Antoine Jean, 1771–1835, historical painter, pupil of David, painted Napoleon at Arcola, drowned himself in a fit of melancholia.

Grouchy, Emmanuel de 1766–1847, distinguished himself in the Napoleonic Wars, failed at Waterloo to prevent the junction of Blücher's and Wellington's armies, his timidity often blamed for the French defeat, Marshal of France.

Hulin, Pierre Augustin, Comte, 1758–1841, general, presided over the court condemning the Duc d'Enghien, as governor of Paris 1812 put down Malet's conspiracy.

Isabey, Jean Baptiste, 1767–1855, French miniature painter, among his works portraits of Napoleon, Josephine and members of the Congress of Vienna.

Jourdan, Jean Baptiste, 1762–1833, Marshal of France, initiated the conscription law known as the Loi Jourdan, defeated by Wellington at Vitoria 1813.

Junot, Andoche, Duc d'Abrantès, 1771–1813, General, met Napoleon at Toulon, accompanied him to Italy and Egypt, took Lisbon in 1807, Governor General of Illyria, committed suicide in a fit of madness, husband of Laure Permon, Duchesse d'Abrantès, q.v.

Kléber, Jean-Baptiste, 1753–1800, distinguished general, took command of the Egyptian expeditionary force on Bonaparte's return to France, assassinated in Cairo 1800.

Lacépède, Bernard Germain de, 1756–1825, musician and scientist, President of the Legislative Assembly, resigned during the Terror, held chair ichthyology at the Museum, Senator 1799, Minister of State 1804, Grand Chancellor of the Legion of Honour.

Lacuée, Jean Girard, 1752–1841, Deputy to the Legislative Assembly and Council of Ancients, temporary Minister of War 1800–4, Councillor of State 1801, Director of War Administration 1810–13, Member of the French Academy.

Lafayette, Marie Joseph Paul Yves Roch Gilbert du Motier, 1757–1834, Marquis de, General, revolutionary and statesman, fought in the American War of Independence, present at Cornwallis's surrender, member of States General 1789, commander-in-chief Paris National Guard, captured by Prussians and Austrians and imprisoned 1792–7, returned to virtual exile in France 1799, Vice President of the Chamber during the 100 Days and demanded Napoleon's abdication.

Lanjuinais, Jean Denis, 1753–1827, Professor of ecclesiastical law and lawyer at Rennes, proscribed by the Jacobins, one of the makers of the constitution of the Year III, Senator 1800, voted against consulate for life and the Empire, Count of the Empire 1803, voted the overthrow of Napoleon, President of the Chamber during the 100 Days.

Lannes, Jean, Duc de Montebello, 1769–1809, joined the army 1792, distinguished himself at Arcola, wounded at Acre and Aboukir, played a decisive part in the victory of Friedland, mortally wounded at Essling, one of the most brilliant of Napoleonic generals for whom Napoleon had great affection. His wife became lady-in-waiting to Marie-Louise but was hostile to Napoleon.

Laplace, Pierre Simon, Marquis de, 1794–1827, astronomer, mathematician and physicist, Professor at the Ecole Normale, Minister of the Interior after Brumaire, Count of the Empire, 1806, Vice-President of the Senate, loaded with honours by Napoleon for whose overthrow he voted in 1814 and rallied to Louis XVIII.

Las Cases, Augustin, Comte de, 1766–1842, emigrated during the revolution, returned after Brumaire, chamberlain to Napoleon, whom he accompanied to St Helena, expelled by Hudson Lowe in 1816, published the *Memorial of St Helena*, a collection of his conversations with the Emperor 1815–16.

Lavalette, Antoine Marie Chamans de, 1769–1830, aide-de-camp to Napoleon, married niece of Josephine, played an essential part in Brumaire, Director of Posts and in charge of Black Cabinet, arrested and condemned to death after Waterloo but escaped with his wife's aid.

Lebrun, François-Charles, Duc de Plaisance, 1739–1824, deputy to the States-General, released from imprisonment 9 Thermidor, member of the Council of Ancients, Third Consul 1799, Arch Treasurer of the Empire 1804, carried out important administrative and diplomatic functions, rallied to the Bourbons, translated Homer and Tasso.

Lecomte, Félix, 1757–1837, sculptor, worked for Madame du Barry, Member of the Institute 1810.

Lemot, François Frédéric, 1773–1827, sculptor, principal work chariot and figures of Victory and Peace on the Carrousel arch and bas-relief on the pediment of the Louvre, restored the Henri IV statue on the Pont Neuf, Member of the Institute.

Lepère, Charles, 1761–1844, architect, member of the Egyptian expedition, architect of Malmaison and Vendôme column in collaboration with Gondoin and church of St-Vincent de Paul in Paris.

Lescot, Pierre, *c*.1510–78, scholar and man of letters, architect, from 1546 worked on the building of the Louvre in collaboration with Jean Goujon.

Macdonald, Jacques Joseph Alexandre, Duc de Tarente, 1765–1840, Marshal of France, fought at Jemappes and under Pichegru, on the Rhine and in Italy, Governor of the Roman states 1798, Naples 1799, defeated by Suvorov at the Trebbia 1799, specially distinguished at Wagram, served in campaigns 1813–14, defeated at Katzbach 1813.

Malet, Claude François de, 1754–1812, General, conspired against Napoleon 1808, imprisoned, tried to rally the Paris garrison and seize power by spreading the rumour of Napoleon's death in Russia 1812, arrested and condemned to death.

Mansart, Jules Hardouin, 1646–1708, architect to Louis XIV 1675, created the final Versailles of Louis XIV, the Orangerie and the Trianon, the domed church of the Invalides in Paris, the Place des Victoires and the Place Vendôme.

Maret, Hugues Bernard, Duc de Bassano, 1763–1839, Director of the *Moniteur Universel*, ambassador in London and Naples, Secretary of State during the Consulate, *chef de cabinet* to Napoleon 1800, Minister of Foreign Affairs 1811, prepared the return from Elba, again Secretary of State during the 100 Days, exiled 1816–20, confidential agent of Napoleon.

Marie-Louise, Empress of the French, 1791–1847, daughter of Francis II, Emperor of Austria, married Napoleon 1810, gave birth to the King of Rome 1811, Regent during the Emperor's absences but played no political role, never saw the Emperor again or communicated with him after 1814, became Duchess of Parma 1816, married the Comte de Neipperg after Napoleon's death and as her third husband the Comte de Bombelles.

Marmont, Auguste de, Duc de Raguse, 1774–1852, Marshal of France, took part in the Egyptian expedition, played a leading part in the organization of Dalmatia, beaten by Wellington in Spain 1812, defended Paris 1814 and betrayed Napoleon, supported Charles X in the July Revolution 1830.

Masséna, André, Duc de Rivoli, Prince d'Essling, Marshal of France, 1756–1817, distinguished himself at Lodi, Rivoli and against the Russians at Zürich 1799 and Genoa 1800, won the battle of Eckmühl, retreated

Spain and Portugal 1811, rallied to the Bourbons 1814, governor of Paris after Waterloo.

Maury, Jean Siffrein, 1746–1817, Cardinal, opposed secularization of church property in the States General, emigrated to Rome, rallied to Napoleon 1806, Archbishop of Paris 1810, again exiled in Rome 1814.

Méhul, Etienne, 1763–1817, composer of twenty-five operas or comic operas, composed celebrated *Chant du Départ*, precursor of Weber and the symphonic poem.

Méneval, Claude François de, 1778–1850, secretary to Napoleon, then private secretary to Marie-Louise whom he followed to Vienna 1814.

Metternich, Clemens Wenzel, Prince, 1773–1859, Austrian statesman, ambassador to France 1806, Minister of Foreign Affairs 1809–48, negotiated marriage of Marie-Louise to Napoleon, re-established Austria as a great Power.

Molé, Louis Mathieu, 1781–1885, Councillor of State 1806, Prefect 1807, Director of Highways Department 1809, Grand Judge 1813, rallied to the Bourbons and filled many offices until 1851.

Mollien, François Nicolas, 1758–1850, studied finance in England, Director of the Caisse d'Amortissement 1799, Councillor of State 1804, Minister of the Treasury 1806, instituted many financial reforms.

Moncey, Bon Adrien Jeannot, 1754–1842, Marshal of France, Governor of the Invalides 1833–42.

Montalivet, Jean Pierre Bachasson, Comte, 1766–1823, Prefect 1801, Director Highways Department 1806, Minister of the Interior 1809, Intendant General of the Crown during 100 Days.

Montebello, Duc de, *see* Lannes, Jean.

Montesquiou-Fezensac, Pierre, 1764–1834, Comte de, former equerry of the Comte de Provence, rallied to the Empire 1804, deputy to the Legislature 1805 and president, succeeded Talleyrand as Grand Chamberlain. His wife, Elisabeth, was governor of the King of Rome and accompanied him to Vienna.

Moreau, Jean Victor, 1763–1813, General, helped in coup d'état of Brumaire, victor of Stockach and Hohenlinden, involved in Cadoudal plot, condemned to two years' imprisonment, reprieved and went to the U.S.A., struck off the strength, returned to Europe and was killed at Dresden fighting with the Russian army.

Mortier, Edouard Adolphe, Duc de Trévise, 1768–1835, Marshal of France, conqueror of Hanover, victor in Spain, commanded the Young Guard, after defence of Paris rallied to Louis XVIII, refused to act as one of Ney's judges, killed in an attempt on the life of Louis-Philippe.

Murat, Caroline, 1782–1839, youngest sister of Napoleon, married 1800 Joachim Murat q.v., Grand Duchess of Berg, Queen of Naples, joined the Austrians 1814, exiled 1815.

Murat, Joachim, 1767–1815, Marshal of France, Grand Duke of Cleves and Berg, King of Naples, one of the most brilliant cavalry generals of the Empire, particularly distinguished himself at Eylau, Friedland and the

Moskowa. Negotiated separate peace with Austria 1814 in the hope of saving his kingdom, defeated by the Austrians at Tolentino 1815, attempted to regain Naples, captured and shot at Pizzo.

Nesselrode, Karl Robert, Count, 1780–1862, Russian statesman and diplomat, directed Russian foreign policy 1813–56, conducted negotiations 1813–15, signed Peace of Paris 1814, present at Congresses of the Holy Alliance 1818–22, concluded Peace of Paris 1856 at the end of the Crimean War.

Ney, Michel, 1769–1815, Duc d'Elchingen, Prince de la Moskowa, Marshal of France, joined the army 1788, during the 100 Days set out to capture Napoleon for Louis XVIII to whom he had rallied but instead joined the Emperor, tried by the Chamber of Peers, condemned to death and shot.

Orloff, Alexis, Count, 1787–1861, took part in the Russian wars against France during the Empire.

Otrante, Duc d', *see* Fouché, Joseph.

Oudinot, Nicolas Charles, 1767–1847, Duc de Reggio, Marshal of France, fought at Zürich, Austerlitz, Friedland, Wagram and the Russian campaign 1812, commanded the National Guard during the 100 Days.

Paër, Ferdinando, 1771–1839, Italian composer of opera, choirmaster to Napoleon 1807.

Paoli, Pascal, 1725–1807, Corsican patriot, proclaimed chief of the island 1755, defeated by the French 1768, took refuge in England, returned to Corsica at the Revolution, invoked English aid, outlawed by the Convention, enemy of the Bonapartes.

Pasquier, Etienne-Denis, 1767–1862, Baron, statesman, imprisoned under the Terror, released 9 Thermidor, Prefect of Police 1810, Minister of the Interior 1815, having rallied to Louis XVIII, Keeper of the Seals 1817, Minister of Foreign Affairs 1819, President of the Chamber of Peers under the July Monarchy, then Chancellor of France, wrote Memoirs.

Percier, 1764–1838, inseparable collaborator of Fontaine, Pierre, q.v. All national ceremonies under the Empire were directed by them.

Peyre, Marie-Joseph the Elder, 1730–88, Member of the French Academy 1762, architect, most important Paris work the Théâtre de l'Odéon.

Pichegru, Charles, 1761–1804, general, distinguished as commander of the Army of the Rhine 1793 and Belgium 1794, suppressed insurrection in Paris April 1795, member of the Council of 500, implicated in Fructidor conspiracy 1797, escaped to England, returned to France to engage in Cadoudal plot, committed suicide or was assassinated in prison.

Pius VII, Gregorio Luigi Barnaba Chiaramonti, 1740–1823, Pope 1800–23. Signed Concordat 1801, came to Paris to crown Napoleon 1804, deprived of his States, later taken as prisoner to Fontainebleau, returned to Rome 1814.

Poyet, Bernard 1742–1824, architect to Duc d'Orléans and the City of Paris, the archbishopric, the university etc., constructed the façade of the Palais Bourbon.

Pozzo di Borgo, Carlo Andrea, Count, 1764–1842, Corsican patriot opposed to the Bonapartes, entered Russian diplomatic service 1803, noted for his hostility to Napoleon, ambassador to France 1814–35, England 1835–9.

Prud'hon, Pierre Paul, 1758–1823, historical and portrait painter, Grand Prix de Rome 1782, among his works are the interview between Napoleon and Francis II of Austria after Austerlitz and a portrait of Josephine.

Prussia, King of, Frederick William III, 1770–1848, King 1797–1848 declared war on France 1806, signed Treaty of Tilsit 1807, lost large amount of Prussian territory, joined War of Liberation 1813, married Louise of Mecklenburg-Strelitz.

Raguse, Duc de, *see* Marmont, Auguste.

Rapp, Jean, Comte, 1772–1822, General, distinguished himself in the defence of Danzig, commanded the Army of the Rhine during the 100 Days.

Raymond, Jean Arnaud, 1742–1811, architect, Grand Prix de Rome 1766.

Raynouard, François Juste Marie, 1761–1836, French poet and scholar noted for works on Provençal literature and language.

Réal, Pierre François, 1757–1834, Comte, politician, public prosecutor, Councillor of State, Prefect of Police during 100 Days.

Récamier, Jeanne Françoise Julie Adélaïde Bernard, Madame, 1777–1849, leader of society during the Napoleonic régime, her beauty and intelligence attracting a brilliant circle to her salon, exiled from Paris because of her friendship with members of the opposition, notably Mme de Staël, sought in marriage by Chateaubriand after her husband's death in 1830.

Regnault de St-Jean d'Angély, Michel, 1761–1819, Comte, lawyer, Deputy to the States General, administrator of the Hospitals of the Army of Italy 1796, Councillor of State 1799, Procurator-General of the High Court, Minister of State during the 100 Days, helped persuade Napoleon to abdicate.

Régnier, Claude, 1736–1814, Duc de Massa, deputy President of the Council of Ancients 1796, Councillor of State 1800, Grand Judge and Minister of Justice 1802–13, President of the Legislature 1813, took a large part in drawing up the Civil Code.

Rémusat, Claire Elisabeth Jeanne Graviers de Vergennes, Comtesse de, 1780–1821, wife of Napoleon's Chamberlain and attendant on Josephine, her Memoirs, largely unfavourable to Napoleon, published 1879.

Roederer, Pierre Louis, 1754–1835, Comte, politician and economist, Member of the Constituent Assembly 1789, administrator under the Empire, confidant of Napoleon whom he supported during the 100 Days, wrote historical works.

Rome, King of, François-Charles-Joseph, 1811–1832, left Paris with

Marie-Louise, his mother, 1814, brought up in Vienna as Austrian archduke, as Duc de Reichstadt, Napoleon II to Bonapartists after his father's death, died of tuberculosis.

Rovigo, Duc de, *see* Savary, Anne Jean Marie René.

Russia, Czar of, *see* Alexander I.

Sacken, Fabian-Gottlieb, 1752–1837, Russian soldier, began as a sergeant, commanded Second Russian Corps under Bennigsen, distinguished himself at Eylau, acted with Blücher in the Battle of France 1813–14, Military Governor of Paris, Field-Marshal 1815.

Savary, Anne Jean Marie René, 1774–1833, Duc de Rovigo, general and politician, confidential agent of Napoleon, presided at the trial of the Duc d'Enghien, engaged in various diplomatic missions, notably in Spain 1808, Minister of Police 1810–14, supported Napoleon during the 100 Days, exiled, commander-in-chief of the army in Algeria 1831–33.

Schwarzenberg, Karl Philipp, Prince, 1771–1820, Austrian general, served at Hohenlinden, Wagram, filled various diplomatic posts in France and Russia, commanded the Austrian contingent in Russia 1812, and the Allies against Napoleon 1813–14, won the victory of Leipzig 1813, Field-Marshal.

Ségur, Philippe Paul, 1780–1873, Comte de, French general and historian, wrote *La Campagne de Russie*.

Sérurier, Jean Philibert, 1742–1819, Marshal of France, fought in the Seven Years' War, in command at St-Cloud 18 Brumaire, Senator, Governor of the Invalides, in command of the National Guard of Paris 1819, disgraced after the 100 Days.

Sieyès, Emmanuel-Joseph, 1748–1836, Abbé, Deputy to the States General 1789, drew up the Tennis Court Oath, one of the founders of the Jacobin Club, voted the death of Louis XVI, member of the Council of 500, ambassador to Berlin, member of the Directory, one of the original three Consuls, then Senator and Count of the Empire, exiled under the Restoration as a regicide, returned to France during the July Monarchy.

Soult, Nicolas Jean-de-Dieu, 1769–1851, Duc de Dalmatie, Marshal of France, volunteer 1785, fought at Fleurus, General 1799, governor of Andalusia, beat the English at Orthez and Toulouse, rallied to the Bourbons 1814, rejoined Napoleon during the 100 Days, exiled 1816, returned to France, Minister of War in 1834 and 1840, Foreign Minister 1839, Marshal-General 1847.

Staël, Anne Louise Germaine Necker, Baronne de Staël-Holstein, 1766–1817, daughter of Jacques Necker, minister to Louis XVI, distinguished writer, exiled by Napoleon.

Talleyrand-Périgord, Charles Maurice de, 1754–1838, Prince of Benevento, statesman and diplomat, Bishop of Autun, member of the States-General, emigrated U.S.A. 1794–6, returned to France, Minister of Foreign Affairs 1799–1807, dismissed for intriguing 1809, played prominent part

in the Bourbon restoration, peacemaker at the Congress of Vienna 1815,
Ambassador in London.

Tallien, Therésia, Cabarrus, 1773–1835, married first Marquis de Fontenay,
secondly J.-L. Tallien, whom she met at Bordeaux and on whose career
she had a profound influence, thirdly after divorcing Tallien in 1802
married the Prince de Caraman-Chimay, popularly called 'Our Lady of
Thermidor'.

Talma, François-Joseph, 1763–1826, tragic actor, friend and favourite actor
of Napoleon.

Trévise, Duc de, *see* Mortier, Edouard Adolphe.

Vernet, Horace, 1789–1863, French genre and battle painter.

Vicence, Duc de, *see* Caulaincourt, Armand Auguste Louis de.

Vignon, Pierre-Alexandre, 1763–1828, architect, built the Temple of Glory,
later the Madeleine.

Walewska, Marie, Comtesse, 1789–1817, Polish mistress of Napoleon by
whom she had a son, visited him at Elba, married 1816 General P. A.
d'Ornano.

Whitworth, Charles, Earl, 1752–1825, soldier and diplomat, Minister
Plenipotentiary at St Petersburg for thirteen years, ambassador in Paris
1802.

Wintzingerode, Ferdinando, Baron von, 1770–1818, Russian general and
diplomat, switched from Austrian to Russian service, helped to form
third and fourth coalitions against Napoleon, beaten by him at St-Dizier
in the Battle of France.

Yorck von Wartenburg, Hans David Ludwig, Count, 1759–1830, Prussian
Field-Marshal, commanded the rearguard after Jena, distinguished
himself at Montmirail, Laon and Paris.

Bibliography

AUBRY, OCTAVE, *La vie privée de Napoléon* (1939)

—, —, *Le Roi de Rome* (1940)

—, —, *La Jeunesse du Roi de Rome* (1933)

AULARD, ALPHONSE, *Paris sous le Consulat*

—, —, *Paris sous le Premier Empire* (1912)

BAINVILLE, JACQUES, *Napoléon* (1951)

BALZAC, HONORÉ DE, *Le médecin de campagne* (1833)

—, —, *La femme de Trente Ans* (1842)

—, —, *Le Cousin Pons* (1847)

BARTEL, PAUL, *La jeunesse inédite de Napoléon* (1954)

BAZIN, GERMAIN, *Le Louvre* (1933)

—, —, *Trésors de la peinture au Louvre* (1957)

BERTAUX, JULES, *Paris à travers les âges* (1951)

—, —, *Madame Récamier* (1947)

BIVER, MARIE-LOUISE, *Le Paris de Napoléon* (1963)

BOULAY DE LA MEURTHE, A. J., *Documents*

CADIOUX, GASTON, *Les finances de la ville de Paris de 1789–1900* (1909)

CASTELOT, ANDRÉ, *Le grand siècle de Paris* (1955)

CHABROL, G., *Recherches statistiques sur la ville de Paris* (1821)

CHATEAUBRIAND, F. R. DE, *Mémoires d'Outre-Tombe: Napoléon*

CHRIST, YVAN, *Le Louvre et les Tuileries* (1949)

CHUQUET, ARTHUR, *La Jeunesse de Napoléon* (1897)

CILLEULS, ALFRED DES, *Histoire de l'administration parisienne au XIXe siècle* (1900)

CONSTANT, BENJAMIN, *Mémoires*

COUCHOUD, P. L., *Voix de Napoléon* (1942)

DOHER, MARCEL, *Charles de la Bedoyère* (1963)

DRIAULT, CHARLES, *Napoléon le Grand* (1930)

DU CAMP, MAXIME, *Paris* (1874)

DUCHÊNE, ALBERT, *Guerres et Finances—Mémoires du Trésor sous l'Empire* (1940)

DUHOURCAU, FRANÇOIS, *Bonaparte peint par lui-même* (1940)

DUNAN, MARCEL, *Napoléon et l'Allemagne*

ERCKMANN–CHATRIAN, *Le conscrit de 1813*

ESTRE, HENRY D', *Bonaparte—Les années obscures* (*1769–98*) (1942)

GABRIEL-ROBINET, LOUIS, *Journaux et Journalistes—Napoléon Directeur de Journaux* (1962)

GARROS, LOUIS, *Itinéraire de Napoléon Bonaparte* (1941)

GEFFROY, GUSTAVE, *Le Palais du Louvre*

HAUTECOEUR, LOUIS, *Histoire de l'architecture classique* (Vol. V)

—, —, *Le Collège des Quatre Nations et l'Institut de France* (1962)

HÉRON DE VILLEFOSSE, RENÉ, *Histoire de Paris* (1944)

HERRIOT, EDOUARD, *Madame Récamier et ses amis* (1924)

HILLAIRET, JACQUES, *Connaissance du Vieux Paris* (1959)

—, —, *Dictionnaire historique des Rues de Paris* (1962)

—, —, *Le Palais du Louvre* (1955)

HAUTERIVE, ERNEST D', *Napoléon et sa police* (1944)

HOUSSAYE, HENRY, *1814* (1894)

—, —, *1815—La Première Restauration*
                Le retour de l'Ile d'Elbe
                Les Cent Jours (1894)

HOUVILLE, GÉRARD D', *L'impératrice Joséphine* (1933)

HUGO, VICTOR, *Les Misérables* (1862)

—, —, *Les chants du Crépuscule* (1830)

IUNG, THÉODORE, *Bonaparte et son temps* (1885)

KAHANE, ERIC, *Un mariage parisien sous le Directoire* (1961)

LAMEYRE, GÉRARD, *Haussmann, Préfet de Paris* (1958)

LANZAC DE LABORIE, L. DE, *Paris sous Napoléon* (1905)

LAVEDAN, PIERRE, *Histoire de l'Urbanisme* (1952)

—, —, *Histoire de Paris* (1960)

LECOMTE, L. HENRI, *Napoléon et le théâtre* (1912)

LÉFEBVRE, GEORGES, *Napoléon* (1935)

LEGRAND ET LANDON, *Description de Paris et de ses édifices* (1808)

LENÔTRE, GOSSELIN, *Napoléon. Croquis de l'Epopée* (1932)

—, —, *Vieilles maisons, vieux papiers—Paris Révolutionnaire* (1905)

—, —, *Les Tuileries* (1933)

LÉVY, ARTHUR, *Napoléon Intime* (1894)

LO DUCA, *Journal secret de Napoléon Bonaparte* (1962)

LUDWIG, EMIL, *Napoléon* (1947)

MADELIN, LOUIS, *Histoire du Consulat et de l'Empire* (1949)

MADELIN, LOUIS, *Napoléon* (1947)

MARTIN-SAINT-LOUIS, F.-L., *Recettes et Dépenses de la Ville de Paris* (1843)

MARTIN, LÉON, *Encyclopédie municipale de la ville de Paris* (1902)

MASSON, FRÉDÉRIC, *Napoléon et les femmes* (1894)

—, —, *Napoléon inconnu* (1895)

—, —, *Napoléon et sa famille* (1897)

—, —, *Joséphine répudiée* (1901)

—, —, *Le sacre et le couronnement de Napoléon* (1908)

—, —, *Napoléon à Sainte-Hélène* (1912)

—, —, *Pour l'Empereur* (1914)

—, —, *Jadis* (1914)

—, —, *Une Journée de l'Impératrice Joséphine* (1933)

MERCIER, LOUIS-SÉBASTIEN, *Tableau de Paris* (1780–8)

MONNERAYE, JEAN DE LA, *Paris* (1946)

MONTORGUEIL, GEORGES, *Bonaparte* (1910)

MORIZET, ANDRÉ, *Du vieux Paris au Paris moderne* (1932)

NERVO, DE, *Les finances françaises* (1863)

NETTEMENT, ALFRED, *Histoire de la Restauration* (1866)

NORVINS, J. DE, *Histoire de Napoléon* (1837)

OLIVIER-MARTIN, FÉLIX, *L'inconnu, Napoléon Bonaparte* (1952)

PASSY, LOUIS, *Frochot* (1867)

PERCIER ET FONTAINE, *Résidences de souverains*

POISSON, GEORGES, *Napoléon et Paris* (1964)

ROBIQUET, JEAN, *La vie quotidienne au temps de Napoléon* (1944)

ROCHEGUDE, MARQUIS DE, *Promenades dans toutes les rues de Paris par arrondissement* (1910)

ROUSSIER, MICHEL, *Le Conseil Général de la Seine sous le Consulat* (1962)

SCHUERMANS, ALBERT, *Itinéraire de Napoléon* (1911)

SÉDILLOT, ROGER, *Paris*

ROSTAND, EDMOND, *L'Aiglon* (1900)

SARDOU, VICTORIEN, *Madame Sans-Gêne* (1893)

STENDHAL, *Histoire de l'Empereur Napoléon* (1840)

SUDRE, CHARLES, *Les Finances de la France au XIXe siècle* (1883)

VANDAL, ALBERT, *L'avènement de Bonaparte* (1903–7)

VILLAT, LOUIS, *Napoléon* (1789–1815)

VOX, MAXIMILIEN, *Napoléon* (1959)

St Helena Memorials

BERTRAND, GENERAL, *Cahiers de Ste-Hélène* Vol. I 1816–17, Vol. II 1818–19, Vol. III January–May, 1821, Manuscript decoded and annotated by Paul Fleuriot de Langle, Preface by Marcel Dunan

GOURGAUD, G., *Journal de Sainte-Hélène*

LAS CASES, COMTE DE, *Le Mémorial de Sainte-Hélène*

MARCHAND, L., *Mémoires*

MONTHOLON, C. H. DE, *Récit de la captivité de l'Empereur Napoléon*

SAINT-DENIS, L. E., *Souvenirs du Mameluck Aly sur l'Empereur Napoléon* (known as Aly)

Memoirs

Abrantès, Duchesse d'

Barras

Bausset

Beugnot

Bourrienne

Carnot

Caulaincourt

Fain

Fouché

Hortense (Queen)

Lafayette

Méneval

Miot de Mélito

Molé

Montesquiou

Pasquier

Rémusat (Mme de)

Roederer

Rovigo

Talleyrand

Thibaudeau

General History

GAXOTTE, PIERRE, *Histoire des Français*

GUIZOT, FRANÇOIS, *Histoire de France: Le Consulat*

HAMEL, ERNEST, *Histoire de France* (1837)

HANOTAUX, GABRIEL, *Histoire de la nation française* (1920)

LAVISSE ET RAMBAUD, *Histoire générale*

MALET, *Histoire de France*

THIERS, A., *Histoire du Consulat et de l'Empire*

Correspondence

General Correspondence of Napoleon

Letters of Napoleon I to Marie-Louise

(Introduction and notes by Louis Madelin)

National Archives

A. F. IV	940–943, 1011, 1012, 1057, 1073, 1221–40, 1329, 1353, 1367, 1490–1563, 1502–63, 1933, 1940
A. F. III	83, 84, 163, 169, 176, 437
F. IV	244
F. lc V	Seine 1
F. 7	260–262, 3040, 3041, 3200, 3705, 3733, 3735, 3738–46, 3773, 3774, 3782, 3783, 3832–35
F. 13	521, 550, 579–96, 601, 645, 707, 806, 866–87, 912–44, 974, 1025–1284
F. 20	255
F. 21	579
02.	225, 303, 305, 306, 307

Murat papers
31 AP 43 – 31 AP 26

Administrative and Technical Works

Ville de Paris	Nomenclature des voies publiques et privées (1951)
Ville de Paris	Actes additifs intervenus dans la gestion des Halles, marchés et abattoirs (1889)
Ville de Paris	Commission des travaux historiques: Documents sur l'état de l'Industrie et du Commerce de Paris et du Département de la Seine (1778–1810) by Bertrand Gille, preface by Michel Fleury (1963)
Préfecture de la Seine	Plan d'urbanisme directeur de Paris, with a commentary by M. Taurand, Ingénieur Div. Services Techniques
Préfecture de police	Direction de la police économique—Lecture given by M. Jean Michaud, Commissaire de Police Principal, Chef du Service actif des Halles Centrales, marchés et abattoirs (1958)

L'Administration de la Ville de Paris et du Départment de la Seine, by Maurice Block and Henri de Pontich (1884)

Le Régime Administratif et financier de la Ville de Paris et du
   Départment de la Seine, by Maurice Félix (1957)
Almanach des Bâtiments pour l'an 1812, F. M. Garnier
Tableau détaillé des prix de tous les ouvrages des bâtiments, by
   M. Morisot, inspector (Year XII–1804)
La Conjoncture Economique dans le Département de la Seine: Les
   Ponts de Paris (1958)
   Les Fontaines de Paris (1961)
Les Travaux de Paris (1789–99). Atlas produced under the direc-
   tion of Alphand, Inspector-General of the Highways Department,
   Director of Public Works in Paris in the administration of
   Poubelle, Prefect of the Seine

Etudes sur les transformations de Paris, Hénard
Les travaux souterrains de Paris, Belgrand (1873–87)

Newspapers and reviews

Le Moniteur Universel
Le Journal des Débats
Le Journal de Paris
Le Courrier de France
Le Publiciste
La Gazette de France
Le Courrier du Commerce
Revue de l'Institut Napoléon
L'Eau, the Fountains of Paris, A. Ragiot (July–August, 1959)

Index